National Pathways to Low Carbon Emission Economies

T0361962

The science is clear: climate change is a fact and the probability is extremely high that it has been caused by humans. At the same time, policy responses are hesitant, rather lukewarm and differ substantially between nation-states. The question is, what drives and what blocks radical action? This book makes the case that institutional settings, path dependence and emerging change coalitions are critical in explaining climate policies across the global political economy.

Technological and social-political innovations are key drivers for dealing with climate change. This class of innovation is very much guided, or suppressed, by a national economy's established institutional settings. By anchoring national case studies in a version of the well established 'varieties of capitalism' approach, the chapters in this book show why some economies are policy leaders and others become policy followers, or even policy interlockers. Moreover, the case studies demonstrate the extent to which external events and institutional constraints from international polity influence national innovation strategies. Taking a unique analytical approach, which combines insights from innovation policies and a variety of capitalism literature, the authors provide genuine comprehension of the interplay between institutional settings, political actors and climate policies.

National Pathways to Low Carbon Emission Economies offers a valuable examination of these issues on climate change that will be of interest to academics and postgraduates researching climate policy, economic policy and social movements. Furthermore, it is relevant for policy analysts and policy makers who are interested in learning from climate policies in the context of innovation strategies from a range of countries.

Kurt Hübner is a Professor at the Institute for European Studies in the Department of Political Science, University of British Columbia, Canada. He also holds the Jean Monnet Chair for European Integration and Global Political Economy and has previously had research stays at Waseda University in Tokyo, Hebrew University in Jerusalem, Ben Gurion University, National University Singapore, University of Birmingham, LUISS University in Rome, and Science Po in Grenoble.

Routledge Explorations in Environmental Economics
Edited by Nick Hanley
University of Stirling, UK

For more information about this series, please visit www.routledge.com/series/REEE

National Pathways to Low Carbon Emission Economies

Innovation Policies for Decarbonizing and Unlocking

Edited by Kurt Hübner

Routledge
Taylor & Francis Group

LONDON AND NEW YORK

First published 2019
by Routledge
2 Park Square, Milton Park, Abingdon, Oxon OX14 4RN

and by Routledge
52 Vanderbilt Avenue, New York, NY 10017

First issued in paperback 2020

Routledge is an imprint of the Taylor & Francis Group, an informa business

British Library Cataloguing-in-Publication Data
A catalogue record for this book is available from the British Library

Library of Congress Cataloging-in-Publication Data
Names: Hèubner, Kurt, 1953- editor.
Title: National pathways to low carbon-emission economies : innovation policies for decarbonizing and unlocking / edited by Kurt Hèubner.
Description: Abingdon, Oxon ; New York, NY : Routledge, 2019. | Series: Routledge explorations in environmental economics ; 53 | Includes bibliographical references and index.
Identifiers: LCCN 2018017203 (print) | LCCN 2018019578 (ebook) | ISBN 9780429458118 (Ebook) | ISBN 9781138312616 (hardback : alk. paper)
Subjects: LCSH: Carbon dioxide mitigation–Economic aspects. | Carbon dioxide mitigation–Government policy. | Emissions trading. | Carbon offsetting. | Environmental policy–Economic aspects.
Classification: LCC HC79.P55 (ebook) | LCC HC79.P55 N37 2019 (print) | DDC 363.738/747–dc23
LC record available at https://lccn.loc.gov/2018017203

ISBN 13: 978-0-367-58734-5 (pbk)
ISBN 13: 978-1-138-31261-6 (hbk)

Typeset in Bembo
by Wearset Ltd, Boldon, Tyne and Wear

Contents

Contributors

Daniele Archibugi is Director of the National Research Council (CNR), Rome, Italy, and Professor of Innovation, Governance and Public Policy at the University of London, Birkbeck College, UK.

Marina Chiarugi is a member of the National Research Council (CNR), Rome, Italy.

Alexander Ebner is Professor of Political Economy and Economic Sociology at Goethe-Universität, Frankfurt am Main, Germany.

Kathryn Harrison is Professor of Political Science at the University of British Columbia, Canada.

Kurt Hübner is a Professor at the Institute for European Studies in the Department of Political Science, University of British Columbia, Canada.

Torbjørg Jevnaker is Research Fellow at the Fridtjof Nansen Institute, Norway.

Miranda A. Schreurs is the Chair of Environmental and Climate Policy in the Bavarian School of Public Policy at the Technical University of Munich, Germany.

Jon Birger Skjærseth is a Professor at the Fridtjof Nansen Institute, Norway.

Preface

Global warming has become a household term, and so has climate policy. The move from obscurity to widely accepted fact took a long time and was met, and is still met, with suspicion – to a significant degree across *a wide range of countries*. However, it seems fair to say that these terms have become accepted within the political mainstream. Moreover, a widely held impression has taken hold that the globe can already feel the effects of the rise in global temperature, even though these effects are distributed very unevenly. Political and economic actors who only care about the present, and thus have short time horizons, do not worry much about the future state of the economy. In contrast, forward-looking economic and political actors are willing to take the future into account and, due to their longer time horizons, have started to worry. These issues have been examined in risk analyses provided by investment and pension funds and by entities such as the Bank of England, which all lay out *challenges* that may occur quickly should sudden policy changes occur in regard to reducing carbon emissions. Companies and whole sectors that are sitting on large, unexploited fuel assets run the risk of facing lower market values in the future, and thus may experience quite serious financial losses.

Still, the gap between knowledge about climate change and its social and economic costs on the one side, and the lack of adequate economic and political action on the other side, has not decreased in recent years. Optimists suggest that this is changing, and that the Paris Climate Agreement is a proper global political framework to close that gap. Our national case studies show that countries are engaging, with varying levels of seriousness, in innovation policies that aim for low carbon emission activities. We also observe that these efforts depend very much on two variables, namely the political intensity of climate change discourse and the quality of national innovation regimes. Societies with strong climate policy voices tend to foster efforts for the creation of low carbon emission activities. Economies with a regime that tends to generate disruptive innovation are, on average, quicker to change established practices and to generate path changes.

And yet, we could not find a single case where the move to a low to zero carbon emission path has happened or is yet conceivable. Path change has increasingly become a politically loaded term rather than a term that guides actual action. Moreover, powerful vested interests try hard to delay, or even block, any change in existing growth models. As a matter of fact, unlocking has become the foremost problem for a climate-oriented innovation policy. State subsidies for fossil fuels in the global economy, to give only one prominent example, are estimated by the IMF at US\$5.3 trillion in 2015. This dwarfs all subsidies for alternative climate friendly technologies. Unlocking is a serious problem for both politically driven and market-driven efforts toward low carbon emission technologies. Defending coal industries may be good politics for governments whose fate depends on critical votes, but it is definitely bad policy, not only in regard to climate change, but also in regard to a forward-looking modernization and competitiveness strategy.

This book presents the joint efforts of a group of international researchers, who tried hard to stick within a common analytical approach that was meant to generate the kind of homogeneity that is required for a meaningful comparative learning experience. Our own learning went far and we had ample opportunities to discuss varying views and insights. The work benefitted not only from our individual and collective learning curves, but also from the many comments and suggestions we received from participants at workshops we held in Vancouver and Berlin. Our thanks also go out to the research assistants and indispensable staff that kept the whole project viable. This includes Yana Gorokhovskaia, Kerstin Lüttich, Andrea Nüser, Stefan Pauer and, in particular, James Thiébault in Vancouver, who was most critical to putting together this book. Obviously, a project like this needs financial as well as intellectual support. Thankfully, the Hans Böckler Foundation provided us with both. As always, none of the above is in any way responsible for the final product.

Kurt Hübner
Vancouver, March 2018

1 Decarbonization and unlocking

National pathways to low carbon emission economies

Kurt Hübner

Carbon conundrums

The science is conclusive. Man-made greenhouse gas emissions are the main driving force for changes in the global climate. According to the most recent synthesis report by the IPCC (2014):

> the period from 1983 to 2012 was *very likely* the warmest 30-year period of the last 800 years in the Northern Hemisphere, where such assessment is possible (*high confidence*) and *likely* the warmest 30-year period of the last 1,400 years (*medium confidence*).

Climate change is not an uncertain future but rather a contemporary reality, and a well established critical threat for the future. The increase in average global temperature is irreversible but, potentially, the rise can be managed and kept to a level that would avoid catastrophic outcomes. A turnaround of current trends however, requires pivotal changes in the pattern of production and consumption. Ultimately, a strict policy of decarbonization is needed at a global scale to keep worldwide temperatures to a non-catastrophic level. And yet, such a global policy project is out of reach. However, climate policies of and within nation-states are currently being enacted. These are moving along at differing speeds, and with differing depth and breadth. Today's decarbonization policies will not result in an immediate transition to a zero carbon emission global economy, but efforts to create such an economy are under way, which indicates that a turnaround is a possibility. In 2016, global CO_2 emissions were approximately the same as in 2015 and 2014 (Jackson et al. 2016). What can be seen as a success still implies that the cumulative amount of CO_2 continues to rise. Also, the emissions stagnation was largely the result of lower economic growth in China rather than the outcome of policy induced emissions changes. A carbon budget perspective shows that the world has already used up two-thirds of its CO_2 emissions quota, presuming a target of a 2°C increase. What is more, the entire budget will be used up in about 30 years if emissions remain at 2016 levels. Action is required to prevent future abatement costs from rising beyond economic capacities.

Any such policy project requires a vision for the transition period, including the ways in which such a transition will be managed in economic, political and social terms. Decarbonization entails a fundamental change in the underlying socio-technical regime that guides current production and consumption patterns, and such a change is as much an opportunity as it is a threat. An opportunity in so far as it opens up new ways of producing and consuming. A threat in that it requires the deliberate obsolescence of established economic and social patterns. One crucial component for fundamental change is related to *innovation*, in both technological and social terms. Staying on the current growth path is not a viable option. As such, a change in course to a climate-compatible growth regime, with corresponding production and consumption patterns, is required. Such a change can be triggered via market processes and/or by political action.

Decarbonization will not happen overnight; rather it will be a time-consuming process that needs to be organized, by political as well as market-driven means. Moving from a high carbon emission path, to a low, or even zero, emission path is demanding on many levels. It is also risky in both economic and political terms. The chapters in this book analyze political efforts to unlock deeply entrenched growth paths and to move toward low carbon emission paths of economic and social development. We do this from a comparative institutional perspective that differentiates various types of capitalism when it comes to climate policies. These variations are critical for understanding emerging national pathways to low carbon emission economies and the reasons why they differ in so many respects. Rather than identifying one pathway, our analysis shows a broad variety of pathways that are guided by established institutional settings.

After the publication of the *Stern Review* (Stern 2006) the debate among economists focused on the proposition that the earlier a profound climate policy is initiated, the lower the marginal turnaround costs will be. Critics of such a view made the point that the discount rate chosen was too low, which meant that future costs were calculated as being too high (Nordhaus 2007; Pindyck 2013).[1] Indeed, if one takes an opportunity cost-based discount rate, then the resulting future costs of climate change would be much lower, and thus the urgency to take action now would be less pressing. However, such a view takes the future as an extrapolation of the past and thus excludes the non-linear dynamics that govern global climate. With these non-linear dynamics, tipping points are a real possibility, even though they cannot be predicted. It may be a fair assumption to see the 'tail' of climate change as a literal fat tail, and thus as a process that may come with high social and economic costs (Weitzman 2014). Consequently, the discount rate should be relatively low. The actual development of CO_2 emissions confirms a non-linear perspective. The Stern Report, as well as similar benchmark studies, all calculate economic costs on the basis of emissions doubling from pre-industrial levels. However, the most recent IPCC, business as usual scenario, indicates at least a tripling, and maybe even quadrupling, of accumulated emissions (see IMF 2008). Such an increase hints at much higher economic costs than initially calculated. Given these characteristics of climate change, economic and political actors with a sufficiently long time-horizon should act today, since procrastinating is associated with higher costs tomorrow. Still, political and economic actors discount the future according to their own short-term preferences. These are influenced by their particular interests, which are enshrined in specific national institutional settings. Also, choosing an appropriate discount rate is not as evident as is often assumed, mainly due to the high level of uncertainty that comes with the aforementioned unknown tipping points for events related to climate change. As a result of this uncertainty, economic and political actors chose to stay on a path that favors exploiting the still available parts of the global carbon budget. And yet, as our case studies demonstrate, change is under way. Relevant countries have started to engage in climate policies that have the potential for path change. However, change occurs very unevenly, both concerning the way it is generated and with respect to the varying speed and depth with which policies are being enacted.

The relations between carbon emissions and economic institutions are complex. In an ideal world of market capitalism this should not be the case. Markets would generate prices that fully cover the social costs of production and consumption, and thus guide actors to optimum outcomes where private and social costs are identical. Yet, markets are not complete and do not automatically include the social costs of production and consumption. Even if markets have – through political action – internalized social costs to deal with this shortcoming, this may not be sufficient to generate a low carbon emission path. This is partly due to the fact that not all economic activities are organized via markets and thus some activities are not subject to market pricing. It is also a result of the fact that sectoral shifts from high to low emission activities have the potential to meet harsh political and social opposition from certain economic agents. These are actors that would lose out with a significant change in direction and thus oppose market-induced shifts.

In analytical terms, the argument that the decarbonization of market economies becomes relatively cheaper if it is started earlier rather than later is well established. And yet, it neglects the fact that the envisioned path change generates *immediate* economic and social burdens, whereas the benefits may only occur later. This time inconsistency has wide-ranging implications. High carbon emission activities will have to shrink permanently at the inception of a sectoral shift. It is to be expected that such actions will provoke resistance from affected sectors. Thus, it is no surprise if otherwise unlikely coalitions between employers and employees form when their interests are challenged. Moreover, time horizons diverge for winners and losers of a path shift. Economic sectors that will be closed down, or at least drastically shrunk, experience immediate costs. Potential winners of a path change may only reap their gains in the distant future. The question then is, from a political point of view, how can both interests be reconciled? Moving from a high carbon to a low carbon emission path requires a substantial reallocation of resources, compensatory measures, and a fundamental change in market economies' institutional settings, to help guide the decisions and actions of critical actors. It also requires adequate infrastructure and private investment to support and grow low carbon activities. Technological innovations can be important drivers in any unlocking and path changing strategy, in addition to their role in expanding markets and stimulating employment opportunities. To achieve all of these outcomes, or any mixture of them, is quite a feat. It therefore seems only rational to assume that an innovation-led path change comes with substantial political and social change, which may in turn result in social and political conflicts that delay adequate action. The Fukushima accident triggered a German case of an *Energiewende* (energy transformation) as a striking example of a purportedly quick political move away from atomic energy, toward renewables, and potentially toward a low carbon emission path. It should satisfy Germany's 2020 target of a 40 percent carbon emission reduction compared to 1990 levels. This goal also implies unlocking from fossil fuels, and thus a decision by the German government to take the oldest and most carbon-intensive coal power stations immediately off the grid. Energy experts make the argument that such a policy would be possible without creating electricity bottlenecks or an increase in electricity prices (Oei et al. 2014). And yet, a powerful coalition of energy sector-trade unions and a Social Democratic Party with a key voting bloc in what can be labeled *coal-land*, undermined such a policy change.[2] Rather than continuing its position as a climate policy leader, the Merkel-Gabriel coalition decided to dilute its climate target by stretching the transition period and offering side-payments to energy incumbents (see Chapter 5, Ebner).

If we follow established science, wherein greenhouse gas emissions are the result of economic activities, and if we further assume that these activities are organized via markets, then climate change can be interpreted as an externality which results in *market failure*. The discipline of Environmental Economics is full of examples of this kind of market failure, as well as of analyses of how to overcome this institutional incapacity. Generally speaking, markets need an adequate social-political embedding to avoid such failures. Most prominent is the proposal for the internalization of externalities, the best-known variety of which is the so-called Pigovian tax, named after Arthur Pigou who made the case that the existence of market externalities justifies corrective interventions by the state (Pigou 1920). Such a tax addresses the social component of overall costs and adds this critical element to the market-determined private costs of production. Other ways to internalize carbon emission costs include cap-and-trade regimes where carbon emissions receive a market price that is charged to the emitting source. By including (the 'true') social costs of private production (and therefore of consumption), market prices would reflect 'true costs' and provide an effective incentive for a more climate-friendly allocation of resources. Such a regime could run into cost competitiveness problems for producers however, if only one or a small number of nation-states opt for such a tool of cost internalization. In this case, companies located in a jurisdiction with a 'Pigovian tax' would have higher costs then companies located in a jurisdiction that does not levy such a tax. Hence, embedding environmental costs in markets may be seen as a necessary condition for a change toward a carbon-reducing regime, but not as a sufficient condition, since the reality that polluters want to avoid such a tax cannot be ignored. At a minimum, these first-movers would need to safeguard their domestic producers and consumers from carbon leakage by introducing carbon-oriented border adjustments, such as taxes and tariffs. As long as not all (relevant) national jurisdictions are following the same internalization of external costs, such a protective policy seems reasonable.[3] At least from an analytical perspective, not participating in a global climate policy treaty would result in a border duty by participating countries so that they can internalize the costs to the level set by the treaty. In such a case, imports would be taxed at a rate that either equals the respective domestic carbon price of the import economy times the amount of carbon embedded in the particular good, or the domestic carbon allowance of a similar domestic producer in the case of a cap-and-trade regime. Either way, imports of non-participating economies would become more expensive.[4] Still, some of our case studies indicate that individually implemented national approaches can work quite smoothly, even in the absence of border adjustment. This is possible either due to a relatively low carbon tax rate and/or due to the installation of cost compensation policies that shelter private businesses from cost disadvantages. In both cases, the chosen level of internalization of social costs is suboptimal in order to protect national interests.

One of the paradoxes of climate change is the large gap between established knowledge about the detrimental economic and social effects of rising temperatures on the one side, and effective political action on the other. Procrastination and half-hearted actions are the preferred way to go when it comes to political responses. Usually, the literature explains this gap through the global public good (bad) character of climate change that induces free riding; actors receive the benefits of particular actions without contributing to the costs of the action. Given that greenhouse gases do not stop at national borders and the fact that cause (production of greenhouse gas) and effect (change of climate) are decoupled, political and economic actors tend engage in free riding. Climate policy deniers, such as the USA under President Trump for example, have used the argument that international agreements are not worth the paper they are written on, as long as the largest global emitters are not fully on board or enjoy privileged treatment. Consequently, inaction by others is used as an argument to defend their own inaction. Rather than becoming politically invested in measures dealing with the increase in carbon emissions, governments passively enjoy the climate initiatives of others, while simultaneously refusing to enact serious climate policies at home. Such a political argument (concerning the futility of independent climate action) becomes progressively more difficult to make, the more countries are willing to contribute to the production of a global public good. Moreover, in cases where inaction is the preferred route on the federal political level, there are still critical policy actions taken on the sub-federal level (see Harrison and Schreurs in Chapters 2, 4 and 7) that can show positive effects. Still, if we assume that managing climate change, either on the 'effect side' or on the 'cause side' comes with immediate tangible economic costs, then it is only fair to assume that economic and political actors have strong incentives to avoid, or at least minimize, such costs. Free riding is facilitated by the 'Westphalian dilemma' (Nordhaus 2015: 1340). The 1648 Treaty of Westphalia established the sovereignty of nations, gave them the right to self-determination, declared all states as legally equal, and set the principle that all nations can manage their internal affairs without outside interference. In legal terms, states have the right to abstain from climate policies. The result of non-action could be a *global tragedy of the commons*. Such a bleak outcome is not inevitable though. The less ingrained the principle of sovereignty in this domain is, the more incentives are in place for climate policy leadership that has the potential to create benefits in the medium term. One incentive can be, as we demonstrate in some of our case studies, that national actors are eager to reap first-mover advantages and to conquer emerging markets when it comes to climate-friendly goods, services and technologies.

The proposition is that the global character of climate change requires coordinated global action that results in a global climate *regime*. Such a regime not only needs to put in place provisions that allow for the successful management of the effects of climate change, but also has to deal with the production and maintenance costs of such a regime, including a cost distribution mechanism that makes membership of such a regime attractive. Moreover, it needs strict supervision and enforcement powers in order to be effective. And finally, it needs to deal with the historical legacy of accumulated greenhouse gas emissions and the claim of some nation-states to have the right to catch-up in economic terms, and thus to emit more than others.

So far, international negations for installing a *binding* regime have not been successful. Part of this failure can be explained by the lack of a true climate policy leader initiating such a regime, and willing and able to carry substantial parts of its production and maintenance costs. Moreover, the brief history of global climate negotiations shows the strong vetoing and blocking powers of some countries, which results in an escalation of production costs. The Kyoto Protocol, which was the most advanced climate regime prototype, ended up as a failure, and it has become obvious since the failed Copenhagen climate meeting that an effective global climate regime will be difficult to establish (Keohane and Victor 2011). It seems fair to state that the 2016 Paris Conference launched a regime that is best described as a second-best version of what is needed to keep the global temperature increase as close as possible to the 2°C target. Our (small) dose of optimism comes, in part, from the generally positive experience of the Montreal Protocol. This agreement was instrumental in successfully dealing with the threat to the ozone layer by banning chlorofluorocarbons (see Molina et al. 2009). This example indicates that global regimes can be successfully established and actually realize concrete outcomes if certain conditions are fulfilled, in particular decisive actions by a few consequential national members. In this regard, the November 2014 bilateral agreement between China and the USA about quantitative constraints on greenhouse gas emissions, even though lacking in detail, was a ray of hope. Especially since it indicated a potential willingness to establish a loosely binding agreement between the two highest emitters. Since then, the change in presidency in the USA has dampened this optimism. The Trump administration's decision to leave the Paris Agreement, while China has simultaneously maintained its climate policy ambitions, has resulted in China's sudden emergence as a global climate policy leader. Given the size of its economy, any successful climate policy depends from China's stance. Another cause for slight optimism is the agreement between the G7 nations in June 2015, who agreed – once again vaguely – to a 40–70 percent reduction in carbon emissions from 2010 levels by 2050. The US federal government does not feel bound by this voluntary declaration. Even so, through economic self-interest, critical private actors are slowly realizing that market-compatible tools that favor low carbon emission technologies, actually improve global competitiveness (Dechezlepretre and Sato 2014). This, in conjunction with climate policies at sub-federal levels, are feeding a more optimistic take on the future of effective climate policies. Moving ahead of the crowd comes with potential advantages. Our case studies show that the self-interest of private actors, in combination with robust institutional settings, can be a powerful driver of climate policies, even in the absence of strong centralized policies. And yet, political and economic hurdles are high.

It is well-known that the production of a global regime does not need to wait until *all* critical actors agree to move. A small group of lead actors, or even a single hegemonic actor can, in principle, design and establish a regime that produces benefits for both members and non-members. Lead actors who introduce Pigovian tax-like policies can, again in principle, easily handle carbon leakage by introducing border adjustments. Such a tool would add costs to actors who are not introducing pricing or taxing schemes on their national levels. Border adjustments, in other words, create an incentive to join the structure that has been established by the leader(s) since political actors would only have the chance to shape the rule making of the climate administration as a member of its regime. Alternatively, organizations can be successfully established and maintained if a few members have the economic and political room to lift (in a non-proportional manner) regime costs.

Given both historical and more recent global emission trends, a drastic decarbonization is needed over a relatively short time period to achieve the 2°C target. It is argued that such a turnaround will not be possible without violating basic mechanisms of capitalist market economies (Jackson 2009). In this strand of literature, decarbonization and economic growth are presented as adversaries or even as pure contradictions. The political writer Naomi Klein is one of the most prominent proponents for "managed degrowth" and argues that individuals will have to consume less, corporate profits need to shrink dramatically, and governments need to engage in extra-market policies. The argument for degrowth often comes with a strong anti-capitalist conception (Brand and Wissen 2013) that sees climate change as a political opportunity for system change. In the academic literature, degrowth has a distinct tradition that goes back to the work of Herman Daly (1975) and Georgescu-Roegen (1971). They laid the groundwork in the 1970s for the argument that capitalist growth imperatives and the carrying capacity of the globe contradict each other. These approaches imply that any political project that wants to avoid catastrophic climate change by means of mobilizing capitalist 'animal spirits' will fail. This can be interpreted as quite a fatalist approach that significantly underestimates the capitalist market economies' efficiency dimension, and thus miscalculates the dynamic effects of profit-driven innovation. Jakob and Eden-hofer (2014: 452) for example, point out that a degrowth policy that reduces carbon emissions by 10 percent through a corresponding reduction in average per capita global GDP, results in an abatement cost of US$2,100 per ton of carbon. This is a much higher mitigation cost per unit of carbon than one could achieve with already known technologies. On the other hand, it is well known that private markets do not automatically favor low carbon technological innovations. Some of the benefits of such innovations cannot be accrued solely by the innovator but are spread to the overall global system. Given this characteristic, chances are that these types of innovations will be under-supplied. Public policy can temper this under-provision by setting out a reliable transition path toward a low carbon emission economy. Appropriate policies provide private businesses and households with the confidence necessary to guide their investment and consumption decisions. Moreover, public policy will have to engage aggressively in the process of managing expectations and generating both technological and social innovations that make a low carbon emission regime attractive, and economically sustainable.

> In the Cold War, the Apollo Programme placed a man on the moon. This programme engaged many of the best minds in America. Today we need a global Apollo programme to tackle climate change; but this time the effort needs to be international. We need major international scientific and technological effort, funded by both public and private money.
> (King, Browne, Layard, O'Donnell, Rees, Stern and Turner 2015)

These are stark words, and to some degree risk irrelevancy for all the reasons provided by the free rider approach. In addition, it seems that the call for a new and truly international Apollo program misses the potential that innovations can be the outcome of particular national innovation regimes.

It is well known that science and research play a substantial role in generating path-disrupting innovations. This is of particular relevance at the nation-state level where innovations are usually generated through a complex interplay between public and private innovation efforts. An elegant way to present the role of innovations and thus innovation policies for climate politics is given by a simple identity equation (Frankhauser and Jotzo 2017):

$$C = C/E \times E/Y \times Y.$$

This so-called Kaya equation demonstrates that carbon emissions C are the product of: (i) the carbon intensity of the underlying energy sources C/E; (ii) the energy intensity of the macroeconomic output E/Y; and (iii) economic output Y. A move toward a low carbon emission economy can come as a decrease of C/E, E/Y, a decrease of Y, or any combination of the three factors. If we exclude the degrowth option, then a reduction in carbon emissions requires energy source changes in favor of low or zero carbon sources, along with a sectoral shift from high carbon economic activities to low carbon activities. Significant changes in C/E and C/Y are only possible via innovations, technical as well as social.

Over the preceding years, an enormous number of scholarly and expert studies have been produced that delve into the aforementioned challenges, as well as other complexities, in the relationship between capitalist market economies and climate change. The chapters of this book add to this body of literature in several distinct ways.

First, we are interested in an understanding of the *unlocking* of carbon regimes and the strategies chosen by various actors. Path change is often envisaged as a generally smooth exercise, which mainly requires political will to create a win–win–win situation for global climate, businesses and employees. Our approach differs from such harmonious views by explicitly focusing on the unlocking phase of a path change toward a low carbon emission trajectory. As a result, it explicitly analyzes political-economic coalitions and strategies that support, or hinder, transition processes. The identification of blocking coalitions as well as of change coalitions is part of our exercise.

Second, we are interested in the role of particular national and supranational institutional settings in moving toward a low carbon emission path. This institutional focus helps us understand the perseverance of existing regimes, as well as identifying the critical institutional settings that guide path change. In particular we are looking for the appropriate mixture of allocation mechanisms in various countries, as well as the role of technological and political innovations.

Third, we are curious about the triggers for unlocking and path change. Path change, as our case studies demonstrate, is more often triggered by unforeseen events than the outcome of well planned political actions. Unseen events can take various forms, from surprising innovations to disasters, and seems of crucial importance in understanding how specific national institutional settings deal with such 'black swans.'

Fourth, we analyze these processes in a comparative way by using a coherent, but flexible, analytical framework. This allows us to compare a large and diversified group of economies. For lack of a better label, we refer to this approach as a *variant of the varieties of capitalism approach* (Hall and Soskice 2001), which deals explicitly with climate policies. Before we present our slightly modified version of this approach, I will explain and justify the cases we have selected for the purposes of this study.

Carbon relevance of our case studies

Our study consists of ten countries that cover – as of 2015 – more than 55 percent of all global CO_2 emissions from fuel combustion (Table 1.1). By including China and the USA it covers the two largest emitters in terms of volume, which are also polar opposites in terms of their institutional settings and growth regimes. By including Canada, we cover a case of a developed economic-political entity that has shown a strong increase in carbon emissions due to a strategy of extensive and intensive exploitation of high carbon fossil fuels. For a long time, climate actions were neglected, and for a few years even denied, but then a change in government created a new situation in which Canada turned into a climate catch-up country. Norway is a carbon-intensive resource economy much like Canada. As its experience demonstrates, at least to some extent, that it is possible to progress down an ambitious carbon path from the outset, if political and social actors are willing to accept such a carbon trajectory. The UK is a case in which a

Table 1.1 Four varieties of capitalism and cases overview

Institution	LME	CME	DME	SME
Dominating Allocation and Coordination Mechanism	Market	Interfirm networks	Intrafirm networks of transnational companies	State-guided markets
Finance	Capital markets	Domestic banks	Foreign banks and FDI	Corporate financing mainly by state banks
Corporate governance	Shareholder control	Stakeholder control	Transnational company control	Mix of state control and private shareholder
Industrial relations	Company-employee	Corporatist consensus	Company-level agreements	Party-controlled unions; Limited involvement
Innovation	Market-driven	In-house	Intrafirm technology transfer	Large-scale FDI in technological lead sectors; state-led innovation targets
"Our cases"	USA, Canada, UK	Germany, Norway, Japan	Czech Republic, Poland, Hungary	China

market-driven and highly financialized economy develops its own low carbon emission strategy, where state actions go hand in hand with private initiatives. The inclusion of Japan allows us to look more carefully into a case where a sudden catastrophe triggered a policy turnaround that came with increasing carbon imports. Germany is a case where an outside catastrophic event – the meltdown of the atomic reactor in Fukushima, Japan – led to the acceleration of a previously planned policy change in the energy arena. And yet, this quick move resulted in – at least in the short-term – an increase in carbon emissions, despite a huge surge in renewable energy utilization. Our Eastern European cases allow us to look deeper into the operating mechanisms of economies that had to undergo deep economic and political structural transformations. These countries are on an economic catch-up path that seems to favor short-term economic gains over long-term productivity gains, where proactive climate policies are on the backburner. In quantitative respects our cases are relevant to the understanding of a transition from a high carbon emission to a low carbon emission growth path. Policy changes in this sample of nation-states are obviously critical with regard to the usage and distribution of the available global carbon emission budget. Rather than analyzing peripheral economies, our sample focuses on a number of key emitters, which allows us to draw – at least preliminary – conclusions on the requirements for successful path changes.

Our cases are similar enough to allow meaningful comparisons, while also showing critical differences in terms of emission activities, institutional settings and economic performance. Moreover, taken individually, our countries offer rich empirical histories of climate policy-relevant political strategies. Our sample encompasses both extremes within the sample range, high as well as low emitters. We also included 'middle-of-the-road' cases that will help uncover specific challenges, and specific routes of action, taken on the move toward a low carbon emission path.

In terms of global proportions of carbon emissions, China and the USA reside at one extreme of our range, both exhibiting the highest shares of

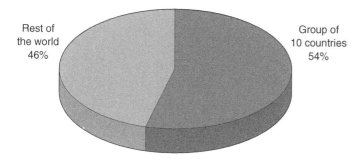

Figure 1.1 CO_2 emissions from fuel combustion in 2014.
Source: International Energy Agency, 2016.

global CO_2 emissions by far. In terms of absolute carbon emissions, China has overtaken the USA and sits at the top position globally. Norway resides at the other extreme with a close to zero share of global CO_2 emissions. Our other cases (Canada, Czech Republic, Germany, Japan, Poland, Hungary and the UK) are located in the middle of this range but differ in many respects (see Figure 1.2). Obviously, potential changes or non-changes in the USA and China are the most critical for developments in global emissions.

If one or both of the high carbon emitting economies opts for a significant move toward a low carbon emission trajectory or, alternatively, if one or both of those economies opts to stick to the high carbon path, this will have consequences for the global carbon trajectory as well as for national carbon policies of other countries. In this respect, the 'Beijing Agreement' of November 2014 between China and the USA signaled that both nation-states *intended* to become climate leaders, and this would have had adjustment consequences for countries whose policies are responsive to initiatives from these integral powers. As it turned out though, a change in the US presidency was sufficient to withdraw political support for an active climate policy (see Harrison in Chapter 2 on the role of federal policy changes in the case of Canada and the USA). This created a gap in global climate policy leadership that has the potential to induce more widespread free riding behavior. Alternatively, it could also encourage some countries to forge ahead and attempt to grasp available economic advantages through bold climate policy.

China and the USA, while critical actors for the understanding of decarbonization policies, are not the only important cases when it comes to understanding the ambiguities of climate policies. The same holds for our EU cases, as well as for Canada and Norway. Unlike for the big emitters, China and the USA, this may not be obvious at first sight. The relevance of our other cases

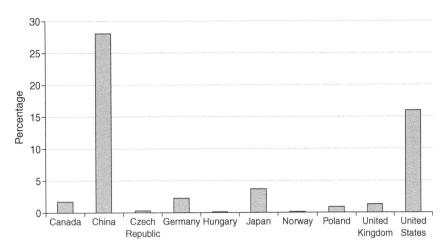

Figure 1.2 CO_2 emissions from fuel combustion in 2014: share in the world total.
Source: International Energy Agency, 2016.

lies not in their absolute emission levels but in their particular institutional and economic positioning in the 'world of capitalism.' As we will argue, any transition to a low carbon emission path has to deal with a country's own institutional legacy and lock-in characteristics; therefore, it is critical to understand the *national character* of pathways. Small emitters can still be critical actors for path change, insofar as they set an example and reap some of the first-mover advantages that are generally gleaned by innovators. The cases in our sample represent four relevant types of growth models. With China, we include the most successful emerging market in terms of economic growth, which also comes with distinctive political and institutional features. China's growth spurt since the early 1980s is as impressive as its growth in carbon emissions. The USA, Germany and the UK represent mature capitalist market economies with strong service sectors, and in the case of Germany a significant industrial sector. They however differ fundamentally in their underlying institutional settings. Canada and Norway are examples of resource sector-driven economies, where carbon-intensive industries are critical for overall economic growth. Despite similarities they also show rather disparate institutional patterns. Finally, the Czech Republic, Hungary and Poland represent Eastern European catch-up economies, they are EU members but they adhere more closely to their respective national policy preferences. They therefore come with a 'layered' structure of economic governance that makes them distinct from other catch-up economies. Our EU cases can also claim relevance for the fact that the EU bloc aims to reduce carbon emissions by 40 percent from 1990 levels, by 2030. Given that this overall EU-wide target encompasses stark differences in emission reduction targets between EU member states, it is self-evident that the national options to move along the EU transition path are highly relevant for the understanding of a path change. National pathways are critical in a situation without a binding international climate agreement. Moreover, our case studies indicate that even a binding and relatively detailed international agreement requires specific national strategies for a fundamental path change. These national strategies reflect economic-political institutional settings, as well as particular economic growth regimes.

Climate change policies and varieties of capitalism

This project goes beyond a standard comparative analysis that lines up case studies one after the other. It also differs from analyses that only look at individual countries and their pathways to decarbonization by focusing on purely technological or modeling aspects.[5] Rather than presenting a loose collection of national cases, our approach works out more general patterns of transition processes that allow (at least modest) generalizations. To achieve this we decided from the outset to guide the various case studies with a necessarily loose, but structured, analytical framework that has become prominent in the last 20 years or so, namely the "varieties of capitalism" (Hall and Soskice

2001). This literature was established to detect institutional comparative advantages through two distinct varieties of capitalism (VoC), specifically a Liberal Market Economy (LME) and a Coordinated Market Economy (CME), by looking into potential complementarities among some key institutions. Hall and Soskice started out by distinguishing five institutions: (i) financial regimes; (ii) structure of corporate governance; (iii) patterns of industrial relations; (iv) vocational systems; (v) innovation systems. Both versions of capitalism differ in their distinct institutional set-ups, while simultaneously being characterized by strong institutional complementarities. These complementarities on the one hand show self-enforcing synergies for the given path, and, on the other hand, make deviations from chosen paths relatively unlikely. Rather, both varieties tend to stick to their respective institutional paths and adjust along those paths to deal with new challenges. In the vein of the original formulation of variants of capitalism, we expect LMEs to excel at responding to climate change by means of technical innovations. Insofar as climate change requires – ceteris paribus – a new technological paradigm, this literature intimates that LMEs will tend to generate more radical and disruptive innovations than CMEs. The latter tend to produce incremental innovations and are superior in incremental reforms that make use of existing comparative institutional advantages, in moving away from a carbon-intensive path. LMEs, on the other hand, are best suited to fundamental path changes.

Such a focus on (technological and institutional) innovation has its rationale in the climate change challenge itself (see above). In order to meet the 2°C target there needs to be a substantial improvement in carbon productivity (i.e. the monetary value of GDP per unit of carbon equivalents). Current carbon productivity on a global scale is calculated at US$740 GDP per ton of CO_2; to meet the target productivity needs to increase roughly ten-fold to US$7,300 GDP per ton of CO_2 by 2050 (Beinhocker et al. 2008). If one applies a 2050 target of 20 gigatons of CO_2, this comes to a carbon budget of 6 kg per head, per day:

> If one had to live on such a carbon budget with today's low level of carbon productivity, one would be forced to choose between a 40 km car ride, a day of air conditioning, buying two new T-shirts (without driving to the shop), or eating two meals.
>
> (Beinhocker et al. 2008: 12)

A drastic improvement in carbon productivity, however, is only a necessary condition for a successful climate policy. The sufficient condition, as the illustration indicates, can only be derived by proportional changes in existing production and consumption styles, which goes much farther than pure technological innovation. The VoC approach seems well suited to providing an analytical framework for the understanding of political and economic responses to the challenges ahead. It promises insights into the dynamics of technical change while at the same time providing a foundation for understanding the role of institutional complementarities that guide production and consumption patterns. It is often taken as a given that, generally speaking, political systems must have the capacity for policy innovation that either deals with new challenges, or proactively prepares the groundwork for new pathways (Jordan and Huitema 2014). Analyses that utilize the VoC approach are much more careful in this respect, as policy innovations are seen as the outcome of established institutional settings and their degree of complementarity (Hübner 2009). Climate policies are relatively new areas of state activity, and we expect that they are connected in a plethora of ways with other national regimes, encompassing institutional settings in different VoC.

Since the publication of "Varieties of Capitalism" the literature on comparative capitalism has gained enormous momentum. This has resulted not only in a fine-tuning of the original contribution, but also in a widening and deepening, as well as partial modification, of the analytical focus. As a result, the original institutional duopoly has made space for a rather large continuum of VoC. We do not intend to add to this enriching procedure. Rather, we make pragmatic use of the widened typology and apply some of its key institutional features in analyzing policy, as well as economic innovation, with regard to climate change. Still, by applying the core ideas of the VoC approach to climate change policies, we do enter new analytical territory to some extent. Up until now such attempts have been rare. One exception is the work by Harrison and Mikler (2014) who make use of the original dichotomy and analyze national paths of technological innovations for the mitigation of climate change. Their empirical work on the USA comes to the conclusion that its actual innovation regime contradicts the analytical expectations of the VoC approach, as it produces inferior climate mitigation innovation outcomes compared to Japan and Germany. Our case study on the USA does not confirm such a harsh assessment, and this has to do – in analytical terms – with the specifics of our approach. It takes into account broader institutional sets in order to explain blockages as well as partial technological push forces (see Harrison, Chapter 2). Tienhaara (2014) discusses green stimuli in the context of economic policy responses to the financial crisis of 2008 and envisions "varieties of green capitalism," but without making the effort to link such varieties to the institutional settings that were put forward in the original VoC literature.

Our case sample goes beyond the dichotomy of CMEs and LMEs. Rather than putting all cases under those labels, we extend the typology to two more varieties for our analysis, in line with recent literature. The version of a Dependent Market Economy (DME) is supposed to cover our European catch-up economies, represented by the Czech Republic, Hungary and Poland (Nölke and Vliegenhart 2009). This variety of capitalism is characterized by a heavy dependence on foreign investment for its underlying growth and accumulation processes, as well as on a financial regime that is dominated by foreign banks. Both institutional features reflect the lack of a strong self-financing domestic industrial core. This is in addition to a weak financial regime that had to be established from scratch, in the process of transformation from a state-planned economy, to a version of a market economy. In this sense, both of our Eastern European cases can be labeled as dependent or peripheral economies. Such a label does not imply there are no strong and developed domestic sectors. Generally, however, both Poland and the Czech Republic are economies with a strong outward-looking orientation and multi-layered ties within the political-economic space of the EU. Our case study (Archibugi and Chiarugi, Chapter 8) draws on this specific trait of DMEs in its analysis of climate policies.

Grouping national economies under the VoC approach is generally an arbitrary undertaking. Any comparative politics approach has to deal, in one way or another, with the problem of comparing the 'right cases.' Comparative capitalism approaches have largely neglected the part of the global economy in which rapid economic growth occurred for quite a long time, namely in Asia. Asian economies were often treated as sui generis cases that would not fit into existing comparative models, and thus as not meeting comparative requirements. This is especially evident in cases like China, where it seems that many different VoCs exist simultaneously within the same nation-state (Witt 2010). More recently, systematic efforts have been initiated to find analytical and methodological ways for bringing Asian 'economic styles' into the frameworks of comparative capitalism approaches. Witt and Redding (2013) give a wide-ranging comparison of Asian business styles by following the main institutional features of the original VoC approach. With the exception of Japan, their other 12 cases are incompatible with the distinctions offered by Hall and Soskice. Japan's business and overall economic system can be treated as a version of a CME, somewhere in the range between Germany and France (Witt and Redding 2013: 285). Though the character of the state as a *developmental state* may need to be stressed as an institutional feature that makes Japan distinct from Germany (see Schreurs, Chapter 4).

In contrast, grouping China in the realm of a comparative capitalism approach is a challenging maneuver. Toyhama and Harada (2013) make the case that China is a sui generis case that does not fit within standard procedures of grouping in the tradition of comparative capitalisms.[6] We have a different take and suggest incorporating China within a cluster of post-communist economies in Asia. An early attempt by Witt (2010) to locate China in the dualistic VoC approach followed the originally suggested institutional dualistic settings rather strictly. It came to the conclusion that China very much resembles the characteristics of LMEs, with the exemption of the financial system that shows rather unique traits. In later work (Witt and Redding 2013), which looked more closely at Asian business systems, a category was made that groups China within a cluster of post-socialist economies. Zhang and Peck (2014) also stress the hybrid character of the Chinese model. We follow Zhang and Peck's characterization of the five key institutional settings of the VoC approach and – in deviation from their own suggestion – group China as a *state-led market economy* (SME). Admittedly, many of China's economic dynamics over the last ten years or so stem from the burgeoning private sector. Despite this, we see state dominance in the financial regime, as well as the type of party-controlled industrial relations and state-controlled technology imports via foreign direct investment, as institutions that make China a case within the SME form of capitalism. This form of capitalism shares features with a small group of other Asian capitalisms (e.g., Malaysia, Thailand; see Boyer et al. 2013). We are aware that such a grouping neglects some key features, for example the role of person-based economic-political networks (see Storz, Amable, Casper and Lechevalier 2013). Still, our reading of the literature leads us to the conclusion that, broadly speaking, the state plays an significant role in Chinese economic development, and this is an important feature in regard to our overarching question of national responses to climate change.

Table 1.1 provides an overview on how we group our nine cases. Our four types of VoC help us generate hypotheses with regard to prevalent channels for policy adjustments, and policy change in general. In line with the original VoC approach, we would expect that our LME cases tend to respond to challenges to the existing growth model through predominantly private actors. These responses would reflect changes in market incentives, or could reflect 'sudden' innovations that have the potential for radical changes in production and consumption styles. The USA is the most well studied case of such a political-economic innovation style. This category also seems to apply to the UK. At least in the distinct sense that the UK's dominant economic sector is the financial industry, where the UK ('aka the City in London') has demonstrated strong levels of innovation. The same does not hold however for other sectors (see Ebner, Chapter 3). Even though Canada can mostly be grouped as a LME, it does not show such innovation styles. On many levels, Canada is a follower of US policy. It is also a part of a North American economic value chain, which makes the country an integral, but often inferior, part of a wider economic network. It needs to be stressed, though, that the expectation for radical innovation does not exclude incremental progress. Rodrik (2014) demonstrates that the USA, in a fashion similar to China and Germany, has established a number of incentives and regulations to generate 'green technologies'. As a matter of fact, such incentive and subsidy programs are a general feature across all of our groupings. We think, however, that identifying dominant innovation styles still offers relevant insights into the dynamics of existing growth paths. With regard to LMEs, the hypothesis thus holds that radical innovations are more often the outcome of economic and political actions of this group of economies than of other groupings.

CMEs, in contrast, are champions of incremental change, in both technological and political arenas. Adjustment and change occur along a given path, very much supported by strong institutional complementarities. Even sweeping policy changes such as the *Energiewende* in Germany follow a strict incremental path, with sectors receiving time 'rebates' in order to adjust to new norms and rules. The same holds for Japan and Norway, not least in their dominantly trust-oriented (Japan) or corporatist political-economic styles (Norway).

DMEs are neither radical technological innovators, nor strong incremental reformers. Much of their innovative capacity comes from outside, due to their inferior roles in European-wide value chains. This position results in low international rankings in technological competitiveness, which is becoming increasingly difficult to compensate for through low wages. Overall low technology levels generate low productivity levels, which then consequently reduce the available space for policy adjustments.

When discussing post-socialist countries such as China, which follow a different growth path, the guiding role of the state is a key contrast to the aforementioned DMEs. State-led market economies give a lot of leeway to private business activities, but also provide a fairly rigid political institutional regime. This provides the state with substantial ex post-control. The state apparatus controls, at least to a large degree, the direction of the overall economy, as well as the type of technology transfer, via its control of foreign direct investment. This is one of the reasons why state-led market economies like China are not institutionally well equipped for radical innovation and policy change. These happen instead in a rather incremental top-down manner.

To fine-tune these rather general hypotheses and apply them to the topic of national pathways to low carbon emission, it would be prudent to provide a clearer understanding of another category, namely, the type of national *carbon regime* in place. By adding this institutional feature to our existing VoC outline, we attempt to fine-tune our expectations for transition paths and unlocking strategies. Table 1.2 presents a broad sample of indicators for our cases.

Despite the fact that our national cases differ in terms of GDP per capita, they show surprising similarity in regard to their underlying carbon regimes. The cases share the commonality that coal is the most important, or at least an important, source of electricity generation. This ranges from 84 percent in Poland to 29 percent in Japan. Canada and Norway are at the other extreme with hydro shares of 60 percent (Canada) and 97 percent (Norway). In terms of carbon emission intensity (per unit of GDP) China has by far the worst record with a value of 3.3 tons, followed by Poland and the Czech Republic. All three countries are post-socialist societies, even though they now represent different VoC. It is puzzling that Canada and Norway, even though they both have a high proportion of hydro electricity generation, differ from each other so enormously in terms of carbon intensity. Norway, along with the UK, ranks at the very bottom in our group of countries (with a value of 0.2), whereas Canada, with its 0.5 tons per unit of GDP, ranks equal with the USA. Less surprising is the empirical fact that across all our cases the energy sector is the dominant source for carbon emissions. National carbon emission records for 1990 to 2012 differ enormously. During this period China has become the largest global emitter. In absolute, and even more dramatically in relative, terms Canada represents another case of significant emission increases. The USA shows a path toward an attenuation of emission growth rates, as does Japan. Germany and the UK, along with the Czech Republic and Poland, are the nations with the best records in our sample. These four countries represent three different VoC, which already begins to suggest that there is no linear connection between a dominant institutional setting and a particular carbon policy outcome. Our case studies show the importance of intermitting variables that help to explain this particular policy outcome. For the quantitative aspect of a national carbon regime it is necessary to take a further look at the balance of CO_2 in trade. Table 1.2 shows that Canada, Norway and China are all net exporters of CO_2. Our case studies show that the reasons for this position differ. In contrast, countries such as the USA, Japan, Germany and the UK are net importers. The trade balance in CO_2 is relevant to the policy dimension for at least two reasons. First, being a net exporter may raise concerns for net importing countries, as they may feel like victims of a free-rider attitude on the side of the net exporters. Second, exporting CO_2 in net terms implies that from a global perspective the country is stuck on a high carbon path. The inherent contradictions are probably best illustrated by a country like Norway, which is on the one hand extremely 'carbon clean', but on the other hand is a relevant energy producer that exploits carbon-intensive energy sources. The situation is slightly different for Canada, which is also on an energy producing economy track, but combines this sectoral trait – unlike Norway – with very high CO_2 emissions per capita. In other words, richness in extractable carbon resources does not automatically need to be translated to a high carbon path.

The Kyoto Protocol, which consisted of formidable emission reduction targets, covered all our cases with the exception of China. Our EU countries all share the EU-wide target of a 20 percent reduction by 2020, with 1990 as the base year. Japan and Norway were even more ambitious with emission targets of 25 percent and 30 percent respectively. Our North American cases of the USA and Canada chose 2005 as the base year, and both came up with an emission target of 17 percent. Canada decided to withdraw from the Kyoto Protocol unilaterally, and the USA was never able to ratify it domestically. From our set of nine cases, three involve further increases in emission projections until 2030 (Canada by 12 percent; China by 78 percent; and Japan by 3 percent). With regard to the launch of institutional incentive mechanisms and provisions, we can see a further differentiation. Four of our cases (Japan, Norway, the UK and one province in Canada) have some form of carbon tax. Moreover, all of our cases, with the exception of Japan, have cap-and-trade systems in place. However, those systems differ in depth and breadth. Our European cases (including Norway), are part of the EU ETS (EU Emission Trading System), which covers a number of critical sectors. China is currently running six provincial pilot trials; Canada has one province with a cap-and-trade system; and the USA has such a system in place in ten states.

Table 1.2 Case metrics

	Canada	China	Czech Republic	Germany	Hungary	Japan	Norway	Poland	United Kingdom	United States
GDP per capita (thousands of constant PPP USD) 2016	$43	$14	$31	$44	$25	$38	$64	$26	$39	$53
Electricity generation (top 3 sources) 2015	Hydro 57% Nuclear 15% Nat. gas/coal 10%	Coal 72% Hydro 19% Wind 3%	Coal 53% Nuclear 32% Bf/W 6%	Coal 44% Nuclear 14% Wind 13%	Nuclear 52% Coal 19% Nat.Gas 17%	Nat. gas 40% Coal 33% Oil 10%	Hydro 96% Nat. gas 2% Wind 2%	Coal 81% Wind 7% Bf/W 6%	Nat. gas 30% Coal 23% Nuclear 21%	Coal 34% Nat. gas 32% Nuclear 19%
Emissions 1990 (Mt CO_2e)	611	N/A	196	1,251	94	1,268	52	468	797	6,363
Emissions 2015 (Mt CO_2e)	722	7,466	127	902	61	1,323	54	385	507	6,587
CO_2 Emissions intensity (kg CO_2/2005 US$) 2014	0.31	1.10	0.46	0.20	0.29	0.21	0.08	0.52	0.16	0.32
CO_2 Emissions per capita (tonnes) 2014	15.61	6.66	9.17	8.93	4.08	9.35	6.87	7.25	6.31	16.22
Emissions sources of total (top 3)	Energy 81% Agric. 8% Ind. pr. 7%	Energy 77% Agric. 11% Ind. pr. 10%	Energy 77% Ind. pr. 12% Agric. 7%	Energy 85% Agric. 7% Ind. pr. 7%	Energy 71% Ind. pr. 12% Agric. 11%	Energy 89% Ind. pr. 7% Agric. 3%	Energy 73% Ind. pr. 16% Agric. 8%	Energy 73% Ind. pr. 16% Agric. 8%	Energy 81% Agric. 9% Ind. pr. 7%	Energy 84% Agric. 8% Ind. pr. 6%

Emissions reduction target for 2012 under Kyoto Protocol (base year)	(Withdrawn) Formerly –6% (2005)	–	–8% (1990)	–21% (1990)	–6% (1985–1987 average)	–25% (1990)	+1% (1990)	–6% (1988)	–12.5% (1990)	(Never Ratified) – 7% (1990)
Emissions reduction target for 2030 under Paris Agreement	–30% (2005)	Soft non-quantitative Target	–14% Signed but not yet joined (2005)	–38% (2005)	–7% (2005)	–26% (2013)	–40% (1990)	–7% (2005)	–37% (2005)	–28% (2005) (Intend to withdraw) (Target is for 2025)
Carbon tax	Yes (2 provinces)	–	–	–	Yes	Yes	Yes	Yes	Yes	–
Cap-and-trade	Yes (2 provinces)	Yes (7 provinces and cities)	Yes (EU-wide)	Yes (EU-wide)	Yes (EU-wide)	Yes (3 prefectures)	Yes (EU-wide)	Yes (EU-wide)	Yes (EU-wide)	Yes (10 states)

Sources: The World Bank World Development Indicators (GDP per capita), 2016; International Energy Agency, 2017 (Electricity Generation); UNFCCC Data Interface, 2017 (Emissions 1990 and 2015, Emissions Sources of Total); International Energy Agency, 2016 (Emissions Intensity, Emission per capita); UNFCCC, 2014 (Kyoto Protocol Reduction Targets); UNFCCC NDC Interim Registry, 2017 & European Commission Climate Action, 2017 (Paris Agreement Reduction Targets); World Bank Group. (2016) *State and Trends of Carbon Pricing*. Washington D.C. (Carbon Tax and Cap-and-trade);

Notes

Emissions data do not include LULUCF or indirect CO_2.

Paris Agreement figures for EU countries come for the European Commission Proposal for an Effort Sharing Regulation 2021–2030 as the EU NDC does not delineate how much each member state will reduce their emissions by. Japan's base year and target year for the Paris Agreement are both based on fiscal years which differ slightly from the other annual timelines.

By adding the carbon regime as an additional institutional set to the VoC components, we get a much richer picture. At the same time, the picture is getting more complex and, to some degree, blurry. In regard to our three LME cases, it turns out that the introduction of a carbon regime variable makes the USA and Canada even more similar. In contrast, the UK becomes a special case inside the LME camp, mainly because it is already on a relatively low carbon path and is covered by at least two critical institutional incentive mechanisms (cap-and-trade and carbon tax). However, as the USA and Canada case studies show, these differences are not as solid as they appear. In particular, the USA moved onto a lower carbon path more recently, not least due to a radical type of technological innovation, as well as the effects of regulatory policies from the federal government.

Our three CME cases also show internal differences due to the introduction of the carbon regime variable. Norway is the most obvious outlier, and this largely has to do with its status as a natural resource economy (i.e., being a net exporter of oil and gas). This status does make Norway a substantial net exporter of CO_2. This position seems to be a significant driver for both its inward, and (even more significantly) outward, looking carbon policies that come with a strong mitigation approach (see Sjkærseth and Jevnaker, Chapter 6). Japan and Germany have both started to move toward a lower carbon path but have run into problems caused by the Fukushima Disaster. In pure carbon terms, this catastrophe resulted in an increase in carbon-intensive imports for Japan to 'keep the lights on.' In Germany's case, the political response to Fukushima was an acceleration of the already planned shutdown of its atomic reactors, and a more pronounced move toward renewables. In its first transition phase, the *Energiewende* resulted in relative price advantages for existing coal plants, and thus in an increase in carbon emissions (see Chapter 5 on Germany). Still, despite the shocking accident in Japan and Germany's policy decision to move out of atomic energy more quickly than initially planned, the dominant policy and innovation response in both cases can best be labeled as incremental. However, what was initially planned as a consensual process between energy providers and the state in Germany, turned into a fight about costs and rents in its first transition phase.

The relevance of our DME cases is stressed by the introduction of the carbon regime variable. Not only do these economies show a technological and innovational dependence on outside, they are also getting an externally imposed carbon regime that, at least to some degree, is not compatible with their internal economic structures. In both cases, the coal sectors are key political drivers for a carbon policy characterized by exemptions and additional adjustment time frames, all of which are granted by the EU. This feature is critical for explaining their position as innovation laggards, which presents medium-term risks that can undermine their competitiveness in terms of quality (see Archibugi and Chiarugi, Chapter 8).

Unlocking dilemmas and path change experiences

Our case studies demonstrate that despite all the rhetoric about transitioning to low carbon emission economies, the world in general, the countries of our sample included, are far from moving toward a low carbon emission path. This is the dispiriting news. The good news is that almost all the countries in our sample are responding to the climate challenge and have more or less ambitious intentions to move toward a low carbon emission path. Our goal is to understand the directions and underlying instruments of these responses, as well as how they are structured in political and economic terms. Based on our institutional framework we expect particular responses from particular countries.

One of the most interesting cases with regard to the underlying analytical institutional framework is the USA. Following our hypothesis for LMEs, we would expect the emergence of radical innovations as their dominant response to the climate change challenge. At first glance this is exactly what has happened in the USA. Due to the two new technologies of horizontal drilling and large-scale hydraulic fracturing, it became possible to reach previously inaccessible oil and gas reserves.[7] In particular, so-called shale gas is seen as an optimum energy source for an economy on its way to a low carbon emission state. In the last few years, the production of shale gas and tight oil has increased enormously. US production of shale gas increased from one trillion cubic feet in 2006 to 4.8 trillion cubic feet in 2010, and to 9.6 trillion cubic feet in 2014 (Sieminski 2014). The production of light tight oil that became accessible due to fracking increased 18-fold between 2007 and 2012 (Blackwill and O'Sullivan 2014). This technological push was very much supported by complementary actions of the US financial system that is, as expected, relatively supportive of innovation. These technology-driven developments can claim four overall effects: (i) the strong increase in US oil and gas production added significantly to global supply levels and contributed to the downward price trend from 2013; (ii) relatively 'cleaner' gas started to substitute for relatively 'dirtier' coal as an energy source, and thus contributed to the emerging turnaround in US carbon emissions; (iii) lower energy prices in the USA improve overall macroeconomic price competitiveness; and (iv) the lower price for gas and oil sends relative price signals throughout the economy that make renewables relatively *less* attractive in price terms.

Climate policies that were based on 'peak oil' assumptions came under stress and may be devalued for quite a while (Helm 2014). In particular, the relative price effect of a technological innovation hints at the detrimental effect for climate policies. The less attractive renewable energy sources become, the less change in production and consumption styles we can expect. In the short-term it seems as if tight oil and shale gas contributed strongly to a decline in carbon emissions. Medium- and long-term this may not be the case, if only for the reason that it will become increasingly more difficult – and expensive – to access these carbon sources. Moving toward a low carbon emission economy is not solely a question of technological innovations and new markets that crowd out existing products. Without strong social and political support, any unlocking becomes highly controversial. As our case study shows, the USA is an example of a highly divided polity with a large *fossil fuel coalition*. This coalition consists of fossil fuel sector companies, trade unions, think tanks and representatives from coal states across both Democratic and Republican parties (Hess 2014). This coalition successfully pushes for financial support of high carbon emission industries; the USA provides state subsidies for the exploration and extraction of fossil fuels of approximately $5 billion per year (Bast et al. 2014: 29). In 2014, 39 percent of US electricity was generated by coal-fired power plants (see Figure 1.3), and this dominance plays a significant role in determining the carbon path. At the same time, the fossil fuel coalition intervenes meaningfully in the national discourse about climate change. It is not an accident that recent elections have seen a wave of politicians elected to the House and Senate who are outspoken climate change skeptics. In this politically divided situation, President Obama decided to take refuge in the Clean Air Act of 1963 and asked the Environmental Protection Agency (EPA) to use its regulatory power to deal with carbon emissions. Consequently, in 2014, the EPA started to target the more than 600 coal-fired power plants with a regulation that would result in a 30 percent reduction in carbon emissions by 2030 compared to 2005 levels. Rather than proposing a uniform strategy to achieve this goal, states were given a menu of options, including side-by-side modernization of existing coal plants along with the installment of low carbon energy sources such as wind and solar generators (US Environmental Protection Agency 2015). The aforementioned renewable sources, including biofuels, enjoy tax credit subsidies of around US$10 billion in 2010, but have so far represented a relatively minor contribution to the reduction of carbon emissions (Murray et al. 2014: 573). Renewable energy sources currently contribute to about 13 percent of all electricity produced (US Energy Information Administration, 2015). This relatively low share still makes the USA the largest global consumer of renewable energy sources.[8] And yet, politics can interfere in various ways. Incoming President Trump used the same presidential power to reverse most of Obama's support for renewable energy and in the framework of his America First strategy moved back to a strong support for coal and nuclear energy. The fossil fuel coalition came back in the saddle and immediately prepared for a turnaround in US energy policy.

Growing a new energy industry in the shadow of a large and politically favored incumbent industry like the coal sector is a difficult undertaking. The problem is even more complicated if new technologies simultaneously drive an extraction and production process that comes with price effects that undermine the viability of alternative renewable energy sources which need, at least in their infant stages, a minimum price level to make them competitive. If such a threshold is not in reach, direct or indirect state funding via industrial policy can help to get them onto markets. This is not necessarily an easy task

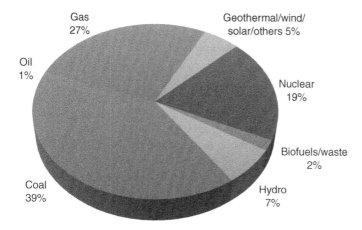

Figure 1.3 US electricity generation by fuel type in 2014.
Source: International Energy Agency, 2017.

to fulfill. President Obama introduced a version of a green industrial policy, as part of the 2009 American Reinvestment and Recovery Act. One of the beneficiaries was the solar cell company Solyndra, which received a loan guarantee from this program of US$535 million. Just two years later the company went bankrupt. This was due, in no insignificant measure, to the enormous fall in silicon prices that was triggered by state-subsidized solar cell production of Chinese companies, which flooded the market and brought prices down (Rodrik 2014).

The technological breakthroughs for accessing fossil fuel sources may restrict further gains in the market share of renewables, as a gap emerges between the minimum price that makes these sources economically viable, and the actual market price for energy, at least in the short term. Moreover, it is not yet clear whether hydraulic fracturing technologies will actually decrease CO_2 emissions in the long term. A recent modeling exercise (McJeon et al. 2014) indicates that the use of more natural gas as an energy source may even increase CO_2 emissions or – depending on the scenario – only provide a small mitigation impact. And yet, our US case confirms our expectation that LMEs are relatively successful in generating radical innovation. At the same time though, the US example also hints at the potential lack of an adequate institutional setting for a viable path change. One that would reflect the social costs of private production and consumption. Even if one sees fracking and hydraulic drilling as innovations for a successful transition path to a low carbon emission economy, it can be argued that the economic effects are highly ambiguous. On the one hand, we see – in the case of shale gas – an energy source substitution that comes with a slightly lower carbon footprint (see Harrison, Chapter 2), while on the other hand it adds to a supply glut that leads to a reduction in overall energy prices. The supply glut induces higher consumption and, more relevantly, makes new alternative energy resources less competitive. The immediate change is largely market-driven, and only gets minor additional support in terms of regulatory actions by the President. The combination of a polity that is highly divided on climate policies, along with an innovation- and market-driven process of path change, makes unlocking an unstable endeavor.

In the comparative capitalism literature Canada is treated as an LME, and for good reason, as Harrison shows in Chapter 2. When it comes to climate policies, Canada shows some unique traits. The relatively small size of its economy and the strong economic integration with the USA has made Canada, in economically sensitive areas, a traditional *policy follower.* Close to 80 percent of Canada's exports go to the USA, and a rather high share of production located in Canada is part of a US-dominated supply chain. This reflects a "re-exporting trade character," where Canada systematically sits on the dominant end of this chain (Baldwin and Lopez-Gonzalez 2014: 5). This asymmetric dependence tends to encourage a wait-and-see attitude, particularly when it comes to policy projects that come with short-term costs. For quite a long time this held for climate policies. The federal government argued over a couple of years that an attempt to upscale climate policies before the USA moved in the same direction would be too risky a strategy in terms of competitiveness. As a result, Canada lacked a far-reaching and coherent federal climate policy strategy (Fertel et al. 2013). This changed with the new Liberal government in late 2015. Canada started to move away from the habit of following policy and turned to a global leadership role – not so much in terms of emission reduction as in terms of policy habit.

Canada is a strongly federal country and thus it is relevant to take into account that not all provinces share this passive approach. British Columbia and Quebec follow a different path and referred explicitly to a potential first-mover advantage, when they introduced a carbon tax and cap-and-trade system respectively (see Harrison, Chapter 2). In 2015, the Liberal government in Canada's industrial heartland province of Ontario provided the same argument when it announced the introduction of a cap-and-trade regime by joining the carbon market constituted by California and Quebec. Additionally, British Columbia introduced fuel quality standards, and with it the Clean Energy Act. This demands that 93 percent of energy emanating from the provincially owned power generator is 'clean' energy. It helps both of these provinces that their provincial energy mix is dominated by hydropower. The test comes for British Columbia if it continues to move forward with its liquefied natural gas strategy. This would increase its carbon footprint enormously, with the consequence that – in a business as usual scenario – the province would fail to reach its climate commitment.

Canada's climate policies were very much determined by its abundance of carbon-intensive resources, and the intention of the federal government to make the country an energy superpower. This political project led to the

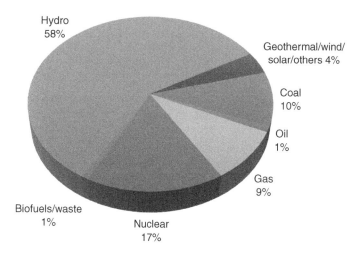

Figure 1.4 Canada electricity generation by fuel type in 2014.
Source: International Energy Agency, 2017.

abandonment of its Kyoto commitments, and to a weak intensity target that was not helpful for guiding producer and consumer decisions in the low carbon emission direction. This strategic choice indicates the strong economic developmental dimension that guides Canada's management of its resource sectors. Domestically, the country is in the position to generate 60 percent of its electricity from hydropower. However, there is significant variance across the country. When it comes to the exploitation of natural resources, it is the provinces that have the say, by constitution as well as in real politics. The most critical political actor in this oil sand coalition is the province of Alberta, which holds the third largest proven oil reserves on Earth and has built its economic future on those reserves. Getting this type of oil out of the ground has already added substantially to emissions in the past few years, and will continue to do so. According to the government agency Environment Canada, the country will miss its Copenhagen obligation of 610 megatons in 2020 by a large margin, if no fundamental policy change occurs (Environment Canada 2013).[9] For quite a time, such decisive action could not be expected to come from the federal level. Former Prime Minister Harper declared in blunt terms that it would be "crazy economic policy" to introduce carbon strategies that would act as an additional tax on the industry.[10] At the same time, various government levels in Canada provided the fossil fuel sector with estimated post-tax subsidies of approximately US$46 billion in 2015 (International Monetary Fund-Fiscal Affairs Department 2015). These allotments provide huge hurdles to the unlocking process, and actually work as impediments for alternative technologies. Rather than moving toward a low carbon emission economy, Canada was on a path that cements the high carbon regime. Breaking this path became a huge challenge for the incoming Liberal government under the leadership of Justin Trudeau. The new government quickly made sure that climate policies become a critical feature of its policies, and actually stepped up its policy advances at the Paris Climate Summit. The planned country-wide cap-and-trade system became a lightning rod of its ambitions, and also demonstrated the political challenges for a project that wants to put a solid price on emissions in a resource-intensive economy. As long as governments are eager to make use of those resources by exporting fossil fuels, mainly to the USA, national emissions will continue to grow (see Harrison, Chapter 2).

Political divisions about climate policies follow the political-geographical distribution of carbon-intensive energy sources rather closely. The more resource-abundant a province is, the more its political actors favor an economic strategy that puts a priority on income and jobs over climate targets (see Harrison, Chapter 2). The same distribution holds for investments in renewable energy. From 2009 to 2013 Quebec and British Columbia invested C\$5.3 billion and C\$6.1 billion, respectively. Only Canada's industrial heartland province Ontario invested more (C\$8.7 billion) over this period. In contrast, Canada's provincial growth engine, Alberta, only invested C\$1.6 billion over those five years (Clean Energy Canada 2014). Given that these funds depend to a large degree on institutional prerequisites that include active state support, it is telling that the provinces with relatively advanced climate policies attract the bulk of investments in renewable energy sources. In a very illustrative way, this connection supports our hypothesis that proper institutional settings and incentives are needed to guide investment decisions.

Climate-friendly institutional settings should not be muddled with costly state subsidies, or other forms of direct and indirect support policies. Institutions can be mechanisms to internalize the external costs of private production, such as the revenue-neutral carbon tax of British Columbia. Climate-friendly innovations can be market-triggered, but due to their higher break-even point may also need direct state support. This holds even more true for radical climate technology innovations as they come – like all radical innovations – with a high level of uncertainty in terms of potential marketization and demand potential. LME governments are not afraid to enact innovation policies, and Canadian state agencies are no exception. The provinces of Alberta and Saskatchewan, with additional support from the federal government, have committed substantial government spending for the installment of trial carbon capture and storage (CCS) facilities,[11] which would allow them to maintain their carbon-intensive energy strategy.[12] This path-stabilizing innovation approach orients public funding toward a 'big technology,' as has happened in the past in many parts of the developed world with the public support of the nuclear industry. Rather than being a carbon emission avoiding technology, CCS starts at the end of the process cycle by storing actually released carbon. This approach may make sense – if the technology were ever to be successfully implemented on a large scale – for a strategic project that aims to turn Canada into an energy superpower. However, it is definitely not an approach to unlock Canada's current carbon path and induce a change toward a low carbon emission economy. Rather, the current state of CCS technologies, and the political hope for future technological breakthroughs, indicate a reluctance for a fundamental path change.

The UK is our third version of an LME, and thus shares fundamental characteristics and institutional settings with the USA and Canada. At the same time it shows at least three distinct features. First, the UK economy is much more 'financialized' than the economies of the USA and Canada, with a share of financial services in value-added terms of more than 10 percent before the financial crisis of 2008. In the year before the crisis, the financial services sector growth rate was more than double the growth rate of UK GDP (Burgess 2011). Financial services are by their nature less carbon-intensive then many other economic activities. Second, as a member state of the EU the UK is covered by the EU ETS. This makes the country a participant in a carbon cap-and-trade regime that provides companies and sectors with overarching rules and carbon prices. Third, the UK is on track to meet its Kyoto obligations to reduce carbon emissions, and as Ebner shows (Chapter 3) this makes the UK an above average performer in the EU. Given its specific institutional settings, one would expect this record to be due mainly to successful radical innovations in the private sector. Relevant innovation indicators indeed do hint at strong British innovation performance. However, a closer look reveals that the UK's institutional setting no longer fits a simplistic LME description. In particular, the innovation regime has added many features that make it a hybrid sub-regime. Prominent additions are public carbon budgets, direct support for low carbon technologies, state regulations and joint public-private funding mechanisms (see Ebner, Chapter 3). This confirms the analytical insight that technological shifts, where social gains are higher than private gains, require non-market actors to play a role in order to successfully transition to a low carbon path. This also holds true for LMEs.

Decarbonization of the UK economy is not inexorable though. Figure 1.5 provides an impression about the role of fuel in electricity production. In 2014, coal was the leading source of electricity with a 40 percent share, followed by natural gas with a 27 percent proportion and nuclear energy with a 19 percent stake. In other words, two 'old' technologies made up about 60 percent of electricity production. If the UK wants to meet its 80 percent emission reduction target by 2050, this energy supply mix needs to change dramatically. Following scenarios provided by the Department of Energy and Climate Change, the electricity grid will have to be fully decarbonized by 2050 to meet these targets. This can only be achieved by giving renewables and nuclear, in combination with CCS technologies, absolute priority. In such a world there is no room for coal as an energy source (Mander, Walsh, Gilbert, Traut and Bows 2012). As Ebner shows (Chapter 3), there are no critical political actors at this point who could drive such a fundamental change toward decarbonization. Whether the UK will stick with, or

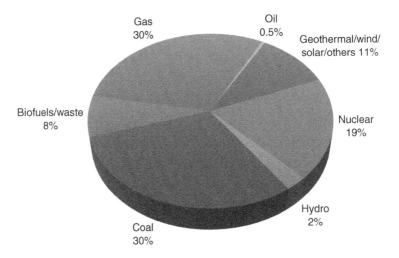

Figure 1.5 UK electricity generation by fuel type in 2014.
Source: International Energy Agency, 2017.

even expand, its nuclear energy supply and/or focus more on renewables is as much a political decision, as one driven by market expectations of innovators.

The VoC literature views Germany as the CME poster child; one can even argue that the overarching category is rooted in the German experience. The German version of a CME contains the ideal typology of long-term firm finance, in conjunction with close banking relations, cooperative industrial relations, high levels of firm-specific vocational training in support of technological learning, and inter-firm cooperation in technology transfer (Ebner, Chapter 5). Following the literature, firms in coordinated market economies prefer incremental innovations within stable organizational settings, based on persistent skills upgrading, long-term capital investments, and cooperative labor relations. It is these traits that led us to the expectation that Germany would move along a given economic-technological trajectory, by more or less smoothly adapting to a carefully designed climate policy. The intense public discourse around nuclear energy and carbon emissions eventually resulted in the transformation of various political movements into a political party that has been electorally successful over the last 40 years. Due to this public interest, various German governments started to engage relatively early in energy and climate policies, not least in the promotion of renewable energy sources. The phasing out of nuclear energy became a hot political topic, especially after the Chernobyl catastrophe in April 1986. And yet, only the formation of a so-called Red–Green Coalition of the Social Democratic Party and the Green Party in 1998 resulted in a law that foresaw the phaseout of nuclear power plants. Existing nuclear power plants were given a maximum lifetime of 32 years and, on this basis, residual electricity volume was calculated for each power plant. The provision of a clearly defined schedule supposedly provided economic security and certainty to the nuclear power sector, only to get overturned in the aftermath of the core melt accident of the Fukushima reactor. The reigning coalition in Germany that had campaigned against the previous phaseout schedule now performed an impressive U-turn that resulted in the decision to decommission the seven oldest nuclear power plants and to phase out nuclear by 2022.[13] This was no small feat given that nuclear electricity generation accounted for around 22 percent of Germany's overall electricity in 2010 (Kemfert, Opitz, Traber and Handrich 2015). To secure a reliable and economically viable energy supply that simultaneously minimizes its carbon footprint, the phaseout of nuclear energy was accompanied by targets to: (i) significantly increase energy efficiency across all sectors; (ii) substantially increase the share of renewable energy sources for final energy consumption; and (iii) to reduce CO_2 emissions by 40 percent by 2020 compared to 1999.

The project of an *Energiewende* has been long in the making, but then the project was accelerated when the Fukushima incident created a sudden and stark loss of confidence in nuclear energy among the German electorate. Rather than being a spontaneous response to Fukushima, the whole project needs to be seen as a political-logical implication of German environmental and climate policies. Germany possesses a strong innovation bedrock, and thus reflects all of the innovation traits inherent in a CME, and embodies even more innovation than might be typically expected in this VoC (Ebner, Chapter 5). The Renewable Energy Act (EEG) of 2000 – which saw intermittent alterations and modifications until 2014 – can be seen as the most critical policy initiative for moving toward an increase in renewables for the provision of electricity. This is mainly due to the setting of – adjustable – firm feed-in tariffs for a period of 20 years. This provided certainty to investors, and consequently triggered substantial investments in renewables. As a result, the share of renewable electricity in overall electricity production increased from around 10 percent in 2000 to around 25 percent by 2013 (Kemfert, Opitz, Traber and Handrich 2015: 39). And yet, the EEG is also a story of two tales. The first tale is about solar energy, where Germany was the largest producer of photovoltaic modules globally, only to become – at least partially – the victim of rapidly decreasing prices for solar panels as the result of strong growth in foreign production. The domestic solar industry was badly hurt, not least as a result of strong government support for the creation of a solar panel industry in China (Hübner 2015), as well as due to a feed-in tariff for solar guaranteed by the EEG which was too high and led to the misallocation of resources. The second tale is about the rise of wind power, where Germany became a global leader in the production of off-shore wind turbines, just shy of Denmark's production. This technological lead is not solely based on domestic innovation potential, but is also the result of smart technology oriented acquisitions by companies such as Siemens. Siemens' main wind power department emerged largely from the purchase of Danish technological competence (Kemfert, Opitz, Traber and Handrich 2015: 41).

German success in increasing its share of renewables in the energy mix is not reflected by a reduction in greenhouse gas emissions. In 2012, 2014 and 2016, CO_2 emissions actually increased, mainly because energy companies opted to burn more so-called hard and lignite coal as opposed to natural gas, which has a comparative price disadvantage. As long as prices for coal and natural gas move in opposite directions, coal-fired power plants will be reactivated as this generates easy windfall profits. It has become obvious, however, that Germany's ambitious climate policies are coming under political stress, including from representatives of the coal sector. Coal interests opposed the Ministry of Economy's plan to drastically curb emissions from coal-fired power plants by 22 megatons by 2020, an amount that would equal the shutdown of eight coal-fired plants. Such a step toward unlocking met fierce resistance and has since led to a much lower reduction target, which allows energy companies to continue reaping windfall profits. Overcoming the short-term interests of the coal sector – in particular the resistance of the interest coalition of coal-based trade unions, regional and state politicians of coal Länder across all parties and from the coal industry – has become a potential stumbling block for *Energiewende*. Especially one which thrives on innovation, but will encounter challenges with respect to following a growth path based on old technologies.

Japan is our next case of a CME with relatively strong neo-corporatist institutional arrangements. Moreover, Japan's version of capitalism has strong features of an entrepreneurial state, in which powerful ministries set rather detailed frameworks for the development of technologies (see Chapter 4, Schreurs).

The relatively high level of administrative capacity – mainly represented by the powerful Ministry of Finance and the Ministry of Economy, Trade and Industry – and the established *keiretsu* structures, pushed particular

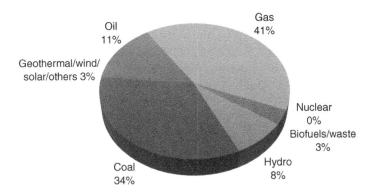

Figure 1.6 Japan electricity generation by fuel type in 2014.

Source: International Energy Agency, 2017.

technological trajectories during the long Japanese growth spurt that came to a halt in the early 1990s. Since 1991, the burst of the real estate bubble, along with state policies toward the over-indebted financial industry, have resulted in long-term economic stagnation and the large accumulation of public debt. The well orchestrated cooperation between large companies and the state apparatus began to suffer, as the latter could no longer provide the input and guidance it was previously capable of proffering.

In terms of factor endowment, Japan has a lack of natural energy resources. Electricity generation was thus mainly based on the importation of oil, natural gas and coal. This import dependence became a huge problem in the early 1970s. The sudden rise in oil prices as the result of successful OPEC cartelization efforts created both a supply shortage, and more acutely (due to the surge in global energy prices) a price competitiveness problem for Japan. The Japanese response was swift and very much in line with its institutional setting, which makes use of the strong ties between large companies and administrative state capacity. The innovation offensive, broadly aimed at energy efficiency technologies and at alternative energy sources, was also simultaneously focused on atomic energy as the main provider of electricity. Strong emphasis was also given to the development of so-called supercritical power plants, that used coal as an input factor. As a result, this type of power plant turned Japan into a global technology leader (Horbach, Chen, Rennings and Vögele 2014). State-driven programs for developing energy efficient technologies helped the Japanese car industry move quickly to achieve the top position in terms of productivity and technology leadership.

Japan's innovation policies and its relatively advanced and ambitious climate policy stance came under pressure for two reasons, which were independent of each other. As for other varieties of coordinated market economies, Japan had experienced a process of slow hybridization since the 1980s, which came with a stronger market orientation of the financial regime and a shrinking planning capacity of the state apparatus (Boyer et al. 2012). When the financial bubble burst at the end of the 1980s – mainly driven by price developments in the real estate sector – Japan entered the long period of deflation and stagnation that still ails the economy. Deleveraging by the private sector, shrinking total factor productivity and low GDP growth were symptoms of these processes that were never overcome by means of fiscal or monetary policies. Despite these serious problems, Japan stuck to its ambitious climate policies, and enacted fairly strong programs at various levels of society. This all unraveled with the Fukushima nuclear accident that fundamentally changed the nature of climate policy challenges. With the shutdown of its nuclear fleet, Japan abandoned its emission targets. Post-Fukushima, the country became the world's largest importer of liquefied natural gas, the second largest importer of coal and the third largest importer of oil. This low self-sufficiency ratio, in combination with a depreciating yen, has resulted in an increased import bill that is threatening price competitiveness (McCracken 2014; Institute of Energy Economics, Japan 2015). Under these economic constraints, nuclear energy is experiencing a revival; at the same time the Japanese government is developing energy policy scenarios in which renewables are receiving a more prominent role. The combination of a structural economic crisis and a failed energy policy has the potential to change the emission path, by making Japan a more self-sufficient energy provider. Schreurs (Chapter 4) hints at the possibility of Japan unleashing its innovation potential in energy policy. At the same time though, the political influence of the nuclear industry has opened the door for a revival of nuclear power, and thus the prolongation of the old path of energy production.

Institutional features of capitalist formation are crucial but not sufficient to explain policy outcomes. This is best illustrated by the case of Norway (Skjaerseth and Jevnaker, Chapter 6), a country that easily qualifies as a CME, where incremental economic and political processes dominate. At the same time, Norway is a fossil fuel-based economy in which gas and oil extraction makes up approximately 25 percent of its gross national product, and half of its export revenues. It is this last feature that may slow down innovation processes toward a low carbon emission path. To be more concrete, the endowment of significant natural resources whose exploitation is highly carbon-intensive makes a transition to a low carbon emission economy challenging. The country's stated objective to be carbon neutral by 2050 is surprising in this perspective. In terms of its ambitions, Norway trumps even the EU, which only belatedly moved to the same emission target (and only did so briefly) before the December 2015 Paris Climate Conference. Compared to the other resource-oriented economy in our sample of cases – Canada – the political goal is an extraordinary step that makes Norway different, and not only from Canada. As a matter of fact, Norway was actively engaged in international climate activities and introduced the world's first CO_2 tax as early as 1991. What is more, this tax explicitly targeted its petrol sector. Today, about 80 percent of its emissions are subject to both the carbon tax and the EU ETS (see below). Like other resource-rich economies Norway is not willing to give up the economic exploitation of its resource endowment. Unlike other resource economies, the country is heavily engaged in low carbon emission projects abroad, while at the same time investing in technologies that can potentially help in dealing with domestic carbon emissions. Most prominent is CCS. In comparison to Canada, Norway takes climate change seriously and has activated relevant policies early on; and yet it is obvious that its economic lock-in to petroleum makes deep decarbonization both a political and an economic challenge. Skjaerseth and Jevnaker (Chapter 6) speculate that the unlocking of its energy path will not be induced within the domestic institutional setting but, if at all, by climate policy actions from the EU that would force Norway to act as a policy follower.

In light of our analytical approach, we argue that institutional settings are guiding policy decisions to a relatively strong degree, and thus that they create some path dependence. In this regard China is a puzzling case. Its institutional setting of market allocation and strong state control – a combination that we label a SME for our purposes – results in an enormous marketization and commodification of economic activities. These, however, are still under a staggering level of direct and indirect state control. Given that its institutional features have been evolving since the start of market-oriented reforms in 1979, and not always linearly, it is not clear how the balance between commodification and state intervention is developing. Strong economic growth has been the hallmark of the Chinese model since the 1980s. Average annual GDP growth rates of around 10 percent may be a thing of the past. But even if growth recedes to a 'normal' rate for a maturing economy in the next few years, the absolute increase in output, and accordingly the required inputs, will still be above the OECD average. It is not yet settled whether China can continue on its growth path or whether it will be the victim of the middle-income trap (Pritchett and Summers 2014). Evidence suggests that China's growth path is meeting serious hurdles, including through a significant environmental costs component. An analysis by the Chinese concluded that it needs an annual US$465 billion over the 2015 to 2020 period just to fulfill its existing pollution regulations (Chenghui, Zadek, Ning and Halle 2015):

> China became the world's second largest economy in 2010, but has been the number one emitter of conventional pollutants since 2005, and by 2011 it was also the largest carbon dioxide emitter. The risk of major environmental accidents, and daily concerns about air, water and soil quality make environmental issues a widespread concern. Only 3 out of 74 cities monitored for air quality met minimum standards in 2014. An estimated 60 per cent of underground water monitoring sites have poor quality, and 19 per cent of arable land is badly polluted. China is actively pursuing industrial restructuring; it is identifying dirty and inefficient industries to be restricted and eliminated, and high-tech, high value-added sectors to be encouraged. However, despite these policies, the fastest growing sectors from 2005–2011 were the 'restricted' industries such as coal, minerals, metals and chemicals.

High and increasing environmental costs are causing both economic and political-social problems, and – as Schreurs argues in Chapter 7 – have become powerful drivers for a change in the underlying Chinese growth models. In particular, air pollution and climate policies have become critical initiatives for the Chinese government. This led to ambitious programs in their Five-Year Plans. And yet, the move toward a low carbon emission economy still seems to be cumbersome, not least under the current conditions of reduced economic growth and a fragile financial system. In terms of social integration, the Chinese growth model is rooted in high annual growth rates. This allowed a relatively smooth transfer of rural workers to the emerging industrial and service sectors, as well as the steady growth of a middle-class. However, this model has reached its limits in terms of system integration, economically as well as environmentally. The government's plan to move from a mainly investment- and export-driven economy, toward a more inward-looking, consumption-driven economy, is a response to these challenges. But this response comes with its own problems. Schreurs (Chapter 7) makes the point that active climate policies can help smooth such a change to a potentially lower, but also more energy efficient, growth path. During its long phase of astounding economic growth, China became a manufacturing locus of the global economy, and thus a leading net export economy. Net exports go hand in hand with the export of carbon emissions, and it was net importers like the USA that imported high carbon amounts in their economic relations with China. Greater sophistication of China's export goods production led to a reduction of carbon intensity per unit of export goods, but this improvement was easily offset by the growth in export volumes (Zhang 2015).

China's state-led growth model, and its specific institutional features, provide ample opportunities for a path change. In particular, the level of effective state control in industry – making up to about 30 percent of China's GDP – in sectors of strategic importance, can be seen as a supportive element in the transition toward a more inward-looking and less carbon-intensive growth path. On the other hand, state-owned enterprises are relatively sheltered from international competition and thus tend to have less impetus to adopt cutting-edge technologies (Zhang and Peck 2014). So far, China has experimented with seven pilot emission trading schemes on the local level that put a price on carbon emissions. The sooner a nationwide cap-and-trade regime is established, and the more comprehensive such a regime is, the higher the cost pressure on emission-intensive production lines and technologies. This move is now planned for 2017 and would add a carbon market that would be significantly larger than the European carbon market.

Our case studies on Poland, Hungary and the Czech Republic (Archibugi and Chiarugi, Chapter 8) demonstrate – in a paradoxical way – what a lack of economic and political incentives means for an active climate policy. All three economies have had to undergo critical and far-reaching economic, political, social and cultural transformations since the end of the Soviet Empire. Support programs from the EU closely accompanied those processes, not least because all three countries embraced the chance to become members of the EU early on. Preparing for membership of the EU required underwriting a vast body of rules, norms and laws – entitled the *Acquit Communitaire* – and thus implied a structural convergence; and yet, all the new members from Eastern Europe reserved some leeway for the design of their own politics and policies. Most critically, two (Poland and the Czech Republic) of our three countries started with emission levels in 1990 that were far above the EU average, and experienced huge economic crises in the early years of their system transformations. This resulted in a significant decrease in GDP, along with shrinking carbon emissions that allowed them to easily to fulfill their obligations stemming from the Kyoto Protocol. The processes of deep transformation included far-reaching sectoral changes and the substitution of inferior production processes. The latter was strongly driven by liberalization strategies put in place in the early 1990s that led to extremely open foreign direct investment regimes, and thus to strong capital inflows – the main reason why we label these economies as DMEs. This inflow of foreign direct investment was nothing less than a technology import that contributed to the gains in energy efficiency for all three economies. The import of technology, however, comes with decreasing marginal effects. This could be compensated for by an active green innovation policy that aims to foster carbon-reducing innovations. Archibugi and Chiarugi show that not one of the three economies took such a route, and thus it is no surprise that the negative emission trends since 2007 slowed down significantly. Our DME cases also share the political shortcoming of a lack of political actors who would push for an unlocking of the established growth path. Rather than forging a forward-looking policy, they tend to stick to the given path. As a result, DMEs display strong resistance to the ambitious climate targets of the EU. In the case of Poland, it is strong coal interests that mobilize against changes in the energy sector; in Hungary the government favors a recourse to Russian atomic plants to decrease carbon emissions. The more coherent the economic status quo block is, the weaker is the coordination of efforts toward an emission-oriented innovation policy, and the less 'modern' the sectoral composition of the national economies.

State and markets – again

Moving to a low carbon emission economy requires disruptive technological change, in tandem with fundamental social and economic change. A common claim tells us that capitalist economies are best equipped to generate exactly this type of change:

> Under capitalism, innovative activity ... becomes mandatory, a life-and-death matter for the firm. And the spread of new technology, which in other economies has proceeded at a stately pace, often requiring decades or even centuries, under capitalism is speeded up remarkably because, quite simply, time is money.
>
> (Baumol 2002: 6)

It is well established that capitalist economies tend to under-produce specific types of innovation, namely ones where the social benefits are higher than the private benefits of the innovating economic actor (Mazzucato 2013). Carbon-reducing technologies tend to fall into this category. The argument is not that capitalist economies do not generate these technologies, but that they do not produce enough of them in a short enough time frame. Insofar as carbon-reducing innovations reach the market, it is mainly due to active state policies that encourage or directly support such innovative efforts (Mazzucato 2013) Moreover, it is widely accepted that not all capitalisms are equal and are thus not equally capable of generating disruptive innovations. Nor are they equally capable of finding an acceptable balance between private innovation rents and social benefits. Our case studies convincingly demonstrate that institutional settings matter, and thus that the type of capitalism is critical with regard to innovation outcomes. And yet, some of the findings are surprising, or at least do not easily harmonize with the analytical expectations derived from the VoC literature. The economy closest to the framework's analytical prediction is that of the USA, where hydraulic fracturing and horizontal drilling have transformed natural gas and oil production. Fracking can be seen as a disruptive innovation that comes with indirect carbon-reducing effects (Golden and Wiseman 2014). At the same time, this particular innovation comes with serious ecological side effects that undermine the implied social benefits (see Harrison, Chapter 2). The USA is also a case where the government has come to realize that climate-friendly, carbon-reducing technologies are not automatically generated by private markets, but need substantial state support, which goes through the existing national innovation system. It also, however, relies significantly on stringent regulations to guide innovation toward those activities that will eventually create social benefits, as opposed to predominantly private benefits. Even though the US version of a LME is no stranger to active state policies, the Obama government struggled to employ policies that favor alternative technologies aimed at reducing carbon emissions. President Trump's strategy of deregulating the energy sector and actively supporting coal and nuclear power production will be a test of the strength and resilience of fracking, as well as of the renewable energy sector.

As stated, not all capitalisms are equal. This statement also holds – to a lesser degree – within the LME variant of capitalism. Most key elements of the Canadian growth regime qualify it as a LME, but one with a highly federalist character, in which respective approaches to climate policy differ enormously within the country. In the absence of a comprehensive central innovation policy and an overall neglect of emission-reducing policies, the Canadian growth regime lacks the political incentives that are needed to organize a successful path change. And yet, climate policies are put forward on the sub-central (provincial) level where we can identify carbon taxes (British Columbia), as well as active state innovation policies that target climate change (Ontario). CMEs, on the other hand, are genuinely characterized by policy-guided market interventions and politically motivated actions of market making. Direct and active innovation policies, as well as industrial policies that are meant to generate new processes and products which are low, or even neutral, in carbon emissions, are key instruments in the effort to move to a low carbon emission path. CMEs are policy leaders in this regard, but it needs to be stressed that LMEs exhibit considerable diversity as soon as we consider sub-center levels of policy-making. The USA and Canada (see Harrison, Chapter 2), along with economies such as Japan and China, which differ in so many respects, have in common active innovation and climate policies that are developed at the sub-central level (see Schreurs, Chapters 4 and 7). And yet, as the cases of Germany, and to some degree of Norway, demonstrate, providing economic incentives for new technologies is a necessary but far from sufficient condition for path change. Moving to a sustainable growth path requires substantial unlocking efforts and thus political decisions to degrade existing technologies that are socially inferior. This holds in particular for the role of veto players that need to be dealt with in order to move to a new growth path.

Economically, the most elegant way to include environmental costs in a market price is to give carbon emissions a price. This can be done by means of a carbon tax and/or by establishing a carbon market. In both cases, as an action by the state as either a market maker or a price-setter for carbon emissions. Carbon taxes, in addition to giving carbon emissions a market price, are also meant to use the 'language' of markets to disincentivize emission-intensive activities, and to consequently favor emission-reducing technologies. These insights guided the decision by the EU in 2005 to launch its own EU ETS. This set a cap on the total amount of emissions for all sectors that are a part of the system. Such a cap was combined with a trade element, that is, the EU provided emissions allowances; in a first round for free and then in a second round, which slowly phased in an auction system. The EU ETS covers more than 11,000 power stations and industrial plants, in all EU member states plus Iceland, Liechtenstein and Norway, as well as civil aviation flights between these countries. Approximately 45 percent of all EU emissions are covered by this regime (EU Commission DG Climate 2013). The EU ETS was designed as the flagship policy approach, that would, by means of harnessing market forces, provide strong incentives for guiding innovation processes and simultaneously generating equally strong disincentives for inaction. Obviously, the effects are strongly related to the price levels per ton of carbon emissions; the higher the price, the stronger the incentive to move toward low emission technologies. In this regard, the EU ETS must be seen as a failure (see Figure 1.7).

Since its start in 2005, the price per ton of carbon has experienced an enormous decline and, even more concerning, the low level was maintained for quite a long stretch. This price drop can be explained by the severe reduction in economic growth since the outbreak of the Eurozone crisis in 2011, the impact of the large amount of so-called certified Emission Reductions in the framework of the clean development mechanism of the UN, the effects of parallel climate policies in EU member states that favored particular technologies, the allocation of free allowances at the very start of the EU ETS that resulted in an oversupply of allowances, or a combination of all of these factors (Koch, Fuss, Grosjean and Edenhofer 2014; Böhringer 2014).

The way the European carbon market was set up alludes to the problem of veto players from emission-intensive sectors. These industries successfully pushed for a market design that resulted in a massive oversupply of allowances. This proved even more disadvantageous for the ETS when the EU economies entered a stretch of low economic growth. Oversupply of

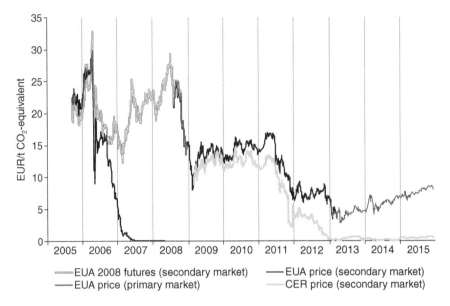

Figure 1.7 EU ETS carbon price.

Source: European Environmental Agency, 2016.

allowances and low demand due to anemic economic growth resulted in downward price pressure. The EU dealt with the problem half-heartedly by withdrawing emissions worth €900 million in 2014, and with the suggestion of introducing a market stability reserve by 2019. This is supposed to smooth too much price volatility by withdrawing or adding emission rights.

Getting prices right requires fighting the political resistance of incumbent industries. Our case studies show that most governments are neither willing nor ready to move speedily in such a direction. This failure can best be explained by time inconsistency: short-term interests of relevant actors and sectors undermine the pursuit of policies that are far more desirable in the long term. Such political behavior then confirms the existing policy path and makes it more difficult to diverge later. Righting prices is a necessary but not sufficient condition for a path change. Adequate carbon pricing is an incentive for producers and consumers to change patterns and habits. What is additionally needed for any successful path change is a climate-oriented industrial policy on all levels that proactively phases out harmful technologies and simultaneously favors clean technologies. The green embedding of markets, which are governed by prices that cover the social costs of production and consumption, is developing only slowly. Versions of coordinated market capitalism are best prepared for such a combination of policies but are currently held back by the sectoral interests of incumbent industries. These industries may not halt policy changes forever but are still strong enough to delay decisive action.

The EU experience is relevant not only in regard to institutional learning on the side of the EU, but also in regard to the prominence of this particular policy. As Figure 1.8 shows, quite a large number of jurisdictions either already have an emission trading regime and/or a carbon tax in place, or have plans to make use of such an instrument. Our case studies indicate that these instruments can be helpful for path change but are far from guaranteeing change. In particular, the installation of a carbon market requires strict state action to guarantee the inclusion of a maximum range of sectors, as well as a price formation mechanism that is not distorted by exemptions. Our case studies indicate that across all VoC efforts have been made or brought under way to install forms of carbon pricing systems.

In this respect, it seems indisputable that the size of the carbon price matters. A recent study by Dietz and Stern (2014) uses a "dynamic integrated

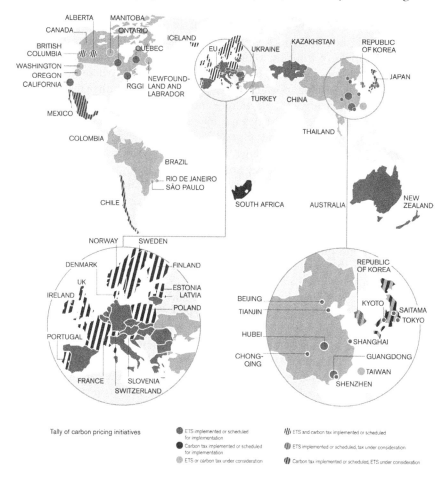

Figure 1.8 Overview of global ETS and carbon taxes.
Source: The World Bank, 2016.

climate-economy model (DICE)" in the tradition of Nordhaus. It takes into consideration the endogeneity of economic growth, the potentially increasing size of damages and the "fat tail" of climate risks. Accordingly, the optimum abating carbon price should have been in the range of US\$32–103/t CO_2 in 2015 (2012 prices), and should increase over the next 20 years to US\$82–260/t CO_2 (Dietz and Stern 2014: 22) to keep global warming to the 2°C increase level. Even though such calculations are, by their nature, very much dependent on modeling assumptions, it is reasonable to conclude that price signals far below such ranges may not be strong guides for a path change.

Our case studies convincingly demonstrate that climate policies have become an increasingly critical part of state policies. Active innovation policies that target low carbon emission technologies, as well as market regulations that favor climate-friendly technologies, have emerged over the last few years across all VoC. The direction, as well as the speed, of change differs however, and the differences very much reflect the institutional settings within our sample of capitalist economies. At the very bottom of the move toward low carbon emission economies is the DME where innovation regimes are weak, and the power of veto players is high. Rather than actively promoting a path change, the economic and political regimes are dominated by strong 'fossil coalitions' that defend the status quo. In contrast, the group of CMEs are moving swiftly but with different climate abatement approaches. Japan is refocusing on atomic energy, whereas an economy like Germany's is moving toward alternative energy sources. Their deeply entrenched policy paths guide both cases. Germany and Norway simultaneously strengthened their innovation regimes by targeting low carbon emission technologies. The USA is characterized by its ability to generate disruptive innovations but has had to realize that the move toward cutting-edge alternative technologies, on both product and process sides, needs state support and active state guidance. And yet, from the perspective of a global carbon budget, such active state policies seem not to be sufficient to keep the global temperature rise within the 2°C target. Fulfilling this target range would require a substantial change in existing production and consumption practices that is currently nowhere to be found.

According to a report by the Prudential Regulation Authority of the Bank of England (2015: chapter 4) annual emissions would need to see a decrease of approximately 6 percent globally, if the transition to a low carbon emission economy were to start in 2020. This level of abatement is needed to keep within the limits of the available carbon budget. The later a global decrease of carbon emissions starts, the higher the annual reduction rates need to be. Hence, procrastination is an economically, as well as politically, expensive strategy. This insight only slowly trickles through economic-political systems. Based on our case studies, one can conclude that the VoC with the densest and most complete institutional complementarities, and thus with a coherent interplay between state and market actions, are relatively better equipped to lead climate policy efforts. At the same time, it seems fair to argue that climate policies may induce a hybridization of the given VoC. CMEs will have to delegate significant parts of their innovation efforts to privately funded markets, and LMEs will have to give direct and indirect state-led innovation policies a more prominent role. And yet, without far-reaching unlocking policies that go against the entrenched interests of veto players, no change to a low carbon emission-path will occur. Such an unlocking may get support in parts of the global financial market where institutional investors are already looking at the implied risks of 'stranded assets', that is, investments in energy companies that engage in the exploitation of fossil fuels which may be kept in the ground due to overarching climate concerns. The later a tougher global climate policy regime is put in place, the higher the risk for financial markets to continue investing in fossil fuels. At the end of the day though, it is the nation-state that decides on the design and precise principles of a global regime. Our case studies show that the political-economic ability and willingness for path changes are coming into place but have so far only led to slow movements.

Notes

1 What is seen as the adequate discount rate is still hotly debated. It does seem though that the overall argument for early action can be sustained. The Stern Review used a discount rate of 1.4 percent per year, and consequently the effects of immediate action were relatively high.

2 This only illustrates the difficulties of unlocking. When the former German Minister of Economics and head of the Social Democratic Party announced in April 2015 that old coal power stations would have to pay a special levy, the first response came from the leader of the powerful multi-service trade union VERDI, who warned about the job losses that come with such a policy. From an analytical perspective, a radical supply-side policy that would close down coal production would be the optimal way to go to be cost-effective while simultaneously lowering carbon emissions (Collier and Venables 2014).

3 This poses the question whether carbon-related border adjustments are allowed under the WTO's rules.

4 Nordhaus (2015: 1348ff.) makes the point that such carbon duty schemes are rather difficult to implement and demonstrate relatively small emission effects. Alternatively, he proposes a general import duty on all goods and services from countries that do not participate in a global agreement. Such a penalty tariff is not aimed directly at penalizing the carbon content of imports, but is designed as an incentive for a nation-state to enter a global treaty to avoid penalizing costs for its producers.

5 See, for example, the 2014 report on pathways to deep carbonization convened by the Sustainable Development Solutions Network (SDSN) and the Institute for Sustainable Development and International Relations (IDDRI).

6 See also the more ambiguous work by Boyer, Uemura and Isogai (2012).

7 US fracking policies and its underlying technologies are the envy of many other countries. It fits well within our analytical framework that this technology has become so prominent in the USA, while at the other extreme, encountering problems in a CME like Germany. The difference has much to do with the VoC in place. The deployment of new technologies in a country like Germany is very

much an object of public debate, where civil society organizations, as well as political parties and trade unions, play a critical role. In such an institutional setting, policy change is supposed to happen in more incremental ways, as the outcome of social dialogues that allow the entering of new domains. The German coalition government, for example, needed quite some time to present a draft law that would allow fracking in the near future, even though some conditions apply. This decision has been pushed not least by the trade union that covers the sectors of mining, chemistry and energy (IGBCE). Its head challenged the German *Energiewende* with the argument that the increase in energy costs drives German companies to low energy price locations, such as the USA, where the social and political acceptance of fracking paved the way to a path of *lower carbon emissions – more jobs – and shrinking energy prices.*

8 Available: www.instituteforenergt=yresearch.org/topics/encyclopedia/renewable-energy/, (Accessed October 23, 2014).

9 In the annual international ranking by the independent climate policy think tank German Watch, Canada was ranked 58 out of 61 in terms of climate protection. The ranking is based on the evaluation of five indicators (CO_2 emissions; CO_2 emission trend; share of renewable energy in overall energy mix; energy efficiency; and climate policies). Out of the OECD group of economies only Australia performed worse, placed 59th.

10 It should be noted that he made this statement in a situation where the Canadian gas and oil industry was confronted with a strong price decline (McCarthy 2014).

11 Alberta allocated C$2 billion for four CCS trials; the federal government provided another C$1 billion for demonstration projects across the country (Einsiedel et al. 2013: 151).

12 In fall 2014 Alberta Premier Jim Prentice announced the winding down of funding for trial projects in the province, with the argument that the province had already committed C$1.3 billion to this technology, and now wants to see some concrete outcome. The province of Saskatchewan continues to fund this technology (Morgan 2014).

13 An excellent summary of the history of the German *Energiewende* is given by Hake, Fischer, Venghaus and Weckenbrock (2015).

2 The challenge of transition in liberal market economies

The United States and Canada

Kathryn Harrison

Introduction

As wealthy countries with abundant fossil fuel endowments, it is not surprising that the United States and Canada have among the highest per capita greenhouse gas emissions in the world. Over time, both countries have built economies that rely on the production of fossil fuels and the consumption of inexpensive energy for lifestyles in which citizens often live in large homes and commute long distances in private vehicles. For such countries, the transition to a low carbon economy demands nothing short of fundamental economic and social reform. Yet that much needed reform is especially challenging *because* of fossil fuel intensity, which gives rise to both powerful opposition from fossil fuel-intensive industries and ambivalence from voters accustomed to prosperous fossil fuel-intensive lives.

In response, policy reforms to reduce greenhouse gas emissions and promote the transition to a low carbon economy have been modest at best in both countries. While neither country has made deep reductions in greenhouse gas emissions to date, the USA has made greater progress in contrast to Canada, where emissions continue to increase. This chapter argues that these emission trends have been primarily a result of economic forces, rather than policy change. Indeed, the same technological innovations that have yielded emission *reductions* in the USA have contributed to emission *increases* in Canada. In the USA, the advent of hydraulic "fracking" has given rise to a dramatic energy revolution, as an increasingly abundant domestic supply of natural gas has rapidly displaced coal as an electricity source. In response, US greenhouse gas emissions have declined to their lowest level in decades, despite steady economic and population growth.

In Canada, the same innovations are having the opposite effect. Fracking and related techniques have facilitated increased production not only of natural gas but also of heavy oil and bitumen, though the latter is also produced in growing quantities via surface mining. Because Canada exports most of the oil and gas it produces, extraction-related emissions are proportionately greater than in the USA, where fossil fuels are produced almost entirely for domestic consumption. Canadian extraction emissions are rapidly growing as a function of both growing exports and increasing emission intensity of production. At the same time, with a lower reliance on coal for electricity production, Canada has not experienced the same benefits of fuel substitution as has the USA.

Strikingly, the increase in extraction-related emissions, which accounts for the majority of emission increases in Canada, has been associated almost exclusively with oil exports to the United States. In comparing emission trends, it is thus critical to consider the economic integration of these two countries, particularly their trade in fossil fuels. In addition, Canada's reluctance to adopt regulatory or tax policies that diverge from those of its main trading partner has been a longstanding challenge in addressing Canada's growing emissions. It is one that looms ever larger as the climate change positions of the Trump administration and the Trudeau government are increasingly at odds.

Economic context

In 2014, US and Canadian per capita greenhouse gas emissions (excluding land use change) were comparable at 20.5 tons CO_2 eq/yr and 20.1 tons CO_2 eq/yr, respectively, though with a population almost ten times greater the USA's absolute emissions also were an order of magnitude greater than Canada's. As illustrated by Figures 2.1 and 2.2, there are important similarities and differences in the emissions profile of these two countries. Transportation emissions account for roughly one-quarter of emissions in both Canada and the USA. Manufacturing and agriculture also account for comparable emission shares in both countries.

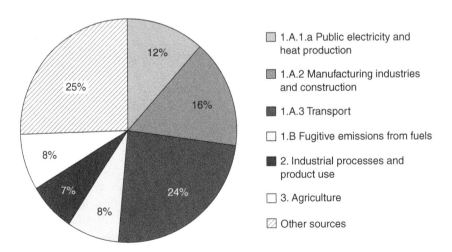

Figure 2.1 GHG emissions by Canadian sources, 2015.

Source: UNFCC submissions.

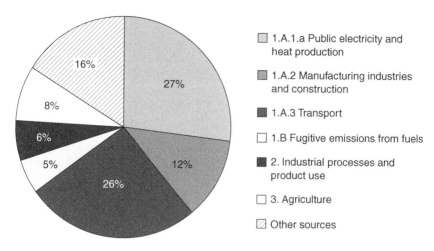

1.A.1.a Public electricity and heat production

1.A.2 Manufacturing industries and construction

1.A.3 Transport

1.B Fugitive emissions from fuels

2. Industrial processes and product use

3. Agriculture

Other sources

Figure 2.2 GHG emissions by US sources, 2015.
Source: UNFCC submissions.

There are, however, two marked differences. Electricity generation accounts for just 12 percent of Canadian emissions, compared to 27 percent of US emissions. This reflects the USA's greater reliance on coal, in contrast to Canada's reliance on hydro-electricity. Canada makes up for its lower greenhouse gas-intensive electricity sector with higher emissions from oil and gas production, including related fugitive and oil sands mining emissions (which appear in the "other" category in Figure 2.1).

Geographic variation in fossil fuel endowments results in significant regional variation in greenhouse gas emissions in both countries. US emissions range from below 10 tons/yr/person in states such as New York, California, and Oregon, to 75 and 110 tons/yr/person in the sparsely populated, coal-producing states of North Dakota and Wyoming respectively (see Figure 2.3). Similarly, hydropower-rich Canadian provinces such as Quebec, Ontario, and British Columbia have emissions in the order of 10 to 13 tons/yr/person, while Alberta and Saskatchewan, both of which produce oil for export and rely on coal for electricity, have emissions in the order of 70 tons/yr/person (Figure 2.4).

A critical difference between the two federations though, is that provinces or states with an emissions intensity greater than 40 tons/yr/person account for roughly half of all emissions in Canada but less than 10 percent of US national emissions. The greenhouse gas emissions story in Canada is largely driven by the two oil-producing provinces of Saskatchewan and Alberta. Individual states have less impact in the USA, reflecting relatively even state reliance on coal for electricity. Subnational climate leadership thus requires commitment by a large number of states in the USA but is less vulnerable to veto by small numbers than in Canada.

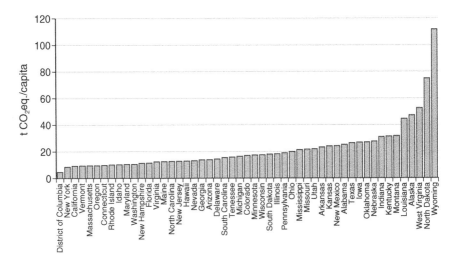

Figure 2.3 US per capita emissions by state (2014).

Source: US EPA State CO_2 emissions from fossil fuel combustion; US Census Bureau.

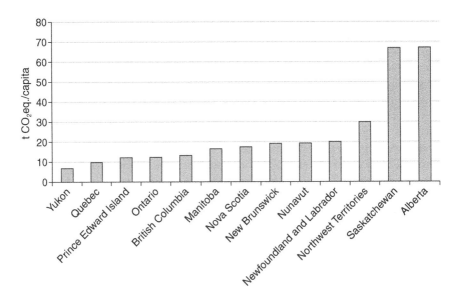

Figure 2.4 Canadian per capita emissions by province (2014).

Source: Canada's National GHG Inventory 2017, Statistics Canada Table 051–0001.

By international agreement, greenhouse gas emission inventories only report emissions released within a country's national borders. This convention masks important differences in carbon footprints based on consumption, defined as the carbon released to produce all goods consumed within a country, regardless of where production occurred. Countries that produce a lot of carbon-intensive goods for export tend to be net exporters of "embodied carbon," with territorial emissions higher than their consumption-based carbon footprints. In contrast, those that import carbon-intensive goods have domestic emissions that understate their carbon footprint based on consumption (Davis, Peters, and Caldeira 2011). The USA is in the latter category, with a carbon footprint of consumption roughly 10 percent greater than its territorial emissions in 2004. Canada is the opposite, with territorial emissions 7 percent higher by virtue of goods it exports, the most significant of which is oil destined for the USA.

Whether the assignment of environmental responsibility in this trading relationship is fair is far from straightforward. On the one hand, Canada benefits economically from the production of fossil fuels for export, yet it evades responsibility for the combustion emissions that result when those fuels are burned in the USA. On the other hand, in relying on imported oil from Canada and other countries, the USA evades responsibility for growing emissions associated with extraction. What is clear is that US imports of Canadian oil make it more difficult for Canada and easier for the USA to meet their respective greenhouse gas emissions targets.

Emissions trends

Both countries experienced steady emissions growth from 1990 to 2008, as illustrated by Figure 2.5. Thereafter, the impact of the global recession was

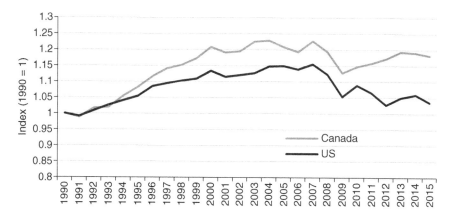

Figure 2.5 Comparison of normalized emissions trends (excluding LULUCF).
Source: UN FCCC.

evident from 2008 to 2010: as both economies contracted, emissions also declined. However, the Canadian and US trends diverged after 2010, with US emissions continuing to decline and Canadian emissions rebounding. Trends in per capita emissions provide additional insight (see Figure 2.6). US per capita emissions were slowly declining even before 2008. The same cannot be said of Canada, which experienced increasing emissions intensity per capita, consistent with its steeper emissions growth than in the USA prior to 2008 (Figure 2.5).

Figure 2.7 reveals that both countries have experienced a steady reduction in emissions relative to GDP (though caution is warranted in interpreting the Canada–USA comparison in this figure given a significant variation in the Canada-USA exchange rate during this period). That this decline was already

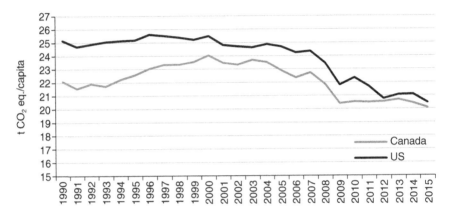

Figure 2.6 Comparison of per capita emissions trends.

Source: UNFCCC.

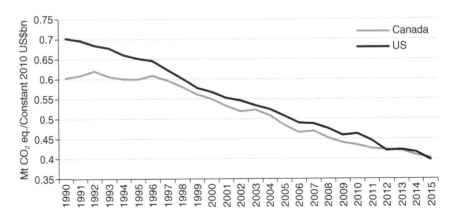

Figure 2.7 Comparison of trends in emissions/GDP.

Source: Emissions from UNFCCC; GDP from World Bank.

evident in the 1990s, before either country began to adopt policies to mitigate emissions, suggests that this trend is not a function of climate policy, but
rather of market forces, as businesses and individuals have responded to economic incentives for energy conservation and the replacement of aging appliances, vehicles, and equipment with more efficient models.

The financial incentive to conserve energy is likely to continue, but it has
been complemented in recent years by a revolution in US energy production.
Between 2005 and 2015, US natural gas production increased by 50 percent,
driven by a seven-fold increase in shale gas production via fracking. As prices
for domestic natural gas have fallen, retiring coal plants have been replaced
almost exclusively by natural gas facilities. The result has been a dramatic
reduction in the USA's reliance on coal, from 50 percent of electricity production to 33 percent over the same decade. The resulting decline in carbon
dioxide emissions from coal combustion, less the increase in emissions from a
greater reliance on natural gas, amounted to a net reduction of 400 million
tons/yr, or roughly 60 percent of the decline in US emissions over that
period.

The gains from market-driven shifts from coal to gas in the electricity
sector have largely been exhausted, however. Absent proposed federal regulation of power plants emissions (discussed below), the US Energy Information
Administration projects that electricity production from coal will rebound
slightly in response to an increase in natural gas prices, then level off. Growth
in demand will be met by renewables, especially wind and solar, driven by
both declining prices and federal tax subsidies (US Energy Information
Administration [EIA] 2017). Still, the net effect is expected to be a leveling
off of energy-related carbon emissions in the USA after 2020 at about the
2015 level.

Trends in Canadian emissions have been less encouraging. While the
recent US trajectory is a story of transition to a *less* carbon-intensive fuel, the
Canadian emissions trajectory is underpinned by growing production of *more*
carbon-intensive oil. Canadian oil production more than doubled from 1990
to 2015. During that period, the fraction of production that was exported
increased even more dramatically, by almost five-fold. By 2015, roughly 80
percent of oil produced in Canada was exported, virtually all of that to the
USA. In response, emissions associated with oil production constitute a large
and growing share of Canadian emissions. Growth in extraction-related emissions has been further compounded by the changing nature of production. As
conventional reserves of oil have declined, Canadian producers have increasingly turned to unconventional tar sands and in situ heavy oil, both of which
produce more emissions during extraction and upgrading.

The combination of growing exports and increasing emission intensity per
barrel of Canadian oil has yielded significant emissions growth from the oil
and gas industry. The oil industry alone accounted for roughly three-quarters
of Canada's emissions growth from 1990 to 2014 (Environment and Climate
Change Canada 2017). Moreover, as illustrated by Figure 2.8, it is the one

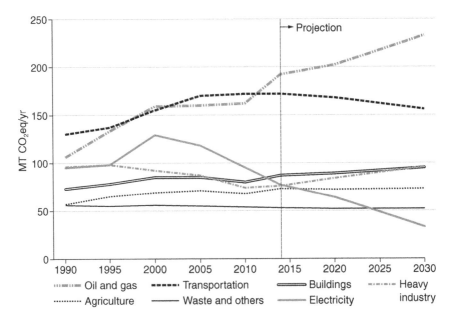

Figure 2.8 Trends in Canadian GHG emissions, by sector (MT CO$_2$eq/yr).

Source: Environment and Climate Change Canada (2017).

sector from which emissions are projected to continue growing. Emission reductions from all other sectors are being overwhelmed by steady growth in emissions from oil and gas production, a growth which is largely contained within a single province, Alberta.

As in the USA, the overall effect is expected to be a leveling off at about the 2015 level, absent further policy measures. However, following emission declines in the USA and growth in Canada prior to 2015, this would have the effect of locking in substantial divergence.

Policy comparison

One can compare policies to reduce greenhouse gas emissions on two levels: national targets, which are often adopted in the context of international nego-tiations; and domestic policies to meet those targets.

International targets

For almost three decades, target setting for greenhouse gas emission reduc-tions in both Canada and the USA has been a story of declining ambitions disguised by shifting the goalposts to ever-later dates. For the most part, it is also one of convergence, with Canada taking its lead from the USA.

It was no coincidence that Canada and the USA emerged from negotiation of the Kyoto Protocol in 1997 with very similar targets: reductions of 7 percent for the USA and 6 percent for Canada relative to 1990 emissions to be achieved over the five-year period from 2008 to 2012. Canadian Prime Minister Jean Chretien directed his negotiators to stay 1 percent behind the US position, the 1 percent intended to account for expected growth in Canadian gas production to displace US coal (Harrison 2010a) Although targets in the single digits may seem modest, to achieve compliance both countries anticipated reductions in the order of 30 percent below business as usual projections for 2010, a more demanding target than that adopted by other advanced industrialized countries in Kyoto (Harrison and McIntosh Sundstrom 2010a).

Canadian and US international targets diverged in 2001 when President George W. Bush announced the USA's withdrawal from the Kyoto Protocol, offering as rationales that it exempted developing countries from making reductions and because of "the incomplete state of scientific knowledge of the causes of, and solutions to, global climate change." On the initiative of Liberal Prime Minister Jean Chretien, Canada forged ahead unilaterally, ratifying the treaty the following year (Harrison 2010a, b). Canada formally maintained its Kyoto target until 2006, when it was abandoned and replaced by a less ambitious goal from a newly-elected Conservative government led by Prime Minister Stephen Harper.

Canadian and US targets re-converged at the international climate negotiations in Copenhagen in 2009. US negotiators, now under the direction of Democratic President Barack Obama, committed that the USA would reduce its emissions to 17 percent below 2005 levels by 2020. Canada immediately announced that it would match the US target, which was in fact slightly less ambitious than that previously announced by the Harper government. Following the necessary waiting period, Canada formally withdrew from the treaty in 2012, joining the USA as the only two industrialized countries outside the Kyoto Protocol.

In 2014 the USA signed a climate agreement with China that laid the foundation for the international agreement achieved at COP21 in Paris the following year. The USA committed that it would reduce its emissions to 26–28 percent below 2005 levels by 2025. The Obama administration subsequently affirmed that as the US target in the Paris Agreement. In advance of the Paris meeting, the Harper government committed to a somewhat greater emissions reduction of 30 percent, but with a deadline of 2030, five years later. A new Liberal government formed under Prime Minister Justin Trudeau just weeks before COP21 maintained that target for Canada in the Paris Agreement.

Canadian and US international targets diverged again in 2017, when President Donald Trump announced that the USA would withdraw from the Paris Agreement. In making the announcement, Trump declared that he, "was elected to represent the citizens of Pittsburgh, not Paris." Under the terms of the Paris Agreement, it will take several years for the USA to withdraw. In the meantime, however, the USA has declined to introduce new emissions targets. When the USA withdrew from the Kyoto Protocol in 2001, Canada reaffirmed its commitment to its target in the Paris Agreement. Achieving that goal will require significant policy change, to which we now turn.

Domestic climate policies

Announcing greenhouse gas emission targets is easy; meeting them is a lot harder. Despite periods of divergent international targets, to date Canada and the USA have always converged in adopting similarly weak domestic policies to reduce greenhouse gas emissions. Both countries relied primarily on voluntary programs throughout the 1990s and the first half of the 2000s, despite a growing body of evidence calling into question their efficacy (Antweiler and Harrison 2007; Morgenstern and Pizer 2007; Takahashi and Nakamura 2001). Thereafter, both embraced subsidies for biofuels, renewable wind and solar power, and energy-saving home renovations. Although subsidies hold political appeal compared to taxes and regulations, the level of spending was never sufficient to achieve significant emission reductions in either country.

US President George W. Bush campaigned on a commitment to regulate greenhouse gas emissions from power plants but abandoned that promise (in addition to the Kyoto Protocol) within months of assuming office. Policy-making to address climate change stalled at the national level in the USA for the next eight years.

During that period, Canada's continued commitment to the Kyoto Protocol would have demanded significant policy change to reduce emissions by roughly one-third below the business as usual trajectory. In practice, the regulatory and tax policies needed to achieve emission reductions also failed to materialize in Canada in response to formidable opposition from the business community, which argued that the Canadian economy would suffer should Canada impose greater regulatory costs on firms than those experienced by their US competitors.

That is not to suggest that domestic policies were not proposed. The Chretien government committed to negotiate sector emissions agreements to cover the large industrial sources that account for half of Canada's emissions, but made no progress before Chretien's retirement and replacement as Prime Minister by Paul Martin. The Martin government dithered for several years before promising to establish a cap-and-trade program for the industrial sources. However, when the Liberals lost the 2006 election, the new Conservative government cancelled virtually all of their predecessors' plans to address climate change, a reversal made easier given that the Liberals' plans were still on the drawing board.

When global warming surged to the top of the public's agenda, however, the Conservatives announced a renewed commitment to a national cap-and-trade program in 2007. The prospect that Canada would establish a regulatory program that diverged from its major trading partner was mitigated by the election of US President Barack Obama in 2008. Soon after assuming office, Obama called on Congress to pass legislation to establish a national cap-and-trade program for greenhouse gases. In 2009 the Democratic-controlled House narrowly passed a bill calling for a 17 percent reduction below 2005 emissions by 2020 (a target embraced by the administration later that year in Copenhagen.) However, a similar bill never attained the super-majority needed to overcome a filibuster in the Senate (Lizza 2010). Prospects for US cap-and-trade legislation died when the Republican Party won control of the House of Representatives in the 2010 election.

Although the Canadian government had expressed hope for a joint Canada–USA trading scheme, with the demise of any prospect of US emissions trading and Canadian public attention to climate change receding with the onset of the global economic recession, the Conservative government also abandoned Canada's commitment to emissions trading.

In the wake of Congress' failure to pass cap-and-trade legislation, the Obama administration took advantage of its existing executive powers to pursue a sector-specific regulatory strategy under the 1990 Clean Air Act. That strategy was underpinned by a 2007 Supreme Court decision, which upheld federal authority to regulate greenhouse gases under the Act should the Environmental Protection Agency (EPA) Administrator make a finding that they "endanger public health and welfare." The case had been brought by US states and cities in response to the Bush EPA's refusal to regulate greenhouse gas emissions from motor vehicles. Although the Bush administration delayed action following the court decision, the Obama EPA published the critical "endangerment finding" soon after assuming office, thus setting in motion non-discretionary mandates to regulate various sources of greenhouse gases.

In response, in his first year in office President Obama committed to national motor vehicle greenhouse gas emissions and fuel economy standards to match those that had been proposed by the state of California. (The Obama administration also granted California the necessary waiver under the Clean Air Act to pursue its own standards, which had been denied by the Bush administration.) US emission standards for light-duty motor vehicles were finalized in 2010 and 2012, to take effect from 2012 to 2016 and 2017 to 2025, respectively. The combined effect is expected to nearly double fuel economy from 27.5 miles/gallon before 2010 to 54.5 in 2025, with a corresponding halving of greenhouse gas emissions from light-duty vehicles. The USA followed a similar strategy for medium- and heavy-duty trucks, with two rounds of standards adopted in 2011 and 2016 that will carry through to 2027.

Given a highly integrated North American automobile manufacturing sector, which primarily serves the much larger US market, it would be to Canada's economic disadvantage not to harmonize regulatory standards with the USA. Canada readily matched all US motor vehicle standards adopted by the Obama administration.

Obama also committed to emission standards for key stationary source sectors, beginning with the electricity sector, which was the largest source of US greenhouse gas emissions up until 2016. The EPA finalized new standards for new and modified gas- and coal-fired power plants in 2015. The New Source Performance Standards effectively prohibit construction of coal-fired facilities unless accompanied by costly carbon capture and sequestration. In practice, the impact of the standard for new plants is likely to be modest for the foreseeable future since few new coal plants are anticipated, given the transition from coal to natural gas in the electricity sector.

More significant environmentally, and more contentious politically, were the Obama administration's standards for existing electricity generators. A draft of the Clean Power Plan was first published in 2014, prompting fierce opposition from coal-intensive utilities, coal states, and the Republican-controlled Congress. Congress had little hope of blocking the regulations, however, since President Obama was relying on his executive authority under the existing Clean Air Act and would have vetoed any bill to revise the Act or otherwise block his proposed regulations. The Clean Power Plan, finalized in August 2016, projected a reduction of power plant emissions by 32 percent relative to 2005 levels by 2030. In contrast to the new source standards, which apply to individual facilities, the Clean Power Plan allocated emission allowances at the state level, granting states considerable discretion with respect to how they would meet those targets, including via renewable energy portfolio standards and within- or cross-state emissions trading.

It is routine for EPA decisions to be challenged in court, typically by those seeking more and by those seeking fewer stringent standards. State governments also line up on both sides: 18 (including the District of Columbia) supported and a majority of 27 opposed the Clean Power Plan. The outcome of judicial review of the Clean Power Plan was especially uncertain given the EPA's novel interpretation of its authority under the Clean Air Act. Section 111(d) of the Act directs EPA to establish "standards of performance" for "any existing source" of pollutants that endanger health and welfare, and also that those standards should reflect, "the degree of emission limitation achievable through the application of the best system of emission reduction." The critical legal question was whether the courts would demand standards specific to an individual "source" or instead endorse a more cost-effective "system" to control emissions from many sources. In February 2016 the Supreme Court stayed the application of the Clean Power Plan pending judicial review by the DC Circuit Court and, should it accept an appeal, the Supreme Court.

Like the USA, Canada also moved first to regulate emissions from electricity generation. In 2012 Canada adopted regulations for coal-fired electricity generators. The standards for new plants were comparable to those proposed and subsequently finalized in the USA. However, the Canadian standard also covered existing power plants several years before publication of the Clean

Power Plan. The electricity sector is an easier target for Canada, since electricity emissions comprise a much lower share of their emissions. In any case, the Canadian standard for existing plants adopted by the Harper government was to be phased in so gradually as to have minimal impact before existing coal plants' end-of-life shutdown.

The comparable challenge in Canada to electricity generation in the USA is the upstream oil and gas sector. While accounting for a lower fraction of total emissions than coal in the USA, oil and gas accounts for the majority of Canada's recent and projected emissions growth. In 2014 Prime Minister Harper announced that regulation of emissions from the oil and gas industry promised since 2006 had been shelved because it would be "crazy economic policy" for Canada to regulate its oil and gas sector unilaterally (McCarthy 2014). Although the federal government acknowledged that Canada was not on track to meet its Copenhagen target – with emissions at the time projected to be 3 percent above, rather than 17 percent below, 2005 levels by 2020 (Government of Canada 2013) – the Harper government did not even pretend to have a plan to close that gap.

Poised for divergence

Recent elections in Canada (2015) and the USA (2016) yielded dramatic changes in leadership with respect to climate change. The election of a Liberal majority under Prime Minister Justin Trudeau ushered in a new era of Canadian climate activism. In stark contrast, the election of US President Donald Trump launched an almost complete reversal of the Obama administration's climate change policies and commitments.

The Canadian Liberal Party's 2015 election platform offered something for all sides in the climate policy debate. For environmentally concerned voters, the Liberals committed: to establish a national carbon price; to adopt an international emissions target at least as ambitious as that promised by the Conservatives; to legislate an oil tanker ban on British Columbia's north coast that would have the effect of prohibiting a major pipeline approved by the Harper government; and to reform procedures for the National Energy Board's (NEB) review of future pipeline proposals. On the other hand, those in more carbon-intensive industries and provinces were reassured by Justin Trudeau's emphasis on the need to get Canada's "energy resources" to international markets, and by the Liberals' commitment that national carbon pricing would be done in partnership with the provinces. Inherent in these commitments were two fundamental tensions. The first was a question of how to achieve increasingly deep reductions in Canada's emissions while also pursuing the expansion of Canada's tar sands exports via new pipelines expected to operate for decades. The second, and related, tension was how to achieve consensus with provincial governments on a national carbon pricing strategy when large differences in the carbon intensity of provincial economies portended unequal costs of emission reductions.

Since winning the 2015 election, the Liberal government has made progress along these two inconsistent paths. The government has proposed a slate of laudable initiatives to promote the transition to a low carbon economy, including reversing the Harper government's approval of the 525,000 barrel/day Enbridge Northern Gateway pipeline to the north coast of British Columbia. The government also established stricter conditions for NEB approval of the 1.1 million barrel/day Energy East pipeline from Alberta to the Atlantic, following which the proponent cancelled the project (though it is unclear to what degree that decision was due to regulatory hurdles, rather than reduced demand projections in the face of persistently low oil prices). In 2016 the Liberals achieved agreement with all provinces but Saskatchewan and Manitoba on a Pan-Canadian Framework on Clean Growth and Climate Change. The plan proposes a broad range of measures, including: an accelerated phaseout of coal-fired electricity by 2030; federal regulation of methane emissions; new building codes; and a national carbon price.

In the lead up to the federal–provincial agreement, Prime Minister Trudeau took a hard line that the federal government would impose a carbon tax, starting in 2018 at \$10/ton CO_2 and increasing to \$50/ton by 2022, in any province that did not establish an equivalent carbon price, whether via a tax or by emissions trading. That federal backstop undoubtedly was critical to reaching agreement at other than the lowest common denominator. However, another foundational element of the federal–provincial partnership was the election in 2015 of a Social Democratic government in Alberta, ending decades of Conservative reign. The new Alberta government had already announced its own climate plan, which included a phaseout of coal-fired power plants and the introduction of a \$30/ton provincial carbon tax.

While demonstrating climate leadership in domestic policy, Prime Minister Trudeau simultaneously maintained support for expanding Canada's oil exports. Trudeau had always been an enthusiastic proponent of the Keystone XL project, which would increase Canada's bitumen exports to the USA by 830,000 barrels/day. Keystone XL is less politically controversial in Canada than other pipeline proposals because it crosses only the oil-producing provinces of Alberta and Saskatchewan. In late 2016 the Liberal government approved two additional pipeline projects, the replacement and expansion of Line 3 to the USA and the twinning of the Kinder Morgan pipeline to the southern British Columbia (BC) coast, which together will expand Canada's oil exports by a further 950,000 barrels/day. The federal government also approved the Pacific northwest liquefied natural gas (LNG) project, which proposed to export fracked and liquefied natural gas from northern British Columbia to Asia (though the project was later abandoned by the proponent). The coincidence of the timing of the announcement of the Pan-Canadian Framework close after approvals of an LNG plant advocated by the British Columbia government and two new pipelines sought by the Alberta government (both provinces that had been resistant to increasing their carbon taxes), suggests a political bargain in which provincial governments agreed to more ambitious carbon pricing in exchange for federal approval of expanded fossil fuel exports.

The Trudeau government has been remarkably successful in avoiding controversy concerning the inconsistency between climate leadership and growing oil production. Canadians have largely been able to ignore the *additional* 2.8 million tons of CO_2 (roughly four times Canada's own national emissions) that will be released when oil from the three new pipelines is burned, since under the UN Framework Convention on Climate Change those emissions are the responsibility of those other countries to which Canada's oil is exported. When questions about climate impacts of fossil fuel exports have arisen, Canadian governments and industry invariably have defended exports on the grounds that if Canada does not provide oil to growing markets, some other country will. Even Prime Minister Trudeau has asserted that Canada needs to grow its oil exports in order to afford the transition to a low carbon economy.

While combustion emissions from Canada's fossil fuel exports are on other countries' books, Canada is responsible for emissions associated with oil and gas production that occurs within its borders. Government ministers' statements about the Pan-Canadian Framework seldom highlight that it is not, in fact, a plan to meet Canada's Paris Agreement target, but rather that it falls short by some 40 million tons, an amount comparable to projected growth in emissions from the tar sands between 2005 and 2030. Similarly, the Alberta climate plan has been applauded, even by some environmental leaders, for placing a "hard cap" on tar sands emissions, but it is seldom acknowledged that the celebrated cap allows for a tripling of the sector's 2005 emissions.

In light of failures by past Liberal and Conservative governments to implement previous climate action plans, it bears emphasis that the majority of the measures in the Pan-Canadian Framework remain to be implemented, whether at federal or provincial levels. As with the numerous previous plans, there is ample pressure for backsliding. The Prime Minister took a hard line in negotiating the Pan-Canadian Framework but has yet to secure agreement from the two last provinces. The federal government's willingness to follow through on the threat to impose a federal tax in those provinces if needed will be critical not only to ensuring a nationally consistent carbon price, but also to maintaining the resolve of other, less than enthusiastic, provinces. The federal government has already delayed the start date of the tax from 2018 to 2019, allowing additional time to win over Saskatchewan and Manitoba and to shore up support in other provinces. An even greater threat looms should the current Alberta government, which is lagging in the polls in part due to the provincial carbon tax, be defeated by their Conservative opponents, who adamantly oppose what they call a "job-killing tax."

A final threat lies in the Canadian business community's opposition to any taxes or regulatory measures that increase their costs beyond those of competitors in the USA. The Trudeau government responded to the USA's proposed withdrawal from the Paris Agreement by insisting that Canada will stay the course. However, the situation is eerily reminiscent of 2001, when a previous Liberal Prime Minister insisted that Canada would fulfill its Kyoto Protocol obligation despite US withdrawal. Canada's subsequent failure to adopt virtually any policies to meet its target provides little basis for confidence. Business and provincial concerns regarding economic competitiveness that contributed to that failure last time round are likely to reemerge as implementation dates draw near and as the gap grows in carbon prices between Canada and the USA.

South of the border, the 2016 election of Donald Trump as President yielded an almost complete about-face in US climate policy. Indeed, it would be difficult to overstate the differences between the Obama and Trump administrations with respect to climate change.

Most fundamentally, the Trump administration does not accept that climate change is caused by human activity. President Trump has consistently appointed senior officials who are climate change skeptics or deniers. These include Energy Secretary Rick Perry, EPA Administrator Scott Pruitt, who as Attorney General of Oklahoma joined states challenging the Clean Power Plan in court, and Secretary of State Rex Tillerson, who previously was CEO of Exxon Mobil, a company that for decades actively undermined public understanding of scientific consensus on climate change. Below the Cabinet level, executive ranks of relevant agencies are being filled by former oil industry lobbyists and staff from climate change-denying think tanks. Career staff are resigning from the EPA in droves.

Although withdrawal from the Paris Agreement will take several years, the Trump administration is not waiting to undo the policies put in place by President Obama. The task of reversing initiatives is made easier by the fact that Obama resorted to executive authority in the face of a hostile Congress. It is thus a relatively straightforward matter for a new President to use that same executive authority to reverse his predecessor's decisions, particular those that have yet to be implemented.

As promised during the election campaign, reversing Obama's rejection of the Keystone XL pipeline was one of Donald Trump's first acts as President. Next up were motor vehicle standards. Although the first phase of standards are already in force, the Obama administration committed to complete a midterm review of the feasibility of second phase standards by April 2018. Following the results of the November election, EPA rushed the mid-term review to completion in January 2017, concluding that no changes to the second phase standards for light-duty vehicles were warranted. In February 2017 the new EPA Administrator received a letter from the Alliance of Automobile Manufacturers requesting that he reconsider that conclusion. The following month, Administrator Pruitt granted the request, announcing that EPA would revisit the second phase standards for light-duty vehicles, and possibly those scheduled for medium- and heavy-duty trucks as well.

The Clean Power Plan was next in the crosshairs of the new administration. In April 2017 the DC Circuit Court accepted EPA's request to stay judicial review while the Agency reviewed the standards. In October 2017 the EPA published a proposal to repeal the Clean Power Plan. EPA Administrator Pruitt announced the decision to an audience of cheering coal miners, declaring that, "the war on coal is over" (Dennis and Eilperin 2017).

It would be premature to conclude that there are no obstacles to the Trump agenda to roll back US climate initiatives. Keystone XL remains tied up in court, facing opposition from state governments. Moreover, while there was considerable musing by commentators after the inauguration, the Trump EPA has not signaled any intention to reverse the endangerment finding. It may be easier to publicly declare climate science to be unsettled than to defend that position in court. Critically, under the Clean Air Act, EPA has no choice but to regulate sources of pollutants found to endanger public health and welfare. The Clean Power Plan and motor vehicle emission standards thus will need to be replaced by regulatory standards in some form.

Finally, regardless of the President's and EPA Administrator's rhetoric, the "war on coal" has been fought and won by electricity markets, not previous regulators. The stream of coal plant retirement announcements has continued since Trump's election. Even among the 27 states that challenged the Clean Power Plan, 21 were expected to comply without additional effort. That said, elimination of the Clean Power Plan will have growing impacts over time. The US Energy Information Administration anticipates that emissions will be 50 million tons/yr higher in 2025 without the Clean Power Plan, but double that in 2040. Most importantly, the reversal of the policy further delays next steps in the transition to fossil fuel-free energy, of which the Clean Power Plan was merely the first.

Subnational climate policy

Thus far, the chapter has focused on national level actions. However, Canada and the USA are both federal countries in which subnational jurisdictions have considerable authority to pursue their own actions to reduce carbon emissions. The vitality of subnational climate action in both countries has been widely documented (Engel 2006; Rabe 2004, 2007, 2008; Thomson and Arroyo 2011; Ostrom 2012; Houle 2015; Boyd 2017). Climate action by states and provinces can be significant in (at least) three ways (Harrison 2013a). First, state and provincial policies can fill a void in the absence of federal leadership. Action by some is better than none. Second, unilateral actions by leading states or provinces can be contagious. Climate leaders can provide reassurance that other states' businesses will not be unduly disadvantaged, which may be sufficient to convince other states or provinces to follow suit. State and provincial governments also may actively coordinate their policies. Third, subnational governments may prompt action by national governments.

There is evidence of all three dynamics in Canadian and US climate policy. In the USA, California has been the clear state leader with ambitious targets and a host of policy innovations, including a renewable fuel standard, motor vehicle standards for greenhouse gases, and a clean electricity standard that mandates that all electricity sold in the state – regardless of where it is produced – must have been generated with emissions equivalent or less than those of a combined-cycle gas plant. It is noteworthy that state climate leaders, including California, New York, and Massachusetts, tend to be the most populous states.

US states have reduced the risks of unilateralism by acting in concert, most notably in the northeast and mid-Atlantic states' Regional Greenhouse Gas Initiative (RGGI), an emissions trading scheme for power plant emissions that has been operational since 2008. Following the lead of RGGI, seven western states and four Canadian provinces promised an economy-wide emissions trading system under the auspices of the Western Climate Initiative.

California's tailpipe standards for motor vehicles are a special case of institutionally facilitated policy contagion. In recognition of the state's unique air quality challenges, the US Clean Air Act grants California, and only California, authority to adopt motor vehicle emissions standards that depart from national standards, though only if a waiver is granted by the EPA. Other states then have the option to adopt California's standards or to stay with the federal baseline. California led the USA in developing the first greenhouse gas emission standards for motor vehicles. Even while awaiting a federal waiver (eventually denied by the Bush EPA, but reversed by Obama), 15 other states comprising 40 percent of the US population committed to match California's tailpipe standards.

The Clean Power Plan would have laid the foundation for the RGGI emissions trading scheme to spread nationally. However, that policy has been reversed by the Trump administration. More successful was the nationalization of California's tailpipe standards in 2009 by the Obama administration, though the Trump EPA's ongoing review of motor vehicle standards may preclude the next step in this state–to–nation dynamic.

The Canadian equivalent to California in terms of policy innovation arguably is BC, which adopted North America's first revenue-neutral carbon tax in 2008 (Harrison 2012, 2013b). BC, Manitoba, Quebec, and Ontario also committed to participation in the Western Climate Initiative, though only Quebec and Ontario have followed through to date. Quebec and California created a joint carbon market in 2014, which Ontario joined in 2018. The Alberta government established a carbon tax in 2017, though like the province's previous cap-and-dividend approach, the province's climate plan anticipates continued growth of emissions from the oil industry. The measure that has had the single largest impact on Canadian emissions remains the Ontario government's unilateral phaseout of its coal-fired power plant.

Provincial actions are poised to have a greater impact at the national level in Canada than has occurred in the USA. In the 2015 election the Liberal Party applauded carbon pricing initiatives at the provincial level and committed that, if elected, they would pursue a national approach that builds on actions already taken by the provinces. The Pan-Canadian Framework and the associated federal government backstop thus allow that each province can devise its own carbon pricing scheme. While this demonstrates the potential for provincial initiatives to go national, it also underscores the risk of locking in a patchwork of inconsistent price- and quantity-based policies.

Unilateral actions by US states and Canadian provinces are unquestionably encouraging. However, their impact should not be overstated for several reasons. First, the leaders among the states and provinces tend to be those with the least emissions-intensive economies (Harrison 2013a). Not only have the more emissions-intensive states failed to follow their greener neighbors' lead but, in the USA, have also repeatedly taken to the courts to obstruct state and federal actions. A majority of US states sued to block the Clean Power Plan. In Canada, recalcitrant provinces have blocked national action on climate change time and again (Harrison 2010a). It is no accident that one of the holdouts to the Pan-Canadian Framework, which will test the federal government's resolve, is Saskatchewan, the province with the highest per capita emissions.

Second, state and provincial commitment can be difficult to maintain in the absence of a national backstop. The failure of proposals for national emissions trading programs in both countries in 2010 prompted backtracking by many states and provinces. The RGGI survived, though largely because electric utilities could easily meet their caps in a depressed economy. In contrast, all US states besides California and all Canadian provinces except Quebec either withdrew from the Western Climate Initiative or put their commitments on hold. A nascent Midwestern trading system was abandoned altogether.

Still, the initiative by California and Quebec was a critical foundation for Ontario returning to the fold and ultimately for a new Canadian national plan. California's actions also leave the door open to other US states rejoining the Western Climate Initiative. In the Trump era, action at the state level, however incomplete, will be the only game in town.

Conclusion

To date both the USA and Canada have failed to adopt ambitious policies to launch the transition from a highly carbon-intensive to a low carbon economy. Although both countries have embraced challenging greenhouse gas emissions reduction targets for more than two decades, neither has made significant progress in adopting the national policies needed to meet those goals. Both belatedly adopted standards to reduce motor vehicle emissions, which are beginning to have an important impact. However, the USA is now reconsidering its standards and it remains to be seen whether Canada will proceed unilaterally, given the integrated nature of North American automobile manufacturing. Despite many promises and proposals, to date neither country has established either a national cap-and-trade program or a carbon tax, though Canada has (yet again) promised a national carbon price in 2019. Neither country has national regulations for the emission sources most critical to their success: upstream oil production in Canada, and power plants in the USA.

The Canadian and US cases are not only similar, but deeply intertwined. To date, economic interdependence has deterred actions to launch a transition to a low carbon economy. The smaller, and thus more vulnerable, of the two trading partners, Canada, has gone to great lengths to harmonize its international negotiating positions and domestic policies with those of the USA.

In the face of weak policies, observed emission trends to date largely reflect market forces. The impact of innovation is a central question in this project. While *policy* innovation has been in short supply, the impact of *technological* innovation on the carbon intensity of the US and Canadian economies is evident – yet mixed. On the one hand, increasing energy efficiency has facilitated a partial uncoupling of economic growth and greenhouse gas emissions in many sectors in both countries. More recently, the advent of fracking has prompted a quiet revolution in US energy, prompting significant emissions reductions as the USA has shifted its electricity sector from coal toward natural gas, a lower if not low carbon path. On the other hand, the same technology is having the opposite effect in Canada, where increasing reliance on unconventional oil reserves is yielding an emissions growth.

Even in the USA, technological innovation alone cannot be counted on to prompt a transition to a low carbon economy. To the extent that a shift from coal to gas in the USA has been driven by market forces, it has already occurred. Absent additional measures, US emissions are expected to level off. There is thus no substitute for policy innovation to direct markets toward a low carbon economy. While that represents a challenge for North American liberal market economies that traditionally have been steered with the lightest of touches, it is much needed and long overdue.

Tragically, the Trump administration rejects the reality of human-caused climate change and is actively dismantling regulations devised by their predecessors. While many US states will fight a rearguard action to limit damage, the USA has chosen a dangerous path for its own economy and for the planet.

Canada, in contrast, is in a mixed position. The current government continues to promote expansion of oil exports, but is also pursuing a slate of praiseworthy policies to reduce emissions in other sectors. Canada has reaffirmed its commitment to the Paris Agreement despite the USA's withdrawal. These signs are undoubtedly promising, but with three decades of hindsight, success is far from assured. Although Canada ratified the Kyoto Protocol after the USA had already withdrawn, that action turned out to be largely symbolic. In the face of formidable pressure from carbon-intensive industries and their provincial defenders, Canada's domestic climate policies have never significantly diverged from those of the USA. They must do so now.

3 Transition to a low carbon economy in the United Kingdom

A case of liberal capitalism?

Alexander Ebner

Introduction

This chapter explores the political-economic process for the transition to a low carbon economy in the United Kingdom. Historically, the United Kingdom has pioneered fossil-fuelled industrialisation, going through distinct periods and phases of industrial change. These have resulted in the formation of the current post-industrial type of economy with an extended financial services sector. The varieties of capitalism (VoC) perspective portrays the United Kingdom as a liberal market economy (LME), characterised by a pattern of predominantly market-based coordination in the operations of firms and their institutional environment. The following chapter explores British capitalism's low carbon transition by addressing the matter of industrial change and technological innovation given these underlying actor constellations and policy strategies.

The first section takes stock of the United Kingdom's decarbonisation profile, by addressing its patterns of greenhouse gas and carbon emissions. The second section outlines the British variety of capitalism in terms of a liberal type of market economy. The third section discusses the related institutional setting and performance of the British innovation system in support of a low carbon transition. The fourth section outlines strategies and policies driving this transition and the fifth discusses the underlying actor constellations and coalitions. The conclusion elucidates how the British path to a low carbon economy involves strong governmental components to accompany market-based governance, which highlights the hybrid elements in the British variety of liberal capitalism.

Profiles of carbon emissions in the United Kingdom

The path towards a low carbon economy in the United Kingdom is exemplified by its institutional foundations of legally binding emission targets: using 1990 as the base year, the 2008 Climate Change Act demands an 80 per cent reduction in greenhouse gas emissions by 2050; the Low Carbon Transition Plan from 2009 outlines a target for a 30 per cent share of renewable electricity by 2020 and an almost complete decarbonisation of electricity by 2030 (Geels *et al.* 2016). The redesign of the energy system that is necessary to reach the decarbonisation targets of the Climate Change Act, includes the expansion of renewables and the phasing out of coal (Staffell 2017: 463n). In light of these ambitious targets, which reach beyond those of the Kyoto protocol and Paris Agreement, British performance in reducing carbon emissions has shown positive results. The decrease in carbon emissions and the parallel improvement in energy efficiency, are both said to be caused by favourable changes in industrial and energy structures, framed by specific policies in support of a low carbon economy (Burck *et al.* 2013). Furthermore, econometric evidence on the effects of the reduction in carbon emissions suggests that this has been achieved with largely positive effects on economic growth and employment (Pollitt *et al.* 2013).

Figure 3.1b outlines the United Kingdom's greenhouse gas emissions performance since 1990. Greenhouse gas emissions were reduced by 36.1 per cent between 1990 and 2015; a pattern that represents a success, and actually outperforms the average reductions in the EU 28 economies, as well as besting most OECD economies during the same time period (see Figure 3.1a). The reductions in carbon and energy intensities have actually outweighed the impact of economic growth since the 1990s. In disaggregating greenhouse gas emissions, the most striking performance was delivered in the non-carbon dioxide gas domain, as a small number of industrial installations accounted for nearly all of these emissions and their subsequent reduction

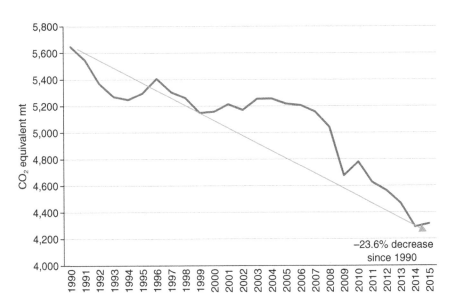

Figure 3.1a EU GHG emissions.

Source: UNFCCC Data Interface, 2017.

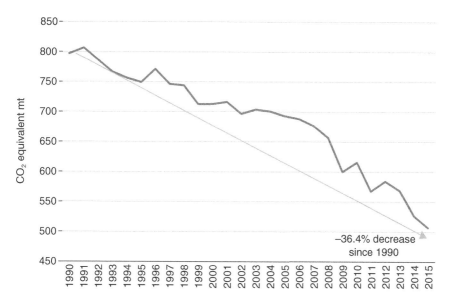

Figure 3.1b UK GHG emissions.
Source: UNFCCC Data Interface, 2017.

(Bowen and Rydge 2011: 6). The economic downturn in the late 2000s seems to have catalysed a further decline in greenhouse gas and carbon dioxide emissions, resulting in a faster average rate of decline per head between 2005 and 2009, driven by a fall in the growth of GDP per capita, along with a fall in both carbon intensity and energy intensity of output (Bowen and Rydge 2011: 8). In addition, the observed reduction in carbon emissions since 2012 is said to be due to falling coal consumption, thus reflecting structural changes in the prevailing energy mix (Staffell 2017: 472). In summary, despite fluctuations in annual emissions performance, the overall trend of decreasing emission levels has persisted as one of the most relevant contributions to the transition towards a low carbon economy (DECC 2013c: 2). This promising performance in the reduction of greenhouse gas and carbon emissions points to the fact that, for 2016, more than half the electricity in Britain was generated from low carbon resources, which includes renewables, domestic nuclear, and French nuclear and hydro imports (Wilson and Staffell 2017).

Figure 3.2 provides an overview of British greenhouse gas emissions by their source, as recorded since 1990. It underlines the high share of the energy sector in total emissions (which is standard for most countries), while the role of manufacturing industries remains comparatively small. This is in line with structural changes in the industrial sector, based on a drive towards a service economy. Emissions reductions by sector between 1990 and 2015

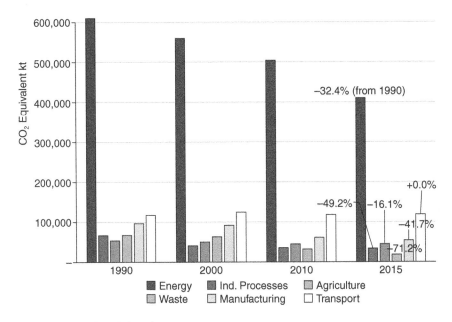

Figure 3.2 GHG emissions by sector.
Source UNFCCC Data Interface, 2017.

proceeded as follows: the energy sector decreased its emissions by about 32 per cent during the 25 years under scrutiny; the agriculture sector by 16 per cent; manufacturing industries and construction by 42 per cent; and industrial processes and product use, including waste, by almost 50 per cent and 71 per cent respectively; the transport sector kept its emissions fairly level throughout the period, following slight increases during the 1990s. With regard to the overall mix of sources of greenhouse gas emissions, however, a downward trend in emission levels is obvious (UNFCCC 2017b). Furthermore, there are decreases in emissions from the residential sector recorded during the most recent decade with a drop by 20 per cent in 2010 alone (DECC 2013c: 6). This decrease in residential emissions reflects temporary influences, such as temperature swings, but it also stands for the overall reduction in demand for electricity, actual modes of residential gas use, and greater use of nuclear power for the purpose of low carbon electricity generation (DECC 2013c).

The British fuel mix provides further evidence on the specific energy base of the United Kingdom. Indeed, the mix of fuel from domestic electricity suppliers has been going through some obvious structural change in recent years. Coal has lost its leading position in the electricity generation mix, gas and nuclear have slightly expanded their shares, while renewables have exhibited impressive growth. This pattern of substituting coal for gas was already visible in the context of a 'dash for gas' during the 1990s, based on short lead times, low capital costs, quick returns on investment, new gas finds and low international gas prices. Coal was therefore under constant cost and price pressures that would contribute to its politically framed, later phasing out (DBEIS 2017; DECC 2013b). It is worth noting that the share of energy from coal has been relatively small compared to other European and OECD economies; a pattern that can be explained as an effect of the politically enforced de-industrialisation processes of the 1980s and 1990s, which predominantly hit coal-based heavy industry. The current policy of phasing out coal as a means of decarbonisation builds on these structural specificities. A further specificity relates to current British plans to promote the utilisation of nuclear energy in the fuel mix, which can build on widespread political support including from labour unions.

Electricity capacity dynamics provide a telling illustration of this decarbonisation process. The fossil fuel capacity fell from 65 GW to 45 GW between 2011 and 2016, whereas renewables expanded from 2 GW to 27 GW. In line with these tendencies, the share of fossil fuels within the electricity supply fell from 83 per cent in January 2009 to 45 per cent by December 2015. The share of nuclear remained consistent at around 20 per cent, and renewables – including gas, biomass, wind, and solar – increased from 4 per cent to 25 per cent. By the end of 2015 wind had overtaken coal's share in the electricity supply. At the same time, electricity imports grew from almost zero to 7 per cent of the total (Staffell 2017: 467n). A further look at the dynamics of electricity generation underlines the pattern of coal collapsing and renewables expanding. In the UK, excluding Northern Ireland, coal held a 9.3 per cent share of electricity generated in 2016, down from over 40 per cent in 2012. At the same time, wind produced a 10.2 per cent proportion of electricity, followed by solar with 3.2 per cent (Wilson and Staffell 2017). This outstanding performance by wind power also reflects the fact that the United Kingdom is the windiest country in Europe and therefore possesses environmental conditions that are conducive to wind energy. Accordingly, the United Kingdom persistently takes one of the top spots when it comes to the new deployment of wind power facilities in Europe (Global Wind Energy Council 2012).

Figure 3.3 depicts data on electricity generation from renewable energy sources as a percentage of gross electricity usage between 2004 and 2015. In 2004 this share was at 3.5 per cent, which dramatically increased more than six-fold to 22.3 per cent in 2015. The corresponding level for 2015 in the EU economies was already 28.8 per cent at this point. In a similar manner, energy from renewables has been experiencing a solid take-off during the 1990s and 2000s; the contribution from renewable energy to total primary energy supply has risen from 0.5 per cent in 1990 to 3.1 per cent in 2009, paralleled by a share in electricity generation which has risen from 1.8 per cent to 6.7 per cent between 1990 and 2009. Still, the contribution of renewables has so far remained comparatively low relative to other OECD economies (Bowen and Rydge 2011: 12–13).

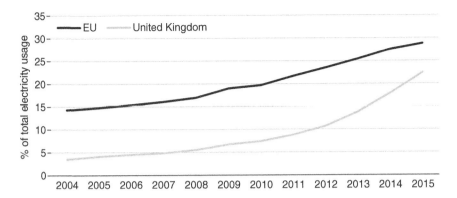

Figure 3.3 Share of renewable energy in electricity.

Source: Eurostat, 2017.

Figure 3.4b provides an overview of the United Kingdom's primary energy consumption from 1990 to 2015. It shows swings of generally increasing consumption during the 1990s and 2000s, followed by levels that only markedly decrease from the mid-2000s. Primary energy consumption only settles below the 1990 standard after the early 2010s. However, the same cyclical pattern of primary energy consumption also holds for the EU 28 economies, as can be seen in Figure 3.4a.

Figure 3.4a EU primary energy consumption.

Source: Eurostat, 2017.

Figure 3.4b UK primary energy consumption.
Source: Eurostat, 2017.

Figure 3.5 outlines the dynamism of resource productivity in the United Kingdom between 2000 and 2013. Given the key role resource productivity plays in resource-friendly ecological transformation, the British metrics are quite impressive, with a resource productivity increase of 71 per cent between 2000 and 2016; a performance that dramatically exceeds that of the EU economies.

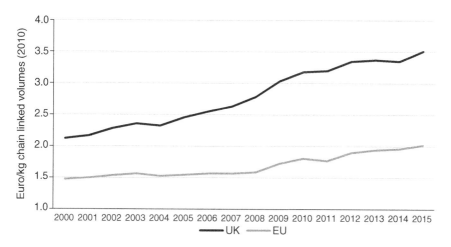

Figure 3.5 Resource productivity.
Source: Eurostat, 2017.

However, the low carbon transition of the British economy also needs to be assessed with regard to import and export dimensions. Available data indicate that the import side of energy supply has been prevailing over exports in recent years with a net import dependency of 43 per cent, a fossil fuel dependency of 87.3 per cent and a low carbon share of 11.9 per cent in 2012. While net import dependency has thus risen by almost 20 per cent in recent years, fossil fuel dependency has shrunk from over 90 per cent in 2010 to just under 83 per cent in 2013 – data which underline the steady turn away from coal (DECC 2013b: 9–10). This shift in the energy foundation is also constitutive for the British position in the European Union's emissions trading system. In this setting, the United Kingdom has been a net seller of emission allowances (DECC 2013c).

The geographic heterogeneity of carbon emissions can be seen by exploring disaggregated emission activities at regional and local authority levels, and in particular sectors and industries, which tend to have evolved into industrial agglomerations in certain regional and local settings. Indeed, changes in greenhouse gas emissions between 2005 and 2011 reflect the spatial concentration of industrial activities. Traditional manufacturing industries are expected to be most prominently affected by emission reduction efforts. During 2005 to 2011 the highest percentage change in greenhouse gas emissions was a 30 per cent decrease in the North East of England (known for its large industrial installations). The region that showed the least progress in decreasing emissions was Northern Ireland, with a decrease of 8 per cent. Northern Ireland is also one of the less developed industrial regions in the UK. Wales and Scotland both exhibit similar percentages of emissions reduction with 11 per cent and 12 per cent respectively. More pronounced is the reduction performance of the North West of England and Yorkshire with 18 per cent, the South East of England with 17 per cent, the East and West Midlands with 16 per cent and 15 per cent, and the Greater London area with 14 per cent. In effect, in 2011 the South East of England remained the region with the highest level of emissions, amounting to 54,634 kt CO_2, followed by North West England with 49,043 kt CO_2 and Yorkshire with 43,382 kt CO_2. In terms of the industrial specificity of these greenhouse gas emissions, the biggest share of emissions was generated by industry and commercial electricity, followed by household domestic electricity and diesel railways (DECC 2013a).

In exploring the inherent dynamics and development of the British economy's carbon emission profile, we will have a closer look at the prevailing institutional framework. This framework coordinates economic transactions in terms of production and consumption, with institutional scaffolds that underlie the low carbon transition being shaped by government activities, and even cultural dispositions that allow for the reconstruction of distinctly national types of capitalism. In the case of the United Kingdom, this national type of capitalism has been commonly perceived as a liberal model, based on competitive market processes for firms and industries, framed by the legal governance mechanisms of a regulatory state. Accordingly, viewed from the VoC perspective, the British transition towards a low carbon economy is expected to be based on market-compatible fiscal and legal frameworks that set incentives for firms to decrease their emission activities. However, the British variety of capitalism's prevailing institutional setting is much more complex than the simplistic traditional VoC LME might suggest.

The British variety of capitalism

From the perspective of the VoC approach, the United Kingdom is typically characterised as an ideal LME, which exhibits a dominant pattern of market coordination through investment in transferable assets (Hall and Soskice 2001). Its common qualities involve market-oriented characteristics in the major sub-systems of corporate governance, industrial relations, skill formation, education and training, finance, technology transfer, innovation and polity. The system of corporate governance echoes the logic of financial markets, as it is marked by an orientation towards shareholders that combines the prevalence of short-term financial resources with publicly assessable market monitoring. This puts high performance pressures on discretionary management. Industrial relations exhibit a market-oriented form of wage formation, with decentralised wage bargaining and few barriers to workforce turnover. Skill formation proceeds largely on the job, without a formal apprenticeship system for vocational skills. This implies a less relevant role for unions in the qualification of these skills. The market-based financial system undergirds the strategic importance of financial markets. These are linked to managerial concerns with shareholder value, market capitalisation, and competitive markets for corporate control. Technology transfer proceeds in terms of a competitive mode of standardisation and market-based mechanisms. The related innovation regime tends to favour radical technological innovations that disrupt established routines and paradigms. This innovation environment provides competitive advantages during periods of changing techno-economic paradigms, with a strong bent for entrepreneurial initiatives. All of this is flanked by a political system that operates as a liberal regulatory state with parliamentary sovereignty and centralised governance mechanisms, driving policies that maintain the primacy of market-based incentives in the regulation of economic affairs (Casper and Kettler 2001: 14).

Based on the patterns of the prevailing sub-systems, and the complementarities between them, comparative institutional advantages sustain the technological and industrial specialisation of firms in the different VoC approaches. Thus, firms in LMEs are expected to realise advantages by generating more radical and disruptive innovations, due to the flexible institutional setting in which they are nested. Therefore, the liberal model may reign supreme in times of rapid and comprehensive change, especially in terms of paradigmatic technologies on an international scale. This is because adaptive flexibility in the institutional domain becomes key in maintaining industrial competitiveness

(Hall and Soskice 2001: 38–41; Soskice 1994). The transition to a low carbon economy poses a distinct challenge for each country's prevailing capitalist variety. From the VoC analytical perspective therefore, one can expect the transition path for the UK to be shaped by the specific systemic institutional complementarities, and industrial specialisations, that constitute a LME (Hall and Soskice 2003).

Recent discussions in the comparative capitalisms domain understand complementarities as an outcome of evolving institutions, which are subject to institutional recombination and change. Accordingly, institutional diversity needs to be viewed as the common state of institutional co-evolution of capitalist varieties, resulting both from internal forces, such as sectoral and regional specificities, and from external impetuses, such as international regulatory regimes and foreign investment activities (Lane and Wood 2009). Implications for a conceptual assessment of institutional change are straightforward: a wide scope for institutional hybridisation may take place, which changes the quality of complementarities by adding ever new institutional components. Speaking of hybridisation then, implies dealing with deviations from empirically grounded ideal types, and thus allows for an adequate understanding of capitalist diversity (Crouch 2005). The political dimension of this process is reflected by a hybridisation of state-market relations, which is shaped by the diversity of interest groups and their organisational patterns across all domains of society (Hancké *et al.* 2007).

Historically, the British variety of capitalism evolved with Britain as the hotbed of industrialisation during the nineteenth century, serving as a 'workshop of the world' that would generate major technological innovation, and promote liberal standards of free trade and market competition under the rule of law. At the same time, London evolved as the major financial centre of the world economy, with a reach far beyond that of the division of labour within the British Empire. These pioneering efforts at industrialisation and the formation of modern industrial capitalism, might explain why the economic impact of British capitalism remained remarkably strong all the way through the twentieth century (Dore *et al.* 1999). The underlying trajectory of economic performance, however, reveals further specificities and allows us to revisit Britain's institutional diversity. Following economic reconstruction during the post-war era, the British economy regained industrial strength in its internationally competitive industries, such as automotive, aerospace and pharmaceuticals. This continued until the 1970s, when the impact of industrial restructuring in traditional heavy industries met with macro-economic turbulence in unemployment and inflation. The onset of Thatcherism in the political domain and its deregulation strategies, pushed structural change towards services, with financial services being an especially prominent example. Ever since, the British economy has been shaped by a rapid drive towards the tertiary sector, although those core activities in manufacturing accompanied by the rise of new science-based industries, such as biotechnology, still prevail (Booth

2001). These changes in the industrial environment are also reflected in the evolution of British capitalism.

In effect, Britain's LME model has been subject to comprehensive reconfigurations that have affected its diverse institutional forms and layers (Crouch *et al.* 2009). Major institutional changes were promoted in a political system characterised by a strong government, based on parliamentary sovereignty and centralised governmental capacities. The voting system favours single-party governments with strong legislative capabilities that are able to support potentially disruptive policies (Wood 2010: 259). In fact, some of the liberal character of the British variety of capitalism was contested by the Labour government during the post-War era, in effect introducing elements of non-market coordination to domains such as labour rights and welfare services, while also expanding the public sector. Remnants of corporatism would even expand during the 1960s and 1970s and business associations and labour unions were even involved in price and income regulation efforts, as promoted by the Conservative Heath government in the early 1970s (Moran 2009: 42–45). Labour governments also tried to strengthen market coordination in the 1970s. Subsequently, major components of the liberal model have been reintroduced, initiated by the reforms of the Conservative Thatcher government in 1979. This included rolling back non-market coordination in areas such as corporate governance, industrial relations and financial markets. As a result, the role of government in the economy at large was redefined by pressing for an extension of state autonomy in economic governance (Howell 2007). These deregulation and privatisation efforts propelled the UK to within striking distance of the idealised LME (Wood 2001).

Crucially, the liberal reform programmes of the late 1970s and 1980s provided further incentives for the expansion of an already strongly liberalised and economically potent financial system. The bias towards financial markets has reinforced the short-term competitive strategies of firms, allowing for constant pressure on returns and profitability (Fioretos 2011: 221). This set of market-oriented incentives spurs radical technological innovation in new industries, because it allows for a more comprehensive reallocation of resources, while simultaneously furthering cost and price competition in established industries (Vitols 2001). However, the combined economic and societal range of these financial markets also needs to be taken into account. For instance, investment and pension funds in the UK hold almost half of all available shareholdings, which is far greater than corresponding numbers in coordinated market economies (Crouch *et al.* 2009). These basic orientations towards a liberal model also prevailed with the shift towards New Labour. The Blair government kept a commitment to these liberal market positions, although some coordinated elements were introduced, such as state involvement in skills upgrading and retraining of the workforce and a more union-friendly outlook in industrial relations (Coates 1999). Regional devolution created further manoeuvring room for regional policy experiments with non-liberal coordination patterns, such as networking and associational governance. The regional authorities in Wales and Scotland in particular would utilise these options in deviating from the hegemonic liberal model at the national level (Moran 2009; Morgan 2007; Amin, Cameron and Hudson 2002).

From a VoC perspective, the decarbonisation of the economy involves a restructuring of institutional complementarities in line with industrial and technological specialisation. This restructuring is driven by strategic coalitions of change and can also be obstructed by adverse coalitions that would like to maintain the status quo, or at least slow down the process of transformation. In terms of the prevailing discourses on the transition towards a low carbon economy, it has been argued that the United Kingdom is stuck between a market competition and governmental control ideology, thus exhibiting a politically entrenched contradictory rationale, which may impede further transitory progress (Keay 2016). A key problem in this regard is therefore the unlocking of path dependence by means of collective action, in both the economic and political systems (see Hübner in Chapter 1; Altenburg and Pegels 2012). Beyond these policy elements, the material driving force of a low carbon transition can be traced to new products, production processes and modes of energy supply, that is, in the domain of technological innovation. In addressing the relationship between institutions and innovation in distinct VoC, it may be argued that the prevailing institutional complementarities also shape the institutional architecture of the related national innovation system (Hübner 2009; Ebner 1999).

Low carbon innovation in the British innovation system

The VoC perspective claims that LMEs exhibit advantages in radical innovation, especially in high-tech industries. This claim derives from the prevailing set of institutional complementarities among the main sub-systems in the institutional environment of business firms (Hall and Soskice 2001). Empirical explorations of OECD economies during the 1990s and early 2000s have largely confirmed the prediction that LMEs tend to specialise in high-tech exports; although aspects of internal diversity and technological dynamics within these classifications need to be taken into account (Schneider and Paunescu 2012). In the case of the United Kingdom, this is exemplified by debates on the advent of biotechnology as an industrial and technological field. Biotechnology is marked by a deep science base with strong university–industry linkages and sustained patterns of entrepreneurial start-up activities, all of which seem to be successful in the context of LMEs (Casper and Murray 2004; Taylor 2004). The British innovation system's institutional setting is distinguished by a pattern of university-related research activities, with an emphasis on research and development (R&D) cooperation. This is most prominently seen in high-tech sectors that are characterised by entrepreneurial activities, such as biotechnology. Empirical evidence shows that, when compared to other European economies, the United Kingdom is distinguished by both the breadth and intensity of university–industry interaction in its science-based industries (D'Este and Patel 2007). Indeed, the British innovation system has been ranked second in an international comparison for university–industry collaboration in R&D by the World Economic Forum. The UK also stands out in terms of R&D funding from abroad, and in scientific output as measured by scientific citations (BIS 2012).

The revealed technological advantage metric provides further insight to this pattern of specialisation. This metric counts the national share in world patents of a certain good, divided by its total share in world patents. During the late 1990s, the British pattern of revealed technological advantage highlighted competencies in pharmaceuticals, chemicals and aerospace (Tylecote and Visintin 2008: 258–259). Accordingly, when it comes to the industrial specialisation of innovation efforts, science-based industries stand out – these include biotechnology, biosciences, pharmaceuticals, defence, aerospace and automobiles. This bias in industrial innovation is accompanied by the eminent role of financial markets in the provision of venture capital (Leijten *et al.* 2012). However, this pattern of industrial and technological specialisation goes along with a comparatively narrow path of R&D operations in the British innovation system. The gross domestic expenditure on R&D/gross domestic product (GERD/GDP) ratio for the United Kingdom has been operating way below the 2 per cent threshold throughout the 2000s – with comparatively high shares of publicly funded and enacted R&D. This GERD/GDP ratio is slightly below the EU average and significantly below global economic powerhouses such as Japan and the United States. The British GERD/GDP profile has also remained below the OECD median value on both the input and output (patenting activities) side (OECD 2012b). With regard to the sectoral performance of R&D activities, the available data show that more than 60 per cent of all R&D in 2010 was carried out by private sector business, 27 per cent in higher education, 9 per cent in government, and the rest in non-profit organisations. In terms of a comparative perspective within the OECD, the British R&D profile underlines the gigantic role of higher education in R&D (OECD 2010c). Thus, public involvement in R&D remains comparatively high in the LME of the United Kingdom. A pattern that may reflect such factors as the short-term market orientation of the private sector, as well as gargantuan uncertainty in science-based innovation that constrains, or even prevents, private sector initiatives with their distinct rationale of investment. The large contribution of higher education to the R&D performance of the British economy is also noteworthy, involving both private and public institutions. It reflects the role of universities as pillars of a British national innovation system that is increasingly oriented towards science-based university–industry relations, with strong market linkages (Mikler and Harrison 2012: 191).

Among the challenges facing the British innovation system is the paucity of privately financed industrial R&D investment, which remains comparatively low according to OECD measures. Other hurdles comprise the maintenance of public funding of the national science base in times of fiscal austerity, the promotion of an adequate supply of venture capital and the ongoing supply of human capital in science and technology. The latter reflects the comparatively low share of science and technology occupations in total employment (OECD 2012a; Cunningham and Sweinsdottir 2012: 12). Knowledge-based entrepreneurship in emerging science-based industrial fields, such as biotechnology, requires an adequate supply of manpower, thus reiterating the long-standing need for extended public–private interactions between firms, universities and government when it comes to strategic efforts in high-level education and training (Casper and Kettler 2001).

The governance and policy dimensions of these distinct innovation and industrial change profiles in the United Kingdom are straightforward. First, the market-based coordination patterns of LMEs as in the United Kingdom tend to rely more prominently on formal regulations and government activities in science and technology. These are meant to promote radical technological change in line with the logic of market competition. In official expositions therefore, the private sector is said to be in the lead, while government facilitates and provides adequate institutional conditions for technological innovation in promising industrial fields, such as renewable energy (DECC 2011a: 12). Accordingly, when it comes to ecologically oriented types of innovation, market signals are dominant in carrying out technological change. Activities of consumer initiatives and related interest groups from civil society remain attached to this market logic, as they aim to alter market signals and related market incentives for innovation (Mikler 2009, 2011). Thus, as the British innovation system and its contribution to the transition towards a low carbon economy indicate, the actual relationship between institutions, innovation and ecological sustainability is quite complex, but the core of the system still clearly reflects a market orientation.

The institutional scaffold of the United Kingdom's national innovation system is constituted by interactions between firms, universities, research organisations, industry associations, unions, political and administrative organs, as well as diverse actors in complementary policy areas such as research, education and finance. The coordination of these interactions combines the competitive dynamics of markets with extensive legal frameworks provided by government. In this setting, a key policy player in the governmental domain has been the Department for Business, Innovation and Skills, which was responsible for several related policy areas, such as technological innovation and intellectual property rights, along with science, research and higher education. It had also overseen the Government Office for Science and housed the Council for Science and Technology with its advisory functions for government. In July 2016 however, it was merged with the Department of Energy and Climate Change to form the new Department for Business, Energy and Industrial Strategy. This measure by the Conservative May government is not necessarily a downgrade. It could possibly be a device for a more integrated industry-oriented climate policy that frames the public support for low carbon innovation (Hepburn and Teytelboym 2017). An important public body has been the Technology Strategy Board, a former advisory body within the Department of Trade and Industry, which had evolved into the United Kingdom's premier innovation agency. It was recently reorganised and renamed InnovateUK. It is now labelled as an executive non-departmental public body that is sponsored by the new Department for Business, Energy and Industrial Strategy. In the past, it had developed several innovation programmes to stimulate technological change. One example is the low carbon vehicles innovation platform, which promotes R&D in low carbon automobile technologies (Technology Strategy Board 2013). A complementing organisation is the Small Business Research Initiative, which offers assistance to entrepreneurial start-ups and small and medium-sized enterprises, in the commercialisation of their innovative products by providing lead customers from the public sector (SBRI 2013). These concerns with commercial viability have also been relevant for new bodies created to support low carbon innovation during the 2000s, these include the UK Energy Research Centre and the Energy Technologies Institute (International Energy Agency 2015).

The former Technology Strategy Board also co-initiated the N8 Industry Innovation Forum, along with the Higher Education Funding Council for England and the N8 Research Partnership. These bring together the leading research-intensive universities and global firms involved with UK R&D, including AstraZeneca, Croda, National Nuclear Laboratory, Procter and Gamble, Reckitt Benckiser, Siemens, Smith and Nephew and Unilever. The Industry Innovation Forum supports linkages among these key players in the national innovation system, by creating collaborations between the established research base and industry (N8 Research Partnership 2013). A further programme in this domain is the UK Research Partnership Investment Fund, which provides financial support to higher education research facilities. It was set up by the Higher Education Funding Council for England in 2012, with a total of £300 million in funds for 22 university projects. It also attracted additional private funds in the process (HEFCE 2013). This strategic thrust to further university–industry relations is shared by sector-specific Research Councils, which are publicly funded research agencies, each providing their own particular funding and support opportunities. The Research Councils UK energy programme is responsible for research on global competitiveness in energy security, affordability and sustainability (Research Councils UK 2013). A related component of these efforts since 2007 is the formation of Innovation and Knowledge Centres, funded by the Engineering and Physical Sciences Research Council, in a comprehensive university and business collaboration initiative (EPSRC 2013). The private non-profit sector also contributes to the British innovation system with activities of the Wellcome Trust in life sciences as a case in point (Leijten *et al.* 2012). A major venture capital fund – initially sponsored by the former Department for Business

Innovation and Skills, the Department of Health and the Department of Energy and Climate Change – has aided technological innovation efforts. This fund, the UK Innovation Investment Fund, promotes venture capital investment in high-tech SMEs and entrepreneurial start-ups. In 2009 Hermes Private Equity and the European Investment Fund were selected as fund-of-fund managers for this fund – which is actually the largest European technology venture capital fund, as well as being a public fund (BIS 2009). Therefore, the finance-innovation nexus in the British innovation system involves shares of public venture capital, and this reflects the persistent involvement of government in the national innovation system.

In view of these innovation profiles, the actual performance of the British innovation system in the low carbon transition is rather ambivalent. In 2011, expenditure on R&D in the fields of energy and environment only comprised 3.2 per cent of total public R&D expenditures, which remains rather low globally. R&D spending in energy-related industries has actually declined over the past 20 years in relation to GDP, with the British government lagging behind other major OECD economies in terms of spending on energy R&D. The more recent resurgence in government R&D is largely due to spending on renewable energy R&D, whereas government funding for clean energy R&D remains underrepresented (Bowen and Rydge 2011: 14).

Similar patterns hold for the output side of low carbon innovation. Although the United Kingdom was ranked high in 'clean' innovation global patent submissions during the 1990s and 2000s, with British patents experiencing sustained growth, its position slipped slightly in the latter period. In addition, their number is still way below the patenting efforts of other leading economies. While the United Kingdom remains a leader in marine energy innovation, its international ranking declined in batteries, electric and hybrid vehicles, nuclear, methane, heating, solar, fuel injection and waste. However, these tendencies are not only the result of a relatively underperforming British innovation system but they also seem to be due to higher growth in patenting activity in emerging economies such as South Korea (Bowen and Rydge 2011: 15). At the same time, British green technology patents have shown a low degree of specialisation throughout the 2000s. The UK's proportion of world patents for environmental management is 4.8 per cent, it is 4.6 per cent for energy generation, 2.9 per cent for transportation, and 2.6 per cent for emissions mitigation technology (OECD 2012a: 69). The sub-field of clean energy patenting comprises the patenting of activities in technologies such as solar, wind, carbon capture and storage, hydro, geothermal, biofuels and the integrated gasification combined cycle. In this particular sub-field, the British share of global clean energy technology patents between 1988 and 2007 was 3.6 per cent, while the in the EU that share was 32 per cent. Also, in this particular sub-field, the United Kingdom exhibits a revealed technological advantage below 1 – that is, no significant advantage at all. In line with this pattern, British numbers of patent applications filed under the Patent Cooperation Treaty for energy generation from renewable and non-fossil sources in 2010 were much lower than those of other leading OECD economies (Veugelers 2011: 4–5).

Accordingly, comparative technology advantages of the UK in green innovation from 1988 to 2011 were most prominent in the fields of wind, hydro, biofuels, and carbon capture and storage (Veugelers 2011). In OECD rankings the United Kingdom holds the sixth place in patents for clean energy technologies; in the hydro/machine domain the UK is ranked fourth, in biofuels fifth, in carbon capture and storage fifth, and in integrated gasification combined cycle fourth (OECD 2012b). These advantages are related to distinct industrial fields. The most advanced green innovation sectors in the United Kingdom are actually in 'pharmaceuticals, medicinal chemicals, etc.' with a green innovation score of 1.8 and a revealed comparative advantage score of 1.9. In comparison 'measuring/testing/navigating appliances, etc.' held a green innovation score of 1.0 and a revealed comparative advantage score of 1.6 in 2012 (Fankhauser *et al.* 2012).

When it comes to venture capital and private equity in financing low carbon technology innovation, the leading economy in this field is the United States. USA investment volumes are almost eight times higher than those generated in the United Kingdom, which is ranked second globally. However, the latter still accounts for related financial operations, which are more than two times greater than the EU average. In fact, along with tidal and wave, biomass, wind and others, carbon finance has evolved as a major low carbon growth sector (BIS 2010). In line with this pattern, the United Kingdom was by far the biggest European investor in renewables in 2015 and 2016, largely a consequence of offshore wind projects. It accounted for almost double the amount of investment of second place Germany (FS-UNEP 2017: 25). In general, energy efficient and low carbon technologies and services, and other renewables, take the largest share of green venture capital and private equity finance, with a particular focus on wind energy. This contrasts with Continental European economies that only hold minor shares in financial services for low carbon transition, which reflects their less market-oriented and more bank-based financial systems (McCrone *et al.* 2013). However, a major step towards the institutional hybridisation of the British variety of capitalism and its national innovation system has been made with the establishment of the Green Investment Bank. This bank is part of the public sector and finances investment activities in projects that contribute to government environmental and sustainability targets (Green Investment Bank 2012). This comes close to the model of a government-owned development bank supporting low carbon innovation; in any case, it can be seen as a major contribution to the moulding of a new financial infrastructure for 'low carbon entrepreneurs', who are set to promote innovative new enterprises with significant effects on the technology landscape (Carbon Trust and Shell 2013). Yet, promoting the dynamism of the low carbon transition requires much more than just the support of entrepreneurship and innovation. It also implies efforts in unlocking path-dependent institutional structures of the established energy systems.

Strategies and policies in the United Kingdom's low carbon transition

The British transformation path towards a low carbon economy is based on the impact of both incumbent firms and actors that promote the established large-scale energy system, involving both cooperation and struggle between industry and government (Geels 2014). The corresponding environmental policy style has been portrayed as pragmatic, with government partnering and consulting with industry. In contrast, environmental groups find it difficult to access governmental decision-making (Bailey 2007). This pattern is driven by a centralised political system that is most accessible to incumbent interests, while small parties like the Greens are disadvantaged. A predominant liberal ideology of market competition and cost efficiency, and comparatively weak structures of environmental organisations in civil society also characterise the British political system. While policies in favour of renewables have become more pronounced since the late 2000s, the basic orientation towards a coalition between government and established utilities remains strong. In effect, renewable electricity technologies in the United Kingdom are mainly related to large-scale centralised modes of deployment, as represented by onshore and offshore wind farms and the biomass conversion of coal power stations. In addition, nuclear power and carbon capture and storage systems add to the prevalence of large-scale varieties of low carbon electricity generation. Indeed, the dominant regime for lighting, heating and power services is still a system of centralised technologies with large-scale transmission and distribution frameworks. Recent policy efforts in support of renewables, such as the Community Energy Strategy, are meant to complement the established large-scale systems. The formation of a low carbon economy means that both this large-scale centralised energy system and its dominant market logic are under pressure from transitional forces. These forces encompass new technologies and transmission mechanisms that allow for decentralisation and small-scale operations, as well as new institutional and cultural patterns of non-market coordination that relate to these alternatives (Geels *et al.* 2016).

Historically, the post-war nationalisation of the electricity supply industry led to a lock-in of a highly centralised, monopolistic and large-scale energy generation system, involving fuel-based technologies and national grid networks. Thus, the energy component of the public sector expanded from the 1950s, run by the Central Electricity Generating Board. However, after the liberalisation and privatisation of the energy sector that was completed in the 1990s, which also involved the abolition of the Department of Energy in 1992, the market logic of competitive efficiency has been dominant. Yet a centralised system has, in fact, prevailed. An oligopolistic market structure emerged with six large vertically integrated firms. The expansion of this market logic has also been paralleled by government activities in support of an adequate market framework (Foxon 2013). Britain's centralised energy system prevents local deviation and niche competition, which are key factors in the promotion of renewables in other, more decentralised, European systems. Unlocking these path dependencies thus stands for a key aspect of policy strategies in the low carbon transition of the United Kingdom (Simmie *et al.* 2014).

As outlined above, a key issue regarding the role of market competition in low carbon transition is the *oligopolistic* market structure of the British energy supply. In fact, 'big six' energy companies dominate the United Kingdom's supply structure, operating three-quarters of British electricity generation, while facilitating over 90 per cent of electricity supply in the British retail market. The leading player among these 'big six' is EDF Energy, a subsidiary of Électricité de France, the major state-owned French energy company. It is followed by Scottish and Southern Energy SSE. Other players are RWE power, a British subsidiary of Germany energy supplier RWE, Centrica British Gas, E.on UK, the British subsidiary of German company E.on, and Spanish company Iberdrola/Scottish Power (New Power Consulting 2011). Data on the carbon intensity and fuel mix of these energy suppliers in the United Kingdom serve as a reminder of the ramifications of nuclear energy in the British energy mix. EDF energy is the biggest supplier of nuclear energy in the United Kingdom and operates with the lowest carbon intensity at $280\,\mathrm{g}\,CO_2/$ kwh. In contrast, E.on UK operates with a negligible share of nuclear energy and therefore has the highest carbon intensity of the major firms at $543\,\mathrm{g}\,CO_2/$ kwh (Friends of the Earth 2011). In a dynamic view, EDF energy has made some major advances in low carbon activities. These are chiefly due to the acquisition of nuclear power plants, which have contributed to a massive reduction of the company's carbon intensity (ElectricityInfo 2013). Corresponding evaluations of carbon savings of the major energy suppliers tend to highlight their overall compliance with official reduction targets, although further improvements are deemed indispensable by the authorities (OFGEM 2013).

Policy efforts in support of the British economy's low carbon transition may be labelled market-oriented, quite in line with the prevailing liberal variety of capitalism and its bias towards market coordination of firms and arm's length regulation by government. Most domestic policies in the United Kingdom that target decarbonisation of the economy use price signals that set incentives for firms and households to adjust their behaviour in a cost-effective manner. Examples are tradable quota markets, as implemented in the form of a Renewables Obligation, and price-based instruments, such as the Climate Change Levy. There are also market regulations in support of specific mandatory actions, such as the labelling requirements for energy efficiency. As a matter of fact, legal measures that are related to programmatic governmental projections play a key role in the British approach to decarbonisation policy, this has become apparent since the late 2000s. An example is the Climate Change Act from 2008, which gave statutory force to carbon reduction budgets, accompanied by the Committee on Climate Change with distinct statutory responsibilities in the management of these carbon budgets (Bowen and Rydge 2011: 16).

Further hybridising mechanisms have emerged that transcend the logic of market coordination by infusing a rationale of governmental involvement. The influence of the public sector in the domain of green finance is a case in point, as outlined above. Transnational governmental influences in the corporate setting of the energy sector may also be addressed at this point. In conceptual terms then, this hybridisation of market and non-market coordination reflects long-standing historical processes in the recombination of governance mechanisms. These shape the institutional architecture of capitalist varieties (Crouch 2005). That being said, the institutional core of British capitalism still remains dedicated to the rationale of market coordination, which was constructed and installed in its current shape by the policy reforms of the 1970s. When it came to the energy sector, these liberal reform efforts involved privatisation in coal, gas and electricity, as well as a liberalisation of the energy market framed by complex regulatory efforts. It is fair to say that these privatisation and liberalisation processes in the energy sector, which paralleled the politically enforced decline of Britain's emission-intensive coal and steel industries during the 1980s, have shaped subsequent efforts in the transition towards a low carbon economy.

The political processes underlying British decarbonisation policies have been shaped by distinct actors and coalitions from across the political spectrum. Until the mid-2000s, the agenda of climate change mitigation was of secondary importance, not least because during the 1990s the United Kingdom was already making some progress in the reduction of greenhouse gas emissions. This reduction was an unintended consequence of the Thatcher government's privatisation of the electricity sector, which resulted in the replacement of coal-fired power stations with gas-fired plants. The instrument of non-fossil fuel obligations was introduced in 1990 as a means to support both nuclear energy and renewables, combined with an auction system that was marred by information asymmetries and benefitted incumbent firms and actors. In fact, the Conservative liberalisation and privatisation programs that were initiated by the Thatcher and Major governments kept a focus on price-regulated market competition and a business-related refocusing of governmental energy policy. This was symbolically institutionalised by the dissolution of the Department of Energy and the transfer of energy policy to the Department of Trade and Industry, in tandem with the establishment of the new regulatory agency Ofgem (Geels *et al.* 2016).

Blair's Labour government, installed in 1997, became a major force in the design and implementation of the low carbon agenda. It actively negotiated the Kyoto Protocol, yet – following extensive consultations with energy providers, industry and experts – it managed to go beyond the Kyoto targets. It also established a Climate Change Programme and introduced related initiatives, such as the Climate Change Levy as a downstream tax on commercial energy consumption. Crucially, Climate Change Agreements with industry would allow for major reductions, in exchange for the commitment to legally binding reduction targets. Furthermore, the Renewables Obligation instrument was taken to the fore in order to encourage electricity generation from renewable sources (DETR 2000). The latter was designed as a market-based instrument that would accompany the established emissions trading market mechanism, which had been settled in the context of an UK Emissions Trading Scheme. Under the Renewable Obligations scheme, utilities would need to meet renewable electricity targets by either producing electricity from renewables themselves, by buying certificates from other electricity generators or by paying a penalty. Again, as in the case of the non-fossil fuel obligations, this mechanism exhibited an inherent bias towards favouring well established and experienced incumbents (Geels *et al.* 2016; Bailey 2007).

However, Blair's actual government activities were largely void of further decarbonisation actions; an aspect that was repeatedly criticised by the opposition. More ambitious governmental activities were hindered by organised interest groups. For instance, the proposal of the Climate Change Levy in 1999 initially met with hostile criticism by organised business interests. A year later, public discontent with increasing fuel prices resulted in organised militant protests led by hauliers' and farmers' organisations (Carter 2008). All of this contributed to delegitimising taxation as an environmental and climate policy. Instead, the government reverted back to the view that carbon markets, as exemplified by the European Union's Emissions Trading Scheme, were the best means of reducing carbon emissions. Intragovernmental conflicts between a less market-oriented policy approach pursued by the Department of Environment, Food and Rural Affairs and adherents of market efficiency in the Treasury, the Department for Trade and Industry and the Department for Transport were decisively solved in favour of the market (Lorenzoni *et al.* 2008).

Brown's Labour government pressed more emphatically for the transition towards a low carbon economy, while being engaged in political competition over the environmental affairs mantle with the Conservative and Liberal Democrat opposition in parliament, framed by green interest groups across civil society. Brown's government established a new Department of Energy and Climate Change in 2008, paralleling the introduction of the Climate Change Act with its ambitious emission targets to implement the emission targets of the Kyoto Protocol. This initiative made the United Kingdom a pioneer in building a credible, legally binding framework for achieving clear targets in the reduction of greenhouse gases. These amounted to a 34 per cent reduction in greenhouse gas emissions by 2020 from 1990 levels, and an 80 per cent reduction in emissions by 2050 from 1990 levels. These targets were to be framed by quinquennial carbon budgets that set the trajectory towards these targets, overseen by a formally independent Climate Change Committee. At the same time, the European Union's targets on renewables were accepted, with 15 per cent of all energy to be generated from renewable sources by 2020. Therefore, the United Kingdom became the first country to operate within a legal framework to tackle the problem of emissions and establish an institutional setting for governing the required adaptations

(Dreblow *et al.* 2013). Moreover, the 2009 Low Carbon Transition Plan presented an almost complete decarbonisation of electricity by 2030, including the expanded use of the renewals obligations for large-scale electricity generation, which had been in place since 2002, as well as feed-in tariffs for small-scale renewable electricity generation from 2010 onwards. This was accompanied by strategic investment in renewables, carbon capture and storage, grid capacity, transportation and storage in sustainable infrastructure, along with related R&D. The streamlined regulation and planning of marine, offshore wind and nuclear power were combined with market-oriented mechanisms of decarbonisation. These involved up-front financing of energy efficiency, internalised through energy bills and supplemented by clean energy cash-back schemes (DECC 2009). Crucially, energy supply and utilisation reform would also include the phasing out of coal, in effect making the United Kingdom the first country to commit to a coal phase out. In so doing, maintaining a decade-old trend of replacing coal with gas, and later on with renewables. Indeed, in addition to the economic pressures on coal, its decline was sped up by political means, such as the Large Combustion Plant Directive and then the Industrial Emissions Directive (Staffell 2017: 463n). Thus, in a historically unique political move, a Labour government would initiate the shut out of coal from the energy mix – finalising the decline of British coal, which had formed a major social basis of the Labour Party in prior decades.

The 2010 elections that resulted in a power shift from Labour to a Conservative–Liberal coalition government were marked by significant concerns with climate change across the political spectrum. Labour's 2010 election manifesto focused explicitly on the transition to a low carbon economy as a key challenge of future governments (Labour Party 2010). At the same time Cameron's Conservative Party had already developed a distinct political brand in terms of 'greening' the economy. The British Conservatives only became visibly interested in environmental affairs in 2005, under Cameron's leadership. This caused the climate change mitigation and emissions reduction agenda to join the mainstream of political debate. This was further intensified by green lobby organisations, such as Friends of the Earth, with their agenda of channelling environmental concerns into legal measures (Carter 2008). Also, since the mid-2000s, the British business community has become more open to tackling environmental issues within the confines of market regulations. The mitigation of climate change has increasingly been viewed as a new field of business opportunities in terms of improving energy efficiency, new green technologies and emissions trading schemes. The low carbon initiative of the Corporate Leaders Group – which formed in 2005 and includes major British corporations such as Shell, Tesco, Unilever and Vodafone – exemplifies this point. The Confederation of British Industry, the United Kingdom's major employers' organisation, would soon set up a task force on climate change that should contribute to the communication of related policy proposals (Strong 2010).

The Conservative Party's 2010 election manifesto combined the call for a reduction of greenhouse gases, with the goal of increasing the competitiveness of British firms in global markets for low carbon technology. Corresponding key projects included the establishment of the Green Investment Bank, meant to leverage private sector capital to finance new green technology start-up enterprises (Conservative Party 2010). In even more sweeping terms, the Liberal Democrat election manifesto emphasised environmental issues regarding climate change and the transition towards a low carbon economy, underlining a green political profile (Liberal Democrats 2010). Accordingly, the Cameron coalition government of Conservatives and Liberal Democrats took off with a distinct pledge to strengthen efforts in mitigating climate change and promoting energy efficiency, in so doing actually pushing for a more interventionist approach. This was done in terms of feed-in tariffs and new emission standards, despite increasingly vocal opposition from interest groups in industry and finance. Indeed, the coalition government continued the established low carbon strategy. Including, among other measures: furthering distinct Energy Acts; accepting the fourth carbon budget through to 2027; creating the Green Investment Bank; establishing a Green Deal for domestic energy efficiency; promoting smart meters in all homes across the nation; and reforming electricity markets. The latter was done in a manner aimed at encouraging companies to do more long-term investment in low carbon energy generation (Carter 2014: 423–424; Foxon 2013: 15). These electricity market reforms were meant to promote a system of feed-in tariffs with different contracts for large-scale renewables and nuclear from 2014 onwards, introducing fixed prices for energy generators along with market price oriented compensation for energy suppliers. Emissions performance standards should limit carbon emissions from new fossil fuel power plants, while long-term contracts are set to provide a high degree of revenue certainty to investors in low carbon generation domains, such as renewables, nuclear and carbon capture and storage (DECC 2011a, 2011b, 2012). Additionally, tendering is promoted as a possible means to mitigate the security of supply risk, in line with European market conditions (Meeus *et al.* 2012).

Crucially, nuclear power remained a debated topic in the politics of low carbon transition during the 2000s. In the coalition government, which initially proposed a major thrust towards decarbonisation, the Conservatives acknowledged the opposition of the Liberal Democrats on the nuclear issue, yet Cameron soon confirmed that the new government's strategic orientation should allow for the construction of new nuclear power plants. This is in keeping with the prevailing fuel mix – and also quite in line with the positions of previous Labour governments (Cabinet Office 2010). Therefore, the 2008 White Paper on Nuclear Power proposed that innovations might allow for the 'eco-friendly' inclusion of the nuclear sector in the low carbon economy strategy. Indeed, nuclear energy is increasingly seen as a relatively clean technology, which is likely to make an important contribution to the energy sector's long-term decarbonisation. The military-political aspects of nuclear capacities also play a key role in this discourse, as is discussed below (Bowen and Rydge 2011: 26). This pro-nuclear stance has not been altered by the international impact of the Fukushima incident. Fukushima may have increased perceived dangers in comparative risk assessments when examining low carbon transition options, yet without damaging the generally positive standing of nuclear energy in the British energy mix (Rhys 2013). In fact, the Conservative Cameron and May governments have voiced continued political support for nuclear power as an energy source. Also, the building of new nuclear power plants is clearly an option for the future. In 2015 the Conservative government announced the construction of new nuclear reactors that should contribute to the low carbon energy system of the future (Pemberton 2017).

However, the matter of climate change mitigation and low carbon transition has recently become the subject of some serious conflict within British politics. While the cross-party consensus on energy and climate policies has largely been sustained, growing divisions within the Conservative Party have turned climate change into an increasingly partisan issue. For instance, the Conservative position on the environment involves cautious support of fracking, while becoming ever more critical of the subsidy-based promotion of onshore wind power and other types of renewable energy sources. During the Liberal–Conservative coalition government, environmental debates were reflected in controversies between the government's economic and environmental affairs departments. Both departments were stacked with Conservative and Liberal Democrat leadership personnel, and repeatedly communicated conflicting policy strategies on these issues, despite belonging to the same administration (Macalister and Harvey 2013). This burgeoning stance towards low carbon policies reflects growing discontent among Conservatives on the economic costs of emissions reduction, which allegedly pose an increasingly unbearable burden on businesses and their competitive performance. Thus, the promotion of subsidies for offshore oil and gas exploration has become a debated topic, while the legally binding definition of decarbonisation targets remains controversial (Carter 2014: 429–430).

In actuality, recent reforms under Conservative leadership have involved feed-in tariff auctions, which provide a competitive market mechanism to counterbalance price distortions; a policy motive that has become ever more pronounced since the Conservatives took over again in 2015. However, with Prime Minister May in charge, the Conservative government seems set to maintain the low carbon agenda of previous governments. A government proposal from November 2015 aims to deliver on the phase-out of unabated coal use by 2025. As coal use is at a historic low, with major coal plants closing, the remaining ones being over-aged, and electricity generation from solar surpassing coal for the first time, it seems as though the Conservatives may be ready to put the finishing touches to the complete phase-out of coal (Littlecott 2016). Still, this does not imply full-blown policy continuity with recent Conservative governments, for the level of support for renewables has been revised. In particular, support for onshore wind and solar photovoltaic has largely been withdrawn in an effort to push the agenda of market-based competitive pressures as key forces in moulding the energy mix (Geels *et al.* 2016). Most specifically then, British low carbon policies signal that renewables might expand, as long as they are driven by markets, whereas nuclear remains a politically charged (and government subsidised) component of the energy mix – while coal is phased out at last (Keay 2016: 248n).

The upsurge of critiques against low carbon transition strategies in the United Kingdom, however, are not only an echo of business interests fighting regulatory measures that may drive up costs and endanger competitive advantages, but these positions also represent substantial criticisms of the efficacy of the implemented policy strategies. A common denominator for both proponents and detractors on energy and climate policies in the United Kingdom, is provided by the insight that the economy's low carbon transition is in need of a solid legal basis that credibly commits government. Given its long-term nature, strategies for decarbonisation may face time inconsistency problems as governments may be tempted to postpone difficult measures. In this respect, the combination of long-term commitments enshrined in law with statutory short-term targets have been singled out as the most promising way forward (Fankhauser *et al.* 2012). Also, the strategic orientation towards credible long-term commitments may in fact encourage the development of new low carbon technologies, as firms prepare for tougher carbon reduction targets and thus channel resources into related technological innovations. Nonetheless, critics of this market-oriented, law-based approach highlight the persistent problem of uncertainty regarding cost-benefit patterns in the decarbonisation of the economy, including with respect to related technological innovations that should serve as the drivers of a low carbon transition.

First of all, the feed-in tariff model that is set to be employed in the United Kingdom means that energy generators are to be paid the difference between the contract reference price and the electricity market price. Allegedly, this measure reduces uncertainty, stabilises expectations and promotes transparent cost calculations in a turbulent technological setting. It has been argued that this model, which resembles pioneering German regulations, is more effective at increasing the share of renewables than the previously adopted approach of renewable obligations (Mitchell *et al.* 2006; Foxon *et al.* 2005). Still, the cost challenges related to the support of new energy industries, such as solar, remain largely unresolved. Levels and directions of subsidising the renewables sector seem to be uncoordinated across industries and technologies, which breeds uncertainty for investors. Moreover, energy and climate change policies seem to overlap, leading to a relatively complex policy regime that differs between business sectors and individual firms. All of this is paralleled by disparities in carbon prices across industries and fuel types – with particularly high price differentials observed between electricity and other fuels, as well as between high and low energy-intensive companies (Bassi *et al.* 2013).

These problems may reflect the overall structure of low carbon policies, for legal frameworks such as the Climate Change Act start by setting mandatory targets from which actual policy strategies are derived. The ultimate process of policy-making is massively influenced by interventions from interest groups. Governance and feasibility problems concerning the extent of decarbonisation and emissions reduction are prevalent in such a complex economic, social and political experiment as the transition to a low carbon economy (Pielke 2009).

Rent-seeking, as well as the stifling of competition and innovation, are critical concerns with price regulation and subsidies. It has been pointed out that feed-in tariffs will also be implemented for nuclear energy, which means that the British government will negotiate long-term contracts for the supply of nuclear energy at the guaranteed price using the feed-in tariff mechanism. This price regulation implies that nuclear power is going to be subsidised on a major scale, regardless of cost and efficiency considerations. A major cost concern that should be addressed is the long-term social cost of nuclear energy (Toke 2011). Additionally, the regulation of nuclear energy industries is among the most politicised in the energy sector. This can be seen in the fact that a major corporate player in the British energy supply – and in nuclear energy – is EDF energy, whose parent company is state-owned French company EDF. In effect, subsidising nuclear energy equals subsidising a foreign government-run enterprise through domestic fiscal resources; resembling a transnational transfer of financial resources that transcends the logic of market competition and its regulation (Theurer 2013).

These issues once again hint at a diversity of economic and political relations that transcends the British image of a LME, and pinpoint direct governmental influences on business affairs, which even reaches the transnational level. In this manner, the transition towards a low carbon economy is subject to governance mechanisms and bargaining relations that are settled well beyond the confines of the nation-state – and thus also beyond the strict limits of national models of capitalism. Transnational and – in the case of the European Union – supranational interactions clearly are of great import. Yet these political–economic interactions increase the complexity of policy-making and, in doing so, invite extended rent-seeking activities of organised interest groups, which push for an agenda of special regulatory treatment and subsidies. Of course, the resulting policies suffer from inconsistency and thus damage the case for long-range strategies and decarbonisation policies. These aspects of rent-seeking and policy inconsistency become ever more complicated once the regional policy level is considered. Strategies for the promotion of a low carbon economy in Scotland and Wales involve regional and urban low carbon energy projects, with these locales possessing their own ambitious carbon agendas. The Scottish regional government in particular uses its competences to further regional economic development in the context of a comprehensive green growth agenda. This is set to transform the Scottish economy into a green regional economy with the goal of 80 per cent of energy consumption emanating from renewables by 2020 (Leijten *et al.* 2012). The recent Scottish referendum serves as a reminder that regional policy concerns, and their underlying deviations from the hegemonic national model of capitalism, remain highly relevant in ongoing policy discourses. As the Scottish exit from the United Kingdom was prevented by a rather narrow majority, regional varieties of transition paths towards a low carbon economy are set to persist. In this regard, the UK case of transition shows similarities with the Canadian case (Harrison, Chapter 2).

Actors and coalitions in the United Kingdom's low carbon transition

Understanding low carbon economy policy efforts requires the re-examination of institutional actors and processes that transcend party politics and governmental affairs. As outlined above in the case of Labour's doomed fiscal approach to the low carbon transition, it is a fact that policy strategies remain subject to institutional constraints. These include policy networks that are dominated by organised business interests, while systematically excluding environmental NGOs and other civil society actors. This may hint at a basic lack of voice when it comes to the communication of environmental concerns within political systems; an aspect that is aggravated by a British electoral system that has stymied the emergence of the Green Party as a political force in the United Kingdom. However, changes in UK climate politics since the mid-2000s reflect a comprehensive reorientation of business interests and political actors. This is based on the persistent activities of environmental interest groups and is framed by wider international, as well as regional, attention to this issue. The temporary alliance between Cameron's Conservative Party and the Friends of the Earth NGO provides a most relevant example of this political agenda and strategy revamping in the context of a comprehensive societal change of perceptions of environmental affairs (Carter 2014: 430–431).

When it comes to the actual operation of the transition towards a low carbon economy, the interactions between businesses and their institutional environments are the most important, involving actors and coalitions from the domain of business associations and labour unions. It is standard reasoning in the VoC framework that the role of associational governance is less relevant in LMEs, such as the United Kingdom, than in relational and associational types of capitalism, such as Germany (Mikler 2009: 105; see also Ebner, Chapter 5). A case in point is the governance-related role of voluntary agreements by business in the political-economic setting of the United Kingdom. They may be quite prominent with regard to corporate commitments to report energy use and emissions, which have nonetheless been subject to legal regulations, yet less so regarding an articulation of associational governance with clear-cut voluntary action. Still, business associations can play a major role in the introduction of low carbon technologies in certain strategically relevant industries, where they take part in the formation of the knowledge base for technology adoption. A fitting example is provided by RenewableUK (formerly known as the British Wind Energy Association), which is the leading renewable energy association in the United Kingdom and focuses on wind and marine energy. Remarkably, collaborative efforts between government and RenewableUK include a Renewables Training Network that assists 77,500 workers in dealing with the prevalent skills gap in the British renewable energy industry (RenewableUK 2014). In this way, it contributes to associational efforts in skills formation as a prerequisite for expanding the supply of renewables. Of course, labour unions also have a stake in the promotion of a low carbon economy at the firm and industry levels.

However, the asymmetrical distribution of business opportunities and economic costs arising from the low carbon transition across firms and industries amounts to a distinct pattern of industrial change, which breeds attitudes of ambivalence among some towards the envisaged low carbon economy. In fact, this ambivalence has largely prevailed in the various business associations and communities that are also involved in the recent Conservative criticism of low carbon initiatives. The Confederation of British Industry, which is the United Kingdom's leading employer federation, promotes a course of 'green growth', which maintains that energy security and affordability need to be tackled through exploring new business opportunities in working towards a low carbon transition. Yet inter-industry differences in energy intensity require specific decarbonisation strategies and targets that fit both the domestic and international competitive situations of firms in each sector, and thus allows for a level playing field with manageable long-term commitments. A stable market framework that promotes competition within the energy sector while prioritising energy affordability is an indispensable basis for further low carbon initiatives (CBI 2012). Low carbon economy ambivalence also applies to British unions, which are historically an active part of the Labour Party and thus have quite an outspoken institutional position in policy-making. The Trade Unions Congress supports renewable energy as a means of low carbon transition. In particular, it demands feed-in tariffs to encourage the sustained use of renewable energy and a corresponding shift in the energy mix towards renewables. However, the remaining coal industries are not completely out of the picture as the TUC has argued that coal and gas should become more environmentally friendly through new technologies such as carbon capture and storage. Reaching technologically viable 'clean' coal has thus been an overarching strategic motive, which contradicts the policy of phasing out coal. Moreover, there is a clear-cut promotion of the building of new nuclear power stations to further reduce carbon emissions, which means that for the TUC nuclear energy is set to remain within the domestic energy mix (TUC 2013).

This aspect of maintaining a reliance on nuclear energy underlines the confrontation of economic and political interests and ideas in the making of a low carbon economy (Hubbard 2014). All the way through the 1990s providers of nuclear power were under constant economic pressure, even though British Energy took over major nuclear plants in 1996. However, despite preceding debates on the social and ecological costs of nuclear energy, policy-makers reverted to promoting the nuclear industry during the 2000s. The 2008 White Paper on Nuclear Power outlined a renewal of the nuclear sector that was met by rather fragmented resistance from environmental groups. While building new nuclear power plants remains an uncertain venture, the British government has been willing to grant subsidies for these endeavours (Geels *et al.* 2016). In 2015 the government announced the subsidised construction of two European-designed nuclear reactors, partly financed by Chinese utility companies. This announcement was largely perceived as a top-down decision without civic participation, thus corroborating the impression that the governance of nuclear energy remains subject to a specific mode of policy design and implementation that lacks basic democratic-deliberative credentials (Pemberton 2017). The question is, why does the British government proceed with such a clear commitment to nuclear power? This strategic thrust is against a global trend of moving away from nuclear. Also, the British nuclear industry has held a rather low proportion of electricity production, exhibited a low degree of innovativeness and has a negligible share of world markets. In these metrics it differs markedly from its German counterpart, which is subject to a national phase-out policy. This British nuclear sector context may be explained by ideological factors relating to military affairs, in particular with regard to the maintenance of nuclear submarine capabilities, which are at the heart of the UK's status as an international political-military power (Cox *et al.* 2016).

The corresponding actors and coalitions that shape the British path towards a low carbon economy can be characterised as follows. Main political supporters of a low carbon agenda are smaller political parties, namely the Green Party, which holds influence primarily when it comes to policy discourses and less with regard to actual administrative capacity, as well as the Liberal Democrats, which have emerged as a third political force in parliament and have consistently promoted low carbon concerns, including when in the former coalition government. The environmental orientation at the regional level should be mentioned, in particular with the Scottish National Party. The Labour and Conservative parties are more ambivalent however. Blair's Labour government introduced the low carbon economy agenda to British politics, involving highly controversial fiscal measures in its support. Yet it was Brown's Labour government that promoted the most relevant legal frameworks and regulatory instruments. At the same time, Labour underlined the need for combining environmental and business concerns into a 'green' growth and innovation model for the British economy. Revamped coal and nuclear energy were to be part of the diversified energy mix. Yet this combination of business and environmental concerns was persistently subject to inter-departmental policy conflicts. These would set proponents of market-breaking measures in the Department of Environment, Food and Rural

Affairs against adherents of market-making and shaping solutions in the Treasury, the Department for Trade and Industry, and the Department for Transport. The Conservative Party then reinvented itself under Cameron's leadership as a political force with a clear-cut environmental agenda, in so doing revamping an approach that aimed to use markets as coordination mechanisms in support of a low carbon economy. This reinvention of the Conservatives was pursued in temporary alliances with civil society actors, in particular with Friends of the Earth. Industry associations also played a major role in the making of low carbon alliances. The Confederation of British Industry, with its task force on climate change, plays a supportive role on this point. This mirrors activities from within the managerial business elite, such as the low carbon initiative of the Corporate Leaders Group, accompanied by industry-specific associations such as RenewableUK in the wind and marine energy sector. On the union side, the Trade Union Congress is quite clear in its support of the low carbon transition and applies a comprehensive cross-industrial approach that involves both 'clean' coal and nuclear energy.

Actors and alliances that are set to slow down or even abolish the transition towards a low carbon economy are most prominently active within the Conservative Party. While business-related public protest against early Labour efforts to promote low carbon policies by fiscal means have led to an abolishment of this policy strategy, current debates address business concerns with the economic costs of low carbon policies. These argue that ambitious national regulations may negatively affect the competitiveness of British industry, and put a monetary burden on domestic energy users and consumers. It may be underlined, however, that the dominant discourse on aligning business and environmental concerns was originally pushed by Blair's New Labour during the late 1990s. In this manner, the Confederation of British Industry also plays a key role in communicating the need for policies that are simultaneously market compatible and business friendly. This, together with persistent concerns with energy security, might actually slow down the transition process towards a low carbon economy.

Whether the recent political turbulence regarding the British exit from the European Union impacts the United Kingdom's low carbon transition in a positive or negative manner is still subject to debate and further observation. The advocacy of 'Brexit' during the referendum campaign did not coincide with specific political positions on decarbonisation. Brexit support came from Conservatives and right-wing forces that sympathised with climate change denial, while more radical environmental elements of the Labour Party's left flank, and other leftist groups who support interventionist climate change policies, also backed the Brexit decision. Apart from these diffuse political constellations, it remains true that the United Kingdom is the only major European economy with legally binding emissions targets that are actually more ambitious than those pronounced by the European Union. This situation is not affected by Brexit. Also, EU directives that would need to be replaced tend to relate to heavily criticised measures such as the Emissions

Trading Scheme. Indeed, as the United Kingdom has been pushing forward and transcending EU regulations with more ambitious goals, even under Conservative governments, a post-Brexit climate policy roll-back seems improbable (Staffell 2017: 474). More significant for the low carbon transition of the British economy may be the impact of Brexit on the national innovation system. For instance, the loss of funds for low carbon energy innovation as encapsulated in EU schemes such as Horizon 2020 need to be considered. Moreover, 'green' funding by means of EU Structural and Regional Funds are at stake and funding by the European Investment Bank may become inaccessible (Hepburn and Teytelboym 2017). This may result in a further intensification of market-based innovation efforts combined with a further extension of 'green' finance in the domain of venture capital, quite in line with the basic structures of the complex interdependencies of the British model of capitalism.

Conclusion

The United Kingdom follows a distinct trajectory in the transition towards a low carbon economy, which combines political-administrative features, such as carbon budgets, with legal frameworks for market regulation and the public support of low carbon innovation. In effect, these measures have promoted a comparatively successful effort at the reduction of greenhouse gas and carbon emissions, based on a rapid phase-out of coal, the expansion of renewables and the persistence of nuclear in the energy system. Also, in the case of the United Kingdom, technological innovation is the key variable in the process of low carbon transition. The corresponding national innovation system is part of an institutional setting that may be labelled a LME from the viewpoint of the VoC perspective. Its market-oriented policy focus, with its logic of arm's length regulation, is inherently combined with hybrid elements that introduce aspects of non-market governance modes. An example is the UK Innovation Investment Fund, a public fund that promotes investment in new high-tech enterprises and which is among the largest European technology venture capital funds. An accentuated role of government can also be traced to the nuclear energy domain.

In the United Kingdom, as in other OECD economies, the transition mechanisms to a low carbon economy are subject to debates on the feasibility of emission targets, energy supply security and the efficiency of market regulations in the face of counter-productive rent-seeking. It remains a key challenge to mediate these concerns, which have recently gained in political weight, with the ongoing need to implement already established targets towards further carbon reduction. The Brexit referendum decision to leave the European Union adds to the complexity of these issues, as it affects the institutional and financial core of the British innovation system – quite apart from its unforeseeable impact on the future position of the United Kingdom in the global division of labour. At this point, it is evident once more that the institutional substance of the British VoC rests on the political construction and regulation of market coordination. This political rationale and its concern with the performance of markets is an indispensable element of the British type of LME; an assessment that is well illustrated by its contested transition towards a low carbon economy.

4 Climate change politics in Japan in the aftermath of the Fukushima nuclear crisis

Miranda A. Schreurs

Introduction[1]

Japan is one of the world's largest emitters of greenhouse gases, accounting for about 3.4 percent of global CO_2 emissions in 2014 (World Bank 2017b). As the host of the climate conference at which the Kyoto Protocol was reached, Japan has been a relatively strong supporter of global action on climate change. Under the Kyoto Protocol, Japan committed to reducing its greenhouse gas emissions by 6 percent of 1990 levels by 2012. Making use of the Kyoto flexibility mechanisms, Japan met its target. At the Copenhagen climate negotiations in 2009, Japan committed to reduce its greenhouse gas emissions by 25 percent below 1990 levels by 2020, a stronger target than the EU's commitment to a 20 percent reduction over the same time frame. Behind this ambitious target were plans for a wide-scale expansion of nuclear energy and further improvements in the country's already strong energy efficiency performance. These plans were, however, abruptly abandoned as a result of the March 11, 2011, triple disaster of an earthquake, a tsunami, and nuclear meltdowns that crippled the Fukushima Daiichi nuclear facility and eventually led to a near total shut down of the country's nuclear facilities. At the time of the Fukushima nuclear accident, Japan obtained over a quarter of its electricity from nuclear energy. Six years after, Japan obtained less than 2 percent of its electricity from nuclear energy, as the process of restarting nuclear power plants has been slow.

The Japanese people rallied together after the triple disaster and combined their efforts in what is the single most impressive energy-saving initiative any country has conducted in recent memory. As a result, substantial reductions in electricity demand were achieved. Nevertheless, the government was forced to abandon its ambitious greenhouse gas emission reduction targets. Carbon dioxide emissions have since risen dramatically as the electricity demand that was previously being met by nuclear energy has had to be replaced by other sources, primarily coal, oil, and natural gas (see Figure 4.1). In 2013, despite the impressive energy-saving initiatives, Japan's carbon dioxide emissions were 10 percent higher than in 1990. At the 2013 climate negotiations in Warsaw, Japan announced it was abandoning its Copenhagen 25 percent emissions reduction pledge and would no longer use 1990 as its

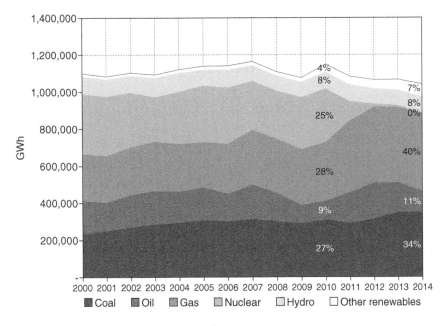

Figure 4.1 Japan's electricity production by source.

Source: International Energy Agency, 2017.

base year. It would instead pursue a far more modest reduction in its greenhouse gas emissions of about 3.8 percent of 2005 levels by 2020 (Kuramochi 2014). Japan's nationally determined contribution (NDC) is to reduce carbon emissions by 26 percent of 2013 levels by 2030 (equating to about a 17 percent reduction below 1990 levels). The plan has been criticized by NGOs, who claim that this commitment is far short of what is needed in light of scientific warnings about climate change (Johnston 2015). In the meantime, efforts are strengthening to expand renewable energy capacities. Japan introduced large amounts of photovoltaic capacity in the period after Fukushima so that it now is a global leader in terms of installed capacity.

Japanese energy and climate policies are at a crossroads, but until a decision is reached regarding how many nuclear power plants will be restarted, it is difficult to predict Japan's future greenhouse gas emission trends.

This chapter explores Japan's climate policies from its decision to host the international climate negotiations in 1997, which led to the eventual formation of the Kyoto Protocol, through to Japan's formulation of its NDC for the Paris Agreement. Several questions are addressed: What explains Japan's ambitious greenhouse gas mitigation targets before the Fukushima nuclear accident? How are the targets related to Japanese style capitalism? And how has the Fukushima nuclear crisis impacted not only Japan's climate change goals, but also the political and economic power structures behind them?

The Japanese political economic context and Japanese style capitalism

During Japan's long period of post-war economic growth, a single political party maintained a hold on government: the conservative, pro-business Liberal Democratic Party (LDP). The LDP has been in power for most of the post-World War II period, with only a few years in which they yielded control of government. Under the LDP's leadership, and with the supportive umbrella provided by its security alliance with the United States, Japan experienced remarkably strong economic growth. It became the world's second largest economy until it lost this position to (a far larger) China in the mid-2000s. The government invested heavily in public works projects – including the construction of roads, bridges, harbors, and airports – and the development of the world-famous bullet train (*shinkansen*).

Cozy relationships developed between the government and major industry. It is therefore not so surprising that various scandals began to hurt the image of the LDP, given the length of time the party was in power. The party was also increasingly held accountable for the country's weak economic performance. Japan has been in a recession or near recession for much of the period from the beginning of the 1990s. In 2009 the Democratic Party of Japan (DPJ) was able to oust the LDP from power. The DPJ however, failed to respond effectively to the country's many domestic problems, in part because it did not gain the support of the bureaucracy it needed to implement its plans. It also had the misfortune of being in power at the time of the Fukushima nuclear accident. The party's dismal approval ratings in the post-Fukushima period led to its downfall in the December 2012 elections to the House of Representatives. In a landslide victory, the LDP was returned to power under the leadership of Shinzo Abe, who became prime minister of Japan for the second time (his first term was a brief stint from 2006 to 2007). Shinzo Abe's government, which is eager to restart the country's nuclear power plants, was soundly re-elected in 2014 and achieved a large majority in the special election to the House of Representatives in 2015.

The LDP's long-term success has been aided by the partnerships it has developed with bureaucratic, industrial, and agricultural interests in what is sometimes referred to as the *iron triangle*. Although a simplification of a far more complex reality, the iron triangle refers to the formal and informal relationships established between the LDP, the bureaucracy, big business, and agricultural interests. In return for rural votes and financial support from industry to fund costly electoral campaigns, the LDP, in tandem with the bureaucracy, supported policies that were favorable to industrial actors and agricultural interests, including efforts to keep electricity prices low.

Bureaucrats are very powerful actors as most bills originate in the bureaucracy rather than in the Diet (Japan's parliament). That being said, important committees in the Diet influence the shape of bills and the Diet ultimately votes on legislation. The Ministry of Finance, with its influence over budgetary issues, and the Ministry of Economy, Trade, and Industry (METI, before 2001 named the Ministry of International Trade and Industry) are particularly powerful when it comes to economic and energy policy. Industry is organized into peak associations, the most important being the Japan Business Federation, often known by its Japanese name *Keidanren*. Big business has helped finance electoral campaigns in exchange for a supportive political environment. There are strong informal institutional ties between bureaucracy and industry. METI and large corporations work together in setting policy goals and targets, including in climate change and energy issues. Some of the businesses that have benefited from this close relationship have been in the automobile, electronics, and nuclear industries. The ministries use various tools to steer industrial directions, including preferential tax treatment, the provision of low-interest loans, information, and connections (Pempel and Tsunekawa 1979; McNamara 1996; Kim 2008).

In explaining Japan's economic success, political economists often follow Chalmers Johnson (1982) in labeling Japan a capitalist developmental state (e.g., Johnson 1987; Wade 1990; Woo-Cummings 1990) in which the government intervenes in private markets with various incentives and restrictions. The extent to which industrial policy has been guided by the state, developed out of negotiated agreements between government and industry, or is market driven is debatable. However, there is considerable agreement that the government has sought to play a strong role in promoting and guiding economic development.

From the perspective of the varieties of capitalism approach, Japan has been categorized as a coordinated market economy with relatively strong neo-corporatist arrangements. In a form of "group-based coordination," the government collaborates with businesses that are organized into families of companies (*keiretsu*) with numerous interconnections that cut across sectors (Hall and Soskice 2001: 33–34). This was historically the case with the nuclear industry. Major producers of nuclear electricity and components, such as Hitachi, Mitsubishi, and Toshiba, are part of such interlocking business relationships. In the *keiretsu*, firms produce both nuclear power plants and appliances that make use of electricity.

Japan also exhibits elements of an entrepreneurial state (Mazzucato 2013). Namely, one in which the state plays an important role in establishing a framework to support the development of particular technologies that would not have been developed if the market had been left to its own devices. Certainly, the ability of Japanese firms to innovate when provided with supportive incentives has been critical to Japan's growth model (Lazonick 2008).

These features, which were heralded as a comparative strength of the Japanese style of capitalism, came under stress with the bursting of the financial bubble at the end of the 1980s. Since then Japan has experienced long years of economic stagnation and deflation. Globalization, the rise of international trade institutions, and the influence of neo-liberal economics, have challenged the developmental state model and Japan's entrepreneurial state. A regime shift did begin as Japan moved toward more international investment (Pempel 1998) and regionalized production chains (Hatch 2002; Yamamura and Hatch 1987) and experimented with efforts to restructure features of its coordinated market economy by introducing more liberal features (Lechevalier 2014). But Japan continued to maintain key features of a coordinated market economy, particularly in the sectors viewed as important for the country's economic stability and growth – including utilities, construction, and transport – in which strong path dependencies remain.

The environmental and social context

To understand Japan's climate policies it is helpful to know the historical context out of which they emerged. Developmental state theorists and scholars in the field of comparative capitalism, have often failed to pay much attention to the externalities of specific growth models, including environmental and social costs. Japan's economic development came at a heavy price to the natural environment and human wellbeing. At the end of the 1960s Japan had one of the largest economies in the world, but this came with severe pollution. Many of Japan's rivers and bays were poisoned by the effluent dumped into them by factories, along with the run-off from mining activities. Air quality in major urban and industrial areas in the 1960s and 1970s was not unlike that in some of the more polluted areas in China or India today. People suffered from horrible pollution-induced diseases that caused nerve damage, turned bones brittle, damaged lungs, led to birth defects, and in some cases resulted in death. There was also serious destruction of natural areas at the hands of Japanese firms, both domestically and in Southeast Asia (e.g., Dauvergne 1987; Ui 1992; Imura and Schreurs 2005).

Several factors helped put Japan on a new less-polluting course. In the 1960s and 1970s the public's growing unease about deteriorating environmental conditions led to protests and demands for change. At first, it was largely the victims of pollution and their supporters who protested to company officials, local government officials, and the national government about harmful emissions. When their cries largely went unanswered, they turned to the courts (Gresser, Fujikura and Morishima 1981). Major court cases addressing mercury and cadmium poisoning, air pollution, and tainted cooking oil, received widespread media attention (Ui 1998; Broadbent 1998).

Japan was also shamed internationally when Minamata mercury pollution victims traveled to the United Nations Conference on the Human Environment (the Stockholm Conference) in 1972. A citizens' group prepared a report for the conference about the state of Japan's environment, describing the diseases caused by pollution in the country. This was done to counteract the government's failure to even mention these ailments in its official report (Ui 1998). Electoral victories by the communist and socialist parties in major cities, including Tokyo and Osaka, added to the pressure on the LDP to alter its policy course.

Corresponding with these environmental protests, the economy was heavily hit by the OPEC oil embargo of 1973 and the oil shock of 1979. At the time, about three-quarters of Japan's electricity was produced with oil (Vivodo 2011). As a group of volcanic islands, Japan lacks fossil fuels, along with most other natural resources. The country is heavily dependent on coal, oil, natural gas, and mineral imports. The oil embargo resulted in immediate and extreme negative repercussions for Japan's high-growth economy.

Once it was clear that without a change of course the developmental state model could be in jeopardy, the LDP responded and made major course corrections. The Japanese government introduced a series of policies to control air, water, and noise pollution, and to protect natural areas. Policies were introduced to develop alternative energies (as part of the "sunshine" program), to promote energy conservation and energy saving (as part of the "moonlight" program), to expand the use of nuclear energy, and to support the development of pollution control technologies and industries. Over the course of the next decade, the policies introduced by the state turned Japan into a global leader in industrial pollution control, energy efficiency, and nuclear energy production. Japanese firms responded to the changes in policy direction by making major investments in pollution control, energy efficient production, and sustainable products. They increased investments from 232 billion yen in 1970 to 1,783 billion yen in 1975 (Hashimoto 1989: 32). Japan's automobile manufacturers' response to the economic, environmental, and energy challenges was the development of lower emitting, more fuel-efficient cars, which helped them become globally competitive players. In the early 1980s Germany was turning to Japan for lessons in environmental pollution control (Weidner 1985).

Linking climate policies and economic innovation

In the 1980s, attention began to turn to a variety of international and global environmental problems: acid rain, biodiversity loss, stratospheric ozone depletion, and global warming. In 1990, in response to growing international demands for action, Japan announced an Action Program to Arrest Global Warming. This was a voluntary program with the goal of stabilizing CO_2 emissions at 1990 levels by the year 2000 (Schreurs 2002; Kameyama 2003; Asuka-Zhang 2003; Sato 2003; Fischer 2003; Broadbent 2002; Japan Center for Climate Change Actions, n.d.). This was the first of several steps Japan took to introduce climate mitigation initiatives. In the following years the Japanese state initiated additional measures to promote industrial and societal innovation, and to coordinate the development of the market in a low carbon direction. For the nuclear industry, which was under pressure after the Chernobyl nuclear crisis, an active climate policy was viewed as a means of securing its future growth.

At the 1992 United Nations (UN) Conference on Environment and Development, Japan signed the UN Framework Convention on Climate

Change (UNFCCC). Then, in 1995, Japan announced its interest in hosting the third part of the UNFCCC conference, where a global climate agreement was expected to be reached. Global agreements tend to be given the name of the city in which they are negotiated, and there were no international agreements with the name of a Japanese city attached to them at this point. As such, Japan's announcement was taken as a strong sign of a commitment to action and an eagerness to be seen as a global leader in climate mitigation.

At the 1997 Kyoto Conference, Japan committed to a 6 percent reduction in its CO_2 emissions relative to 1990 levels by the first commitment period (in 2008–2012). In international comparison the reduction target was quite ambitious, especially considering Japan's relatively high energy efficiency at the time (Ohta 2009: 38). Given Japan's traditionally close relationship with the United States, it is noteworthy that Japan ratified the Kyoto Protocol in 2005 even though the United States had rejected it in 2001.

This proactive position on climate change was motivated by the political leadership's interest in enhancing Japan's foreign policy role, strengthening the country's international image, and promoting key industries (including its automobile industry, which had become a world leader in producing hybrid cars). Over time, the bottom-up push for a green climate policy became stronger. This push came from both from the environmental community, which was eager to promote a low carbon energy transition, and the business community, which was beginning to see potential in environmental pollution control, alternative energy technologies, and new opportunities for nuclear energy. The fact that the international agreement bore the name of Japan's ancient capital, certainly put pressure on policy makers to maintain support for the agreement (Tiberghien and Schreurs 2007, 2010).

In 1998 the Japanese government issued global warming measures that defined global warming as a serious problem and stipulated the responsibilities of both national and local governments, as well as how industries and citizens should address it (Government of Japan 1998b). Guidelines on how the Kyoto Protocol targets were to be met were issued. They stated that the share of electric power supplied by nuclear power plants should be increased by over 50 percent from fiscal 1997 to 2010. To achieve this the government specified that it would "seek to rebuild public confidence in nuclear power that was shaken because of a series of mismanagement incidents and accidents surrounding the fast breeder reactor." It would also seek the understanding of local governments for these plans (Government of Japan 1998a; Ministry of Environment 1998).

In addition, new legislative measures for alternative energies were introduced and existing energy efficiency regulations tightened. The Law Concerning the Rational Use of Energy, which was originally passed in 1979 during the second oil shock, was amended. This legislation mandated energy management in the manufacturing and commercial sectors, and set energy efficiency standards for houses, building, manufacturing, and equipment. Many of these measures indicate the state's strong interest in linking climate mitigation strategies to finding ways to maintain or develop new industrial strengths, which is what one might expect of an entrepreneurial state.

A particularly innovative and climate-relevant program was launched by the government in 1999. This "Top Runner Program" was introduced to spur innovative production and promote the development of more energy-efficient appliances to curb rising emissions in the residential, commercial, and transportation sectors. For products covered by the program, the most efficient product on the market sets the standard the entire industry is expected to meet. Industry is usually given four to eight years to meet the new standard. Initially the program covered 11 product lines, this increased to 18 in 2002, 21 in 2005, and 23 in 2009 (Agency for Natural Resources and Energy, Ministry of Economy, Trade and Industry 2010). Product lines include refrigerators, washing machines, television sets, passenger cars and freight, heating and cooking stoves, and vending machines. The program names and shames firms that fail to meet the new standards, while rewarding products that meet the standard with a label (Kimura 2010). There is now also a Top Runner standard for houses, along with requirements for annual energy efficiency improvements for transport operators and the cargo sector. This program has helped Japanese manufacturers obtain a first-mover advantage in global markets while reducing the energy use of specific ventures.

The government's interest in linking economic competitiveness to its climate policy is a common refrain in Japan's climate documents. The 2002 Climate Change Policy Program stated that Japan's climate change policy should contribute to both the environment and the revitalization of the economy "through innovative initiatives of industry." In the run-up to the June 2007 G8 Summit in Heiligendamm, Germany, Prime Minister Shinzo Abe announced the Cool Earth 50 program that set out Japan's positions on a post-Kyoto framework. Japan accepted that global emissions should be halved by 2050 but stipulated that the approach to doing this should involve all major emitters, including China, India, and the United States. A global framework should be based on flexibility and consider the national circumstances of each country, and thus work under the principle of "common but differentiated responsibilities and respective capabilities" (Abe 2007). The framework also needed to achieve compatibility between environmental protection and economic growth through energy conservation and other technologies.

In response to the Cool Earth concept, METI launched the Cool Earth Innovative Energy Technology Program. The program looks at: technologies that are expected to deliver large reductions in carbon dioxide emissions by 2050; innovative technologies that will deliver substantial performance improvements; and technologies in which Japan can be a world leader. Based on these concepts, 21 innovative energy technologies were selected. These included: high-efficiency natural gas and coal fired power generation; carbon dioxide capture and storage; innovative photovoltaic power generation;

advanced nuclear power generation; high-efficiency superconducting power transmission; intelligent transport systems; fuel cell vehicles; plug-in hybrid vehicles; and electric vehicles; the production of transport biofuel; innovative iron and steel and material making processes; as well as various household areas (high efficiency houses and buildings; next generation, high efficiency lighting; ultra-high efficiency heat pumps; stationary fuel cells; high efficiency information devices and systems; and local level, environmental management systems); high performance power storage; power electronics; and hydrogen transport and storage (Ministry of Economy, Trade and Industry, Japan 2008).

In 2005, Prime Minister Junichiro Koizumi's environment minister, Yoriko Koike, introduced the "Cool Biz Campaign" in an effort to link climate action to the retail industry and the population as a whole. As Japan's electricity demand peaks during the hot summer months when air conditioning is used, the campaign was a clever way to try to implement demand-side management. The campaign asked people to set their air conditioners no lower than 28°C (82°F) and wear clothes designed for the season. The idea was creative, as it had the dual goal of stimulating the retail industry while simultaneously cutting energy use. By getting citizens out of their jackets and neck ties in the summer and having them wear climate-appropriate summer shirts and slacks instead, the program was meant to stimulate new summer clothing designs and sales. As air conditioners are one of the most energy-intensive appliances, lowering demand for air conditioning was expected to cut CO_2 emissions substantially.

A counterpart campaign for the winter, "Warm Biz," was also introduced. Individuals and businesses were asked to set their room temperatures to no warmer than 20°C. Other campaigns, such as "Smart Move," which encouraged low carbon forms of transport and "Morning Challenge," aimed at convincing people to reduce their use of lighting, air conditioning, and television by one hour per day were also launched. The Akari campaign, launched in June 2012, sought to convince manufacturers and retailers to stop producing incandescent lamps to save energy (lighting accounted for 13 percent of residential sector energy use at the time, the second largest after refrigerators) (Ministry of Environment, Japan 2013).

As is true in other parts of the world, climate policy is viewed by urban communities as a means to achieve economic revitalization (Schreurs 2008). In 2003 the city of Kyoto issued a proclamation entitled, Stop Global Warming: "Kyoto, as the city where the Kyoto Protocol was created as a promise to work to prevent global warming around the world, is dedicated to supporting efforts to stop global warming." In 2004, it became the first Japanese municipality to enact a Global Warming Countermeasures Ordinance.

The Tokyo Metropolitan Government also began to act. As part of the Tokyo Climate Initiative it established a Ten-Year Project for a Carbon-Minus Tokyo in June 2007. The plan called for a reduction in Tokyo's greenhouse gas emissions by 25 percent from 2000 levels by 2020. A key step taken was the launch of the Tokyo Greenhouse Gas Emission Trading System (Tokyo-ETS). Under the ETS 1,332 facilities were designated as being subject to the Mandatory Emission Reduction and Emission Trading Scheme.

The national government also has initiated programs encouraging local action (Sugiyama and Takeuchi 2008). The Low Carbon Planning: Act on Promotion of Low Carbon Cities was passed in response to the energy situation change after the Fukushima crisis. It promotes low carbon cities through the centralization of community infrastructure, the promotion of walking and cycling routes, improved transportation systems, and the revitalization of the housing market and local economies through investment in low carbon buildings and energy planning. This includes ideas such as making efficient use of heat from wastewater, expansion of green spaces, and the use of solar panels and storage batteries.

Linking nuclear energy to energy security and climate mitigation

No single industry has been more powerful in shaping Japanese climate policies than the nuclear industry. There are also few sectors that better tell the story of the Japanese government's efforts to steer a policy sector and promote a specific technology. In this vein, there are also few sectors that demonstrate as saliently how such efforts can fail. Supported and encouraged by the United States, and despite its experiences as a victim of atomic bombings, Japan embarked in the 1950s on the development of a conventional nuclear energy industry. In response to the oil shocks of the 1970s, the LDP introduced further support mechanisms for nuclear energy research and development. This also included the building of nuclear power plants. Communities that agreed to accept nuclear power plants were provided with large amounts of compensatory investment. Japan became the world's third largest producer of nuclear energy after the United States and France, as well as a major exporter of nuclear technology. This nuclear position would change dramatically as a result of the Fukushima nuclear crisis.

Japan has ten regional electricity providers: Hokkaidō, Tōhoku, Chibu, Hokuriku, Kansai, Chūgoku, Shikoku, Tokyo, Okinawa, and Kyūshū (Federation of Electric Power Companies, Japan 2014). Each holds a monopoly on distribution in their respective region. In 2010, nine of these regional electricity providers (Okinawa was the exception) joined the three large nuclear plant manufacturers (Hitachi, Mitsubishi, and Toshiba), along with the Innovation Network of Japan (a public-private joint venture), to form the International Nuclear Energy Development of Japan Co. Its purpose was to propose nuclear power plant projects in developing countries since the nuclear industry was seen as important for meeting domestic energy demands, and as an export industry.

Japan's relatively ambitious climate policy goals before the Fukushima nuclear accident were strongly supportive of the nuclear industry. Nuclear energy was marketed as a clean, low carbon energy. Targets for nuclear energy production rose steadily, until disaster struck.

One of the largest earthquakes in recorded history hit the coast of Japan in March 2011, unleashing a series of tsunami that devastated its northeastern coast and triggered a nuclear disaster at the Fukushima Daiichi Nuclear Facility by flooding the plant's nuclear reactors. Loss of electricity to the cooling systems resulted in hydrogen explosions and partial meltdowns in three reactors and serious damage to a fourth. The hydrogen explosions carried plumes of radioactive material over the Pacific Ocean, and over land to the northwest of the plant after a shift in the wind direction. Hundreds of thousands of people were evacuated and some areas remain off limits due to dangerous levels of radioactivity (Schreurs and Yoshida 2013).

In 2010, just before the Fukushima nuclear accident, about 26 percent of Japan's electricity was produced from nuclear power. As a result of the explosions and meltdowns at the Fukushima Daiichi nuclear plant, major changes are being forced on the nuclear industry. The Fukushima facilities comprise six of Japan's 54 nuclear reactors which were operable at the time of the Fukushima accident. These six reactors were permanently shut down. While new nuclear reactor safety standards were developed for Japan's other nuclear facilities, all the remaining reactors were shut down (US Energy Information Administration 2015). The nuclear power plants must now pass new safety standards and obtain approval from the governor of the prefecture in which they are located before they can be restarted. Court decisions can also play a role in determining their fate. Although the government has indicated its interest in maintaining a 20 percent share of nuclear energy in the electricity mix through to 2030, public opinion is against restarts.

Critics argue that the Fukushima nuclear crisis was not simply a product of a natural disaster, but rather a consequence of the "nuclear village" (*genshiroku mura*) that supported and protected the nuclear industry. This term refers to governmental, bureaucratic, industrial, media, and academic supporters of nuclear energy that have formed a mutually reinforcing support structure for the industry. This concept paints a far more pointed critique of Japan as a capitalist developmental state than is common in the mainstream literature. It suggests that a highly collusive relationship among these interdependent actors formed to protect nuclear energy's privileged position in the electricity mix. It was a system that limited critical debate and allowed for the emergence of a culture that favored the protection of the industry over the implementation of a system of checks and balances, or even the enforcement of safety measures (Funabashi and Takenaka 2011; Fukushima Nuclear Accident Independent Investigation Commission 2012; Schreurs and Yoshida 2013; Inaba 2013).

There were some oppositional voices to the government's strategy for addressing climate change through a greater reliance on nuclear energy. One example, from April 2007, was a letter sent to Dr. James Lovelock questioning his position that maximizing nuclear fission energy was an appropriate way to combat global warming by 14 Japanese NGOs: Citizens' Nuclear Information Center (CNIC); Consumers Union of Japan; Global Peace Campaign; Green Action; Greenpeace Japan; Group of Ten Thousand Plaintiffs for the Lawsuit to Stop the Nuclear Fuel Cycles; Institute for Sustainable Energy Policies (ISEP); Japan Congress Against A- and H-Bombs (GENSUIKIN); Kiko (climate) Network; Osaka Citizens against the Mihama, Ohi and Takahama Nuclear Power Plants; Peace Boat; Peace Food action net; ILFA (the international life and food association); Sun & Wind Power Trust for Citizens; and Women's Democratic Club Greenpeace Japan. They wrote:

> At present there are 55 nuclear power reactors operating in Japan. These reactors produce approximately 30 percent of total electricity and 20 percent of total primary energy. About 145 new reactors will be required in Japan if the same conditions indicated above prevail, where new reactors replace old ones and additional reactors are built to replace fossil fuel plants which currently produce about 60 percent of electricity. This is assuming that electricity demand remains flat. If this is to be accomplished by 2050, then every 3–4 months, a new reactor will need to go online.

Almost predictive of the future they also wrote:

> Nuclear power carries with it the latent risk of serious accidents. Therefore, if there is some kind of problem or accident at one reactor, it may be necessary for other reactors of the same model to be shut down simultaneously for inspections.
>
> (CNIC 2007)

Prior to the Fukushima nuclear accident, most opposition to nuclear energy came in the form of "Not in My Backyard" protests (Lesbirel 1998; Aldrich 2008). Japan's NGO campaigns only infrequently focused on nuclear energy, although they did, at times, take anti-nuclear positions. In a 2010 position paper responding to a climate policy plan announced by the DPJ that called for nuclear expansion, the Citizens' Alliance for Saving the Atmosphere and the Earth (CASA) critiqued the assumption that nuclear energy is necessary to reduce greenhouse gas emissions (2010). ISEP, which was founded in September 2000, also pushed for the use of renewable, rather than nuclear, energy. A group of Japanese NGOs pointed out that Japan's business structure has led to developments that are contrary to Japan's energy conservation goals, since firms promoting nuclear energy use are also trumpeting "schemes to increase demand for electricity, such as the 'all electric' campaign for residential buildings" (CASA 2010).

These kinds of pronouncement were the exception rather than the rule. Nuclear power had strong support across Japanese society and few questioned the government's nuclear energy plans. Nuclear energy was equated with clean, climate-friendly energy (Hayakawa 2014; Schreurs 2014). This is no longer the case. In fact, a majority of Japanese would now prefer to see no nuclear power use in Japan, a stunning departure from previous broad-based nuclear acceptance.

After the Fukushima nuclear accident, numerous NGOs and citizen groups mobilized. Having gained much experience from their involvement in the 2006 Hanshin earthquake rescue, many groups played a crucial role in helping to address the needs of the communities that were ravaged by the Tōhoku earthquake, tsunami, and nuclear crisis (Aldrich 2012). They also started expressing their opposition to Japan's nuclear energy policies. Various anti-nuclear groups held protests, organized teach-ins, and supported anti-nuclear candidates in elections. Particularly prominent were the Friday protests held every week in front of the prime minister's office.

The accident has forced reconsideration of how energy policy decisions are made. Although path dependencies remain strong, citizens are demanding a greater say in energy policy-making and are challenging the state's understanding of its role as an entrepreneurial state.

Climate policy planning in a period of uncertainty

The Fukushima nuclear accident has had a tangible impact on Japanese greenhouse gas emissions. Japan was already struggling to reduce its emissions prior to the Fukushima nuclear accident. In 2006, Japan's emissions were 6.2 percent above 1990 levels (and thus about 12 percent above its Kyoto Protocol target) (Kiko Network 2008). They rose again in 2007, but then dropped substantially in 2008 and 2009 due to the global economic downturn. In 2010, they rose once again but remained 0.3 percent below 1990 levels (Ministry of Environment, Japan 2010).[2]

The Fukushima accident not only became a hugely expensive accident in its own terms, but it also meant a sharp rise in Japan's CO_2 emissions following the shutdown of Japan's nuclear power plants. In 2012, total emissions were 2.8 percent higher than in 2011, 6.5 percent higher than in 1990, and 12.5 percent above Japan's Kyoto Protocol target (of −6 percent). Japan still managed to achieve its Kyoto target, but to do so government and business had had to invest billions of dollars in the Kyoto flexibility mechanisms and in enhancing carbon sinks (Ministry of Environment, Japan 2012; National Institute for Environmental Studies 2012). In the meantime, by increasing reliance on natural gas (rather than coal), with energy savings, and a greater use of renewable energy, the rise in CO_2 emissions has been checked and is again coming down (see Figure 4.2). Nevertheless, the challenge of greenhouse gas emission reduction has intensified dramatically as a result of Fukushima and the government's response (National Institute for Environmental Studies 2014).

Although the LDP, which was responsible for the decades-long promotion of nuclear energy, returned to power in 2012, there has been a clear shift away from the government's earlier vision of a large-scale nuclear energy

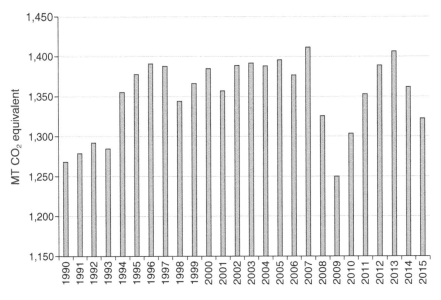

Figure 4.2 GHG emission trends in Japan.
Source: UNFCCC Data Interface, 2017.

expansion. Society at large continues to debate what role nuclear energy should play in the energy mix and in Japan's climate mitigation strategies, but it is clear that nuclear energy will play a far smaller role than had originally been envisioned by the Japanese state.

Various measures have been introduced to promote further energy efficiency and energy savings. Campaigns were launched to encourage individuals and companies to reduce their energy use. As of June 2012, 920,000 individuals and 25,000 companies had signed up to participate in the campaign (Ministry of Environment, Japan, n.d.). Total energy demand dropped in Japan from 503 million tons of oil equivalent in 2010 to 481 million tons in 2011, 478 million tons in 2012, and 474 million tons in 2013. This is a substantial change that should help Japan remain one of the world's most energy efficient industrial economies.

A focus has also been placed on renewable energy. Until the early 2000s, Japan was the world leader in solar photovoltaic installation. In 1994 it introduced the 70,000 Roofs Program to boost solar innovation, this initially covered half of the installation costs. This later dropped to 10 percent as the cost of photovoltaics (PV) came down. Japanese manufacturers Sharp and Kyocera became some of the biggest in the industry. In 2004 Japanese solar PV production accounted for 49 percent of the world's total. In 2002, Japan had 144,000 residential systems installed and was a global paragon in installed solar power. There were also additional support funds for research and development (Jiménez 2004). Despite its success, the program was stopped in the early 2000s by a government that was more interested in nuclear energy expansion than renewable energy development. Renewable energy development thus languished. Japan lost its leadership position in solar PVs to other countries during the latter half of the 2000s. After the Fukushima accident however, faced with a serious energy crisis and demands to do more to support renewable energy, the government followed the German example and introduced a feed-in tariff system in the summer of 2012. This policy was implemented to incentivize renewable energy as a whole, with an emphasis on photovoltaics. A target of 33 GW of PV and 9 GW of wind was set for 2020. By way of comparison, the installed capacity in Germany at the end of 2013 was 35.6 GW and 32.5 GW of wind) (Fraunhofer Institut für Solare Energiesysteme ISE 2014).

Japan now has one of the largest markets for photovoltaics globally; an impressive 42.8 GW of capacity had been installed by 2016. To put this in perspective, the six reactors at the Fukushima Daiichi nuclear power station had a combined capacity of 4.7 GW (Tokyo Electric Power Company 2014). Prior to the Fukushima nuclear accident, total installed photovoltaic capacity in the country was a rather limited 1.66 GW (Clover 2014). PV capacity growth has been so rapid that grid operators have started to refuse to take electricity from photovoltaics, arguing that their grids do not have the capacity for so much fluctuating electricity.

In sum, as a result of the nuclear disaster there are now intensified efforts to promote energy savings, to develop new energy efficient technologies, and to expand the use of renewable energies. The disaster has forced the Japanese state to reconsider its approach to ensuring energy security and to open the door to new actors and more decentralized production.

Since Fukushima, climate change mitigation efforts have taken a back seat in the public debate. Civic discourse is now much more focused on concerns over nuclear safety and finding alternatives to nuclear energy, than it is on concerns with rising global temperatures and finding alternatives to fossil fuels. The Ministry of Economy, Trade and Industry, along with energy companies, has announced plans to build over 40 new coal-fired power plants to replace older and less efficient plants. However, the Japanese Environment Ministry has challenged these plans, arguing that they will put Japan's climate pledges at risk by locking the country into coal use for many decades (Obayashi and Miyazaki 2017).

Conclusion

Due to earlier environmental disasters and the oil shocks of the 1970s, Japan emerged as a global leader in industrial pollution control and energy savings. Policies to further promote leadership in energy efficiency technologies have been supported by Japan's climate mitigation policies. The nuclear industry benefited the most from Japan's climate mitigation strategies. Japan's governmental and industrial leaders saw the expansion of nuclear energy as the main means for addressing greenhouse gas emissions and setting the country on a low carbon trajectory.

In the aftermath of Fukushima Japan's energy policies, and thus its climate policies as well, are in limbo. All of Japan's nuclear power plants, which had produced over a quarter of the country's electricity, were idled and required to undergo safety checks under new, more stringent, regulations and standards. Most remain off line although the government, industry, and some local communities are eager to resume nuclear power generation. There is still strong public opposition against the return of nuclear energy, and opposition voices have succeeded in obstructing the government's plans. Since the Japanese government's climate change commitments were based on the premise that nuclear energy would provide the main source of Japanese electricity in the future, the government has had to rethink its climate strategies after the Fukushima accident. The Copenhagen goal to reduce emissions by 25 percent of 1990 levels by 2020 therefore was abandoned, and the Paris Climate Agreement goal remained relatively modest.

The implications of the Fukushima nuclear disaster for Japan's climate change policies are still unfolding. What is clear is that Japan will be far less dependent on nuclear energy than was planned before the Fukushima crisis, and new strategies for achieving a low carbon economy will have to be promoted. Japan now relies heavily on natural gas and coal to meet its electricity demand. Yet the crisis is also being used by the state, business, and society to help develop new industries. Renewable energy is growing rapidly, albeit from a very humble base. A new focus is being placed on energy conservation processes and the development of environmental technologies. Japan is likely to become a leader in the development of many, next generation, green technologies, including hybrid electric vehicles, robotics, renewable energy technologies, and smart information systems.

Japan's ability to regain its economic strength will be dependent on its ability to build a new vision for the future. This vision might maintain elements of Japan's earlier forms as a capitalist developmental state, but it will also require more transparent and open decision making (Yamamura 2003). This will also be important in terms of the country's energy and climate change policies. Path dependencies are difficult to change, so it is likely that long entrenched energy interests will continue to hold considerable influence over the direction of the country's energy and climate change policy choices for the foreseeable future. Society, however, is demanding new approaches and more influence in a policy field from which they have been largely shut out. Japan's climate change policy was closely linked to the country's nuclear policy. This linkage has been badly shaken by the Fukushima nuclear accident. The crisis could be an opportunity not only for considerable structural change and technological innovation, but also to develop a more participatory approach to decision making in the Japanese model of entrepreneurial capitalism.

Notes

1 The author has researched and worked on Japanese climate and energy policy extensively since the early 1990s. She has visited the Fukushima region numerous times since the nuclear accident and met with citizens' groups, government officials, and academics to discuss Japan's energy policy plans and possibilities.
2 Total greenhouse gas emissions were 0.3 percent below 1990 levels for CO_2, CH_4, N_2O and below 1995 levels for HFCs, PFCs, SF_6.

5 The transition to a low carbon economy in Germany's coordinated capitalism

Alexander Ebner

Introduction

This chapter presents the key patterns of technological and institutional change in Germany's transition towards a low carbon economy and explores which actor constellations and institutional configurations in its political-economic system have shaped its path, with particular emphasis on efforts in technological innovation. This question is explored within the framework of a comparative capitalism approach perspective in which Germany is characterised as a coordinated market economy (CME), This leaves considerable room for manoeuvring relational and associational governance modes in the coordination efforts of firms. Accordingly, it is important to examine the institutional scaffolds of the German variety of capitalism. Especially how they relate to the challenges of coping with the complex and radical institutional and technological changes that are required in the formation of a sustainable low carbon setting of economic affairs.

The first section of the chapter outlines the empirical patterns and structures of carbon emissions and related indicators in the development of the German economy. The second section highlights the institutional specifics of the German variety of capitalism as a CME. The third section explores innovation efforts in the formation of a low carbon economy. The final section examines those actor constellations and policy strategies that drive institutions towards a low carbon economy in Germany.

German emission patterns and structures

In exploring greenhouse gas (GHG) emissions in Germany, the fact that power generation before the start of low carbon transition was from fossil fuels and nuclear power, augmented by minor shares of hydropower and oil, needs to be reiterated. Hard coal provided the traditional backbone of this energy mix, yet the structural crisis in the coal and steel industries led to massive closures of mines and plants in key regions, such as Ruhr and Saar, during the 1980s, leaving only a handful of highly subsidised coal mines. Brown coal, however, largely remained in the market because of its cost advantages. Its relative decline since the 1990s was mostly due to the closure of mines in Eastern Germany (Jacobsson and Lauber 2006). Also, it is prudent to remember that Germany is highly dependent on the import of energy; more than two-thirds of the German energy supply, most prominently oil and gas, are imported from abroad (BMWi 2012). This situation already underpins the transnational dimension of economic decarbonisation and alludes to the limits of those strategic actions that are confined to the national domain. Given these constraints, Germany has made significant efforts in the domain of environmental affairs, in particular with regard to CO_2 emissions reduction. A study commissioned by the European Research Area Board states: 'Today, Germany is one of the world leaders in environmental issues, climate protection, greenhouse gas emission reduction and alternative energy technology' (Leijten *et al.* 2012, p. 109). This may appear surprising given that Germany is one of the leading global industrial net exporters. Based on available data, the German reduction in carbon emissions seems to have been quite successful since the 1990s.

Figure 5.1b offers a first glimpse at the profile of GHG and carbon emissions in Germany since 1990.

First, the data provide telling evidence for the relative success of German efforts on GHG emissions, which were reduced by 27.9 per cent between 1990 and 2015. Yet recent developments indicate a slowdown in emissions reduction, especially when considered with the more precipitous downward trend seen recently for the EU as a whole (see Figure 5.1a). A factor in this development may be the general increase in energy use resulting from economic and population growth, combined with a lack of energy productivity

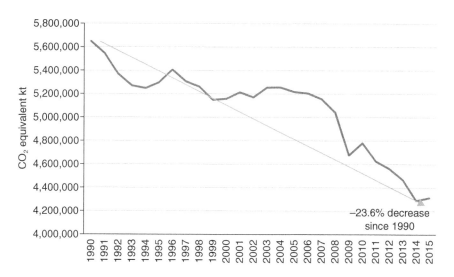

Figure 5.1a EU GHG emissions.

Source UNFCCC Data Interface, 2017.

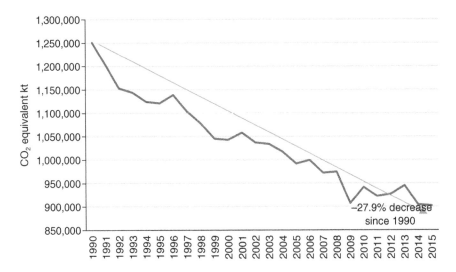

Figure 5.1b German GHG emissions.
Source UNFCCC Data Interface, 2017.

and resource efficiency (Wörlen and Gebauer 2017). Second, the data illustrate the massive carbon footprint that is caused by economic activities in Germany when compared with the European Union 28 countries. GHG emissions in Germany accounted for almost one-fifth of the EU 28 whole during the 1990s and 2000s, making it the largest national emitter in the EU and the third largest in the OECD after the United States and Japan. However, in terms of emissions per capita, or relative to GDP, Germany remains well below the OECD average (Klein 2012). The sheer size of the German economy, its manufacturing base and its specific energy mix translate into a relatively high national share of European carbon profiles.

All these efforts towards the formation of a low carbon economy are within the context of international commitments and regulations, most prominently represented by the Kyoto Protocol. Germany reached its Kyoto commitment for 2012 early, namely a 21 per cent reduction of GHG emissions from 1990 levels, having already reduced GHG emissions 26 per cent below the 1990 baseline by 2009. This is one of the best performances among high-income OECD countries. To proceed further, additional national goals in the reduction of emissions have been put forward, aiming at a 40 per cent reduction relative to 1990 by the year 2020. This emissions target seems to underline further advances in the decarbonisation of the German economy (Leijten *et al.* 2012). More recent trends cast some doubt on Germany's previous success. The slowdown in emissions reduction, in tandem with the level of ambition in these 2020 targets, means there is some concern they will not be met. According to a recent report from Germany's environment ministry, the country is at risk of missing its 40 per cent reduction target. The ministry had expected greater emission cuts from government policies and has now had to revise these forecasts upwards (Reuters 2016). This could have implications for the Paris Agreement. The EU Effort Sharing Regulation 2021–2030, which underlines the expected contribution for each member state leading up to the EU's 2030 Paris commitment, expects Germany to reduce emissions by 38 per cent from 2005 levels (European Commission DG Climate Action 2017a). For comparison, since 2005 levels are lower than 1990 levels, the 40 per cent reduction since 1990 for 2020 was actually a 14 per cent decrease from 2005 (EUR-Lex 2009). This 2030 commitment is quite a lofty goal given current trends.

Figure 5.2 provides an overview of GHG emissions by sector in selected years since 1990. The largest share of these emissions consistently emanated from the energy supply. When it comes to the sectoral dynamics of emissions reduction, the reductions in manufacturing, trade and construction illustrate decarbonisation efforts in the domain of Germany's industrial specialisation. Also, contrary to many other OECD countries, emissions were even slightly reduced in the transport sector, notably in road transportation, which is strategically relevant for the German automobile industry – the key industry in the German export-oriented manufacturing sector. Higher gasoline prices and the implementation of the so-called eco tax and energy standards in the automotive sector played a major role in creating related incentives for energy savings all the way through the 2000s (OECD 2011b).

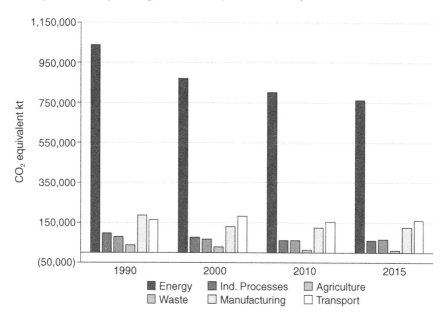

Figure 5.2 German GHG emissions by sector.

Source: UNFCCC Data Interface, 2017.

The same pattern holds for sectoral carbon emissions (Umweltbundesamt 2012). However, as outlined above, recent data on carbon emissions underline setbacks, as the trend of decreasing GHG emissions has been slowing down. The rise of carbon emissions results from an increase in coal burning and it is lessened only slightly by the impact of a parallel increase in renewable energy replacements (Umweltbundesamt 2013a). This development may be viewed as the unintended outcome of the *Energiewende* – the 'energy turn' project discussed below. However, the revival of coal in the energy mix of the German economy is the key challenge for future efforts on emissions reduction (Umweltbundesamt 2013b). Relations between carbon emissions, stationary facilities of industry and energy supply in Germany confirm the trend of carbon emissions reduction, which is intimately related to the activities of energy suppliers (Umweltbundesamt and Deutsche Emissionshandelsstelle 2012).

Patterns in the generation of electricity during the 1990s and 2000s provide further evidence for changes in the specific mix of energy sources. Germany's electricity production has been shockingly carbon intensive. This is due to a relatively high share of fossil fuels, in particular coal, in the energy mix. Levels of coal use are considerably higher than the average levels in other European OECD economies (Égert 2011). Still, the largest shares of electricity generation that came from both brown coal and stone coal declined from a share of 56.7 per cent in 1990 to 44.2 per cent in 2012. From 2011 to 2012, however, the percentage of electricity generated from coal rose again from 42.8 per cent to 44.2 per cent, while the share of nuclear energy was reduced from 17.6 per cent to 15.8 per cent in both years, remaining way below the 1990 level of 27.7 per cent. During the same period from 1990 to 2012, the percentage of renewables in electricity generation increased continuously from a level of 3.6 per cent to 22.6 per cent (Arbeitsgemeinschaft Energiebilanzen 2013). In 2016, shares of energy types in gross electricity generation were: brown coal 23.1 per cent; hard coal 17 per cent; nuclear 13.1 per cent; renewables with a share of 29.5 per cent, of which wind held 12.3 per cent, biomass 7 per cent, and solar photovoltaic and geothermal 5.9 per cent (BMWi – AG-EE-Stat 2017).

When it comes to the expansion of renewable energy in Germany, results are outstandingly positive and have taken off in a most remarkable manner since the mid-2000s. The corresponding pattern of transition resembles a process of technological substitution driven by the entry of new firms and actors challenging the incumbents. This has been possible because electricity technologies in Germany are represented by small-scale decentralised actors in onshore wind, solar photovoltaic and biogas (Geels *et al.* 2016). Figure 5.3 outlines the generation of electricity from renewable energy sources in Germany between 2004 and 2015. The share of electricity from renewable energy sources in gross electricity usage accounted for 9.4 per cent in 2004 and continuously rose to 30.7 per cent by 2015, in fact exceeding the share present in the EU as a whole, despite having had a smaller proportion of

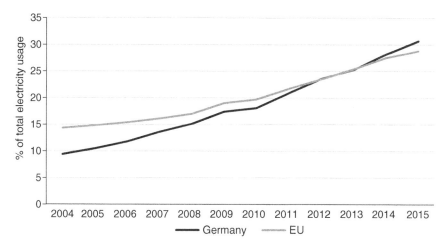

Figure 5.3 Share of renewable energy in electricity.
Source: Eurostat, 2017.

renewables in the energy mix just over a decade prior. The EU 28 has also seen significant growth with an increase from 14.3 per cent to 28.8 per cent. This expansion is mirrored by German renewable electricity generation capacity and not just usage. Between 2000 and 2015, conventional capacity stayed roughly the same from 100 to 110 gigawatts. Total renewables, however, accounted for an increase from 11.75 to 97.92 gigawatts – with onshore wind increasing from 6.1 to 40.99 and photovoltaics from 0.11 to 39.7 gigawatts. Indeed, during the 2000s and 2010s, electricity from renewables has almost reached the total gigawatt level of conventional capacity (BMWi 2016).

Energy consumption also provides a rather positive picture. Figure 5.4b illustrates Germany's primary energy consumption since 1990. Notably, the level of primary energy consumption was reduced by over 10 per cent during this time despite significant GDP growth, whereas the performance of the EU 28 proved less convincing, with less significant decreases in primary energy consumption. The fact that renewables only account for roughly one-third of energy consumption, despite much higher shares in electricity generation capacity, is due to the fact that wind and solar power are only temporarily available under given environmental conditions in Germany (BMWi 2016; BDEW 2016). In terms of resource sustainability, similar patterns hold for energy intensity in Germany, defined as primary energy supply over GDP. It decreased in a manner that was well above the OECD average, thus standing out as a success (Klein 2012). Mirroring these developments, Germany's resource productivity, defined as gross domestic product to the domestic use of natural resources, has improved throughout the 2000s. Figure 5.5 provides evidence for these efforts that parallel related patterns in Europe.

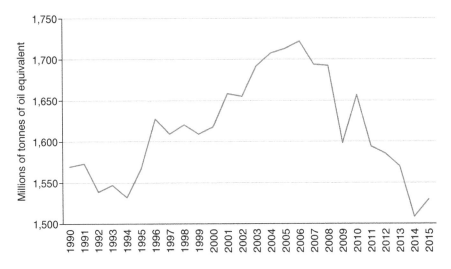

Figure 5.4a EU primary energy consumption.
Source: Eurostat, 2017.

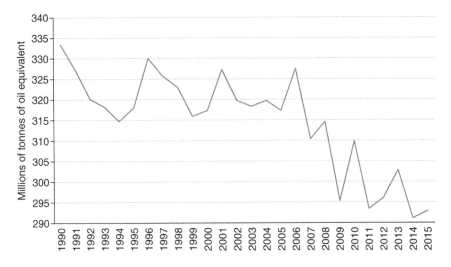

Figure 5.4b German primary energy consumption.
Source: Eurostat, 2017.

Regarding the combined industry and market structures, it is worth noting that the liberalisation of the electricity sector in the late 1990s happened in the context of a system of monopolistic structures. Specifically, there were nine vertically integrated, strictly regulated and regionally demarcated public utilities, accompanied by a set of regional supply companies and municipal

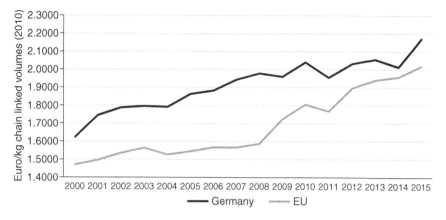

Figure 5.5 Resource productivity.
Source: Eurostat, 2017.

utilities. The result of liberalisation has been a distinct set of suppliers that form the oligopolistic structure of Germany's current energy supply market. These 'big five' energy suppliers are RWE, Vattenfall, E.on, Evonik and EnBW. They emitted a volume of 240 million tons CO_2 in 2011. In relation to the total volume of CO_2 emissions of 351 million tons, this amounts to a share of almost two-thirds of total emissions, predominantly caused by brown coal power stations in Western Germany. Moreover, with approximately 107 million tons of CO_2 emissions in 2011, RWE alone produced by far the largest amount among Germany's 'big five' and it is also a leading player in the European market for energy supply. The operations of the other firms have been recorded as: Vattenfall emitted 73 million tons; E.ON emitted 38 million tons; Evonik emitted 13 million tons; EnBW emitted nine million tons. In comparison, all the emissions of Germany's joint venture power plants, operating on the level of local authorities, amounted to 15 million tons (Umweltbundesamt und Deutsche Emissionshandelsstelle 2012). In view of the challenges of innovation in energy markets, most of these large suppliers have diversified into renewable energy supply since the late 2000s and have set up new divisions: RWE Innogy, Vattenfall Europe New Energy, E.on Climate and Renewables, and EnBW Renewables. However, their activity in Germany has so far remained marginal.

The observed pattern of industrial concentration in energy supply parallels the spatial differentiation of carbon emissions across Germany. Regional profiles of energy-related carbon emissions, which are produced during the conversion and use of energy, underline that the Nordrhein-Westfalen region stood out with a share of almost one-third of German emissions in 1990, followed by Sachsen, Bayern and Baden-Württemberg. During the 1990s and 2000s, all *Bundesländer* (the German name for these regional subdivisions) exhibited a more or less pronounced decline in carbon emissions. In Nordrhein-Westfalen, the hotbed of Germany's carbon-intensive industry, these changes were comparatively modest. This reduction of emissions shows a distinct East–West differentiation after reunification. Indeed, carbon emissions in Sachsen and the other Eastern German regional states have been cut by about 50 per cent during the two decades since 1990. Regional levels of process-related emissions, produced during the use of energy for the purpose of industrial production, also show a decline in emissions. The most impressive efforts are recorded for Nordrhein-Westfalen, a core industrial area of the German economy that has been shifting away from its basis in the heavy industries (Länderarbeitskreis Energiebilanzen 2013).

German efforts to reduce carbon emissions need to be evaluated in the context of the extended industrial basis of the German economy, with its specialisation in manufacturing industries, such as automobiles, and its continued use of coal as a politically shaped energy source. Both of these areas are crucial to the issue of decarbonisation and German efforts to reduce emissions tend to take place in a challenging and highly politicised industrial context. However, as the de-industrialisation of the former Eastern Germany, following reunification in 1991, is included in the data profiles, it needs a more concise interpretation of the general data. A large proportion of reduced carbon emissions may be due to the effects of industrial change related to market-oriented systems transformation in the former Eastern Germany. These are set apart from strategic concerns and concerted policy efforts for decarbonisation. During the 1990s, 50 per cent of the reduction of carbon emissions occurred thanks to the restructuring of the East German economy as heavy industries largely broke down. Outsourcing of manufacturing industries to Eastern Europe also contributed to this effect (Weidner and Mez 2008). Obviously, Germany is no longer going to benefit from these one-off reductions. As the overall trend in the reduction of emissions has been rather promising so far, it remains to be seen whether future developments keep that pattern, or whether it is going to be halted or possibly even reversed.

A major challenge comes from more immediate emissions reduction requirements, which task Germany to reduce its emissions not covered by the European Union Emissions Trading System a further 14 per cent by 2020, as compared to 2005 levels. This target is set by the binding regulations of the Effort Sharing Decision within the European Union. The latest data actually suggest that Germany is currently not on track to meet this target. Projections of emissions scenarios indicate that Germany will only meet its 2020 Effort Sharing Decisions targets if additional measures are implemented across the economy (Donat *et al.* 2013). This buttresses the recent report by the environment ministry that current measures might be insufficient to meet the challenge of the even more ambitious 2030 Paris targets, embodied in the 2021–2030 Effort Sharing Proposal with current policies. However, the implementation of additional measures relies on a political agenda of the major players – which is currently the subject of debate on the potential for further emissions reduction to put a damper on the competitiveness of German industry. So far, it seems that the *Energiewende* – the so-called energy turn, with its phasing out of nuclear energy and its promotion of renewables – has successfully promoted the latter. Yet, counter to its original intentions, it has also been pushing the use of electricity production from brown coal, which has reached its highest level since the early 1990s, while the share of gas-fired power has been declining. Germany's prominent use of coal as an energy source continues to mark its position as the economy with the highest per capita carbon footprint in the European Union (Rhys 2013). A net effect of this confluence of energy factors has been a short-term increase in the emission of GHGs. The political dimension of this problematic scenario becomes clear when it is put in the context of Germany as the world's largest miner of brown coal, with a regional concentration of mining in Nordrhein-Westfalen, a contested battleground for all political parties (*The Economist* 2014). In order to understand the institutional aspects that interlink the economic and political systems, and their role in shaping the trajectories of transition towards a low carbon economy, it is useful to reference the varieties of capitalism approach. This analytical approach addresses the German model of capitalism with its decidedly associational and relational modes of coordination.

An outline of the German variety of capitalism

In the varieties of capitalism tradition, Germany belongs in the CME category. These economies exhibit a dominant pattern of strategic coordination through investment in specific assets. The strategic behaviour of firms is coordinated to a much larger extent through non-market mechanisms than in liberal market economies (LMEs), such as the United States or the United Kingdom. This incorporates long-term company finance, cooperative industrial relations, high levels of firm-specific vocational training in support of technological learning, and inter-firm cooperation in technology transfer. Firms in CMEs are said to prefer incremental innovations within stable organisational settings, based on consistent skills upgrading, long-term capital investments and cooperative labour relations (Hall and Soskice 2001; Soskice 1994). An important implication of this view on complementarities, is that viable policy change must be compatible with existing institutional patterns, that is, they must be incentive compatible with the coordination mechanisms of the prevailing political-economic system. This includes its particular bent towards market, or non-market, coordination. The predominant dynamism of institutional change is predicted to be incremental, for it needs to contain a wide array of linkages among the institutional sub-systems. Accordingly, proponents of the varieties of capitalism approach consider those economies that are situated between the poles of the liberal and coordinated varieties as being less efficient than the pure types. Despite market-oriented reforms in the latter variety, coordinated types are not seen as fragile. Thus, there is no uniform drive for institutional convergence towards a liberal model (Hall and Soskice 2003). Therefore, the varieties of capitalism approach predicts gradual institutional change that remains within the parameters of the complementarities in the CME.

Recent discussions in the comparative capitalisms domain have taken issue with this inherently static reasoning. They stress internal contradiction and conflict in the evolving varieties of capitalism. Accordingly, institutional diversity needs to be viewed as the common state of the co-evolution of capitalist varieties, resulting from both internal impulses, such as sectoral and regional specificities, and external catalysts, such as international regulatory regimes (Ebner 2015; Lane and Wood 2009; Crouch 2005). Corresponding political dimensions of this internal diversity involve varieties of government–business relations and interest group activities, which inform mechanisms of associational governance (Hancké, Rhodes and Thatcher 2007). Moreover, institutional change may involve both gradual and radical effects, involving gradual institutional changes that can cause radical effects in path alteration, as the complex features of the underlying processes generate manifold unintended consequences. This complexity of political-economic interactions fuels the persistent hybridisation of varieties of capitalism beyond pure types and forms (Hall and Thelen 2009; Streeck and Thelen 2005).

In addressing the underlying relationship between institutions and innovation in distinct varieties of capitalism, complementarities also shape the institutional architecture of the kind of sub-system that is predominantly concerned with technological innovation. Namely, the relevant national innovation *systems* and the corresponding innovation *regimes* (Hübner 2009; Ebner 2009, 1999). Accordingly, the varieties of capitalism approach supports the argument that CMEs exhibit advantages in incremental innovation, predominantly in medium-tech industries. Empirical explorations of OECD economies during the 1990s and early 2000s have confirmed the assessment that CMEs specialise in medium-tech exports, although internal diversity and dynamics within these classifications need to be taken into account (Schneider and Paunescu 2012). In this setting, firms are expected to cooperate extensively with government and industry associations in a regulatory and associational governance regime, which differs from a mere reliance on market signals (Mikler and Harrison 2012).

Organise

Echoing the logic of this production regime, the German variety of capitalism, with its relational approach to the governance of relationships between firms and their institutional setting, is characterised by systemic complementarities that have been operating from the 1950s well into the 1990s and beyond. The complementary institutional sub-systems of the German variety of capitalism, include a specific system of corporate governance that combines a stakeholder system of long-term financial resources with relational and reputational monitoring. The system of industrial relations involves regulative patterns of coordinated bargaining and situational moderation in a centralised wage setting. This arrangement is governed by employer associations and labour unions, paralleled by institutional constraints on workforce dismissals in large firms, which gives German unions a strong influence on human resource issues. The corresponding system of skill upgrading is based on wide-ranging industry involvement, framed by a system of education and training that underlines firm- and industry-specific requirements. The underlying rationale of long-term investment also resonates with the basic logic of Germany's bank-dominated financial system. In terms of corporate governance, it promotes a mechanism of stakeholder engagement across industries. Inter-firm relations also permit the diffusion of common standards and practices in support of a cooperative mode of technology transfer (Hall and Soskice 2001). These qualities of German capitalism also mould the patterns of technological innovation, which are at the heart of the transition towards a low carbon economy. Based on the prevalence of diversified and quality-oriented industries, such as automobiles, in the German economy's industrial mix, the basic pattern of technological innovation is incremental, as it capitalises on the long-term of effects of industrial learning. The involved firms exhibit advantages in innovation processes that are pursued within the framework of an established techno-economic paradigm, which implies reduced uncertainty and allows for long-term expectations and relational strategies (Casper and Kettler 2001).

In addition to the technological dynamics of industrial change, and the changes in the knowledge base of both production regimes and consumption behaviour, governance structures in the political system also play a key role in the transition towards a low carbon economy. Crucially, the distinct rationale in the German model of capitalism, with its system of relational non-market coordination, involves comprehensive institutional constraints that favour a consensual pattern of decision-making and implementation. This can be found in the domains of both business and politics (Kitschelt and Streeck 2004). The German political system is accurately described as a constrained democratic government, with a strong constitutional court and multi-level federalism, encompassing a complex relationship between local, regional and national organs of government and administration. This amounts to a system of decentralised government, which is of particular relevance in policy fields such as science and education. In fact, regional governments such as Baden-Württemberg's Conservative government in the late 1980s, have become role models of modern innovation policies with distinctly regional approaches to industrial change. This pattern of subsidiarity and cooperation is in line with the ideological setting of the social market economy. This may be approached in terms of a neo-corporatist consensus democracy, which is actually perceived as the political-institutional backbone for the international competitiveness of Germany's production model (Abelshauser 2004). Regarding the transition towards a low carbon economy, such a characterisation of the political system implies that institutional changes are predicted to be incremental, involving relational decision-making through industry associations and civil society.

This holds for the hybridisation of the German variety of capitalism, which is a result of reform efforts driving a flexibilisation of the institutional constraints on business strategies since the early 2000s. For instance, the local flexibilisation of wage bargaining, industrial relations and labour market regulations, all contribute to a restructuring of German neo-corporatism in its industrial core areas, which combines market and non-market elements in a hybrid model of coordination (Streeck 2009). All this has contributed to a less egalitarian outlook in economy and society. Still, the institutional core of industrial affairs in German capitalism remains within the framework of a CME, with a strong grounding in relational and associational governance (Hall 2007; Carlin and Soskice 2009; Glassmann 2009). Also, despite reforms to strengthen financial markets, Germany's bank-based financial system differs considerably from market-based liberal systems in the United States and the United Kingdom. Most relevant global innovation has been propelled by the advent of venture capital. The emergence of rather volatile stock market segments for entrepreneurial ventures in Germany indicates that institutional transplants from a liberal variety of capitalism may be unsuccessful due to an institutional mismatch (Vitols and Engelhardt 2005; Busch 2005). In conclusion, it seems apparent that the German variety of capitalism is well characterised as a hybridised type of coordinated capitalism. One that combines market and non-market modes of coordination, in accordance with the logic of selective adaptation to ever changing internal and external conditions (Bathelt and Gertler 2005).

The transition towards a low carbon economy is a part of these adaptive efforts that are set to restructure institutional complementarities, in line with the prevailing patterns of industrial and technological specialisation. This transition to a new path of economic growth requires major efforts in technological innovation, which implies the introduction of new products and production processes in an established economic system; a view that also addresses the use of new sources of energy and increases in energy efficiency. This puts the knowledge base of firms and the dynamism of entrepreneurship at the centre of any analytical endeavour. Yet this 'greening' of national and regional innovation systems is driven by strategic coalitions of change, whose formation cannot be taken for granted – and which can be obstructed by adverse coalitions. The structuration of governance regimes in the German energy sector, provides a telling example of specific market and non-market coordination features in the transition towards a low carbon economy.

As outlined above, German energy markets are oligopolistic, with the largest shares being held by the 'big five' companies. In considering the energy supply structure in Germany, it is imperative to address ownership and governance aspects of the involved firms. First of all, four of Germany's 'big five' – RWE, E.on, Evonik, and EnBW – are essentially German companies when it comes to their ownership structure and corporate headquarters. This implies that the internationalisation of large firms in the German energy market is less nuanced than, for instance, in the UK. This home nation bias reflects the fact that energy supply has traditionally been considered a public good, to be provided by public sector monopolies. Deregulation and privatisation efforts, which have been prevalent since the 1980s in most OECD economies, promoted a more dynamic approach to business activities with an international scope. While Germany's big energy suppliers evolved as players in international markets, they still held a firm grip on their home market. E.on emerged out of VEBA AG and VIAG AG, two major German energy suppliers. It is currently the largest German company in the energy sector. RWE emerged out of Rheinisch-Westfälisches Elektrizitätswerk AG, a key German energy supplier based in the Ruhr area. Currently, RWE is the second largest company in the German energy sector. EnBW, Energie Baden-Württemberg AG, is the third largest company in the Germany energy sector. It is owned by the state government and regional authorities in Baden-Württemberg, Germany's primary location for manufacturing industries. Evonik emerged out of Ruhrkohle AG, a major company in coal and mining production from the Ruhr area. Finally, there is a foreign company among the 'big five': Vattenfall, a state-owned Swedish company. All these companies are subject to the kind of institutional legacy of relational governance and non-market coordination that is usually associated with the capitalist varieties found in Western Europe and Scandinavia. Accordingly, from a varieties of capitalism perspective, societal negotiations on strategies towards a reduction of GHG emissions will be deeply entrenched in the political domain.

This is not to say that market competition does not matter. In fact, recent regulatory initiatives have contributed markedly to the introduction of competitive market pressures in the German energy sector, in particular when it comes to the supply of electricity. Since 2007, the unbundling process and the appointment of an independent regulator, the *Bundesnetzagentur*, has contributed to a slight fall in the market shares of the biggest players, while integration with EU energy markets further progressed in a potentially competition-enhancing manner (Bundesnetzagentur 2010). Even more obviously, market competition is quickly developing in the environmental goods and services markets, which are of particular relevance to the domain of renewable energy. The entrepreneurial drive in the evolution of renewable energy industries, such as photovoltaics, has been well documented and is clearly a key aspect in its performance (Brachert and Hornych 2011). Remarkably, these entrepreneurial efforts tend to contradict the predictions of the varieties of capitalism framework, with its claim that CMEs will face a dearth of entrepreneurial initiatives, due to an unfavourable institutional setting. However, the large proportion of these endeavours that are exported implies that international market competition puts enormous pressures on local firms. These domestic companies tend to face difficulties in preserving their markets. For instance, the German export market share of the global market in photovoltaics decreased from over three-quarters in 2004 to only one-third in 2009, while photovoltaic equipment was increasingly imported from China and Japan. A different picture emerges with regard to wind energy with three-quarters of equipment bought in Germany produced by German manufacturers. At the moment, the manufacturing expertise of German industry still pays off (Klein 2012).

The relative success of wind energy also relates to historically rooted political-institutional factors that shape the path dependence of electricity supply systems. In the case of Germany, the prevailing multi-level supply system has allowed for the evolution of alternative technological trajectories at local and regional governance levels. This is best exemplified by the entre-preneurial dynamics of wind power energy in Germany, whose small-scale local dynamics are in contrast to more monopolistic settings in other segments of the energy sector. These other segments are prone to lock-in effects, which prevent path alterations in the transition to a new energy system (Simmie *et al.* 2014). Consequently, it may be argued that the German production and innovation regime, with its reliance on high-quality and knowledge-intensive manufacturing, is set to successfully continue on its low carbon path. This is fundamentally due to the multi-level and multi-actor bargaining processes that are typical of Germany's CME, for they allow for the seamless inclusion of new interest groups and political parties, such as those emerging from the environmental movement (Geels *et al.* 2016). In coping with the low carbon transition, therefore, the varieties of capitalism perspective hints at two inter-related factors. First, the dynamism of technological innovation in support of a low carbon economy and its embeddedness in the institutional configura-tions of the national innovation system. Second, the political making and shaping of the transition towards a low carbon economy, which is subject to policy interventions and interest group activities.

The 'greening' of the German innovation system

From the varieties of capitalisms perspective, it is commonly argued that the German innovation system is biased towards continuous learning and incre-mental innovation. These are set apart from the types of radical change that are driven by the disruptive introduction of new technologies, based on strong science–industry linkages that contribute to the evolution of new para-digms of knowledge. This modelled constellation allegedly reflects the specialisation pattern of the German production model and its key comple-mentarities. Chief among these are relational monitoring in corporate gov-ernance, bank-based long-term finance, a skilled workforce that is subject to continuing training and education, and modes of technology transfer that allow for cooperative relations framed by industry associations. The resulting pattern of long-term coordination that combines market competition with relational and associational governance, has been relatively successful in past settings of established technological paradigms. However, it may lead to rigidities and a loss of efficiency in the context of rapid and disruptive techno-logical change, compared to more flexibly adaptive and short-term market-oriented approaches (Harding and Soskice 2000; Hall and Soskice 2001). When it comes to the underlying competitive strategies, German firms tend to pursue a strategy of non-price competition in favour of an approach based on product characteristics and quality features. this is inherently grounded on incremental innovations (Vitols 2001). In effect, the combination of estab-lished industrial skills and capabilities, along with new knowledge on low carbon technologies and their innovative implementation, poses a key chal-lenge for the German innovation system. This includes its role as a sub-system of the German variety of capitalism that consists of quite a number of key players.

The main institutional actors in the German innovation system are the Federal Ministry for Education and Research (BMBF), the Federal Ministry for Economy and Technology (BMWi) and other ministry departments that deal with science, research and innovation on the federal level, augmented by the regional ministries of the *Bundesländer* that retain key competences in the education domain. This actor assemblage also exhibits strong ties with innovation policies at the European level. The science system is well repres-ented by the national research association *Deutsche Forschungsgemeinschaft* and related public organs of the science system such as the *Wissenschaftsrat*. Non-profit organisations that run specialised research institutes include the *Max-Planck-Gesellschaft*, with a focus on basic research across the natural and social sciences, the *Helmholtz-Gesellschaft*, with a focus on basic research in the natural and life sciences, the *Leibniz-Gesellschaft*, with its applied research across the natural and social science disciplines, and finally the *Fraunhofer-Gesellschaft*, with its focus on applied research across the natural and social sci-ences. This last hosts the *Fraunhofer Institute for Innovation Research* in Karlsruhe, which is a key player in applied technology and innovation research. This set of organisations is engaged in partnerships with universities (predominantly public ones) and the business sector, shaped in its innovation activities by both large firms and the *Mittelstand* of small- and medium-sized enterprises (Ebner 2010; Ebner and Täube 2009).

Since the 2000s a number of key technological innovation policy pro-grammes have been launched. First, a pact for research and innovation, *Pakt für Forschung und Innovation*, has run since 2005 and was recently extended until 2020. It provides governmental funding for non-university research institutes and in its current phase receives a 3 per cent increase in its funding each year (German Federal Ministry of Education and Research 2016). It is meant to operate as a counterpart to the *Exzellenzinitiative*, which provides additional funding for research and teaching excellence at select universities. The federal government's High-Tech Strategy is designed to push innovation in new technologies and industries, which are expected to become integral in the future economy. This strategy has recently been developed further with an aptly named New High-Tech Strategy. This strategy has a distinct ecological bent, targeting the sustainable economy and energy as one of six priority tasks (German Federal Ministry of Education and Research 2014). It combines these concerns with 'future projects' such as the decarbonisation of cities, the broad-based use of renewable energy and an intelligent energy supply that uses smart grids. A further initiative geared towards innovation in promising economic and technological fields, is the Central Innovation Programme of the Federal Ministry for Economy and Technology, which is meant to support the innovation efforts of small- and medium-sized enterprises. The Ministry of Education and Research governs a distinct Framework Programme for Research and Sustainable Development, with a focus on climate and energy issues, paralleled by the Master Plan for Environmental Technologies with a focus on lead markets and resource efficiency in new environmental technologies. Further programmes with an explicit focus on the support of technological change as a key force in the low carbon transformation of the economy, relate to the Integrated Energy and Climate Programme that has been running since 2007. Its key objectives follow the European Union 20-20-20 goals. These include a reduction in GHG emissions by 20 per cent, an increase in the share of renewables in primary energy consumption to 20 per cent, and ameliorating fuel efficiency by 20 per cent, all to be achieved by 2020 (Leijten *et al.* 2012; OECD 2012a).

In terms of output, the regular set of indicators allude to the German innovation system's strong performance in terms of a sustained output of triadic patents (patents for the same product are filed at the European Patent Office, the Japan Patent Office and the United States Patent and Trademark Office) (OECD 2016). In terms of inputs, Germany has a shortage of human capital in high-tech industries, an insufficient supply of private venture capital and slow growth in knowledge-intensive services (Ebner and Täube 2009; EFI 2009; Grupp, Schmoch and Breitschopf 2008). The strengths of the German innovation system, however, are still predominant. Indeed, it is safe to state that Germany remains one of Europe's most innovative economies. According to the European Innovation Scoreboard, Germany is established within the group of innovation leaders, with an innovation performance far above the EU 28 average – although they remain the laggard among those countries regarded as innovation leaders, and in real terms performance has declined relative to the EU by 3.7 per cent (European Commission DG Internal Market, Industry, Entrepreneurship and SMEs 2017). The share of German gross expenditures on Research and Development (GERD), when compared to GDP, equalled about 2.5 per cent during the 2000s, approaching 3 per cent at times, and thus operating well above OECD average, with both public and private research and development (R&D) expanding. From a comparative perspective, this German GERD/GDP ratio is way ahead of other major European OECD economies such as the United Kingdom and France. At the same time, basic research accounts for only 20 per cent of overall R&D, far below the OECD average. This is exacerbated by the fact that international R&D investment in Germany amounts to just under 20 per cent in overall R&D efforts, a notably low figure (OECD 2012b). Moreover, data for gross expenditures on R&D by sector of performance in the year 2014 show that private business accounted for a strong share of almost two-thirds of total R&D expenditures (OECD 2017).

The R&D profiles reflect patterns of industrial specialisation in medium-tech industries with a strong presence of manufacturing industries. The corresponding pattern of revealed technology advantage "is defined as a country's share of patents in a particular technology field divided by the country's share in all patent fields" (OECD 2009). During the 1990s and 2000s, this pattern highlighted German advantages in manufacturing industries such as automobiles (Tylecote and Visintin 2008). More specifically, industrial contributions to GERD are predominantly based in traditional high-skill, high-quality industries such as automobiles, electronics, chemicals, pharmaceuticals, mechanical engineering and machine tools, whereas newly emerging high-technology industries like biotechnology are comparatively underrepresented. The same applies to services at large. This assessment still holds despite recent advances in technological niches, such as nanotechnology and environmentally friendly technologies (Legler, Krawczyk and Leidmann 2009; Rammer *et al.* 2004; Prange 2005). When it comes to the transfer of new technological knowledge into productive uses however, the German nexus between R&D and manufacturing seems to generate positive stimuli for the introduction of low carbon innovations that drive the transition path towards a low carbon economy. Building on these existing skills and capabilities in competitive industries provides the foundations for a technological transition that is set to establish new comparative advantages in an environmentally friendly low carbon setting. The institutional set-up of the German innovation system has maintained a focus on supporting innovation for research consortia among large established firms. This is reflected by the empirical tendency for public institutions in scientific research to be most intimately connected to the R&D facilities of large enterprises. Whereas entrepreneurial spin-offs, which tend to be highly relevant in newly emerging science-based industries, remain comparatively underdeveloped (Belitz and Kirn 2008). Thus, the bias towards mature industries in the German model of diversified quality production may obstruct entrepreneurial start-up dynamics, which are typically most relevant in new industries with a high level of new market entrants (Sapir *et al.* 2003). Indeed, German small and medium enterprises (SMEs), and especially entrepreneurial new firms that could trigger more radical innovations, are lagging behind other more entrepreneurial OECD economies. During the late 2000s only 7 per cent of patents were filed by firms less than five years old, half of the corresponding US-share (OECD 2010b).

Nonetheless, evidence on new knowledge-based industries, such as biotechnology, suggests that CMEs may provide a niche for these science-based industries as a result of cooperative research and commercialisation agreements between firms, universities and non-university research institutes (Knie and Lengwiler 2008; Kaiser and Prange 2004). In biotechnology, for instance, this may hold more for areas that are specialised in platform technologies, and less in the high-risk domain of research in therapeutics (Casper and Kettler 2001; Casper, Lehrer and Soskice 1999). Therefore, the distinct style of Germany's CME does not preclude entrepreneurial dynamics in general, but does seem to delineate certain niches for thriving entrepreneurial activity (Ebner 2010). According to the methodology of the European Commission's Innovation Scoreboard, there are positive signs of a German entrepreneurial turn that should be taken into account. Germany is well above the EU average regarding the sheer number of SMEs innovating in-house, SMEs with product/process innovations and the average R&D spending among top R&D enterprises (European Commission DG Internal Market, Industry, Entrepreneurship and SMEs 2017). At the same time, young high-tech firms in Germany are mainly financed by cash their flow and their own resources, as venture capital financing is comparatively underdeveloped (EFI 2011). Thus, it is fair to state that the evolution of cooperative relations between research institutes, large enterprises, new ventures and capital providers will be decisive in the further greening of Germany's production and innovation regime.

Germany is considered the economy with the strongest record on green innovation in Europe, with a performance that is in the upper range of OECD countries, particularly in the domain of environmental technologies. Germany excels with an innovation score that is well above its revealed comparative advantage. In terms of industrial specialisation, the pattern of green innovation in Germany holds in particular for motor vehicles, with a green innovation score of 2.2 and a revealed comparative advantage score of 1.2. The domain of 'parts and accessories for automobiles' comes with a green innovation score of 1.6 and a revealed comparative advantage score of 1.5; whereas 'other fabricated metal products' stands at a green innovation score of 1.6 and a revealed comparative advantage score of 1.3 (Fankhauser *et al.* 2012). Thus, in terms of green innovation performance, Germany's key manufacturing industries, such as automobiles, perform most impressively.

German input indicators for green innovation depict a mixed performance. The share of public R&D expenditure in the relevant 'green' domains of 'control and care for the environment' and 'production, distribution and rational utilisation of energy' in total public R&D expenditure has been negligible, amounting to about 3 per cent on average all through the 2000s. Still, this is above corresponding expenditure levels in the United Kingdom (Aghion, Veugelers and Serre 2009). Moreover, the general tendency has been for expenditure to increase, R&D in energy and environment as a percentage of total public R&D expenditures in 2011 increased to a moderate level of 7.1 per cent (OECD 2012a). However, in assessing R&D data, it should be taken into account once again that German industry is not specialised in high-tech segments with gargantuan R&D intensive activities. Rather, German manufacturing industries are predominantly active in medium-tech segments. Thus, many innovations are not necessarily recorded by R&D data, for they will be related to more informal procedures of learning by doing.

The performance profile on the input side of the innovation process, corresponds to a mixed specialisation on the output side, as measured by patenting activity. The same caveat as with R&D as an innovation input indicator applies. Namely that patents may not show the true level of outputs as a consequence of slow and incremental change in medium technology not requiring patents. Green technology patents during the 2000s exhibited the following country shares and specialisation patterns for Germany. The German contribution to world patents for energy generation was 13 per cent of total global patents, which amounts to a clear-cut specialisation. The German share for transportation was at 31 per cent, which is also a clear indicator of industrial specialisation. Another domain of specialisation is environmental management with a 13.1 per cent share. Germany applied for 11.2 per cent of total patents in technologies for emissions mitigation, which is also indicative of related specialisation efforts (OECD 2012a). Between 1988 and 2007 the relative strength of Germany in green patenting could be observed as follows. On average, 15.2 per cent of patents originated from Germany, amounting to half of all European patents in that segment, and almost at the same level as the United States with its 15.9 per cent, while Japan stands out as the global leader with a share of 29.7 per cent (Veugelers 2011). In 2007 Germany was the third largest producer of triadic patents in renewable energy sources; it also ranked third with the number of patent applications in technologies related to climate change mitigation (OECD 2010a).

A related overview of the OECD ranking of the main patenting countries in clean energy technologies from 1988 to 2007 shows that Germany takes the rank of third overall in performance among clean energy technologies, leading in Europe yet well behind the global leader Japan and second place United States. In particular, German rankings in the diverse technology fields under consideration are: third for solar photovoltaics, first for solar thermal, first for wind, second for geothermal, second for hydro/machine, second for biofuels, second for carbon capture, fourth for carbon storage ranks, and third for integrated gasification combined cycle. Thus, German industry is most prominent in areas of clean energy technologies such as solar thermal and wind, accompanied by similarly good rankings in geothermal, biofuels and carbon capture (OECD 2012a). This assessment is in line with calculations that depict German comparative technology advantages in green innovation between 1988 and 2011 as a marked pattern of technological advances in the areas of solar thermal, wind, geothermal, and biofuels (Veugelers 2011).

This positive performance persisted during the 2010s. In 2011 applicants from Germany held half of the European patents in climate change mitigation technologies – with German performance in the renewable energy domain four times higher than that of second ranked France, while its lead in the domain of road transport technologies is even higher. Major German inventive businesses in the field of climate change mitigation technologies are Siemens and Robert Bosch – with Siemens dominating the field of clean energy technologies (EPO 2016). When it comes to patents in renewable energy technology, patent registrations with the German Patent Office indicate consistently strong performance, with solar and wind comprising major segments. In 2013 more than 900 patents were registered for solar photovoltaics, while about 800 were registered for wind. Crucially, as indicated by the German Patent Office, the newly established legal framework for the support of renewable energies may have played a stimulating role in this regard (Morris 2014).

The dynamic setting of green innovation is also reflected by the market performance of green-tech firms and the overall profile of green investment in Germany. First of all, in 2011, German green-tech firms attained a 15 per cent share of global markets for clean technology and resource efficiency. These firms represent a booming global industry, which has already seen major increases in market shares in the preceding years from 2007, with corresponding increases in growth projected for the forthcoming years (BMU 2012). A technological take-off for wind energy was recorded for the 1990s, while solar energy took off in the early 2000s (Jacobsson and Lauber 2006; Wong 2005). These developmental dynamics of green-tech industries in Germany feed upon the established knowledge base of the economy, with its set of industrial skills and capabilities in manufacturing. This is augmented by the science and technology infrastructure of the German innovation system. An example is the evolution of competitive advantages in the industrial domain of wind turbines, which has developed from existing expertise in the related industrial domain of high-precision machining. This field is notable as a particularly outstanding area of expertise in the quality-oriented German production model (Huberty and Zachmann 2011). This view of the formative role of manufacturing industries is further corroborated by re-examining the spatial dimension of green innovation in Germany; that is, its geographical concentration in regional centres of green innovation, the states of Baden-Württemberg and Bayern. Both are also key locations for the most competitive branches of German manufacturing industries.

Germany still holds its place for the highest volume of small distributed capacity investments. Yet investment in low carbon innovation requires the availability of adequate financial resources. When it comes to the types of finance that comprise green investment, the most usual forms of asset finance are small distributed capacity, public markets and venture capital – private equity can also be taken into account. Germany is ranked behind China and the United States with regard to the overall volumes of green investment in 2012, with these two economies possessing especially pronounced investment capacities when compared to their global counterparts. In comparison to most other major economies, Germany is characterised by green investment in which small distributed capacity makes up the largest share, more than asset finance, venture capital or public markets (McCrone *et al.* 2013). Also, public credit facilities play a considerable role in the allocation of loans and related financial support for the use of renewable energy and environmentally friendly technology. A highly relevant initiative is the *Marktanreizprogramm*, which provides financial incentives for green investment. Administered by Germany's third largest bank, the public Kreditanstalt für Wiederaufbau, this programme provides low-interest loans and grant support to installations using heat emanating from renewable energy in residential buildings. In effect, it contributed significantly to the expansion of technologically advanced heat networks with reduced carbon emissions. In 2012 the German government increased the financial volume of the programme, with a focus on solar thermal power, biomass installations and heat pumps (Donat *et al.* 2013).

The innovation dynamics of the low carbon transition in Germany are also well developed in terms of lead markets. Altogether, five lead markets with distinct submarkets can be explored. These include: environmentally friendly energies, with the submarkets of renewable energies and storage technologies; energy efficiency, with submarkets of energy efficiency of buildings and efficiency-oriented technologies in industry; sustainable water management, with submarkets in decentralised water management and effluent disposal; sustainable mobility, with submarkets in alternative propulsion technologies and environmentally friendly infrastructure and transport management systems; and the market domains of recycling, sustainable agriculture with organic farming and green services with a focus on sustainable finance. In this profile, the highest shares are taken by the domains of energy efficiency, environmentally friendly energies and energy storage and water management. All these green lead markets combined amounted to a market volume of €285 billion in 2011; this comes close to the automobile sector, Germany's lead industry, with its 351 billion volume. Yet the future expansion of these new green markets on a global scale is not only determined by the economic factors of private sector supply and demand, but also by government support concerning the actual use and consumption of green technologies and products (Kahlenborn *et al.* 2013).

Policies in support of the greening of innovation activities are subject to the interventions of diverse economic and social interests, which may support or hamper an innovation-based low carbon transition. Environmental policies may be viewed as one of the main drivers of innovation in low carbon technologies, as they create a need for abatement solutions while providing market opportunities to innovative firms. Also, the diffusion and adoption of these new technologies benefit from implemented environmental policies, as demonstrated most convincingly in the German case of policy support to renewables (Johnstone *et al.* 2010). However, industrial interest coalitions that involve firms, business associations and labour unions, may have concerns with the costs associated with a low carbon transition. Their apprehension revolves around seeing these costs as posing a danger to industrial competitiveness. This can hinder further advances in emissions reduction, although these advances could have provided dynamic incentives for further innovations. As the German production model seems to favour incremental change along established technological trajectories over the setting up of new trajectories, the matter of static versus dynamic competitiveness also alludes to the quality of innovation at large. The introduction of hybrid motors and electric motor vehicles is a case in point. Key inventions underlying these technologies have been established in Germany, yet German automobile producers have been reluctant in recent years to push for corresponding innovations. In this context, emissions-related interventions by the German government on behalf of the automobile industry proved to be counter-productive. They may have been in the short-term interest of an industry that is focused on fuel-based engines, yet they preclude incentives for long-term innovations in non-fossil fuel technologies (Ruhkamp and Rossbach 2013; Lamparter *et al.* 2013).

The international dimension of these issues is exemplified by the prevailing difficulties with solar energy. Major German firms have been rethinking their subsidised activities in photovoltaics, in part due to competitive pressures from subsidised foreign competitors, in particular China and Korea. A case in point is the decline of Saxony's 'Solar Valley', with its low carbon technology cluster (Schultz 2012). Then again, one can examine the current revival of coal power plants in the new low-emission technology environment, which has been created based on well established industrial capabilities and promoted by large enterprises such as Siemens, which is a key player in German private sector R&D (Fuchs and Wassermann 2013; Pahle 2010). With this revival of coal as an energy source, some of Germany's big energy suppliers, such as E.on, see their envisioned expansion of low-emission gas power plants (which had been singled out as future substitutes for nuclear power plants) as endangered. Other suppliers, like RWE with its extensive activities in coal, tend to benefit from these developments. American exports of coal and gas have pushed international prices for coal into an even steeper decline than those for gas, which provides further incentives for the continued use of coal (Steltzner 2013).

In other words, both national and international policy actors, with their particular strategies, take centre stage in the making and shaping of a low carbon economy. Following the analytical framework of the varieties of capitalism approach, the analysis now turns to the influence of associational governance, which complements regulatory governmental influences in Germany. Concerns with the degradation of the environment and the challenges of climate change are well represented, yet are also persistently contested. This happens through coordination efforts by both business associations and labour unions, with their particular interests, as the forces that determine the actual dynamism of the low carbon transition (Mikler 2009, 2011).

Policy actors and strategies in the German transition towards a low carbon economy

The German economy's prominent position in the field of carbon emissions reduction, and the expansion of energy emanating from renewables during the 2000s, is reflected in public opinion that considers climate change to be a policy priority that requires continued action (UBA 2010a). This is consistent with a long-standing pattern of policy-making and public discourse on climate change, part of an evolving environmentally oriented policy agenda from the 1970s. The oil and energy crisis of 1973 provided the first impetus for economic-political concerns about the resource efficiency and sustainability of established energy systems to come to the fore in the industrialised world. The debate on substituting renewable energy sources for fossil fuels evolved together with the rejection of nuclear energy. Indeed, public opposition to nuclear power became a political factor, with demonstrations against the building of new nuclear power plants in Whyl in 1975 and Brokdorf in 1976, further fuelled by the nuclear accident in Harrisburg in the United States in 1979. In the 1980s these protests continued with efforts focused on preventing the construction of nuclear reprocessing plants in Wackersdorf and Gorleben. The foundation of the Green Party in 1980 provided this broad-based environmental movement with a strategic platform, one that would criticise the use of nuclear energy as a mode of energy supply as prone to major uncertainties. This new social movement combined anti-nuclear sentiments and the push for resource sustainability with a critique of large-scale energy systems and their lack of democratic control. Energy from renewables, in contrast, was hailed as a decentralised, democratic small-scale alternative. This position was further instigated by the Chernobyl accident in the Soviet Union in 1986. Crucially, these debates would parallel campaigns for nuclear disarmament as organised by the peace movement. In this context, a specificity of the German situation derived from the fact that nuclear power did not play the same strategic role in national prestige as it did in countries such as the United Kingdom and France. There were never nuclear weapons under German sovereign command, which gave nuclear power a different political standing, making its use more accessible to economic reasoning in cost-benefit terms. Even after the end of the East–West confrontation, anti-nuclear protests continued, with demonstrations against the transportation of nuclear waste continuing throughout the 1990s and 2000s (Klein 2012). One might add that the Green Party played a key role in transmitting civil society protests to parliamentary and governmental operations. This was also due to Germany's political system, with elections based on proportional representation that promoted the entry of the Green Party as a regional and national force in various coalition governments with both Social Democrats and Conservatives, at times also including the Liberals (Bailey 2007).

Set in this context, German debates on environmental policy in the late 1980s approached a gradual restructuring of the energy mix, by expanding the share of renewable energy sources. A first step towards supportive legal regulation of energy from renewables, was realised with a heavily contested first law on feeding in renewables, *Strom-Einspeise-Gesetz StrEG*. It was introduced by the Liberal–Conservative Kohl government in 1990, four years after the Chernobyl nuclear disaster in Ukraine. In its basic orientation, it took up an initiative of the European Commission, which had been pushing for an expansion of renewable energy. Originally, most policy actors did not expect it to generate major economic and technological effects, but this law provided the institutional background for the introduction of the feed-in-tariff system, providing a building block in the transition of the energy system. In particular, it provided economic incentives for the supply of onshore wind, which would soon be accompanied by regional industrial policies in support of northern German coastal regions, framed by the competitive success of Germany's well positioned wind turbine builders (Jacobsson and Lauber 2006).

The act on renewable energy, *Erneuerbare Eneregien-Gesetz (EEG)*, was introduced in 2000 by the red–green Schröder government. It continued with the established approach of using feed-in tariffs as a means of promoting renewable energy. Crucially, it formulated a legal framework for obliging grid operators to prioritise feeding in electricity from renewable energy technologies, based on a minimum payment for electricity. Its design catered to specific technologies, in particular onshore wind, solar photovoltaic and geothermal, while outlining a long-term, 20-year time horizon in its financial and legal support architecture. The advocacy coalition of this act included a broad array of societal forces, involving environmental organisations, labour unions and even industry associations from within the German manufacturing sector. This effort at promoting renewables was soon followed by the *Atomkonsens*, a formal consensual agreement between government and business with regard to the phase-out of nuclear energy in 2002. This fulfilled a demand for which German environmentalist groups, the Green Party and the left flank of the Social Democrats had spent several decades struggling. Crucially, despite the fact that the nuclear industry was challenging this phase-out in both legal and political terms, it was still possible to find some common ground in a public agreement. Indeed, nuclear power had faced serious troubles in economic terms for some time, not least due to the high cost of risk management with regard to waste disposal. Thus, even before the red–green government pushed forward with a plan to phase out nuclear energy by legal means in 2002, the sector had been under constant criticism from various political and business-related angles (Jacobsson and Lauber 2006).

While the grand coalition of Conservatives and Social Democrats did not alter these regulations after taking power in 2005, the Liberal–Conservative Merkel government overturned the earlier phase-out procedure following the 2009 election. Crucially, this did not mean that nuclear energy was reinstated as a future component of Germany's energy system. Rather, it meant a rearticulating of the phase-out process, for the red–green phase-out strategy was viewed as unrealistic. In particular, as a business-friendly move, the lifetimes of nuclear power plants were extended by eight or 14 years – depending on when they were built. This was accompanied by a new energy concept that put forward the ambitious goals of achieving a of 35 per cent share of renewable electricity by 2020, and 80 per cent by 2050. Mounting energy costs and questions of energy security were provided as key arguments for this move. Yet these plans for slowing down the nuclear phase-out were reversed after the Fukushima nuclear accident in March 2011. Indeed, after this accident, German public opinion shifted massively against nuclear power. The Green Party won elections in the Christian Democratic heartland of Baden-Württemberg, which is a major region in terms of modern manufacturing industries and technological innovation, while simultaneously being a regional champion in environmental affairs. The Fukushima disaster led to the swift adaptation of policy proposals by the Merkel government, which decided to accelerate the phase-out of nuclear power, reversing its 2010 decision to increase the lifespan of nuclear power plants. After a moratorium including the shutdown of eight of the older nuclear plants, and general security checks at all of the nuclear power plants, the German parliament voted for a definitive nuclear phase-out by 2022, in line with the original red-green initiative of the late 1990s (Klein 2012).

This most recent effort concerning the phase-out of nuclear energy should be operated in tandem with a phasing in of clean energy. This incorporates renewable energy as the new cornerstone of the energy supply, replacing the current prominent role of emissions-intensive coal. Both the phase-out of nuclear energy and fossil fuels in the generation of electricity, and the phase-in of energy from renewable energy sources, primarily onshore wind and solar photovoltaics, constitute the so-called energy turn, *Energiewende. Energiewende* is a historically unique societal project, which strives for a multi-decade effort at transforming the national energy system. To achieve this transformation the Liberal–Conservative government put forward a detailed set of goals. Next to the complete phase-out of nuclear energy by 2022, the share of renewables for electricity generation should be increased to at least 38 per cent by 2020, 50 per cent by 2030, 67 per cent by 2040 and 80 per cent by 2050. This is to be paralleled by increases of the share of renewables in final energy consumption to 30 per cent by 2030 and 60 per cent by 2050. As a consequence, GHG emissions as compared to 1990 levels should be reduced by 40 per cent by 2020, 55 per cent by 2030, 70 per cent by 2040 and up to 95 per cent by 2050. Furthermore, energy efficiency is meant to be optimised. Energy consumption from buildings should be reduced by 20 per cent in 2020 and by 50 per cent in 2050. Also, energy consumption from transportation should be reduced by 10 per cent in 2020 and by 25 per cent in 2050. This shift to a new energy supply and use structure should proceed in line with a strategic decarbonisation of the supply of electricity, substituting gas for nuclear power during the energy transition (IEA 2013b; BMU 2012). Crucially, this set of quantitative goals has come together with a further transformation of the structural features of the energy system. This is particularly evident with regard to the increasing role of decentralised, small-scale energy providers that accompany the large-scale operations of the oligopolistic energy companies. The second 'grand coalition' government of Christian Democrats and Social Democrats that came to power in 2013 did not modify these objectives. However, it entered further bargaining processes with regard to the speed of the transition. Thus, the 2014 amendments to the law on renewable energies confirmed its basic orientation (Hirschhausen 2014).

The combination of phasing out nuclear power and shifting energy use towards decarbonisation has been the subject of comprehensive policy efforts in market regulation and governmental subsidisation. Major investment incentives have been set up in the domains of wind, photovoltaics, biomass and hydropower, combined with feed-in tariffs that have contributed to an ever more complex system of price control. In effect, however, the protectionism that has essentially resulted from this these price regulations and subsidies may end up reducing incentives for competitive strategies in German firms entering new markets. Moreover, and more visible in the short-term, is the problem of the social distribution of the energy transition's economic costs among public sector, private business and households. This is the subject of price-setting for energy supply and use as regulated in the law on renewable energies, *EEG*. This law was put into legislation for the first time in the 2000s, as a cornerstone of the German institutional framework for low carbon energy transition, and has been subject to a multitude of amendments and adaptations. German electricity users pay a specific charge, based on a feed-in tariff that is used for funding renewable energy generation, with the aim of supporting its diffusion. In a positive light, this law on renewable energies and its mechanism of feed-in tariffs has contributed to the international acclaim of the high predictability and positive performance of German policies in support of renewable energy sources (Butler and Neuhoff 2008).

In assessing the actual costs of these wide-ranging transformative endeavours, it is useful to first account for the social costs of nuclear energy and coal, that is, the major energy sources that are set to be replaced in the *Energiewende*. The social costs of nuclear energy primarily relate to the risk of nuclear accidents, costs which make nuclear the most expensive source of electricity. The social costs of coal reflect issues such as environmental degradation and health problems from pollution. These stunningly high social costs can be compared with a mechanism of social cost degression to learning effects that result from the use of solar photovoltaic and onshore wind, among others. Therefore, the calculation of costs and benefits needs to account for cost factors beyond the immediate cost concerns of firms, households and the public sector (Hirschhausen 2014).

Still, the coincidence of Germany phasing out nuclear energy and pushing renewable energy sources at the same time, has caused a set of problematic short-term effects. These may affect the overall legitimation of the political project for a low carbon transition. First of all, German electricity imports increased significantly to compensate for the loss in generation capacity that resulted from the first wave of nuclear power plant closures. This effect points directly to the matter of energy security in an increasingly uncertain international political environment, with Russia becoming a much less reliable partner for energy imports. Most relevant for the emissions reduction strategy, however, is the current trend of increasing GHG and carbon emissions. This is a result of the phase-out of nuclear power and the increased use of fossil fuel fired power plants. Paradoxically, then, and quite contrary to the goals of climate change mitigation, the elimination of nuclear energy from the German energy mix is set to promote a revival of emissions-intensive coal as an energy source (Klein 2012).

In effect, the aforementioned additional costs for energy consumption associated with this transition to renewable energy may hit both the industrial sector and private households. Indeed, due to the higher than market price of electricity, the net costs of the promotion of renewable energy in Germany have amounted to an estimated €125 billion since 2000. Households carry one-third of the financial surcharge in support of electricity from renewables, which has been further increasing in recent years. In technological terms, solar photovoltaic holds the largest cost share, with 43 per cent of the total costs of renewable energy sources, while comprising only 6 per cent of German electricity generation. The impact on consumers has been straightforward; electricity prices more than doubled between 2000 and 2015 and household prices for electricity were among the highest in the European Union, almost double the price paid in neighbouring France. Also, industry prices are among the highest across Europe (BMWi 2016; BDEW 2016).

The additional costs for business are especially subject to extended debates and lobbying efforts. These are usually based on arguments concerning a distortion of national competitive conditions, which is most pronounced in international markets that matter a lot for export-biased German manufacturing industry. This international dimension to the exemptions that have been granted for certain industries also hints at the contested compatibility of this national regulation with supranational institutional frameworks, in particular with the institutional setting of the European Union. The European Commission has repeatedly stated that it is set to counter Germany's renewable energy law for an alleged breach of EU competition regulations (IEA 2013b). Indeed, the impact of price distortions due to feed-in tariffs on the international competitiveness of domestic manufacturing industries has become a leitmotif for industry associations such as the Federation of German Industries (BDI). This is paralleled by infrastructural debates that highlight aspects of energy security. These include the fact that nuclear energy, which is being phased out, still provides almost 15 per cent of gross electricity generation, while electricity grid expansion and the risk of power grid instability remain largely unresolved problems (Borshchevska 2016). In fact, these uncertainties related to the energy transition have put the stock price performance of Germany's major utilities under stress. These issues have come together with the matter of competitiveness in the expansion of renewables. In particular, mounting costs for the operation of renewable energy technologies and international competition, in particular from East Asia, pose problems that are accompanied by the unsolved matter of energy storage and demand management (Geels *et al.* 2016).

These conflicts of interest are further reflected within the political system, most obviously in persistent intra-governmental rivalries that echo the conflicting orientations of vested interests in the industrial sector. For instance, in the former Conservative–Liberal government, the Conservative Minister of Environmental Affairs pushed for price increases in carbon emission licences in order to set further incentives for emission reduction, whereas the Liberal Minister of Economy and Technology would block these initiatives due to concerns about the additional costs that could arise for German industry. In the more recent grand coalition government of Conservatives and Social Democrats, these conflicts persist, even though both the economic and environmental affairs ministries are headed by Social Democrats. In fact, the Minister of Economic Affairs underlines the need for the continued use of coal to prevent major price shocks for German industry and private households. Doing this directly rejects further governmental interventions regarding the utilisation of specific power plants, while the Minister of Environmental Affairs insists on the elimination of the most emission-intensive coal-fuelled power plants. The pro-coal coalition among Social Democrats and Conservatives has seemed to hold (Meiritz 2014), and may even persist beyond the September 2017 federal elections .

In view of these bargaining processes and wide-ranging conflicts over interests and ideas, the German style of environmental policy has been outlined as a regulatory state with a strong legal basis. This is accompanied by inter-party bargaining involving regional interests in a federal multi-level system, with corporatist patterns of interest mediation between government, private sector and civil society. All of this is located within culturally rooted concerns with environmental affairs. The ensuing policy style resembles a pattern of 'regulated self-regulation'. This is because business actors take part in sector-specific and allegedly voluntary agreements, with self-commitments that are moderated by government, and also allow for the inclusion of interest groups from civil society (Bailey 2007). Examining the actual mixture of governance structures that operates in the 'energy turn' of Germany's coordinated capitalism, yields an institutional pattern that involves market mechanisms, regulations and private sector governance. All these mechanisms are contested with regard to their functional efficacy in the transition towards a low carbon regime.

Market instruments include participation in the European Union's carbon emissions trading scheme since it began in 2005, which built on Germany's preceding liberalisation of electricity and gas markets starting in the late 1990s. Yet this market-based scheme has suffered from an over-allocation of allowances, which has lowered the carbon price in a manner that obstructed further encouragements for a significant reduction in emissions. New caps on emissions defined at the EU level, and set to be progressively reduced, should hopefully contribute to more effective market operations. In fact, the most crucial problem with this emissions trading system relates to the fact that national success in emissions reduction leads to a release of emission certificates, which means that emissions might increase in other European countries. Thus, in the context of tradable emission certificates, the overall effectiveness of national efforts in emissions reduction might be called into question (Andor *et al.* 2017).

Policy-driven regulations include aspects such as technological and emissions standards, as well as politically moulded price regulations. A critical element of these market regulations is the system of feed-in tariffs that is used to promote electricity from renewables. As outlined above, this German feed-in tariff system implies that electricity generated from renewable energy sources has preferential access to the grid, priced on the basis of feed-in tariffs that outline technology-specific pricing above market rates over a 20-year period. This system has actually become an international role model, despite its disadvantages with regard to the distortion of price signals and corresponding disincentives for the suppliers of electricity from renewables (Andor *et al.* 2017). Indeed, the latter problem currently informs the tendency towards a market-oriented shift in regulations to support renewables. Auctions have recently been introduced to augment the feed-in tariff system, with a more competitive and potentially cost-reducing mechanism. First rounds were held for solar photovoltaic in 2016, while further auctions are also planned for onshore wind (FS-UNEP Centre 2017).

Private sector governance includes the operations of industry associations and voluntary agreements among private sector firms, as applied to carbon emissions in the automobile industry for example. The latter may be singled out as a characteristic of the relational mode of coordination in the German variety of capitalism. Indeed, when addressing these voluntary agreements on emissions reduction, one could even speak of a German brand of eco-corporatism. This is illustrated by the major roles played by BDI and the German federal government in the promotion of industrial commitments to emissions reduction (DIW *et al.* 2001). An initial Climate Change Self-Commitment was signed in 1995 as a largely symbolic gesture, followed by more ambitious agreements in 1996 and 2000 that would involve various energy-intensive sectors and related industry associations in undertaking a reduction in carbon emissions. However, the impact of these private sector and associational forms of governance in driving the low carbon economy transition is subject to ongoing analysis. In fact, self-commitments were soon replaced by fiscal efforts for an ecological tax reform, that would resemble policy-driven regulations. In 1999, initial steps were taken by introducing a so-called eco tax on the consumption of fossil fuels, originally excluding coal due to its political relevance to the electorate. Manufacturing firms were initially granted 80 per cent in tax reduction, a concession that was later downgraded to 40 per cent (Bailey 2007). In the longer run, thus, it seems that the German model of industrial self-regulation has not been successful in markedly reducing carbon emissions in its own right. Nonetheless, it may be argued that it facilitated the introduction of market-oriented instruments in climate change policy, as implied in the negotiations on the implementation of the EU emissions trading scheme. In this manner, the regulatory drive of associational governance may have paradoxically contributed to a further marketisation of the instruments of climate change mitigation (Klein 2012).

The actual design and implementation of these policy strategies and governance structures is subject to the interventions of distinct coalitions of actors. In broad terms, advocacy coalitions in the renewable energy policy area include actors from business firms, industry and employer associations, unions, civil society organisations, political parties and government. While most decisions are made on the level of the federal state and nationwide organisations, the regional level also needs to be taken into account in Germany's federal system. The regional states, *Länder*, are particularly relevant in the support of wind and solar thermal energy, for they play a key role in spatial planning. In terms of the representation of distinct interests and related ideologies, however, one can distinguish between business and ecological concerns – and related advocacy coalitions (Dagger 2009). Business concerns tend to focus on the profitability of renewables. Major players in that domain are the major energy suppliers of E.on, RWE, Vattenfall Europe and EnBW. The related industry association is the Bundesverband der Energie- und Wasserwirtschaft (BDEW). Unions also take part in this advocacy coalition as they articulate the interests of the workforce in the concerned firms and industries. Importantly, the corresponding union in mining, chemicals and energy, the Industriegewerkschaft Bergbau, Chemie, Energie (IG BCE), stands out as an advocate of more conventional energy sources, such as coal. This coalition is well represented in government, in particular in the Ministry for Economy and Technology, BMWi. In political terms, the liberal FDP party has been this faction's most outspoken representative, along with large segments of the conservative CDU and also by certain Social Democrats, who have been politically strong in the traditional heavy industry region of the Ruhr area (Reiche 2004).

Ecological concerns stand for the equal funding of all renewables. They tend to strive for a fundamental transformation towards renewables as quickly as possible, and they are in favour of feed-in tariffs to accomplish that transformation. Industry associations involve the following organisations: Bundesverband Erneuerbare Energie (BEE), Bundesverband Solarwirtschaft (BSW-Solar), Bundesverband Windenergie (BWE), Verband Deutscher Maschinen- und Anlagenbau (VDMA). Unions in this coalition include IG Metall, which is prominent in Germany's competitive industries, such as automobiles and machine tools. Yet the union of the integrated service sector, ver.di, and the union of agrarian and environmental industries, IG Bauen-Agrar-Umwelt, also promote a proactive attitude towards renewables.

The related organisation in government is the Ministry for Environmental Affairs, the Bundesministerium für Umwelt, Naturschutz und Reaktorsicherheit (BMU). Also, the interest association of German farmers needs to be taken into account, as organised in the Bauernverband (DBV). It is well represented in the federal Ministry for Agrarian Affairs, the Bundesministerium für Ernährung, Landwirtschaft und Verbraucherschutz (BMELV). Corresponding political camps are more difficult to detect. The Green Party stands out in this regard, yet parts of SPD, CDU/CSU and the former Communists of the Linke also take part in these endeavours.

Examples of this kind of ecological alliance building are manifold. Quite prominently, a working group on the trade of emission licences has been set up by organs of the federal state, including the BMU, accompanied by major firms, industry associations and even organisations from the environmental movement. In this manner, the Arbeitsgruppe Emissionshandel zur Bekämpfung des Treibhauseffekts (AGE) has been instrumental in sorting out workable regulations for the trade of emissions licences (BMU und AGE 2012). Also, industry unions are a part of key consultations with government and business, as documented by diverse declarations on resource efficiency, environmental innovation and emissions trade, involving IG Metall along with BMU (BMU and IGM 2006; 2008). Representatives from IG BCE have also been invited to join the Council for Sustainable Development, which is a consultative platform for environmental affairs established by the government in 2001. Industry-specific dialogues on environmental issues between labour unions and employer associations are also common, such as that between IG Metall and the German association of aluminium industries (IGM und GDA 2009).

Furthermore, the expansion of renewables was initially driven by new entrants to the market, involving business firms, citizen cooperatives and professional environmental groups, who combined the environmental and social concerns of a social movement for sustainability in a discourse that would later shape the discussions and practices of the *Energiewende* . Their impact on the expanding sector of renewables was most obvious in onshore wind, biogenic fuel, biogas and solar photovoltaic. Subsequently, business actors would gain in influence as large firms came to enter promising market segments (Geels *et al.* 2016). For instance, the initial introduction and adoption of wind turbines on a small scale was driven by utilities, as well as by farmers and environmental groups who, in the 1980s when Germany's new social movement of ecologically concerned protests gained in influence, combined an ecological programme of sustainable development with anti-nuclear anxieties (Jacobsson and Lauber 2006). Also, in its early stages the photovoltaics industry in Germany seemed to be driven not only by business firms, industry associations and government, but also by civil society and environmentalist social movements. On the regional and local levels, these alliances have driven cluster formations in this industry, and thus contributed to the diffusion of related 'green' technologies (Fuchs and Wassermann 2013).

In effect, the low carbon transition of the German economy proceeds on a hybrid basis with both market and non-market coordination, in a manner that reflects the institutional specificities of the German variety of capitalism, and its ongoing institutional evolution.

Conclusion

Germany follows a distinct trajectory in the transition towards a low carbon economy. The corresponding patterns of industrial and technological specialisation reflect the specificity of the prevailing national production model, as well as the institutional conditions and settings. The production model of the German economy is still biased towards diversified quality production in the manufacturing industries, with the automobile industry as a paradigmatic lead sector. The corresponding German innovation system, with its specialisation in gradual types of technological change, is part of a hybridised coordinated variety of capitalism. This hybrid character of German capitalism is reflected in the policy mix of market-oriented, regulatory and associational approaches to the governance of low carbon transition. The transition towards a low carbon economy relies on these industrial structures and institutional patterns, which provide opportunities for new low carbon innovations, which are particularly relevant in the domain of renewable energy sources. Indeed, German efforts in the expansion of renewable energy have been impressive, including with regard to their innovative impact. However, as a specifically German phenomenon, nuclear energy is set to be phased out in the coming decades. The corresponding transition mechanisms in this *Energiewende* are subject to ongoing controversies regarding the efficacy of market-breaking price regulations and subsidies, versus market-conforming instruments such as auctions. Thus, while the share of renewables in the energy mix is increasing further, the transition towards a low carbon regime of production and innovation also needs to account for the private costs of this process. Accordingly, the German transition towards a coordinated 'green capitalism' remains both economically and politically contested.

6 Norway's low carbon strategy

Internal and external drivers

Jon Birger Skjærseth and Torbjørg Jevnaker

Introduction

Norway's stated objective is to become carbon neutral by the year 2050. This will prove extremely challenging, particularly as fossil fuels continue to dominate the Norwegian economy. Oil and gas contribute 14 per cent of the state's revenues and 40 per cent of total exports. The transformative effect of oil and gas has had significant ramifications for other sectors of the Norwegian economy by opening up huge markets for shipbuilding, engineering, information technology and other business services. It has benefited national manufacturing industries and strengthened the economy through rapidly increasing tax revenues, which are filling up the world's largest sovereign wealth fund. Production of oil and gas is the cause of more than one-quarter of Norway's greenhouse gas (GHG) emissions. Leading up to 2050 the Norwegian government will be faced with the dilemma of managing the key national interest of maximising profits from the oil and gas sector on the one hand, while decarbonising the economy on the other. This chapter explores how, why and to what extent Norway has embarked on the transformation towards a low carbon economy, as a response to the global challenge of climate change.

Norway's low carbon strategy and the prospects for change are analysed from two perspectives with different relevances for varieties of capitalism (VoC) theory (Hall and Soskice 2001). The first, a domestic politics perspective, indicates that the key drivers of change in the face of an international challenge can be found at the domestic level, rather than emanating from abroad. As such, Norway's low carbon strategy – its national response to the international challenge of climate change – is expected to be the product of domestic factors. Domestic drivers are essential in VoC theory, which places particular emphasis on relationships between companies and the national institutions in a state's political economy. Differences in national responses to common problems are explained by the state (or government itself), the society, or the relationship between state and society.

The second perspective takes us from domestic politics to the external context, particularly the European Union (EU). The EU's decarbonisation target – reducing GHG emissions by 80–95 per cent by 2050 – may affect Norway's climate policy and energy strategies in various ways. First, EU legislation may directly affect Norwegian public policy for low carbon transformation. Although Norway is not an EU member, it is deeply integrated into the EU energy and climate regulatory system through the Agreement on the European Economic Area (EEA). This agreement gives Norway access to the EU's internal market in exchange for harmonisation with relevant EU legislation (UD 2012a). Second, EU policies may affect domestic alliances and institutions by strengthening alternative energy technologies. Finally, the EU has a market effect that may weaken the fossil fuel regime. As the EU takes almost all Norwegian gas exports today, any significant reduction in European gas use will hurt the Norwegian economy. Oil is traded globally and, in theory, can be sold beyond Europe, but large reductions in European oil use will represent a challenge to any Norwegian finance minister. Norwegian oil and gas interests would be challenged even further if the EU should develop into a firm and credible global force for decarbonisation, contributing to reduced worldwide petroleum demand. According to this 'Europeanisation' perspective, the key sources of Norway's low carbon strategy are found within the context of EU climate, energy and innovation policies. The possibility that external policies may develop and affect a country partly outside national control, and that country's economic energy interests, is not an integral component of VoC theories.

The following section briefly introduces some key institutional features that, when combined with petroleum interests, make radical transformation a challenge in Norway. The third section analyses Norway's low carbon strategy. The fourth section explains the development of this strategy and assesses the prospects for change from both domestic and EU perspectives. The chapter ends with concluding remarks.

Institutional context

Norway is generally classified as a coordinated market economy (CME) in the VoC literature, along with nine other OECD countries (Hall and Soskice 2001). These economies are characterised by institutions that promote strategic interaction among firms and other actors, informal contracting in the legal system, high rates of unionisation, equal income distribution, incremental innovation and policies that encourage collaboration among firms. Most of these factors also depict Norway's low carbon strategy, in particular that of incremental change and innovation.

Norway is characterised by at least three state-society features that impede a radical transformation towards a low carbon economy. First, Norway can be seen as a neo-corporatist country in which institutionalised rights of participation in policy-making are provided to non-state interests in all phases of governmental policy (Katzenstein 1985; Gullberg 2011). However, business (and labour) interests enjoy better access than environmental organisations and other groups pushing for sweeping change in climate policy. Second, low carbon transformation requires policy integration among sectors of society, such as energy, transport and agriculture. The disjunction between the 'holism' of the natural world and the fragmentation of the administrative and organisational relationships for developing and implementing change, has often been criticised (Weale 1992). The suggested 'cure' is some version of an integrated climate policy, or policies, that can penetrate all the policy levels and governmental agencies involved in its execution. Low carbon policies in Norway have traditionally been fragmented and developed within the con-fines of affected sector ministries. There is, for example, a deep split between the Ministry of the Environment, which has the main responsibility for climate policy, and the Ministry of Petroleum and Energy. The exception is the Ministry of Finance, which has exerted pressure on sector ministries to make technology-neutral and cost-efficient climate instruments. Finally, strong interest alliances related to the petroleum and energy intensive indus-tries hamper fundamental change towards a low carbon economy. These include the major political parties, corporations, industry associations, employer organisations and labour unions. The upshot is that the combina-tion of strong neo-corporatism, sector-based policy-making and strong interest alliances representing traditional economic interests make radical change difficult.

Norway's low carbon strategy

Norway has been actively engaged in international climate negotiations ever since the issue first attracted international attention. During the UNFCCC negotiations in 1991 Norway argued – unsuccessfully – for common and quantitative cuts in emissions. It focused on the 'cost-effectiveness' principle and argued that Norwegian money would be better spent abroad, since climate change is a global problem and abatement costs are high in Norway. Domestic emissions were expected to rise significantly, due mainly to the increase in offshore oil and gas production. To counter this rise in emissions, Norway adopted a national stabilisation target and one of the world's first CO_2 taxes in 1991. The tax was focused on the petroleum sector. In the early 1990s, Norway also started to explore carbon capture and storage (CCS) for oil recovery and natural gas (Skjærseth and Skodvin 2003).

The main principles and direction of Norway's climate policy have remained the same throughout: cost-effectiveness, carbon pricing, solutions abroad and research and development (R&D) within low carbon technology (Miljøverndepartementet 2012). Norway's climate targets are, first, to reduce global GHG emissions to 30 per cent of Norway's emissions by 2020, when compared to 1990 levels.[1] This creative wording shows that Norway intends to fulfil a significant part of this obligation abroad (Miljøverndepartementet 2012). Second, Norway seeks EU cooperation to achieve a 40 per cent reduction within the EU by 2030. The 40 per cent target serves as the EU's commitment to the Paris Agreement. Third, Norway aims to be 'carbon neutral' by 2050. Although this resembles decarbonisation by entailing the neutralisation of emissions, the term carbon neutral differs in the sense that emission reduction carried out elsewhere can be considered.

With regard to international commitments, Norway was allowed to increase its emissions by 1 per cent compared to 1990 during the Kyoto negotiations. Under the Protocol's second commitment period (2013–2020) Norway is expected to reduce GHG emissions by 30 per cent by 2020, when compared to the projected growth in emissions for this date. Norway is not bound by the EU's headline targets for 2020, 2030, or its vision to decarbonise by 2050. However, Norway has implemented parts of the EU climate and energy legislation following from the 2020 targets,and is expanding its cooperation with the EU 2030 climate policy.

An important component of Norway's low carbon strategy is to promote low carbon solutions abroad. Besides purchasing external credits under the Kyoto Protocol's flexible mechanisms to over-comply with its Kyoto obligations, Norway is investing in the reduction of deforestation in developing countries.[2] At the Bali climate conference in 2007 Norway launched a major deforestation programme, pledging to contribute NOK 3 billion annually until 2015 to counter deforestation. The innovative part of this financial mechanism lies in its basis in partnership and verified results. Norway has partnered with Brazil, Indonesia and Guyana, which will get funding after they have verified deforestation results compared to a baseline (Miljøverndepartementet 2012).

Domestically, the most important cross-sector policy instrument is still carbon pricing, which creates incentives for companies to invest in low carbon solutions. The petroleum sector (mainly offshore oil and gas production) has been subject to CO_2 taxes since 1991, which has had tangible effects, such as facilitating CO_2 storage at Norway's Sleipner gas field since 1996 (Christiansen and Skjærseth 2005; 2006). From 1998 on, the tax rates on oil and gas in the North Sea have dropped significantly (Christiansen 2002). In 2009, this sector became part of the EU Emissions Trading System (EU ETS). The CO_2 tax was subsequently reduced according to the anticipated ETS allowance price, based on the principle that total emissions costs for the petroleum sector should remain unchanged.

In parallel with the initiation of the first phase of the EU ETS, Norway adopted a domestic emissions trading system in 2005. All allowances were allocated free of charge. From 2009, the Norwegian system became fully integrated into the EU ETS, which was in its second phase (2008–2012). This integration meant that more allowances had to be paid for and that all allowances to the petroleum sector had to be auctioned. About 40 per cent of Norwegian emissions were covered in this period. In the current third phase (2013–2020), around 50 per cent of emissions are covered (Statistics Norway 2016). The change from free allocation to auctioning as the main method for distributing emissions allowances for electric power production did not directly affect Norway – electric power production in Norway is based almost entirely on hydropower. To comply with the EU ETS, Norwegian companies, like other EU companies, may purchase a certain number of international credits. Norway has also been allowed to use state aid to compensate energy-intensive companies for expected increases in electricity prices as a result of the EU ETS (ESA 2013). While this is intended to counter so-called carbon leakage, it also acts to counter company incentives to save energy.

Norway has adopted sector-based climate action plans for transport, buildings, agriculture, forests, petroleum, industry and energy. In 2015, petroleum (28 per cent of total emissions) and industry (22 per cent of total emissions) were the main sources of GHG emissions (Statistics Norway 2016).[3] In the petroleum sector, emissions increased by 83 per cent between 1990 and 2015, and are projected to continue increasing towards 2020, before levelling out. Policies and measures in this sector have focused on limiting the growth in emissions. Since 1996, oil companies have been mandated to consider electrification from land to offshore installations as part of the licensing process. Four offshore fields covered energy needs from on-shore electricity in 2012 (Miljøverndepartementet 2012).[4]

Finally, R&D on CCS has been an important aspect of Norwegian climate policy vis-à-vis the petroleum sector. Between 2007 and 2011, the government granted almost €1 billion to CCS technology development and the CO_2 Technology Centre Mongstad was opened in 2012 as a test facility for various CO_2 capture technologies (Miljøverndepartementet 2012). The centre was partially owned by the state through its CCS agency (Gassnova) and through Statoil (two-thirds state-owned), as well as other companies (BBC 2012). Preparations for full-scale CO_2 capture at Mongstad gas-fired power plant and refinery took place in tandem with the development of the test facility.[5] Described by former Prime Minister Jens Stoltenberg as 'Norway's moon landing' in his 2007 New Year's speech, the full-scale capture project was cancelled after the elections in 2013, officially due to unforeseen technological challenges and high costs (OED 2013).

Land-based, energy-intensive industry was the second most important Norwegian emission source in 2015, accounting for 22 per cent of GHG emissions. Since 1990, CO_2 equivalent emissions have decreased by 39 per cent (Statistics Norway 2016), due mainly to new technologies in aluminium (PFK gases) and fertiliser production (nitrous oxide) and lower activity. The sector receives the majority of its required ETS credits free of charge, and a mechanism for compensating companies for indirect ETS costs was adopted in 2013 (ESA 2013). The main plan for this sector, in addition to carbon pricing, is R&D for climate-friendly technological development. Following the climate agreement between the political parties in 2012 (see below), a new climate technology fund was established, estimated to grow to €6 billion in 2020 (total capital was roughly €4.3 billion in 2013). From 2013 onwards, the fund received substantial allocations (€1.2 billion in 2013, €0.6 billion annually 2014–2016) (Adressa 2013; TU 2012d). In part, the allocations stem from a support scheme for renewable energy, which was made redundant by the introduction of green certificates in 2012 (Miljøverndepartementet 2012). Returns from the fund are meant to strengthen technological development in energy-intensive industry.

Norway differs from other countries since most inland stationary energy consumption is covered by electricity – with renewable hydroelectric power accounting for about 96 per cent of total electric power consumption (Miljøverndepartementet 2012). For these purposes, then, energy savings and new renewable energy will have a limited effect on GHG emissions in Norway, compared to most other countries. The development of new renewable energy has remained roughly stable since 1990 – but this is slowly changing. In January 2012 a green certificate system was launched in conjunction with Sweden, to subsidise renewable energy. The goal was to increase the joint production of renewable electricity by 26.4 TWh by 2020. In Norway, most of the increase would come from more hydroelectric, with some wind power. However, most of this clean power has been built in Sweden, due to its more favourable tax regulations (TU 2014a). The green certificate system is the main instrument for achieving Norway's target under the EU Renewables Directive.[6] While Sweden has decided to continue with the system beyond 2020, Norway will not participate after 2020.

Despite these climate policies, Norwegian CO_2 equivalent emissions increased by 4.2 per cent between 1990 and 2015 and are projected to continue increasing towards 2020 (Statistics Norway 2016).

Assessment of Norway's climate strategy

Norway aims to become carbon neutral by 2050. Depending on the share of this burden taken within the country, this will require policies and strategies for radical change. The innovation literature distinguishes between incremental and radical change (Smith 2011). Incremental innovation comprises small changes in known techniques, products and production processes, such as the electrification of offshore installations or more effective car engines. Radical changes entail the introduction of new products and processes that (over time) fundamentally alter the production process or the quality of the outputs (Freeman and Perez 1988). Such changes tend to challenge existing markets and companies within traditional production systems. Innovations like CCS, may form a part of radical change. Since companies that are strong in traditional production systems tend to resist radical change, public policy is needed. Transformation towards a low carbon economy is likely to require forceful public policy, such as carbon prices that are sufficiently high to facilitate low carbon innovations, or subsidies that are adequate to make renewables competitive.

Thus far we have focused mainly on the policy dimension. Carbon pricing based on the cost-effectiveness principle has been Norway's dominant climate policy instrument since the early 1990s. While the number of sectors exposed to pricing has increased, the carbon price has actually decreased. The EU ETS has encountered major problems due to the economic crises and generous imports of external credits, leading to an over-allocation of allowances and a very low carbon price. A low carbon price means weak incentives for companies to invest in low carbon technologies – the lock-in of old polluting technologies is therefore the most likely result of an insufficiently high carbon price (Skjærseth 2013). How the carbon price will develop in the future depends on the implementation of new EU climate and energy policies towards 2030, including reforms of the EU ETS (see below).

Electricity production from renewable energy has remained high and roughly stable since 1990. Renewable production is set to increase by 26.4 TWh between 2012 and 2020 as a result of subsidies generated by the green certificate system with Sweden (OED 2011). Norway will fund half of this and, although it is intended that new capacity is evenly distributed between Norway and Sweden, economic calculations will ultimately be the decisive factor. During its first year of operation, the green certificates market led to an increase of 3.2 TWh in renewable electricity production, of which 0.4 TWh was in Norway, mainly consisting of hydropower (NVE and Energimyndigheten 2013). Green certificates are a technology-neutral instrument that supports the most mature technologies. In Norway, this basically means more hydroelectric power and some onshore wind power (Bergek and Jacobsson 2011). Due to limited capacity on existing and planned interconnectors to non-Nordic countries, the certificates market is expected to contribute to a Norwegian, as well as Nordic, electricity surplus in 2020 (TU 2012b, 2012c). There has been a lively debate in Norway as to whether this should be exported (and if that would, in fact, contribute to reducing total emissions in Europe, given the overall cap set by the EU), or if it should replace the use of fossil fuels in the transport and petroleum sectors. Two interconnectors are currently being constructed, one to Germany and one to the UK.

Norway has increased its R&D spending on low carbon technology, particularly CCS. Large sums have been spent on CCS innovation, especially linked to capture and storage from natural gas. To date, this effort has failed to realise full-scale CCS plants. The most innovative change in Norwegian climate policy seems to have taken place abroad. The forest initiative, for example, may bring significant global achievements by counteracting deforestation in developing countries. It should also be noted that changes have taken place in sectors not specifically covered here. For example, Norway has more electric cars per capita than any other country, due to state incentives (DW 2013).

The main conclusion is that Norway's current domestic policies are directed towards incremental, rather than radical transformation towards a low carbon economy. The incremental element essentially involves limiting expected domestic growth in emissions by carbon pricing, and by increasing renewables in the short term. There have also been serious attempts to instigate CCS innovation. This situation gives rise to several questions: Why is it so difficult to bring down emissions in the petroleum sector? Why did the production of energy based on renewable energy sources (RES) remain fairly stable until 2012, and why is it set to increase only in the short term? Why has Norway focused increasingly on low carbon technologies, CCS in particular? Finally, why has Norway adopted a relatively ambitious climate policy, given its reliance on the petroleum sector and traditionally high level of renewable energy production?

Explaining Norway's low carbon strategy: stability and change

Norway's low carbon strategy is characterised by both stability and change. Stability includes a reluctance to adopt new sources of renewable energy (except for hydropower) and making investments in low carbon solutions abroad based on the cost-effectiveness principle. It also encompasses political priorities that have led to steady increases in the importance of the fossil fuel regime for domestic emissions and the economy as a whole. Change includes wider use of carbon pricing, a temporary break with the previous stability in renewable energy production towards 2020 and a greater focus on climate-friendly technologies. In the following, we explore the causes for both observed stability, and change from both domestic and EU perspectives.

Domestic politics, transformation and innovation

Public policy for transformation[7]

Public policy is important for innovation processes. In democratic systems, societal demands represent a significant force in shaping public policy. Public policy, however, is not driven solely by societal demands. Governments have their own views and the capacity to act independently. In the late 1980s, a green wave of public concern for the environment washed over Norway. In 1987, the UN Commission on Sustainable Development – led by the then Prime Minister, Gro Harlem Brundtland – issued what has become known as 'the Brundtland Report'. This report, titled *Our Common Future*, emphasised climate change as a major problem. Thus, it came as no surprise that Norway was the first country in the world to adopt a unilateral stabilisation target for CO_2 at 1989 levels by the year 2000. Moreover, in 1991 Norway was, as previously noted, among the first countries to introduce a CO_2 tax, which mainly covered offshore petroleum activities. That move encountered strong opposition from the entire oil industry – including Statoil, even though it was a fully state-owned company at the time.

However, initial political enthusiasm was soon replaced by pragmatic economic concerns. As a petroleum exporter, Norway was expecting a steep increase in its emissions of CO_2 from petroleum activities (to the order of 60 per cent from 1989 to 2000). Stringent policy instruments could affect petroleum markets and exports – and almost one-third of total Norwegian export income came from petroleum exports. Moreover, as Norway's electricity production is based overwhelmingly on hydropower, this limits the country's potential to reduce emissions by changing onshore electricity consumption patterns. This leaves the offshore petroleum sector as one of the largest sources of domestic CO_2 emissions. New renewable energy sources, such as wave, wind, solar and bioenergy, have not traditionally been high on the Norwegian political agenda. In 1997 the first specific target for bioenergy and water-borne central heating was set. Unlike the situation in many other European countries, incentive-based instruments to increase renewable energy usage had only seen limited use in Norway (Christiansen 2002). The structure of Norway's energy consumption and its dependence on petroleum exports led Norway to seek solutions abroad rather than at home.

The debate over a Norwegian CO_2 target started in 1987 and culminated with the stabilisation target adopted in 1989. The ambitious target came as a result of a 'green beauty contest' between the political parties in the Storting (the Norwegian parliament) (Bergesen *et al.* 1995). With the adoption of the CO_2 tax, Norway kept a high international profile during the negotiations that started in early 1991 – in fact, Norway had leadership ambitions in international climate politics. The Norwegian climate strategy was based on a range of principles, including quantitative targets, timetables and flexible international mechanisms. By autumn 1991 flexibility had come to overshadow domestic cut-backs, and Norway was not prepared to sign an agreement that lacked joint implementation (Tenfjord 1995). The UNFCCC resolved Norway's main concerns, and Norway ratified the Convention in 1993.

After Rio, it became evident through work on the national climate action plan that strong and far-reaching domestic policy instruments would be needed to break the expected growth in GHGs by 2000. It was clear that the stabilisation target could be reached only by much tougher policy instruments than the CO_2 tax (Reitan 1998). In 1995, after a significant delay due to conflicting interests, Norway published a white paper on climate policy that formed the basis for its reporting to the UNFCCC in which Norway officially abandoned its stabilisation goal (Miljøverndepartementet 1995). In the final approach to the Kyoto Protocol, Norway focused on differential commitments and flexibility mechanisms. The government proposed that Annex 1 countries commit themselves to a 10–15 per cent emissions reductions by 2010. However, Norway did not want to take part in the reductions and argued for emissions targets of 5 per cent above 1990 level for 2008–2012. However, this figure was reduced to 1 per cent during the negotiations. Norway was actually among the few OECD countries that came to Kyoto without a national target.

In 1996, Naturkraft – owned by the companies Norsk Hydro, Statoil and Statkraft – applied for a licence to build two gas-fired power plants.

This application triggered a fierce environmental struggle in Norway that highlighted the tension between national versus international reductions. Opponents of the project took the position that new plants would increase total national emissions, whereas proponents argued that Norwegian gas could replace Danish coal and Swedish nuclear power. The Labour government supported the new plants. Their problem was to convince the opponents that the gas would actually replace coal, and not come in addition to it.

In 1997 the Labour government was replaced by a centrist coalition consisting of the Christian Democratic, Liberal and Centre (formerly Agrarian) parties. In 1998 this coalition re-adopted a national target aimed at bringing emissions back to 1989 levels by 2005. In a white paper on climate policy, the coalition government argued that a combination of domestic policy instruments and flexible international mechanisms were needed to fulfil international commitments (Miljøverndepartementet 1997). The coalition opposed gas-fired power plants that would result in increased domestic emissions and proposed a tax of NOK 100 per ton of CO_2 to cover – at minimum – land-based energy-intensive industries exempted from the existing CO_2 tax. The government combined their proposal for a tax extension with opposition to gas power based on current technology.

The proposal encountered strong opposition from industry. It was defeated in the Storting, and the majority decided to assess a future emissions trading system instead, envisioned as one that would allow for free or very cheap allowances to the industry (Kasa 1999). Eventually, the coalition resigned due to its divergent position vis-à-vis the majority in the Storting, with respect to gas-fired power plants. The Labour government that followed subsequently signalled a shift back to a predominantly international approach. That shift was countered by yet another coalition government, consisting of the Conservatives, Christian Democrats and Liberals. In 2002 this new government proposed the implementation of an emissions trading system for 2005. The system focused on companies exempted from the CO_2 tax. This approach was continued by successive governments.

Norwegian climate policy has, as shown above, been characterised by deep political conflicts. However, 2008 saw a broad based political compromise ('the climate compromise') being agreed to by all the major political parties in parliament, (with the exception of the Progress Party). The compromise included both the red/green coalition government (Labour, Socialist Left and the Centre Party) and the opposition parties (Conservative, Liberal and Christian Democratic). Once again, the main issue was reductions at home versus abroad. The compromise underpins the main direction of Norway's present low carbon strategy, which comprises domestic reductions to the tune of a two-thirds decrease in GHGs, reinforcing R&D on low carbon solutions, and projects to counter deforestation in developing countries (Miljøverndepartementet 2008). The resumption of negotiations with Sweden on a green certificate system was also part of the compromise.[8] In 2012, the same parties as before adopted a new iteration of this climate compromise, which included some new measures, more research on low carbon technologies and a strengthening of the climate technology fund, but the main picture was one of maintenance rather than renewal of Norway's low carbon strategy. In 2013, the red/green coalition was replaced by a new minority coalition consisting of the Conservatives and the Progress Party, which declared that it would continue to base its climate policy on the climate compromise, thereby bringing the Progress Party on board.

We may conclude therefore that the development of Norwegian climate policy was marked by deep political conflicts until 2008. The dilemma had been how to combine an ambitious climate policy with industrial use of gas power on land and a strong petroleum industry. The conflict has now been dampened by a formal climate compromise involving all the main political parties. This compromise gives weight to the policies already adopted but may also block the way for more radical policies.

Societal demands for transformation

Societal demands for transformation affect not only politicians, but also companies engaged in activities associated with environmental risk. Organised societal interests can influence consumer behaviour and thus be important determinants for corporate decision-making, creating pressure and opportunities.

Norwegian attitudes to climate policy and the environment have fluctuated significantly over time. Regular surveys on the importance of environmental and energy issues, conducted as a part of national election research show quite dramatic variations. In 1989, environment and energy ranked as the second most important political issue overall, and 37 per cent considered it be the most important. By 1993, it had dropped to fifth place, and was considered most important by only 7 per cent of those surveyed (Aardal and Valen 1995).

Fluctuations are also shown in Norsk Monitor studies. In 1989, 61 per cent of those surveyed characterised the situation as 'grave' and agreed that there was a need for 'drastic action'. By contrast, the corresponding figures in 1997 and 1999 were 34 per cent and 28 per cent respectively. Of five environmental problems, global climate change was ranked after ozone depletion and acid rain in the Norsk Monitor study. In addition, general fears about climate change decreased significantly. In 1989, 40 per cent of those surveyed said they were very worried, whereas only 22 per cent were worried in 1997.

Norsk Monitor's tracking of environmental concerns shows that the downward trend continued until 2001–2002, peaked in 2007 and decreased again to 2011. Concerning climate change, about 10 per cent said they were *very* concerned in 2001, nearly 30 per cent in 2007 – and only 13 per cent in 2011 (Hellevik 2013). Another poll indicates only a minor decline in concern since 2008 – about 40 per cent of those surveyed said they were concerned about climate change (Klimaløftet 2011). Despite these differences, the change in attitudes in Norway seem largely in line with the patterns following from Downs' (1972) idea of issue-attention cycles.

There had not been a truly 'green' party in Norway until the 2013 elections, when the Green Party *(Miljøpartiet de Grønne, MDG)* secured one seat out of the 169 in the Storting. This party promotes a radical policy, including a reduction in petroleum activities and large-scale investments in renewables. Its low representation has been explained by the general sensitivity of the political system to new societal demands. Up to the present day, existing political parties have largely managed to absorb a potential 'green' party electorate. Few voters perceive environmental issues as important for party choice, except for two smaller parties – the Socialist Left and the Liberal – which have, to some extent, filled the niche for a 'green' party. In the 2013 elections, the Socialist Left received seven of the 169 seats in the Storting, and the Liberal nine seats.

Norwegian green NGOs are well organised, and they have mobilised against gas-fired power stations. It was actually a Norwegian NGO – Bellona – that first proposed CCS as a compromise between proponents and opponents of gas power (Tjernshaugen and Langhelle 2011). Norwegian NGOs were spilt on the issue of CCS, but support for CCS has grown and significantly influenced the position of others, including the Socialist Left Party (Tjernshaugen and Langhelle 2011). As the Socialist Left Party was a part of the red/green coalition government, its shift in position contributed to the building of the political foundations for CCS. Following the 2013 election – when the centre-right parties gained a majority – the Office of the Auditor General of Norway published a report criticising the government's management of CCS projects (Riksrevisjonen 2013). The new government – comprised of the Conservatives and the Progress Party – followed up by announcing a rethink regarding Norway's CCS strategy (OED 2013).

Thus, societal concerns and demands for climate policy have fluctuated but have not proven stable or strong enough for politicians to embark upon a policy for radical change, or for consumers to demand significant changes in corporate strategies. There has essentially been no strong societal demand for a truly *low carbon* strategy. A low carbon strategy is mainly favoured by some small political parties and green NGOs.

Linking supply and demand for transformation

People and governments, or states and societies, are linked by institutions that channel influence. One important influence channel is the corporate channel whereby industry, interest organisations and government decision-makers meet formally and informally to consult, negotiate or collaborate. Non-governmental interests do not respond solely to societal demand and governmental policies; they represent a societal interest group with the potential to influence government policy for transformation and innovation. Norway is, as previously mentioned, traditionally classified as a neo-corporatist country. This means that institutionalised rights of participation are provided to non-state interests in all phases of governmental policy. Norwegian politics are characterised by corporate interests, particularly coalitions and alliances between interest groups, industrial interests, employer organisations and trade unions. These alliances are capable of exerting a significant influence on energy and climate policies (Hanson *et al.* 2011).

Reducing oil and gas exploration and production on the continental shelf can contribute to bringing down domestic emissions. More importantly, a reduction in oil exported for consumption elsewhere can help to bring *global* emissions down (Fæhn *et al.* 2013). However, Norway's oil industry, with Statoil in the lead, has no such intentions – instead, it has been pushing to extend exploration further north. This has encountered significant opposition from the green movement and the small green political parties, which have temporarily succeeded in limiting expansion somewhat, due to fishery and environmental concerns. The Norwegian state is the majority owner of Statoil (67 per cent since 2009), which has traditionally served as the key state instrument for protecting Norwegian petroleum interests. The link between Statoil and the state is therefore particularly strong, and Statoil has a privileged status as a 'core' insider. However, there is also a broad-based alliance composed of the largest political parties, industrial interests, employers' organisations and trade unions that supports a strong and expanding petroleum sector in Norway.

This support may decline as a result of the rise in exploration costs, declining export markets and prices or domestic macroeconomic concerns. A government-appointed committee consisting of representatives from the Ministry of Finance, the two largest employers, trade unions and Statistics Norway has argued that Norway should slow down its exploration and development of new fields, for economic reasons (NOU 2013).[9] That proposal was promptly dismissed by the government but, in a related development in March 2014, it decided to solicit a comprehensive study of the pros and cons of moving the €700 billion sovereign wealth fund out of fossil fuels (which currently comprise almost 10 per cent of the fund's investments). The fund has an ethical board that can make decisions on withdrawal of investments from specific companies based on moral considerations. The fund is required to divest from companies that derive at least 30 per cent of their business from coal. In 2014, the fund divested from 53 coal companies around the world.

The transformative effect of oil and gas has been significant to the Norwegian economy. The development of the Norwegian petroleum sector since the 1970s has opened up a huge market for other companies, such as shipbuilding, engineering, information technology and other business services. It has also benefited national manufacturing industries and strengthened the economy through rapidly increasing tax revenues. Norway has avoided the 'poverty of plenty', or Dutch disease syndrome, by building up the world's largest public pension fund – a sovereign wealth fund managed by the Bank of Norway. State revenues from the petroleum sector are placed in the fund. The fund's investment strategy is to maximise profit, although with a low-risk strategy, with a broad spread of investments. Although this has been subject to political controversy, successive Norwegian governments have exerted self-restriction regarding use of the fund. It has become customary practice not to use more than its annual returns, estimated to be about 4 per cent. Without these funds, there would have been a deficit in the state budget, making the oil fund important for state expenditures (Ministry of Finance 2013).

The country's petroleum industry has been characterised as possessing a strong innovation system that has also enabled Norwegian companies to become globally competitive as production and supplier companies. As a consequence, economic growth has been consistently higher and unemployment lower than in Western Europe as a whole (Fagerberg *et al.* 2009). Norway (like most of the world) is essentially locked into a fossil regime in which resources, knowledge, policy, technology, organisations and business are directed towards exploration, production, distribution and consumption of fossil energy (Hanson *et al.* 2011). A key challenge is to transform this fossil energy regime into a regime based on low carbon energy and solutions.

The issue of non-methane volatile organic compounds (NMVOC) emissions represents a concrete example of how oil companies can block public policy. An effort was made to reduce NMVOC emissions from shuttle tankers that indirectly lead to CO_2 emissions.[10] Negotiations began in 1998 between the Norwegian authorities and the oil industry on an agreement for reducing such emissions from shuttle tankers loading crude oil. The negotiating parties were the Ministry of the Environment and the oil industry, represented by 18 companies with licence interests on the Norwegian continental shelf. The aim of the agreement was to apply best available technology (BAT) on all 20 relevant ships by 2005.[11] In the end major US oil companies refused to support the deal, and the agreement collapsed. This example demonstrates that multinational companies can affect government policies of host countries, in addition to their influence in their home countries. Moreover, it points to the link between policy instruments and the climate strategies of influential companies.

Even though the oil industry in general, and the Norwegian petroleum industry in particular, exercise significant influence, the Norwegian government was still able to adopt a CO_2 tax in 1991 that had a specific focus on this industry. In 1989 the Environmental Tax Committee was established to assess the foundations for a CO_2 tax. This committee was expert-dominated and did not include representatives from interest organisations. The first report, which provided the basis for the 1991 tax was not even made public. Thus, industry and environmental organisations were effectively prevented from formally influencing the premises for the tax. Moreover, the parliamentary decision to mainly implement the tax on offshore activities, was made in the face of strong resistance from the entire petroleum industry (Reitan 1998; Kasa 2000). There was also heavy opposition from energy-intensive land-based industry, which feared that the tax would be expanded.

In the end, the Norwegian petroleum industry – offshore oil and gas production – lost in their opposition to the CO_2 tax.

Whereas the petroleum and energy-intensive industry regimes make the transformation towards new renewable energy more difficult, some of the same alliances have exerted influence on climate-friendly technology policy. The industrial opposition to the extension of the CO_2 tax to land-based energy intensive industries helped to shift political attention towards technology and CCS (Kasa 2011). The energy-intensive industry has traditionally been supported by the Conservative and Labour parties and it is well organised through both trade and employer organisations.[12] Its opposition was combined with a proactive policy for solving Norway's key climate policy dilemma, that of combining an ambitious climate policy with industrial use of gas power and a strong petroleum industry. The main answer to this dilemma was CCS, characterised as 'political glue' in Norway (Tjernshaugen and Langhelle 2011). With CCS, the basic aim was to continue industrial development within the framework of new climate policy restrictions. An alliance of environmental NGOs, industrial actors, research institutes, trade unions and employers' organisations were the driving force behind this development (Kasa 2011).

In conclusion, Norway's neo-corporatist nature is still important for understanding the country's climate and energy policy. The dominant interests are linked to the petroleum and energy-intensive industries, which have evolved through strong alliances that have the power to shape Norway's low carbon strategy. These alliances can also block new energy technologies that appear to lack strong support, such as new renewable energy. Norway has not succeeded in building strong innovation systems for new RES-electricity production, heat or transport (Wicken 2011). The stability of this influence persists despite some mobilisation for policymakers to reduce exploration for domestic economic reasons. It promotes incremental change and policies on low carbon technologies that combine preservation of these interests with an ambitious climate policy. That in turn raises a further question: How to build up new technological regimes within the boundaries of a fossil fuel regime?

EU policy, transformation and innovation

Although not a member of the EU, Norway has participated in the EU's internal market since 1994 through the Agreement on the European Economic Area. This agreement grants Norway access to the single market in exchange for Norwegian implementation of EEA-relevant EU legislation. Norway's non-membership excludes it almost entirely from EU decision-making (Tallberg 2012). During negotiations on the EEA Agreement, EU climate and energy policy was not expected to have much significance for Norway, being less developed at the time. However, these policy areas were significantly boosted over the next two decades. Beyond domestic politics, then, it is to be expected that Norway's low carbon strategy has been affected by EU policies.

EU policy directly affects Norway's national public policy for transformation. The most important measures in the EU climate and energy package from 2009 – the EU ETS and the Renewable Energy Directive – have been implemented in Norway. The EU ETS has become an important part of Norway's low carbon strategy by expanding the number of sectors subject to carbon pricing. However, the government was sceptical towards the other measures included in the EU's climate and energy package, fearing that these could undermine the effect of the ETS (Miljøverndepartementet 2012). Increasing the production of power from renewable sources was not regarded as something that would reduce Norway's emissions, as the country's power supply was already almost entirely RES-based (offshore excluded). Despite resistance from Norwegian authorities, Norway had to accept a commitment to increase its share of renewables in total energy consumption to 67.5 per cent by 2020, up from 58.2 per cent in 2005 (UD 2012b). To increase its RES-based electricity production, Norway established the common green certificates market with Sweden.

Concerning CCS, the Norwegian government regarded itself as having played an important role in the development of the EU's CCS Directive (UD 2012a). Implementation was delayed for years due to details on liability and permitting storage of CO_2 offshore that were not welcomed by the Norwegian petroleum administration (Jevnaker 2015). However, the Directive will not fundamentally change Norwegian practice on CCS. In contrast, the *Fuel Quality Directive* (FQD) might fundamentally change Norwegian practice. A reference year for reducing emissions from fuels was set to 2010, a decision that spurred controversy because Norwegian companies had taken steps to increase efficiency prior to this date. Major stakeholders in Norway – Statoil, Esso/ExxonMobil and the Federation of Norwegian Industries – were therefore opposed to this proposal, and were supported by the Environmental State Secretary (deputy minister) at the time. Norway did not get derogation on this issue, which means that it will need to enact strict requirements on its fuel producers to increase efficiency.

The EU climate and energy package and other EU policies have affected Norway's major sectors in different ways. Concerning petroleum, the government has repeatedly underlined that the EEA Agreement does not apply to the Norwegian continental shelf – but the EU has had some direct impact on Norwegian policies for oil and gas. This includes being partially responsible for removing the preferential treatment Norwegian companies received in licensing, and was the direct cause of the disbanding of the *Gassforhandlingsutvalget* (GFU), a centralised state body for managing Norwegian gas sales (Austvik and Claes 2011; NOU 2012). The EU has also affected Norwegian low carbon strategies in the petroleum sector, which is regulated by CO_2 taxation and emissions trading. During the second trading phase of the EU ETS (2008–2012), companies within the Norwegian petroleum sector had to purchase ETS allowances, but the third phase (2013–2020) defined them as vulnerable to carbon leakage. This allows them to receive allowances free of charge.[13] The Norwegian government was initially opposed to granting free allowances to the petroleum industry, but failed to get a concession on this from the EU (Klif 2011). As a result, in 2012 the government made revisions to allow flexible adjustments of the CO_2 tax to sustain the costs of petroleum sector GHG emissions (Finansdepartementet 2012).

Energy-intensive industries exposed to international competition, have been subjected to less stringent climate measures in Norway (Miljøvern-departementet 2012). Voluntary agreements have been extensively used. EU legislation has led to wider usage of carbon pricing, covering some 90 per cent of industrial emissions from 2013 (Miljøverndepartementet 2012). It has also resulted in changes to industrial policy, by targeting the Norwegian schemes for providing this sector with long-term contracts for cheap electricity. While the support was more or less sustained, the system had to be changed in a more market-oriented direction to be compatible with EU legislation. A system of guarantees provided by the state, with a market-based premium paid by the companies, was established (NOU 2012). Similarly, the geographically based exemptions from Norway's electricity tax had to be removed. This was circumvented by setting the national tax level so low that industry in the special geographical areas could be exempt from paying this levy under EU state aid rules (NOU 2012: 562).

EU legislation has also affected the structure of the power sector in Norway. The differential treatment of state and private owners of hydro-power plants – the former being granted never-ending licences, the latter not – had to be abolished; although the government used the opportunity to adopt legal changes that meant two-thirds of any hydropower project had to be owned by the state (NOU 2012). The EU's steps towards integrating electricity markets put pressure on the delicate balance between energy-intensive industries and power producers due to the latter's conflicting views on electricity export. Moreover, the EU's 2009 electricity market directive challenges the current setup of the public administration, as it requires that energy regulators are to be independent of their sector ministries.

Concerning energy technology and innovation, Norway participates in the EU Strategic Energy Technology (SET) Plan and contributed to the EU-wide research programmes for 2007 to 2013 (Seventh Framework Programme for Research and Technological Development, FP7) and 2014–2020 (Horizon2020: the EU Framework Programme for Research and Innovation).[14] The SET Plan in particular may strengthen Norwegian interests linked to new RES technologies, such as offshore wind power.

If realised, the EU 2050 decarbonisation strategy will be challenging for Norwegian petroleum-export interests, particularly as long as affordable CCS technologies are not available. From a Norwegian perspective, the big picture is that fossil fuels are under pressure. Future developments will depend first on developments in Norway. For example, Norwegian gas production is expected to fall after 2020 (TU 2012b). Combined with the uncertain future role of gas exports to the EU, investments in new infrastructure and the renegotiation of long-term gas supply contracts will be a challenge for

Norwegian petroleum interests. Moreover, the development of the energy mix in the EU is uncertain. With the low carbon roadmap towards 2050, the future role of fossil fuels after 2030 will depend heavily on the development and commercialisation of CCS. Norway has invested significant resources in CCS development applied to gas, as noted, albeit with limited success so far. Finally, the realisation of a low carbon economy in the EU will hinge on whether key states implement the Paris Agreement.

EU as key for unlocking the carbon path?

The main impact of the EU with regard to decarbonisation has been on Norwegian public policy. EU climate and energy policy account for a large part of Norway's wider use of carbon pricing, as well as for the subsidies and targets to increase the share of renewable energy towards 2020.[15] The greater focus on climate-friendly technology, CCS in particular, has been largely domestically driven. The EU SET plan will underpin and promote further emphasis on other types of climate-friendly technology related to renewables, buildings, energy storage and electro-mobility.

Norway has put a heavy emphasis on national sovereignty over its energy mix, strategy and policy. As an important supplier of oil and gas to EU member states, Norway could be expected to enjoy greater leverage vis-à-vis the EU in energy issues, as compared to other policy areas. Instead of merely accepting EU legislation, Norway has contributed to the shaping of EU policy, as with the CCS Directive. However, Norway's influence on EU policies may have been weakened as a result of the deep split in interests between the Ministry for the Environment, with main responsibility for climate policy, and the Ministry for Petroleum and Energy. This split obstructs the ability of the government to develop a unified Norwegian position at the outset of EU policymaking processes, while also making it more difficult for the EU to manage its relations with Norway with regard to decarbonisation.

Norwegian societal demands for transformation are not likely to be directly affected by the EU. Norway has an EU-sceptical population and few decision-makers or voters tend to consider Norway in an EU context. Still, EU climate and energy policy has strengthened Norwegian green groups in domestic policymaking, particularly Bellona, whose presence in Brussels gives it expertise that it can employ strategically at home.

The EU may also affect Norwegian processes that link supply and demand for transformation. First, Norwegian stakeholders have less influence on EU policies (that will affect Norway) than they have on domestic policymaking. Although companies like Statoil can seek to influence decision-making processes at the EU level directly, or indirectly, through European industry associations, their relative influence compared to Norwegian decision-making processes is substantially lower. Second, EU policies have necessitated institutional changes, such as the removal of differential treatment in licensing

within the petroleum and the power sectors and the removal of the GFU –
yet these have failed to lead to significant changes in practice. However, EU
energy market legislation might bring about greater changes in Norwegian
energy regulation.

Third, the expansion of power production could, over time, affect traditional alliances and decarbonisation policy. The increase in electricity production due to the RES Directive strengthens the power sector's interest in
expanding capacity for cross-border trade (to avoid depressed electricity
prices), thereby bringing it into direct conflict with the energy-intensive
industry's interest in lower prices. Although other options exist – like increasing the use of electricity in other sectors such as transport and petroleum – it
hardly seems surprising that the power industry has turned to export as a
viable strategy for selling surplus power. While the government has been
ambitious regarding electric vehicles, total electricity use for such purposes
remains relatively small. Green parties have fought for change, but the government has not pushed for electrification of offshore petroleum installations
remains, which to be decided on a cost-benefit basis for private companies.
The government has taken a careful approach not to alienate the energy-
intensive industry, seeking only gradual expansion of capacity for cross-border
electricity transmission capacity to non-Nordic countries (interconnectors are
planned to the UK and Germany).

Finally, a potential avenue for change lies in the involvement of Norwegian actors within the framework of the SET Plan. As Norwegian companies
and researchers participate in research programmes that prioritise specific
alternative technologies, this could serve to strengthen domestic groups that
promote these solutions, as contrasted with groups that promote technologies
not supported through EU research.

Concluding remarks

This chapter explored how, why and to what extent Norway has embarked
on a transformation towards a low carbon economy. Norway's stated long-
term objective is to become carbon-neutral by the year 2050. This chapter's
main conclusion is that Norway's current policies and measures are directed
towards incremental, rather than radical, transformation at home, despite
serious attempts to instigate CCS innovation. This strategy is combined with
significant investments in low carbon solutions abroad. Norwegian policy
essentially involves an attempt to reduce the growth of domestic emissions
through carbon pricing, and by increasing renewables somewhat in the short
term. Thus far, this strategy has not reduced domestic emissions as compared
to 1990, which have continued to grow despite carbon pricing.

Norway's carbon strategy has been characterised by both change and
stability. The first conclusion is that domestic factors appear most important
for understanding stability. These include reluctance towards adopting new
sources of renewable energy, other than hydropower, and investments in low

carbon solutions abroad based on the cost-effectiveness principle. It also includes political priorities, which have led to steady increases in the importance of the fossil fuel regime for both its contribution to domestic emissions and the economy.

Public policy for transformation has been marked by deep political conflicts on how to combine an ambitious climate policy with industrial use of gas power on land and a strong petroleum industry. This conflict was dampened in 2008 by a formal climate policy compromise between the main political parties. Societal demands for transformation have not been sufficiently stable, or strong enough, for politicians to embark upon a policy of radical change. Another key to understanding Norwegian policy stability lies in the link between state and society. The dominant interests are linked to the petroleum and energy-intensive industries, which have evolved through strong alliances that have had the power to shape Norway's low carbon strategy. These alliances can also block new energy technologies that appear to lack support equivalent to their clout. The stability of this influence promotes incremental change, and policies on low carbon technologies that can combine preservation of these interests, with an ambitious climate policy such as CCS. Domestic drivers and incremental change is largely in line with VoC expectations concerning coordinated market economies.

The second conclusion is that external influences, particularly the EU, appear most important for understanding change in Norway's strategy. Changes include wider use of carbon pricing and a temporary break with the previous stability in the proportion of renewable energy production towards 2020. EU climate and energy policy largely explain Norway's wider use of carbon pricing, enacted through the EU ETS along with subsidies and targets to increase the share of renewable energy towards 2020. EU policies have also necessitated institutional changes and may affect traditional alliances underpinning current policies. By prioritising alternative energy technologies, EU policies can serve to strengthen the domestic groups that promote these solutions, as contrasted with groups that defend traditional technologies.

We have also seen that EU policies have been 'filtered' through domestic interests and institutions. This is in accordance with expectations from the VoC perspective. However, the EU has also affected institutions by channelling interaction and influence between state and societal actors, including the interrelationship among firms and between firms and the state. It seems that the VoC approach is slightly more static, because it regards external input as being filtered exclusively by existing institutions. As such, domestic change should occur in the *direction* set by existing institutions, making this change 'path-dependent'. However, as we have seen in this chapter, external developments could place pressure on a country to respond in ways in which its domestic institutions would not predispose it. EU policies, in part, have pulled Norwegian low carbon strategy in a direction other than the one its domestic institutions would have pulled it. The most striking example of this is the RES Directive, and more long-term EU policies – decarbonisation by 2050 – might very well place further pressure on the Norwegian low carbon strategy.

The EU's long-term decarbonisation policy is essentially at odds with the interests of Norway as a large petroleum exporter. According to Hall and Soskice, a country's stance on cooperation and new regulatory initiatives will be influenced by whether these will sustain or undermine the comparative advantages of the nation's economy. Governments will be inclined to support initiatives that do not threaten the institutions most crucial to the comparative advantages enjoyed by their firms. By downplaying external influences, VoC seems to ignore the possibility that, over time, external polices may develop partly outside national control. The main reasons are a combination of EU policy development since Norway signed the EEA Agreement, and Norway's exclusion from EU decision-making. As noted above, external policies developed by the EU and internationally may actually be the cause of the most change, which could – under certain conditions – unlock the Norwegian carbon pathway in the long term.

For 2030, EU climate and energy policies are in the making. Norway will be subject to the implementation of these policies, scheduled for adoption by the EU before 2019. Their ambitiousness will affect the Norwegian carbon pathway in the long term.

Notes

1 Facts and figures in this section are largely based on Miljøverndepartementet (2012), Statistics Norway and the Norwegian Environment Agency.
2 Norwegian companies also purchase a certain number of external credits to comply with the EU ETS.
3 Other major sources of emissions are road transport (19 per cent) and air/ship/ fishing (12 per cent).
4 By the end of 2013, 92 fields were in operation (Oljedirektoratet 2014).
5 As for CCS, Norway has been storing CO_2 in geological structures on the continental shelf (i.e. offshore) since 1996 (Sleipner field) and has worked with industry to implement CCS on gas-fired power plants (Miljøverndepartementet 2009).
6 Norway has agreed to increase its share to 67.5 per cent RES-based energy consumption in 2020, from 62 per cent in 2010.
7 This historical survey is based on Skjærseth and Skodvin, 2003.
8 Sweden introduced a green certificate system in January 2005. Norway started to negotiate a common system with Sweden, but these negotiations were abandoned in 2006. The official reason was that the system would be too expensive for Norwegian consumers.
9 One argument is that Norway's dependence on petroleum revenues requires a controlled reduction in activities to meet the expected drop in future revenues (NOU 2013).
10 The formation of ground-level ozone is, however, the main problem associated with NMVOC in combination with NOX.
11 In total, this would cost about NOK 2 billion and lead to reductions to the tune of 70 per cent from each ship. Introduction of BAT on shuttle tankers is

considered the most effective means to redeuce NVMOC, in terms of costs and effects to the petroleum sector (Dragsund *et al.* 1999).

12 This alliance stems from the importance of energy intensives in smaller, urban areas outside Norway's major cities, providing value creation and employment, and thus also ensuring continued settlement, which has been important for district interests.

13 The reason is that the European oil industry was able to change their proposed status from energy industry (subject to auctioning) to energy-*intensive* industry (subject to free allowances based on performance benchmarks) in the 2008 EU ETS reform.

14 Norway's gross annual contribution to FP7 was more than one billion NOK (NOU 2012).

15 However, emissions trading might have been implemented in Norway in any case.

7 China

Greening China's state-led growth regime

Miranda A. Schreurs

Introduction

As China faces growing pollution problems and political pressure to deal more effectively with environmental damage, the political leadership is turning its attention to how it can improve the economy's environmental performance. Climate change, although not the highest priority for China's leadership, has been put more firmly on the agenda. China was a signatory to the Kyoto Protocol but was not obliged to reduce its carbon emissions under the agreement. For many years China's leadership argued that China had the right to develop, and that the main responsibility for climate change lies with rich countries, namely the United States, Europe, Japan, and others that have historically been the greatest emitters of global warming gases. China's stance appears to be evolving however. In November 2014, President Xi Jinping announced that China would work to cap its greenhouse gas emissions by approximately 2030. With China now the world's largest emitter of greenhouse gases, this announcement was heralded as a potential turning point in global efforts to address climate change. This soft 2030 target was ultimately incorporated into China's Nationally Determined Contribution for the Paris Agreement. This may also be a sign of change from the Chinese model of state-led capitalism, toward a form of capitalism that more strongly embraces energy, resource efficiency and pollution control.

China as a type of state-led capitalism

During the Mao era (1945–1976), the Chinese state nationalized industry and collectivized agriculture. In the post-Mao era, China's leaders focused on ways to raise the nation out of poverty and into the ranks of middle-income countries. In a step-by-step process, the state privatized significant industries and opened up markets to foreign investment. Many steps were taken to promote rapid growth. Local cadres were rewarded with career advancement based on their region's economic performance. Energy prices were subsidized to support industrial production and to encourage economic growth. In 2012, China ranked sixth in the world in the amount of fossil fuel consumption subsidies, estimated to be worth about 0.3 percent of gross domestic product (GDP) (International Energy Agency 2013a). Tax breaks were also offered to promote new industries. As a result of these and related policies, within just a few decades China emerged as the world's manufacturing capital for both domestic consumption and export.

There has been a substantial shift away from the social market model. Private firms now dominate in many sectors, with only about 25 percent of industrial output by state-owned firms, down from roughly three-quarters at the end of the Maoist era. Whereas in 1995 about two-thirds of China's total exports emanated from state-owned firms, in 2010 they only accounted for about 11 percent. Where state-owned firms still lead is in strategic industries, including electric power, water, coal, and steel. They also continue to monopolize the oil and gas extraction industries (Lardy 2011: 76–87).

With its transition from a primarily socialist market-based economy toward a more capitalist-dominated one, China does not fit neatly into the standard varieties of capitalism typology. Some scholars have found similarities to the developmental state concept coined by Chalmers Johnson for Japan as China has become increasingly capitalist. Johnson (1982) defined a developmental state as a plan-rational system, in which a government with a strong administration fosters industrial development in a capitalist economy. It does this by working closely with industry in setting priorities and creating supportive policy frameworks for investment. As a late industrializer, the Japanese state intervened in the market to encourage the growth of those sectors deemed important to long-term economic and societal well-being (Johnson 1982; Woo-Cummings 1990). This concept has subsequently been applied across East Asian countries of different political orientations (ranging from democratic to authoritarian), including China, as a state in which the central government has played an active role in promoting particular forms of industrial policy (Haggard 1990).

Drawing on Robert Wade's work related to the governed market, Seung-Wook Baek also identified elements of the developmental state in China:

> the high rate of domestic savings, the huge infrastructure of heavy industry, the promotion of industrial policy, the legacy of central planning, labor-intensive industry [accompanied] by import substitutive capital-intensive industry; a strong central government with a huge bureaucracy; and corporatist control over the society.
>
> (Baek 2005: 487)

Nee, Opper, and Wong similarly noted the important role played by the strong authoritarian national leadership and the elite state bureaucracy in pursuing "developmentally-oriented policies, including direct means of governing the market" (2007, 20). They questioned however whether state intervention has facilitated growth in China, or if growth has largely been the result of labor market liberalization, the growing openness to foreign trade, infrastructure investment, property reforms, and quasi-privatization. Following a similar line of argumentation, Andrzej Bolesta (2015) has termed China "a post-socialist developmental state," which, he argues, aims to guide the trajectory of development while also carrying out a systemic transformation that includes economic liberalization, market institutionalization, and microeconomic restructuring.

China is a Communist state with a market that still exhibits some vestiges of socialist elements, but that has an increasingly dominant capitalist structure. Some of these capitalist components are closer to the liberalized economic model and others more closely resemble a coordinated market model. As such, it is not surprising that the country does not fit easily into the categories identified in the varieties of capitalism literature. China could be classified as a system with a type of "variegated capitalism," or capitalism with Chinese characteristics, including a relatively stronger state than other cases of this type (Zhang and Peck 2014). This chapter takes up this notion by labeling China a state-led growth regime, that is increasingly incorporating environmental considerations into its planning.

Greening Chinese development

Throughout the post-Maoist period, Chinese leaders have emphasized the need for economic growth and development. Deng Xiaoping, widely revered in China for his vision and leadership, promoted economic reform and socialist modernization through the development of a socialist market economy. Economic catch-up with the West was a driving goal. Many steps were taken to promote rapid growth. Local cadres were rewarded with career advancement based on their jurisdiction's economic performance. Energy prices were subsidized to support industrial production and to encourage the growth of an automobile sector. Tax breaks were offered to promote new industries. The Chinese state's efforts paid off. China emerged as the world's manufacturing capital, producing for both domestic consumption and export, and is now the second largest economy in the world.

China's rapid economic development however, came at a high environmental price. Swift economic expansion, population growth, and problems with enforcing environmental laws, all contributed to China's serious pollution challenges. China suffers from grave levels of essentially all forms of pollution. The poor air quality found in many urban and industrial areas is brought about by the burning of coal, oil, wood, and agricultural crops, all of which contribute to the release of particulates, air pollutants, and greenhouse gases. Acid rain has spread and become significantly worse since the 1980s. Desertification, a consequence of groundwater loss, contributes to the country's sandstorm problems. Climate change could contribute to more rapid desertification as water availability is reduced. The deforestation of vast parts of the country in the previous century reduced China's natural carbon sinks (NDRC 2013).

Pollution was dismissed for a long time as a necessary, if undesirable, by-product of economic growth. Environmental laws were only laxly enforced, if at all. The growth first, pollution control later mentality is slowly beginning to change for a variety of reasons, including the high cost of pollution-related damage, rising public dissatisfaction with pollution, international efforts to influence Chinese approaches to growth, concerns about long-term energy security, and improved awareness of the economic opportunities in the green economy.

Perhaps most alarming to Chinese leaders are the various reports highlighting the large economic losses that pollution is causing the Chinese economy. The World Bank estimated that the total health and ecological costs of China's air and water pollution in 2003 equated to between 2.67 and 5.78 percent of GDP, depending on the methodology employed (World Bank and State Environmental Protection Administration, PRC 2007). A joint report issued by the World Bank and the Development Research Center of the State Council in 2014, noted that the economic costs of poor health from air pollution have been estimated at between $100 billion and $300 billion (World Bank 2014: 452).

The Organization for Economic Cooperation and Development put the cost of outdoor air pollution in terms of lives lost and ill health at $1.4 trillion in 2010 (OECD 2014).

The model of economic growth to catch up and develop at all costs started to be questioned by an increasingly well-off population. There is rising public dissatisfaction with environmental conditions, concern about the impacts of pollution on human health, and anger about government corruption, which has been displayed in widespread public protests against pollution (Sun and Zhao 2008; Moore 2009; Li 2008/2009; Ma 2009). Quite a striking number of pollution complaints have been lodged by citizens and this figure has been rising over the years. From 1991 to 1993 Chinese environmental authorities reported receiving 130,000 complaints about pollution (Dasgupta and Wheeler 1997). By 2006 the number of pollution complaints had risen to 600,000 (Liu, Dong and Wang 2011). The government no longer announces complaint figures at the national level but there is other evidence of widespread dissatisfaction. In the first five months of 2014 the public registered 12,599 formal complaints about smog with the Beijing Municipal Environmental Bureau (a 124 percent increase over the same five-month period in the previous year) (Reuters 2014).

Related to this are concerns about the large inequalities and unbalanced distribution of benefits and burdens. Due to China's substantial economic inequality, there are 'First World–Third World-like' dichotomies between urban and rural areas, and between the coasts and the interior. There are substantial differences in terms of which regions of China are the most and least polluted, along with the chasm between regions with the strongest and weakest pollution control capacity. It is largely the urban coastal regions of China that are booming economically and thus are the biggest resource consumers. The richer coastal areas are enjoying China's growing wealth and large-scale investment, while many inland and western regions are primarily resource suppliers to the rest of the country. It is therefore, in the coal-producing regions and industrial manufacturing centers where pollution is most severe. Thus, efforts to address greenhouse gas emissions are being linked to efforts to deal with development inequalities across the country.

Chinese government leaders are aware that if conditions do not improve, there could be more unrest and even political destabilization, as happened in central and eastern Europe in the lead-up to the collapse of the Soviet Union. Some of China's biggest challenges lie with policy implementation. The problems range from a lack of sufficient societal awareness, an incentive structure that still favors economic growth over pollution control, inadequate monitoring and enforcement capacity, to an environmental administration that has neither sufficient capacity nor power to effectively implement many of the rather progressive environmental laws found on the books. The main objective of the new laws and programs being introduced by the central state is to strengthen environmental performance through improved environmental governance.

International actors have played a role in shifting understandings of the relationship between economic development and environmental protection. This is demonstrated by the conversion from a view that pollution control is an impediment to economic growth, to the idea that environmental protection and efficiency improvements can enhance economic sustainability. International actors have also brought many new ideas to China. Multinational companies are increasingly demanding that their suppliers meet higher environmental and labor standards.[1] After the US Embassy in Beijing began publicly monitoring and reporting air pollution levels, pressure increased on Chinese officials to do the same. Daily air pollution readings are now reported in much the same way as the weather is presented. International environmental NGOs, such as WWF, Natural Resources Defense Council, and Greenpeace, have opened offices in China and are engaged in pollution abatement, nature conservation, and climate change campaigns, with the acceptance of Chinese state authorities (although their activities are closely watched).

There is also growing anxiety among Chinese authorities about how to supply sufficient energy and resources to keep the growth model going. The country is becoming increasingly dependent on energy and other resource imports. With a population increase of several hundred million expected over the next decades, the country is focused on promoting energy efficient, resource efficient, and low carbon urbanization.

Linked to this, are a growing number of political and economic actors who are beginning to see considerable innovation potential in the green economy. The Global Commission on the Economy and Climate notes:

> China offers perhaps the most striking example of new policies. It has embarked on a historic structural transformation that has global implications: both directly, because of China's role in the world economy, and

indirectly, by the lessons it provides to other developing countries. China is moving away from a development model based on rapid growth in capital accumulation and energy-intensive industries, powered largely by coal. It is seeking to move toward an economy based on growth in domestic consumption and services, with stronger innovation and more efficient resource use, powered increasingly by cleaner forms of energy.

(2015: 22)

China is already well on the way to becoming a global leader in green technology development and exports, alongside the United States, Germany and Japan (Schreurs 2012).

Environmental governance reform

Statements from the top leadership reflect a growing recognition that China's development path must change, with greater attention being given to environmental protection, resource efficiency, and wealth distribution. In April 2006, Prime Minister Wen Jiabao in an address to an annual national environmental congress stated:

We must be fully aware of the severity and complexity of our country's environmental situation and the importance and urgency of increasing environmental protection. Protecting the environment is to protect the homes we live in and the foundations for the development of the Chinese nation. We should not use up resources left by our forefathers without leaving any to our offspring. China should be on high alert to fight against worsening environmental pollution and ecological deterioration in some regions, and environmental protection should be given a higher priority in the drive for national modernization.

(Wen 2006)

Aware that pollution could derail Beijing's plans to host the Olympics, extensive efforts were made to clean up the environment through a mix of long-lasting and temporary measures, including restricting diesel truck traffic, limiting automobile traffic through a license plate numbering system, shutting down heavily polluting factories, raising auto fuel emission standards to European levels, and halting construction.

In 2013 President Xi Jinping made a statement suggesting that for the first time, the environment would not hold second rank to the economy in China's development. The president stated that the environment should not be sacrificed for temporary economic growth and pledged to establish an ecological "red line," requiring all levels of government to ensure that industrial development occurs within the constraints of natural conditions. "We have to understand that to protect the environment is to preserve our productivity and to improve the environment is to develop our productivity.

Such concepts should be deeply rooted" (China Council for International Cooperation on Environment and Development 2013).

The Central Committee of the Communist Party has issued a series of decisions to guide economic, political, social, and ecological planning over the coming years. It has also called for deepening reforms to help realize an "ecological civilization system." This is to include reforms in environmental protection management, environmental monitoring and enforcement, and ecosystem conservation and restoration.

China's energy structure, air pollution and greenhouse gas emissions

China's air pollution and climate change challenges are intertwined with its energy structure. Fossil fuels are dominant in the energy mix. As a result of economic restructuring, energy-saving measures, research and development, and the diffusion of energy-saving technologies, China's energy intensity has been decreasingly sharply. China's GDP grew 18-fold between 1980 and 2010, but its energy consumption grew a relatively paltry five-fold (World Bank 2014).

Environmentally, China's biggest problem is its heavy dependence on coal. But there are some indications that coal use may have peaked. The share of coal in the primary energy mix decreased from 76 percent in 1990 to 69 percent in 2005 and remained fairly constant at that level for the next decade, then declined once again to about 65 percent of the total, but China is still the world's largest producer and consumer of coal (US Energy Information Administration 2014). In a promising development the Chinese government did decide to cancel plans to build over 100 additional coal fired power plants (Forsythe 2017).

Changing energy consumption patterns and improving energy efficiency will be critical in the way China deals with climate change. Despite improvements in energy productivity of close to 5 percent per year since 1990, China now accounts for about one-third of the global growth in oil consumption (World Energy Council 2013).

In 2012, per capita greenhouse gas emissions in China (7.1 tons) were still well below those in North America (16.4 tons in the United States and 16.0 in Canada) but almost on par with the EU average (7.4 tons). They exceeded France's levels (5.8) and are approaching those of the United Kingdom (7.7) and Germany (9.7) (PBL Netherlands Environmental Agency 2013). With its enormous population that is nearing 1.4 billion, its increasingly large middle class, and its rapid economic growth rates (averaging 9.1 percent per annum from 1989–2014), China overtook the United States as the world's largest greenhouse gas emitter around 2007 (Trading Economics, n.d.).

A considerable share of these emissions is embedded in international trade (according to one estimate, around 29 percent of the country's greenhouse gas emissions in 2007 were embedded in exports), reflecting the strong carbon intensity of the manufacturing sector (Qi 2013: 102). According to the Stockholm Environment Institute, China would not have a carbon export surplus (exporting more carbon than it imports) if each of its industries had the same carbon intensity as its US counterpart. China's competitive advantage is in low-cost labor, not in low-cost carbon, and its exports tend not to emanate from its most carbon-intensive sectors (Ackerman 2009).

Launching a war against air pollution

The State Environmental Protection Administration was upgraded to the Ministry of Environmental Protection in 2008 and to the Ministry of Ecology and Environment in 2018. In the past, the ministry was small in terms of personnel numbers (about 300 in Beijing, 150 in regional offices, and another 2,000–2,500 in supporting agencies) and budget. The successive elevation of the status of the ministry is symbolic of the government's growing environmental commitments (Gang 2008). The Ministry of Ecology and Environment prepares annual State of the Environment reports and participates in international environmental cooperation. It is also responsible for preparing and administering environmental laws, formulating environmental standards, and addressing air pollution matters.

An Air Pollution Control Action Plan was issued in late 2013 covering ten main areas for action, including combining government regulation with market adjustment mechanisms, enhancing monitoring and enforcement, and strengthening regional cooperation. Numerous specific goals were set within the action plan's framework. Overall, national air quality was to be improved within five years, with heavy pollution levels to come down specifically in Beijing-Tianjin-Hebei Province, the Yangtze River Delta, and the Pearl River Delta. Control of particulate matter is a major focus of the legislation. Other measures in the plan included: better treatment and reduction of discharge from multiple pollutants; accelerating the introduction of desulfurization, denitrification, and dust removal equipment; eliminating older vehicles; promoting public transportation; controlling the introduction of energy-sapping, high-pollutant industrial facilities; and fostering environmental industries, including the use of clean energy. The consumption of coal in the energy mix was to drop to 65 percent by 2017 (from 66.8 percent in 2012) and its use was to be reduced in major urban centers. The national action plan also called for the development of provincial level action plans, encouraged the setting of absolute coal consumption caps, and aimed to slow down the growth of coal consumption. Twelve of the country's 34 provinces, cumulatively responsible for just under half of total coal consumption, have made pledges. Combined, the pledges equate to a 350 million ton reduction by 2017, and a 655 million ton reduction by 2020, compared with a business as usual growth rate (Ministry of Environment of the People's Republic of China 2013). At the opening of the annual meeting of the National People's Congress in March 2014, Premier Li Keqang declared war on air pollution: "We will resolutely declare war against pollution as we declared war against poverty" (Blanchard and Stanway 2014).

In 2014 the Standing Committee of the National People's Congress also approved the first revisions to China's 1989 framework environmental law. The revisions placed a stronger emphasis on environmental monitoring and enforcement, and introduced a system of cumulative daily fines for not meeting environmental standards. Polluting enterprises were also to be publicized in an effort to shame companies into action. The law strengthened the hand of the Ministry of Environmental Protection, although this was still not sufficient given its small size and weak status relative to other ministries (Tiezzi 2014; CCICED 2014).[2] Hence, the ministry's status was enhanced in 2018.

Significantly, the law puts a far greater focus on reporting, monitoring, and enforcing the standards. It stipulates that local governments must take measures to protect threatened areas and stay within "ecological redlines." The law further prohibits construction projects where environmental impact assessments have not been conducted and establishes pollution fees for discharges. The fees are to be used exclusively for environmental protection purposes. The new law also emphasizes the importance of environmental performance reviews for local government officials, which are now mandatory. Also noteworthy are provisions that strengthen citizens' rights to participation, supervision, and information. Greater expectations are also being placed on citizens to assist with reporting violations. The biggest changes to the law have to do with strengthened legal liability. This includes the imposition of penalties that are to accrue daily on firms that fail to follow orders to comply with standards, and even criminal detention for up to 15 days for responsible persons.[3] Through both this initiative and previously mentioned environmental measures and institutions, the Chinese government is strengthening its environmental governance capacities. This is important if the Chinese government is serious about shifting toward an ecologically sensitive, state-led, capitalist growth regime.

Energy efficiency and renewable energy as measures for addressing climate change

The National Development and Reform Commission (NDRC), China's powerful economic planning body, has the lead responsibility for climate change. This responsibility was shifted to the Ministry of Ecology and Environment in 2018. The NDRC linked China's national climate strategy to its energy resource constraints. Once energy self-sufficient, China must now import coal, oil, and natural gas to meet domestic demand. Requiring firms to become more energy efficient and less polluting serves the government's modernization and reform goals. The NDRC introduced policies focused on ways to reduce energy consumption per unit of GDP. This includes developing new energy and environmental technologies, such as clean coal technologies, nuclear power, combined heat and power generation, and renewable energy.

In the logic of a state-led growth regime, the NDRC drafts five-year economic development plans that contain significant industrial policy components. These Five-Year Plans (FYPs) are an important signal to both industry and the public regarding leadership priorities and preferences. The government also uses these climate and environmental goals to fulfill its modernization goals. Decisions to shut down old and inefficient facilities serve the two purposes of environmental improvement and economic restructuring. Measures targeting energy efficiency and renewable energy have featured increasingly prominently in these plans.

The 11th FYP (2006–2010) emphasized for the first time "that economic growth does not equal economic development, economic development does not necessarily result in society's development and that growth is not the goal, but the means of development" (Pan 2005). It set a national annual growth target of 7.5 percent, to be accompanied by a 20 percent reduction in energy consumption per unit of GDP (NDRC 2006). A special program focused on improving energy efficiency in China's top 1,000 energy-consuming enterprises was also initiated. The program targeted the steel, iron, utilities, petrochemicals, and construction material industries, which accounted for approximately 47 percent of national industrial use in 2004. Enterprise targets were negotiated with provincial and local governments based on each company's specific context (Price, Wang, and Yun 2008). The program exceeded its energy-saving target of 100 million tons of coal equivalent by the end of the 11th FYP and was expanded to a Top 10,000 Program by the 12th FYP (2011–2015), covering two-thirds of total energy consumption and about 17,000 enterprises (Institute for Industrial Productivity 2015).

The 12th FYP (2011–2015) continued the focus on energy savings, renewable energy promotion, and sustainability. It targeted a reduction in energy consumption by 16 percent per unit of GDP and, for the first time, introduced a target to reduce carbon dioxide emissions by 17 percent per unit of GDP. The forest coverage rate was also supposed to increase, to cover 21.6 percent of the country. The 13th FYP set further far-reaching energy efficiency goals (a 15 percent cut per unit of GDP compared with 2015 by 2020), carbon reduction goals (an 18 percent cut compared with the 2015 level by 2020), and renewable energy goals (15 percent of the energy mix comprising non-fossil fuel sources by 2020). The share of coal is to drop from 64 percent in 2015 to 58 percent by 2020 (Climate Policy Observer 2017).

In addition to the economy-wide five-year plans, there are also sector specific plans. The 13th FYP for renewable energy set highly ambitious goals: 20 percent renewables in the energy mix by 2030 and 680 GW of installed renewable energy capacity by 2020.

Various specific laws have been introduced to encourage the transition to a new development path. For example, the 2005 Renewable Energy Law and related enabling measures introduced a feed-in-tariff model, establishing fixed and government-guided subsidies for renewable energies (www.martinot. info/China_RE_Law_Beijing_Review.pdf). A surcharge for renewable energy was to be paid by end users. Highlighting the importance placed on the development of a domestic industry, the law mandated that technology must include at least 70 percent Chinese content to receive subsidies. This operated as an incentive to develop Chinese companies and engineers in this field and helped spur the development of China's renewable energy industry, eventually allowing China to become a world leader in these technologies. In the 2007 National Renewable Energy Development plan, Chinese authorities set a target of 15 percent for renewable energy as a share of the total energy mix by 2020. An amendment to the Renewable Energy Law was passed in 2009 as a result of mounting problems with grid owners failing to connect renewable suppliers to the grid. The amendment required grid operators to buy all the renewable energy that is produced. Operators failing to comply are fined double the amount lost by the renewable energy producer (Li 2008/2009).

Since 2014 China has been investing more in renewable energy than any other country, while simultaneously possessing the largest amount of installed capacity in the world. In addition to being the biggest investor in renewable energy overall, China claims the mantle of largest investor in hydropower capacity and generation, wind power capacity, solar water collector capacity, and geothermal heat capacity. China has now even overtaken Europe in total wind energy capacity (Ren21 2015). Hydropower dominates renewables, accounting for 22 percent of electricity production and wind brings in another 5 percent. While solar accounts for less than 1 percent of electricity consumption, in 2013 China set a world record for most new solar installations in a year (12 GW). In 2016 China installed a whopping 34.5 GW of solar PV, more than Japan, Germany, and the United States combined. Total installed capacity in China also surpassed Japan, Germany and the United States, approximately double their combined capacity (Ren21 2017). Trade disputes related to "unfair" state support for solar PV modules and wind turbines placed the Chinese government's efforts to promote renewable energy under harsh international scrutiny. This may be one reason for the trend to develop the domestic market.

As a non-Annex I party to the Kyoto Protocol, China had no greenhouse gas emission reduction obligations. It was a major beneficiary of the Clean Development Mechanism (CDM) of the Kyoto Protocol. The CDM was established to permit industrialized countries to obtain emission credits for greenhouse gas reduction projects they initiated in developing countries. China accounted for over 60 percent of all certified emission reduction units registered worldwide at the beginning of 2014 (United Nations Framework Convention on Climate Change n.d.). China's CDM projects were primarily in renewable energy, energy savings, efficiency improvements, and the capture and destruction of greenhouse gases with high global warming impacts (such as methane).

The stricter energy and resource efficiency standards, along with renewable energy goals, have started to create green jobs and export markets. The International Renewable Energy Agency estimated 1.7 million people were directly employed in the Chinese renewable energy sector (Ferrouhki et al.

2013). REN21 put the number at 3.1 million just a few years later (REN21 2017). The NDRC declared that by the end of 2012, China's energy saving and environmental protection industry was worth over 2.7 trillion yuan (NDRC 2013).

Climate change and the Chinese modernization agenda

A National Climate Change Program was released in 2007. Although its opening premise was that developed countries bear the main historic responsibility for climate change and therefore must shoulder the bulk of the requisite emission reductions to prevent global warming, it set climate change relevant goals for 2010. These goals included a 20 percent reduction in energy consumption per unit of GDP, renewables to comprise 10 percent of the primary energy supply (compared to 3 percent in 2003), and raising forest coverage to 20 percent of the country, thereby also increasing carbon sinks. The program noted the progress China had already made in energy efficiency and lowering emission intensity by almost half between 1990 and 2004. Other important measures China had taken that contributed to climate change mitigation were also addressed. These included China's progress in developing low carbon and renewable energy, its national tree planting campaigns, and its family planning and one child policy (a globally unique, and controversial, component of its climate change policy). The program also pointed out the importance of further expanding climate change institutions and laws and research capacity (NRDC 2007).

In mid-2007 a National Leading Group to Address Climate Change and Manage Energy Saving and Emission Reduction Work – chaired by then Premier Wen Jiabao – was established to coordinate climate change policies among China's 27 central government ministries and agencies (Qi et al. 2008; Gang 2008). The State Council indicated that provinces should set up parallel structures. Governors at all levels were required to report on their efforts to save energy and reduce pollutant discharge (Qi et al. 2008). The Chinese government is now strongly encouraging local experimentation in low carbon development and has recognized a growing number of eco and low carbon city initiatives. In these cities, local governments coordinate with industry in an effort to restructure the local economy toward more hi-tech and service oriented industries, to encourage renewable energy deployment, and to develop green industries (Baeumler et al. 2012). Plans to encourage the development of energy efficient, environmental protection industries have also been launched (NDRC 2013).

At the United Nations General Assembly meeting in New York in September 2009, Chinese President Hu Jintao stated that China would take steps to reduce the growth of its greenhouse gas emissions by "a notable margin" by 2020, and would increase the percentage of nuclear and renewable energy in the total energy mix to 15 percent by 2020 (MacFarquar 2009). Then, in November 2009, the Chinese government announced it would reduce the country's greenhouse gas emissions per unit of gross domestic product by 40–45 percent by 2020 (Graham-Harrison and Buckley 2009).

At this point in time it was still not evident whether China would be willing to commit to a binding greenhouse gas emission target. A post-Kyoto climate agreement was supposed to have been drafted at the December 2009 Copenhagen climate summit. China was widely perceived by European and US negotiators as both obstructionist and a major reason behind the failure of the Copenhagen negotiations (Rapp, Schwägerl and Traufetter 2010). In contrast, Xinhua News Agency's (2009) coverage of the Copenhagen negotiations reported that countries were debating intensely on whether to continue action within both the United Nations Framework Convention on Climate Change (UNFCCC) and the Kyoto Protocol (i.e. a two-track approach), or only under the UNFCCC. Criticizing developed countries, especially the United States and Japan, the news agency reported:

> While developing countries insisted on the two-track approach, developed countries were trying to throw away the Kyoto Protocol and replace it with a new single deal. Their real intention was to dodge their mandatory obligations under the Kyoto Protocol and force developing countries to do more, which ran counter to the principle of common but differentiated responsibilities.

At the end of the negotiations, no agreement on an international treaty was achieved. China's position changed significantly in the next years.

The Sino-US Climate Agreement

China and the USA together account for slightly less than half of global greenhouse gas emissions. From an economic standpoint they are strongly dependent upon each other, while also being competitors. In the USA, one argument frequently made to justify the US withdrawal from the Kyoto Protocol was that China was not obligated to make any emission reduction cuts. Republicans and Democrats from fossil-rich US states often argued that as long as China was not planning reduction measures, the playing field would not be level and thus the USA could not be expected to take on binding commitments either (see Harrison, Chapter 2). China, on the other hand, usually countered with the argument that climate change is the historic responsibility of developed countries, and thus mainly the USA.

Starting under the George W. Bush administration and continuing through the Barack Obama administration, efforts to find mutual ground with China on climate change began (Lewis 2010). An early initiative was the, now defunct, Asia-Pacific Partnership on Clean Development and Climate, which ran from 2006–2011 and sought to enhance both the development and diffusion of clean energy technologies. In 2007, the NDRC's vice chairman,

Xie Zhenhua, indicated China's interest in cooperating with the United States on carbon capture and storage, along with other climate technologies. Although these initiatives did not immediately lead to a memorandum of understanding, they did help set a new process in motion (Goldenberg 2009). In July 2009, the USA and China signed a Memorandum of Understanding to Enhance Cooperation on Climate Change, Energy and the Environment, a type of trust-building initiative (US Department of State 2009). Various technology cooperation agreements on energy-saving buildings, smart grids, and energy efficient cars were also signed. In June 2013 China and the USA agreed to phase out hydrofluorocarbons (HFCs), a very potent greenhouse gas whose use was expanding rapidly.[4]

The real breakthrough, however, seems to have occurred as a result of US Secretary of State John Kerry's decision to pursue bilateral climate negotiations with China in February 2014. His visit was followed by an exchange of letters between President Obama and President Xi. These concerned moving in tandem on climate change, with both states taking domestic actions that would bring them closer together on climate action (Goldenberg 2014). Obama announced plans to substantially reduce greenhouse gas emissions from the country's coal- and gas-fired power plants, using his authority under the Clean Air Act. This announcement signaled to China that the administration was serious in its intentions. China responded favorably to the US move.

A side agreement was reached in September 2014 at the UN Climate Summit in New York between President Obama and Vice President Zhang Gaoli, who is responsible for climate and energy issues. At the Climate Summit Zhang Gaoli announced that China will "make greater effort to more effectively address climate change" and said that China would announce post-2020 actions, including "marked progress in reducing carbon intensity" and "the peaking of total carbon dioxide emissions as early as possible" (Dugan 2014). The culmination of these moves was a joint announcement by President Obama and President Xi on emission reduction targets and clean energy cooperation. Obama announced a target to cut US emissions by 26–28 percent below 2005 levels by 2025. For his part, Xi Jinping announced a goal of having emissions peak by around 2030, with plans to increase the non-fossil fuel share of energy to 20 percent by 2030. In addition, an agreement was reached to deepen cooperation on a range of energy efficiency and clean technologies. This included an extension of the USA-China Clean Energy Research Center's mandate, renewing funding for: building efficiency; clean vehicles; carbon capture, use, and sequestration; and a new track on the interaction between energy and water. A climate-smart/low carbon cities initiative is also to be launched (White House, Office of the Press Secretary 2014).

Despite US President Donald Trump's decision to pull out of the Paris Agreement, China has joined the EU in choosing to stay in. It may even be that China is using this as an opportunity to exert greater global leadership in this area, even if it still has problems in fulfilling all of its own domestic targets.

In the coming months and years, there will certainly be a deepening of efforts to improve environmental governance and policy implementation. This will include experimentation with more market-based policy mechanisms and public-private partnerships, measures that will further shift relationships between the state and the market. China has launched pilot emission trading schemes in seven cities and is launching a national emissions trading system (Chen and Reklev 2014). Meeting the climate change targets will be challenging but it is an important method for China to modernize its economy and move it toward a new form of state-led, green, economic development.

Conclusion

Pollution levels have reached crisis point in many parts of China. Air pollution threatens human health, tap water is undrinkable, and chemical pollutants are poisoning the land. China is also under growing international pressure to reduce the country's carbon intensity and its greenhouse gas emissions. The Chinese government has started to respond more aggressively to these pressures. Efforts are underway to strengthen environmental governance— developments that could have positive spin-offs for climate mitigation efforts. As a result, Chinese authorities have made efforts to increase energy efficiency, modernize or shut down the most polluting plants, regulate pollution from automobiles, and expand renewable energy. Many new environmental laws and programs have been introduced in an effort to address environmental pollution and create an "ecological civilization," efforts that are also important for climate change policies. The central government has also required that specific climate change policies be established by all levels of government.

The basic argument of development state theorists is that the Chinese state makes use of various tools to guide industrial and societal development. Chinese authorities set a directional tone for the country's economic and social development, and firms, many of which are now private, make investment decisions. National goals are elucidated in both five-year development plans and more specific policy statements. The pronouncements of top leaders are closely monitored, studied, and followed in a manner not seen in other developmental states. China's signaling of its willingness to eventually cap its greenhouse gas emissions should be viewed as part of a larger transition in China's state-led capitalist growth model. It is part of a grand effort to modernize, green the economy, and stabilize the country politically.

Chinese government leaders view climate mitigation policies as an avenue for modernizing the economy, and shutting down heavily polluting, inefficient, older firms. More and more government leaders and industrial entrepreneurs are seeing possibilities for the development of new green industries

and export sectors. A new mode of Chinese capitalist development that continues to highlight economic growth, but which pays far greater attention to
the environmental consequences of that growth, may slowly be emerging.
China may indeed be moving in the direction of an ecological, state-led, capitalist economy.

Notes

1 Discussion with Apple Inc.'s Environmental Director, Lisa P. Jackson, July 21,
  2015.
2 The author was a member of the international task force set up in 2014 by the
  Chinese Society for Environmental Sciences under the China Council for International Cooperation on Environment and Development (CCICED) to conduct
  special policy research on "Institutional Innovation for Environmental Protection
  in the Context of Ecological Civilization," and to advise the government on
  environmental governance matters. She was also a member of the international task
  force set up in 2015 by the CCICED to make recommendations regarding steps to
  be taken to improve China's environmental governance capacity.
3 Peishen Wang, unofficial translation of the New Environmental Law provided to
  the CCICED Task force on environmental governance, May 2014.
4 HFCs were originally introduced as a substitute to replace chlorofluorocarbons in
  refrigeration and air conditioning to address another environmental issue, that of
  stratospheric ozone depletion, but their high global warming impact made them a
  target for elimination.

8 Climate policies in dependent market economies

The cases of Poland, Hungary and the Czech Republic

Daniele Archibugi and Marina Chiarugi

Introduction

Eastern and Central European (ECE) countries went through radical political, social and economic change with the fall of the Berlin Wall in December 1989. Most, if not all, aspects of social life were deeply transformed, and this also holds for the environmental positioning of these countries. The established regimes of production and consumption were radically modified, which had a dramatic impact on greenhouse gas (GHG) emissions. The list of macroeconomic and political factors that contributed to these changes is long and encompasses: the transition from a centrally planned economy to a market economy; the end of the provision of oil and gas at regulated prices within the COMECON (Council for Mutual Economic Assistance); the change of trading partners from the Soviet Union and other Eastern European countries to the members of the European Union (EU); the efforts put toward gaining EU membership, which for most of these countries occurred in 2004; and the massive foreign direct investment (FDI) from transnational corporations (TNCs) into those economies. Since their independence, ECE countries have managed to substantially reduce GHG emissions. This was less a result of deliberate environmental policy or green innovations and more a consequence of emissions being very high at the outset. Emissions largely came down in ECE due to massive deindustrialization and the overall processes of sectoral change. This chapter focusses on Poland, Hungary and the Czech Republic as paradigmatic cases of dependent market economies (DMEs), whose institutional underpinnings are critical for the set-up of their climate regimes. In analyzing Poland, Hungary and the Czech Republic, the main objectives are: to assess their performance with regard to the emission targets of the Kyoto Protocol (KP); how they are performing vis-à-vis the more demanding and ambitious targets of the EU 20-20-20 strategy; and how the nascent Paris Agreement figures in emission reductions.

An overview of emission evolution

Environmental issues have become of more explicit public concern in ECE countries, mainly triggered by the international campaigns of Western civil society organizations, as well as by EU initiatives (which included the new eastern member states). This led to the first embryonic features of an *ecological culture* that, for many years, did not have much opportunity to unfold. It is difficult to single out the endogenous and exogenous components of these environmental concerns, but it is fair to argue that the desire to become 'a normal member' of the EU and to share (and accept) the administrative and regulatory schemes of the EU, certainly played a major role. On the one hand, the targets and international regulations that Poland, Hungary and the Czech Republic signed are in line with those of other EU member states. On the other hand, given the unique context for ECE countries, the international environmental regime was indulgent with them and asked for policy and political changes that they could handle relatively easily, at least in the first years of EU membership.

Poland, Hungary and the Czech Republic were among the early signatories of the KP. Poland and the Czech Republic signed in 1998 and ratified it, in 2002 and 2001 respectively, while Hungary joined in 2002. KP entered into force on February 15, 2005 in all three states. The KP targets for these economies were very generous. So generous in fact that between the signing and ratifying of the KP, their targets had already been met as a result of ongoing deep economic restructuring arising from the fall of communism. Poland, Hungary and the Czech Republic also joined the EU 20-20-20 strategy, which put EU member countries under stricter emission rules than required by the KP. The EU 20-20-20 strategy uses a wealth of directives aimed at obtaining three key objectives by 2020: (i) increasing the share of EU energy produced from renewable resources to 20 percent; (ii) improving energy efficiency by 20 percent; and (iii) reducing GHG emissions by 20 percent from 1990 levels.[1] The Paris Agreement has now been ratified by the EU as a whole, and by Poland and Hungary themselves (UNFCCC 2017a). The Czech Republic has signed up to the agreement but not yet ratified it, following hurdles in the lower house, but it should eventually pass (J n 2017). Even though the EU has already ratified the agreement, since member states are responsible for implementing parts of the deal they also need to become parties (Jůn 2017).

The KP base year for most countries almost coincides with the fall of the Berlin Wall in 1990, a very symbolic year for ECE countries. It was not considered an appropriate base year since the political revolution also had an important impact on production and consumption. In all ECE countries 1990 coincided with a deep economic crisis and the transition from a planned and widely closed economy, to a variety of capitalist market economy that necessitated the collapse of existing regimes of production and consumption. A result of this deep crisis was a strong reduction in GHG emissions. This emission performance had implications for many ECE countries that were assigned a base year earlier than 1990, when emissions were much higher. Poland was assigned 1988 and Hungary 1985, while the Czech Republic was allowed to make use of the year 1990 as its benchmark.

Signing the KP came with important internal administrative consequences. Government agencies devoted to environmental issues are quite recent policy innovations, with the exception of Poland, where an environment ministry was formed in 1973. Hungary and the Czech Republic did not establish environmental agencies until 1988 and 1990, respectively. These ministries have been put in charge of dealing with the emerging international environmental regime, including the need to collect national data and report to the KP monitoring system. All nations bound to reduce their emissions must present a yearly report (NIR, National Inventory Report) to show the progress toward their target and the efforts made toward implementing the protocol.[2] The KP gave its members emission targets that reflect the specific situation of each nation's production system. Figures 8.1 (per capita emissions) and 8.2 (total CO_2 emissions per unit of GDP) give a general overview of the performance of these three countries with regard to KP targets and the achievements of the EU as a group.

Poland, Hungary and the Czech Republic all report strong emission reductions from their respective KP base years, up until 2015 (the year with the most recent available data). During this period Poland reduced its emissions by 32.4 percent, Hungary by 44.2 percent and the Czech Republic by 35.1 percent (UNFCCC 2017b). In contrast, during the same period the EU bloc managed to reduce its emissions by only 23.6 percent. As a result these three countries were 'overachievers' in terms of KP targets, and indeed the reduction in GHG emissions is substantial. However, a closer look raises some questions about this success. It has already been mentioned that the KP targets were obsolete when these countries eventually ratified the KP. Also, the reduction is very much driven by the enormous economic downturn during the post-communist transition period. This means that the reduction of emissions is not so much the outcome of smart climate policies, as the result of a deep transformation crisis that came with high economic and social costs. Interestingly, if we compare the most recent data for 2015 with data from 2014, all three countries and the EU have seen an uptick in emissions. For the EU however it was 0.6 percent while for our ECE countries it ranged from 1 percent to 6 percent, and we see this as a clear sign that the initial advantages have started to peter out.

In spite of the general similar trends with regard to emissions, our country cases show that the three economies had rather different starting points, as can be seen by their per capita emissions (Figure 8.1). In 1990 the Czech Republic had the highest level of per capita GHG emissions at 14.51 tonnes, a level which was significantly higher than the average 8.42 tonnes per capita emissions for the EU28 (IEA 2016a). The levels of per capita emissions in Poland were only slightly above the aforementioned EU figure, but it was

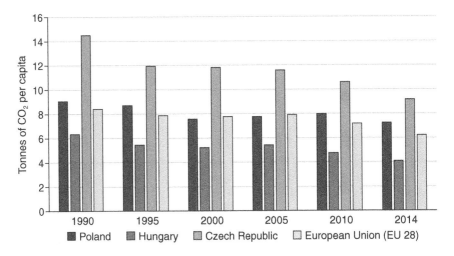

Figure 8.1 CO$_2$ emissions per capita.
Source: International Energy Agency, 2016.

Hungary that had the most favorable starting point at 6.34 tonnes per capita, considerably below the EU average. Over 20 years later, the countries remain in similar positions relative to each other. Hungary still leads the pack with 4.08 tonnes per capita in 2014; the Czech Republic at the other extreme remains a high polluter for its population. Poland retains a middle position and in 2014 still possessed emissions per capita slightly above the EU average (IEA 2016b).

Another way to look at progress made is to relate CO$_2$ emissions to the overall income level of these countries, that is, their GDP. As indicated by Figure 8.2, in 1990 Poland, Hungary and the Czech Republic had a ratio of CO$_2$ emissions per GDP higher than the EU28, and generally even higher than the average of OECD member countries (Hungary was the exception at a infinitesimal 0.1 higher than the OECD average). Again, the differences between the three are significant: Poland in 1990 had a carbon intensity, (measured as kg of CO$_2$ per unit of GDP in 2005 US\$), that was more than two-and-a-half times higher than the average of the EU28; carbon intensity of the Czech Republic was also more than twice as high as the EU28 average. The outlier is Hungary whose carbon intensity was similar to the EU average. This left enormous adjustment space for Poland and the Czech Republic and, as the data shows, both economies have decreased their carbon intensities enormously. Taken as a group, the three countries have more than halved their emissions per GDP units since 1990.

We have noted a slowdown and even reversal in emissions reduction in DMEs that has occurred 'passively' as a consequence of structural change which has either come to a halt, or at least slowed its pace. That being said,

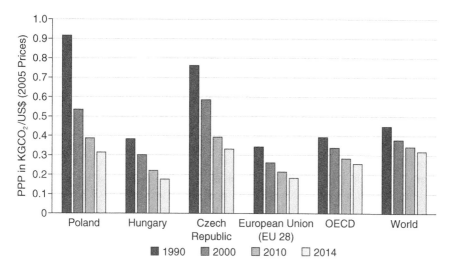

Figure 8.2 CO$_2$ emissions/GDP.
Source: International Energy Agency, 2016.

however, data on the share of renewables in the energy mix indicate that efforts to increase clean energy usage have been successful, at least to a degree. As Figure 8.3 shows, Poland, Hungary and the Czech Republic have all increased the share of renewables in their mixes during 2009–2015. Hungary saw its proportion of renewables spike from 8 percent to 14.5 percent, and significant increases have also been achieved by the Czech Republic and

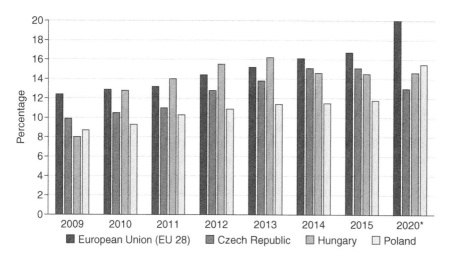

Figure 8.3 Share of renewable energy in gross final energy consumption.
Source: Eurostat, 2017.

Poland, though with some year-on-year fluctuation. Still, all three countries performance is below the EU28 average. Given that the European core is moving along a stricter reduction path, we conclude that these three economies need to increase their efforts, while simultaneously dealing with a broad spectrum of policy initiatives, in order to catch up in terms of income growth.

ECE economies in general, and our three countries in particular, benefited from the international climate regime that emerged with the launch of the KP. The Emissions Trading Mechanism – the first of the flexible mechanisms that were adopted to lower the costs of meeting KP objectives[3] – was of foremost relevance. It allowed member states to buy emission permits from other parties to help achieve their national emission reduction targets. Each Assigned Amount Unit (AAU) corresponded to a megaton CO_2 eq. Given that ECE countries were favored by their initial conditions and reduced emissions more than expected by the KP, this institutional framework provided them with tangible gains. This advantage continued to exist when the EU Emission Trading System (EU ETS) was enacted, as most of the emissions allowances sold in the ETS belong to ECE countries.[4] A recent assessment has confirmed that Eastern European nations benefit from EU climate policy (Landis and Heindl 2016).

Poland, Hungary and the Czech Republic were among the early movers in the now defunct carbon credits trade system of the KP. The exploitation of the trading systems' mechanisms initially guaranteed noteworthy carbon 'revenues,' especially during the first period of their implementation. The AAU for these three countries was in surplus. However, these surpluses were less profitable than expected (and hoped for), with carbon credit prices collapsing from a range of US$8–10 for AAU in 2009 to an amount of US$0.5 at the end of December 2012.[5] This system of the KP has now effectively ended with phase 2 never having entered into force (UNFCCC 2014a).

Many aspects contributed to fall in the price of AAUs, including: the arrival of new sellers from other Eastern European countries; Poland/ Hungary/Czech Republic's huge surplus in AAUs; and the shrinking demand from buyer's due to the fulfillment of their KP obligations. Moreover, the economic crisis that started in 2008 led to a significant reduction in CO_2 emissions, and thus diminished overall trading volume, resulting in a corresponding decline in prices. In other words, supply and demand constellations changed fundamentally in the first couple of years.

All three ECE countries (but especially the Czech Republic), were also active under the Joint Implementation mechanism, carrying on numerous common projects with other Annex I parties (i.e., those industrial countries that, according to the KP, have obligations to reduce GHG emissions). Hungary gained noteworthy amounts of credits deriving from LULUCF activities, principally through financing a strong reforestation program that increased the national forestry cover by 13 percent (World Bank 2012).[6] A typical example of how funds raised from the sale of emission credits were profitably used is the Green Savings Program adopted by the Czech Republic in 2008. The revenues from the sale of these credits were invested in a government program that financed the diffusion of renewable energy heating installations, together with investments in the energy efficiency of new buildings. This program was seen as immensely successful and, after its conclusion in April 2013, it was extended until 2020.

Poland, Hungary and the Czech Republic as a particular VoC: DMEs

The overarching framework of this book utilizes case studies within the well developed and broadly discussed literature on varieties of Capitalism (VoC). In particular, we are interested in explaining national pathways to low carbon emission economies by way of national institutional settings that either facilitate or restrict particular strategies. Extrapolating from the classic VoC typology pioneered by Hall and Soskice (2001), we explore whether liberal market economies (LME) and coordinated market economies (CME) have specific transition routes toward low carbon economies. ECE countries do not seem to generally fit into the typical dichotomy suggested by Hall and Soskice, as they cannot be characterized as either LME or CME. The rather recent transition to a market economy, as well as the legacy of nearly half a century of planned economy, makes them rather different from the categories suggested by Hall and Soskice. So much so that ECE countries provide an impetus to enlarge the original dichotomy. The categories that have been used for the USA and the UK on the one hand and for Germany, Japan and Sweden on the other hand are not pertinent for the ECE countries. Two main reasons are critical for the insufficiency of the original VoC dichotomy with respect to ECE countries. First, LMEs and CMEs can count on public institutions that have the authority to act as market regulators in LMEs or as direct organizers of markets in CMEs. Analogous public institutions are not well developed in ECE countries. Second, LMEs and CMEs both have a significant number of large national firms which are critical for innovation policies. Again, such 'lighthouses' are critically missing in the newly capitalist market economies of Eastern Europe. Instead, FDI has become of the foremost importance, both for finance and production.

Nölke and Vliegenthart (2009) have convincingly suggested introducing a new category to the VoC framework, namely DMEs. With this term, they refer to a market economy typology that is heavily influenced by FDI, and where many economic regulations are relegated to transnational instead of national institutions. Similarly, Bohle and Greskovits (2007) argued that transnational influences have shaped the transformations in ECE economies and suggested a further distinction among ECE economies that puts the Baltic states into one sub-group and the Visegrad states (Czech Republic, Hungary, Poland and Slovakia) into another sub-group. Both the Baltic countries and the Visegrad states are heavily dependent on foreign capital. In the former, liberalization and privatization led to rather free market economies, which created economic and political transformations that came with a relative increase in social inclusion and welfare protection. As noted by Nölke and Vliegenthart (2009), the penetration by TNCs of the three ECE economies this chapter is examining has been impressive. Critical economic sectors, including significant industrial plants and enterprises of the formerly state-run planned economies, were acquired and consequently restructured. Significant parts of the financial sector came into the hands of foreign banks, and FDI became prominent not only in the manufacturing sector, but also in the service sector (Medve-Bálint 2014). The enormous inflow of foreign capital resulted in technology transfer, which imported production methods that were relatively more efficient in material output and ecological throughput (McKinsey 2013). In contrast, the majority of national firms are small and dedicated to domestic markets. Only the most successful managed to integrate their production into the global chains of transnational companies.

This project makes use of a DME variety of capitalism by stressing three key characteristics (see also Hübner, Chapter 1). First, we see FDI as a critical component of these countries' institutional set-ups as they are absorbing not only capital in a monetary sense, but also specific production methods and technologies and industrial relations practices. FDI adds a strong transnational layer to the institutional setting. DMEs are, of course, not the only economies receiving FDI. For some time, China was the most prominent destination for FDI. Unlike in the DMEs, China made deliberate political efforts to keep foreign capital under control; this was possible due to China's strong central political power. For the DMEs, in contrast, there is neither a willingness to control foreign capital, nor a strong enough central political power base to restrict FDI to a specific national institutional setting (Medve-Bálint 2014).

Second, DMEs are not only economically, but also politically, integrated into Western institutions. Primary in this political integration is the governance structure of the EU and its underlying political values. This makes DMEs distinct from state-led VoC, as in China, where free expression is seldom found in the political processes.

Third, DMEs are governed by EU regulations, including environmental regulations. TNCs operate in these countries to do more than just serve local markets, they also have their production integrated across the European economic space. If they operate in Poland, Hungary or the Czech Republic, they cannot ignore that imports, intermediate products and final products can come and go freely to other EU member countries. Even though some national exemptions may hold for DMEs, it still broadly holds that they are part of an overarching international political institutional layer.

In terms of business regulations, there is a general expectation that TNCs do not contribute to improving environmental standards (see Lee 2013). Does this also apply to Eastern European countries in the EU? These countries are mostly rule-takers from the EU, and therefore environmental regulations tend to be similar to those applied in other EU countries. EU directives are the most important sources of environmental regulations. In some cases, these regulations are applied with less exactitude than in other EU countries. In some cases, ECE countries have also managed to obtain longer periods of transition from old to new regulatory regimes. However, both the political and business communities are looking to Brussels rather than to their national capitals, to understand how environmental regulations will evolve. Cross-border trade, which has been growing steadily since 1990, is mainly driven by TNCs, and they are obliged to comply with EU regulations. Our interviews with TNC managers active in several European countries, including ECE countries, have clearly indicated that it is too costly to organize production differently for each individual member country, and that it is crucial to have interchangeable production lines and standards across countries. Apparently, there is not a risk of ECE countries being used as "pollution havens" by TNCs (see Smarzynska Javorcik and Wei 2004). When investing in ECE countries, TNCs say that they are required to apply the same modular production, including in terms of environmental standards, as in any other EU member country.[7]

The issue of how TNC investment is shaping economic development in Eastern Europe has generated large debate and controversies (see for example, Szent-Iványi 2017). The determinants of FDI have been different across countries, and the majority of these dynamics are beyond the scope of environmental policy. There is the general expectation that TNCs can organize their production strategies in order to benefit from advantageous regulations and enforcement, including in the environmental sphere (see Sanna-Randaccio and Sestini 2011). Whether EU regulations are a sufficient deterrent against TNC selectivity in environmental practice should be tested.

DMEs are a distinct category in the realm of capitalisms, in both economic and political terms. We will show how this variant deals with climate policy, in particular how its institutional design results in innovation policies that contribute to low carbon technologies. It is important to note that within DMEs FDI penetration has been impressive in various sectors, including those that are only indirectly related to environmental issues (such as banking, insurance and hotels). The penetration in industries that are more sensitive to environmental issues, such as manufacturing and natural resources, has also been significant, with appreciable differences across countries, as is highlighted below.

Innovation systems in Poland, Hungary and the Czech Republic

In the tradition of VoC literature, specific attention needs to be devoted to the set-up of national innovation systems. The possibility of reducing CO_2 emissions while maintaining social and economic standards, depends on the ability to introduce environmentally friendly innovations.[8] This holds all the more true as all three of our economies saw their initial advantages rapidly dissipate, as elaborated on earlier. As a result, they were required to become proactive to fulfill their emissions commitments. As Beisea and Rennings (2005) have argued, regulations can play an important role in promoting environmental innovation, but this relies on existing technological capabilities and the possibility to respond to changing societal needs. To assess the potential of our DMEs to further reduce emissions, it is therefore crucial to assess their specific innovation systems.

All three countries have considerable scientific and technological traditions. Hungary and the Czech Republic, along with the former GDR, were seen as the most technologically advanced countries of the Eastern European trading bloc during the Cold War. Despite their economic problems and a significant 'brain drain' after the collapse of communism, these countries have still managed to retain, and even develop, substantial research and development (R&D) capacity. Still, the legacy of a knowledge infrastructure that lacks the capacity to translate its considerable quality into effective industrial innovation has persisted over the last two decades (Hanson and Pavitt 1987). Another communist era institutional peculiarity is that both the knowledge institutions (universities, academies of sciences and other public institutions) and the production regime were formally under the control of the government. Remarkably, it was difficult to induce the research institutions to generate the knowledge needed by the production units, or to convince the production units to use the knowledge made available by the scientific and technological research institutions.[9] This led to a situation in which academic institutions did not contribute to economic development, and production units often did not have the needed scientific and technological expertise. The outcome was a failure in technology transfer from knowledge generating to knowledge using organizations (Radosevic and Lepori 2009). The transition to market economies drastically changed the innovation landscape, as privatization and liberalization made the private sector independent from direct government control. And yet, most of the scientific and technological institutions were still funded and controlled by the government. In spite of the transition, the link between public scientific institutions and companies, so vital in any well functioning national innovation system, was not well established and thus tended to be weak or even non-existent (Radosevic 2011). The transition to a market economy has not yet created effective technology transfer or collaboration between public scientific institutions and business.

As discussed in the section above, the massive penetration of FDI has been one of the key economic characteristics in Poland, Hungary and the Czech Republic. Among the reasons why TNCs find it attractive to invest in these countries, besides the relatively low wages, are the highly qualified workforce and good quality of higher education. This has resulted in knowledge flows transmitted by foreign companies' headquarters to their subsidiaries in ECE countries. As such, the activities of TNCs have been very positive in terms of modernizing production and introducing best practice techniques. TNCs have allowed local production units to learn, assimilate and diffuse the production techniques and standards dictated by their headquarters. However, this has not led to an automatic burgeoning of endogenous inventions and innovations. The contribution of TNCs to the innovation system of ECE countries has remained a short-term commitment. TNCs seem reluctant to locate core R&D activities in host economies, or to significantly invest in upgrading the local workforce's competences. They are more likely to benefit from the endowment of these countries, especially in terms of human resources, and to simply integrate local units into their global strategy. A few indicators illustrate this argument.

In terms of R&D, Poland has the lowest share of R&D intensity among the three ECE countries examined, which is less than half of the EU28 average. The three ECE economies have however seen a broad trend toward increasing R&D expenditures, with top performer Czech Republic being just shy of the EU average. Expanding on this, Hungary and the Czech Republic have a higher R&D intensity than Southern European countries such as Italy, Spain, Portugal and Greece. Even torpid Poland still exceeds Greece and is within relative striking distance of these other southern European countries. The breakdown of R&D expenditure by major sources of performance is shown in Table 8.1. On the one hand, we have the Polish economy, larger and less R&D intensive, especially in its business component, and on the other hand the Hungarian and the Czech economies, smaller but also with a greater emphasis on private sector research and innovation. Buttressing this, business R&D is much more important in Hungary and the Czech Republic than in Poland, where this component comprises a paltry 0.47 percent of GDP. The share is more significant in Hungary and the Czech Republic where TNCs have acquired and often restructured the industrial knowledge base of previously state-owned enterprises. Government R&D is in line with the EU28 average in all three countries, but the R&D in higher education is substantially lower than in the EU28 (with an important exception for the Czech Republic, where there has been a gargantuan catch-up). The higher education sector was heavily underfunded in the post-transition years, leading many scholars to quit their jobs or search for academic positions abroad. If we compare this data with an indicator of innovative output, such as patent applications at the European Patent Office (see row 7 of Table 8.1), the gap between these economies and the EU28 average is much larger; the value of patents per million inventors is 26 in the Czech Republic, 23 in Hungary and only 16 in Poland, against an average of 112 in the EU28. A very large proportion of the R&D carried out seems to be devoted to learning, adoption and diffusion of innovations generated elsewhere rather than to an endogenous generation of innovation. This impression is further reinforced by the fact that the already rather limited number of patent applications are often owned by foreign companies; TNCs own more than 60 percent of the patents generated in Hungary and more than 35 percent of those generated in Poland and the Czech Republic, against an EU28 average of 12 percent.

Table 8.1 Key indicators for the innovation systems of Poland, Hungary and the Czech Republic

	Poland	Hungary	Czech Republic	European Union (EU28)
1 R&D intensity (R&D/GDP) as a % of GDP, 2015 % of GDP	1.00%	1.38%	1.95%	2.03%
2 Business enterprise R&D on GDP, 2015	0.47%	1.01%	1.06%	1.30%
3 Government R&D on GDP, 2015	0.25%	0.18%	0.40%	0.24%
4 Higher education R&D on GDP, 2015	0.29%	0.17%	0.48%	0.47%
5 Share of government R&D devoted to environment, 2015	6.4%	2.2%	2.2%	nd
6 Share of government R&D devoted to energy, 2015	1.9%	3.1%	4.4%	nd
7 Patent applications to the EPO per million inhabitants, 2014	16	23	26	112
8 Foreign ownership of domestic inventions in patent applications to the EPO (% of total), 2013	37%	67%	49%	12%
9 Mitigation or adaptation to climate change; patent applications to the EPO per million inhabitants, 2013	0.05	0.24	0.45	1.69

Sources: Rows 1–4, 7–9 Eurostat, 2017; Rows 5–6 OECD Government budget appropriation or outlays on R&D (GBOARD), 2017.

It is difficult to gather specific data on 'green' R&D for our three DMEs. However, we have acquired data on: (i) the amount of government R&D expenditure devoted to the environment (row 5 of Table 8.1); (ii) the amount of government R&D expenditure devoted to energy (row 6 of Table 8.1); (iii) the patent applications related to the environment per billion of GDP (row 9 of Table 8.1). These indicators can provide preliminary information on the extent to which public and business sectors are actually engaged in 'green' innovation efforts. There is a caveat though: government R&D is classified into 14 broad categories and it is often very difficult to single out the additional impact of specific R&D.[10] For example, public R&D devoted to 'defense,' 'industrial production and technology' or even 'health' can have an indirect effect in generating environmentally friendly knowledge. In contrast, the objectives of 'environment' and 'energy' are more directly associated to GHG emission reductions. Given the difficulties in properly assessing 'green' innovation efforts, we can still make some judgments on the data we do have.

With regard to public R&D devoted to environmental concerns, the proportions have fluctuated somewhat as a share of total R&D in our ECE countries. However, there is an unmistakable trend downwards in all three countries in terms of the actual dollar figure. In the last three years of available data, all three of these economies have seen less government money devoted to R&D research in the environment category. Public sector R&D in the energy domain provides a much less clear longitudinal picture. That being said, the proportion of public investment in energy is far from gargantuan and still represents quite a small fraction of the total, as is also the case with environmental R&D.

The situation looks even worse if we move to the business sector and consider the patent applications at the EPO associated with the environment per GDP billion (see row 9 of Table 8.1). The aforementioned caveat should be kept in mind while looking at this indicator, given that patents in a variety of different technological areas can have a beneficial effect on the environment. This indicator still provides us with a useful comparison between the EU and these three ECE countries. It is estimated that in the EU28 there are 1.69 environmental patents per million residents. In the three DMEs this proportion is much lower. Radosevic (2011) has convincingly shown that most ECE region countries have difficulty building appropriate linkages for the promotion and diffusion of innovation. While intra-firm, and thus international, linkages seem to operate quite well in the dissemination of knowledge and innovation, inter-firm linkages and collaboration between public actors and the business sector are not achieved with the same ease. Apparently, this general view also applies with reference to environmental innovations.

A conclusion can already be surmised from these basic data: Poland, Hungary and the Czech Republic's GHG emissions performance and, more generally, the emissions performance of ECE countries as a whole, cannot be the result of deliberate green innovation policies. It is more likely that this is associated with the diffusion of innovations generated abroad and to the introduction of already available processes, as in the case of renewable energy (see Table 8.1). Let us now look at the situation in each country, with the aim of exploring the contribution, if any, played by green innovation and climate policies to overall GHG emissions and emission reductions.

Emission trends, policies and prospects in Poland

The main obligation resulting from ratification of the KP by Poland was to reduce its GHG emissions by 6 percent from 2008 to 2012, compared to the base year (1988). The GHG inventory in 1988 amounted to 568.9 megatons of CO_2 eq. Table 8.2 shows that Poland's 2015 emissions have been reduced to 384.5 megatons of CO_2 eq compared to the base year, a 32.4 percent reduction. The Polish reduction of emissions has been nearly five times

Table 8.2 GHG Emissions in millions of gigagrams CO_2 eq (excluding LULUCF) and Kyoto Protocol Targets for 2008–2015 in Poland, Hungary, Czech Republic and the European Union

Country	KP base year	1990	2015	Change base year-2015 (%)	Change 1990–2015 (%)
Poland	568.9 (1988)	466.7	384.5	−32.4	−17.6
Hungary	109.5 (1985)	93.9	61.1	−44.2	−34.9
Czech Republic	195.8 (1990)	195.8	127.1	−35.1	−35.1
European Union (EU 28)	5,647.7	5,647.7	4,313.8	−23.6	−23.6

Source: UNFCCC Data Interface, 2017.

higher than that requested by the KP. The data show that the decrease has not been uniform across time. The greatest single reduction occurred immediately after the base year 1988, and emissions continued to exhibit a downward trend, but at a slower rate and with some fluctuation after this initial period.

Active climate policies, or for that matter innovation strategies, which focus on energy efficiency and clean technologies, are **not** at the forefront of the political agenda in Poland. The availability of coal has resulted in the development of a strong regime of political parties and trade unions, backed by buisness, who all support the current situation and see no national advantage to switching trajectory. As a matter of fact, Poland tends to oppose the more ambitious environmental targets and programs defined at EU level (Ecological Institute 2012a). Specifically, Poland was very reluctant to join the EU ETS, and when it eventually presented its National Allocation Plan, the EU Commission was not in a position to approve it (European Commission 2010). This torpidity reflects in large part the priority given to economic growth and catch-up, in order to improve social conditions for Polish citizens. It is even more directly a result of the fact that the country is heavily dependent on coal, the main source of domestic production. "We use coal because it is cheap."[11] "Cheap fuel makes for cheap energy" is the view shared by most energy specialists and average citizens in the country. When the EU Commission asked Poland to drastically reduce the allowances handed over to the coal industry and other CO_2-intensive industries Poland took legal action against it (the Czech Republic, Hungary, Estonia and Slovakia were also a part of this effort). More recently, the Polish government declared that it would vehemently oppose the Commission's proposal to reduce emissions by 40 percent from 1990 levels by 2030, as this would risk the survival of its coal industry and lift energy prices to a level that would risk the international price competitiveness of Polish products (*Financial Times* October 10, 2014).

However, Poland has made commendable efforts in recent years to comply with EU requirements, both with the progressive liberalization of its gas and electricity markets, and with the adoption of the EU 20-20-20 strategy. This is particularly true of renewables, where EU directives and plans have become key elements of Polish policies (Skjærseth 2014). Through the 20-20-20 strategy, Poland has committed to: (i) increase the share of renewables in final energy consumption to 15 percent; (ii) improve energy efficiency by 20 percent; and (iii) reduce CO_2 emissions by 14 percent from 2005 levels by 2020. The Polish government approved a concrete energy policy framework in 2009, the Energy Policy of Poland 2030.[12] This outlines the future direction of energy policy to improve economic development and environmental sustainability and to achieve energy security in a comprehensive document that: draws strategic policy objectives; formulates concrete targets; and suggests courses of action related to each target.

The primary goals of recent Polish energy policy have been: improving energy efficiency; enhancing energy supply and security; diversifying the electricity generation mix by introducing nuclear energy; increasing the use of renewable sources, with particular attention paid to biofuels; developing a competitive energy market; and reducing the environmental impact of the power industry. This plan was not seen as ambitious enough, though. The International Energy Agency – in its yearly review of the energy policies of its member states[13] – suggested that the weakest items of Poland's strategy are: (i) the insufficient integration of energy and climate policies; (ii) a lack of competition in its national energy markets; and (iii) the heavy reliance on national coal reserves instead of promoting diversification of energy sources, with particular attention on the role played by natural gases in the decarbonizing process of the energy system.[14] It is worth noting that there is some flux with respect to these energy policies. A process in 2015 began to formulate a new energy policy that would extend through to 2050. The election of a new government put this on hold temporarily but a new reformulating of this 2050 energy policy is expected to be delivered very soon (perhaps even by the time this book is published) (IEA 2017a)

Climate change policies require important investments in technology and innovation, and this is one of the main steps described in many national documents on economic development strategies. In the National Programme for Scientific Research and Development Activities, adopted in 2008, energy is defined for the first time as one of the five strategic priorities of R&D policy. As seen in lines 5 and 6 of Table 8.1, these good intentions are not (yet?) reflected in a substantial amount of government R&D being devoted to environment and energy objectives.

The National Programme for Scientific Research and Development Activities specifically identifies three principal objectives for energy research: (i) reducing energy consumption by developing energy-saving solutions; (ii) managing national fossil fuel resources in an environmental friendly way; and (iii) developing alternative energy sources, such as renewables, nuclear and hydrogen technologies. The Energy Policy of Poland 2030 goes in the same direction by underlining the importance of diversifying technologies in order to enhance energy security, the need to modernize all energy sectors, and the importance of innovation in all areas of energy efficiency – including renewables, clean coal and carbon capture and storage.

However, in spite of some connection between R&D and general energy policy, there is a lack of a developed and coherent innovation strategy with clear objectives, long-term funding and the monitoring and evaluation of results. Targets seem to have little to no association with instruments. Aside from enacting business regulations, it does not seem that the public sector is willing to commit resources to provide solutions. An increase in financial resources is needed today. Government spending on total R&D and, more specifically, the share of government R&D devoted to energy, are both among the lowest in Europe.[15] The combination of defending its coal-based energy supply for cost reasons, along with an underdeveloped innovation regime that is 'conquered' by the interests of foreign-owned companies, makes Poland a climate policy laggard.

When discussing emission trends it is prudent to have a brief look at the Paris Agreement. Poland and the EU have both ratified the agreement, with the EU outlining a 40 percent reduction across its member states from 1990 GHG levels (UNFCCC 2017a). There is an element of burden sharing with the understanding, as has been the case in prior agreements, that ECE countries in general bear less of the GHG reductions. The EU 20-20-20 has already been outlined extensively and this comprises the first part of reaching the Paris target. After 2020 though there is a proposal from the European Commission for an Effort Sharing Regulation 2021–2030 to match up with the timeline for the Paris Agreement for emissions not covered by the ETS (European Commission DG Climate Action 2017a). This proposal stipulates a 7 percent reduction by 2030 for Poland, with only three EU countries having lower targets (European Commission DG Climate Action 2017a). This continues, at least in relative terms, to buttress Poland's climate laggerd status.

Emission trends, policies and prospects in Hungary

By ratifying the KP, Hungary committed to reducing its GHG emissions by 6 percent compared to the base year 1985, when emissions were calculated as being 109.5 megatons Gg CO_2 eq (UNFCCC 2014b).[16] Today, emissions are 44.2 percent lower than in the base year (see Table 8.2). The reduction was seven times greater than that requested by the KP. As has already been explained, this success was an automatic outcome of the initial KP negotiations. By the time the KP had been signed and ratified, Hungary had already fulfilled its obligations. According to the EU 20-20-20 strategy, Hungary set the following targets: (i) increasing the share of renewable energy sources in final energy consumption to 13 percent; (ii) improving energy efficiency by decreasing thousands of tonnes of oil equivalent to 24.1; and (iii) limiting the rise of GHG emissions to 10 percent (European Commission 2017). As in

Poland, environmental issues in general, including climate change, are not at the forefront of public opinion, and thus are not high on the political agenda. Nor is there a relevant civil society voice that could apply pressure around environmental concerns (Ecological Institute 2012b). Hungary had managed to keep emissions on a downward track for an extended period of time. Despite some slight backsliding they are still fairly level. This is particularly impressive, given that per capita emissions in Hungary from the very start has been lower than in the Czech Republic and Poland (IEA 2016a). In Hungary, the energy market and energy security policy depend strongly on regional cooperation.

Because of its dependence on imports, especially of natural gas and electricity, Hungary has taken several steps to manage its energy supplies. These consist of enhancing storage capacity, developing new supply routes and trying to attract investment in energy-sensitive sectors – the latter to increase capacity and replace aging plants. The main reason for Hungary's relatively low emissions is the prominent role of nuclear energy. Nuclear made up more than 50 percent of Hungary's overall electricity supply in 2014 and is widely seen as the most suitable strategy for the national interest (IEA 2016a). The National Energy Strategy 2030, adopted by the government in 2012, addressed some critical energy issues and provided guidelines for investors.[17] The main government instruments for achieving the reduction objectives are: increasing energy savings and efficiency; a rise in renewable energies; integrating the Central European grid network (with construction of the required cross-border capacities); maintaining and improving the existing nuclear capacity; and utilizing domestic coal and lignite resources in an ecofriendly manner. Hungary is intent on maintaining the key role of nuclear energy in its energy mix. It has also set ambitious targets for renewable energy use by 2020, with particular attention to biomass production. Although per capita energy consumption in Hungary is below the EU average, there is still considerable energy efficiency potential across all sectors (World Bank 2017b). Improving the efficiency level must become one of the government's priorities. An element that needs particular attention is the management of the old district-based heating systems, which requires greater liberalization and a wiser administration of subsidies. Similar to Poland, the national innovation policies with respect to alternative energy sources are increasingly determined by EU programs, and yet its national policy has chosen to devote massive resources to the nuclear sector.

Interestingly, Hungary is one of only three EU member states (along with Italy and Cyprus) that signed up to phase 2 of the KP (UN Treaty Collection 2017; UNFCCC 2014a). With the second phase emanating from the Doha Amendment, meant to cover the time span from 2013 to 2020, seemingly unlikely to ever have enough ratifications to enter into force this is little more than a footnote and has already been basically replaced by the EU 20-20-20 targets (European Commission DG Climate Action 2017b). Still, it seems to reflect at least some ambition from the government with respect to environmental issues. Of more consequence is the Paris Agreement. Hungary has ratified it and is subject to the EU-wide contribution previously elaborated on. It also has exactly the same (low) proposed reduction target as Poland at a 7 percent reduction from 2005 levels by 2030.

Emission trends, policies and prospects in the Czech Republic

The Czech Republic has committed to decreasing its GHG emissions by 8 percent compared to the 195.8 megatons CO_2 eq from the base year of 1990 (European Commission DG Climate Action 2017c). The total GHG emissions and removals in 2015 were 35.1 percent below the base year level (see Table 8.2). As in the other DMEs, the actual emissions reduction has been considerably greater than that requested by the KP. In spite of this achievement, per capita emissions continue to be higher than in the EU28 but the trend is downward sloping (IEA 2016a). As for the 20-20-20 strategy, the Czech Republic has committed to: (i) increasing the share of renewable energy sources in its final energy consumption to 13 percent; (ii) improving energy efficiency by 20 percent; and (iii) reducing GHG emissions to 9 percent above the 2005 level by 2020 (European Commission DG Climate Action 2017b). The most significant reduction in emissions so far has occurred in agriculture, where emissions have been cut in half since 1990 (UNFCCC 2017b). In contrast, the reduction in emissions from energy, the most significant GHG emitter, has been a bit more muted (UNFCC 2017b). Electricity generation is dominated by coal (53 percent in 2015 or the fourth highest in the IEA) and nuclear (32 percent, eighth highest in the IEA), and a significant share of this production is being exported; in 2015 the country had net exports of 12.6 TWh (IEA 2017b).

The Czech Republic's emissions situation is markedly influenced by its historical legacy. Until 1989 its economy was based on energy- and material-intensive industrial production, in which heavy industry – including basic metallurgical material, cement and basic chemicals industries – played an important part. The energy requirements were mainly covered by domestic brown coal and nuclear energy. Heavy industrial production and energy supply sources continue to be important in the Czech economy, as is the share of traditional energy sources. The State Energy Policy that was adopted in 2004 regulates the Czech Republic's energy policy framework.[18] The main priorities are: (i) to strengthen national independence from foreign energy sources; (ii) to maximize the safety of energy sources (including nuclear); and (iii) to promote the sustainability of economic development. After a 2005 review, noteworthy efforts have been made to improve the security of the oil and gas supply. In addition, the electricity and gas markets have been further liberalized. With regard to climate policy, the document's goals were even more ambitious than the targets agreed to under the EU 20-20-20 strategy.

However, this policy focus lost political support, particularly as regards the goal to increase the share of renewables in the policy mix, which has become less of a priority; the government chose instead to augment its efforts toward nuclear power (Ecological Institute 2012c). Emission reduction targets mainly focused on the reduction of energy intensity in production and consumption.

The Czech innovation system can be described as highly centralized and with one of the highest shares of private investment in the EU. The government has continued to announce plans to further increase R&D spending in order to modernize the Czech economy. In the 2007 reform, the development and implementation of sustainable technologies was added to the list of priorities. Only two years later, the Technology Platform for Sustainable Energy was introduced and has become one of the main instruments for implementing the European Strategic Energy Technology Plan. However, despite its centralized character, a lack of coordination among R&D funding opportunities, along with politically set priorities, has hindered the efficient dispersion of funds. The National Research Development and Innovation Policy 2016–2020 aims to address some of these issues. Its focus is on improving the management of the R&D system, evaluating research organizations and strengthening the role of enterprises in launching research and innovation (Section for Science, Research and Innovation of the Government of the Czech Republic 2016; CzechInvest R&D Support Department 2016).

The Czech Republic has run into a bit of a bump in the road with respect to the Paris Agreement. At the time of writing it is one of only two EU member states not to have ratified the Paris Agreement. Interest groups, such as the Confederation of Industry of the Czech Republic, have vehemently opposed the deal over concerns with the effect it will have on the economy. The last hurdle is for passage in the lower house, but that has proven a not insignificant block. As of July 10, 2017, a fifth attempt was being made to pass the Paris Agreement bill through the lower house. It has never made it to a vote, being prevented by procedural mechanisms from opponents in the opposition Civic Democratic party, in the Communist party and even some defectors from within parties who otherwise do support the agreement (Jůn 2017). All of this is against the interesting backdrop by which, according to the proposed EU Effort Sharing Regulation 2021–2030, the Czech Republic will have one of the highest required emission reductions in the ECE region, at a 14 percent drop (Eurpoean Commission DG Climate Action 2017a), which is double that of Poland or Hungary.

Leveling national policies

Most ECE countries' environmental policies are directly guided, or at least strongly stimulated, by EU regulations. The provision of considerable financial resources from Brussels, which is of course conditional, also has a strong influence on the environmental policies of ECE nations. Social and political pressure for more proactive and forward-looking climate policies, comes more from external than internal actors. The Framework Programmes on Research and Technological Development in the field of R&D, along with the Structural and Cohesion Funds from the EU, in which energy supply and climate change play an essential role, are the most prominent tools for pushing the DME's climate agenda. Generally, these EU funds can be seen as powerful tools for attracting investment to finance new technologies and activities (Streimikiene et al. 2007), and all of our countries do benefit from these programs. In the framework of regional policy for the 2014–2020 period, all regional units in our three ECE countries are less developed regions which receive the lion's share of funding, with the exception of the major capital regions of Budapest, Prague and Warsaw (European Commission DG Regional and Urban Policy 2015). This means that for the 2014–2020 period, Poland is being allocated almost €64 billion (by far the largest beneficiary in the EU) (European Commission DG Regional and Urban Policy 2015). Among these funds, a whopping €27.4 billion were dedicated by the EU to the operational programme entitled Infrastructure and Environment (European Commission DG Regional and Urban Policy 2017a). This indirectly results in the EU being the largest climate policy actor in Poland, with at least 45 percent going to fund the low carbon economy, climate change adaptation and low carbon transport infrastructure such as rail (European Commission DG Regional and Urban Policy 2017a). The Czech Republic received 18.2 billion from EU Regional Policy, 5.4 billion of this is dedicated to the environment operational programme (European Commission DG Regional and Urban Policy 2015; European Commission DG Regional and Urban Policy 2017b). The program's funds are earmarked to improve water quality, air quality, reduce environmental burdens from waste flows, energy savings in the public sector and nature conservation (European Commission DG Regional and Urban Policy 2017b). Somewhat similar to in Poland, the separate operational program on transport in the Czech Republic encompasses a mélange of transportation-related investments, which include: funding for green programs such as rail and tram lines; increased capacity for recharging e-vehicles; and support for alternative fuel stations (European Commission DG Regional and Urban Policy 2017c). Both environment and transport operational programs receive over half of EU Regional Policy resources. Finally, in Hungary, of a total budget of €21.5 billion provided by the EU, €3.2 billion are dedicated to the operational program Environmental and Energy Efficiency (European Commission DG Regional and Urban Policy 2015; European Commission DG Regional and Urban Policy 2017d). These focus on interventions in the waste and water management sectors, climate change adaptation, waste management and the use of renewables.

These financial support schemes are relevant, but cannot fundamentally change the overall innovation and climate policies of the DMEs. These are still driven by economic catch-up considerations and short-term policy attitudes of the elites. One factor that explains the gap in political attitudes between climate forerunners and climate laggards is the level of public awareness and, even more importantly, the ability of civil society to effect-ively champion climate concerns. Political concerns debated in the public arena and pushed by civil society organizations, often lead governments to introduce new rules and procedures, and have forced companies to adhere to environmental regulations. Under the communist regimes there had been limited tolerance of dissent, although some environmental organizations with a strict non-political nature were able to operate, at least on a minimal level (O'Brien 2011). In other words, up until 1989 environmental organizations provided a substitute for other forms of forbidden and repressed dissident political organizations. Yet, these environmental organizations have not pros-pered after the collapse of the ancient regimes. Environmental and climate topics rarely play a role in these three countries. Poland has a Green Party – founded in 2003 – but it is not represented in parliament. The other political parties do not see environmental concerns as relevant and green issues are rarely discussed on any kind of meaningful level. Polish civil society, in fact, seems to be more vigorous in campaigning *against*, rather than for, environ-mental protection. Polish government attitudes in EU decision making are usually against more ambitious reduction targets. Climate change policies have failed to transpose several climate and energy directives into national law, and this reflects the role of active opposing strategies. Among the most recent of these strategies was Poland's threat to challenge the EU basis for climate policy at the European Court of Justice, during EU negotiations on burden sharing to meet the EU's Paris targets. This was considered especially extreme, even for Poland (de Carbonnel 2017). This opposition, as previ-ously mentioned, reflects strong industrial interests, in particular from the coal industry and its workers. For example, the Central European Energy Partners (CEEP), mostly composed of state-owned Polish energy firms, is promoting many public initiatives to support the use of coal. CEEP argues that the inter-ests of Central and East European states contradict those of Western EU countries, and they urge the EU to develop a separate energy policy for member states with different economic and energy profiles.[19]

Environmental awareness is similarly underdeveloped in the Czech Republic, where the Green Party also has no parliamentary representation and received a paltry 2.4 percent of the vote in recent elections. Nuclear lobbies play a powerful role in the debates on nuclear policy and were suc-cessful in pressing the government to subsidize nuclear production and in encouraging the enlargement of the Temelín Nuclear Power Station with two new reactors. The latter project was cancelled, mainly due to cost con-siderations, and with political pressures from active organizations having little influence.[20]

Hungary also has a Green Party – founded in 2009 – that won 7.5 percent of the votes in the 2010 elections and 5.3 percent of the votes in the 2014 elections, and also won a seat at the 2014 elections for the European Parlia-ment. Born out of an NGO, it mixes an ecologist and a liberal program, but has lately been accused by some observers of being inexpert and too idealistic, without a concrete ecologist nature (Müller 2011). In any case, the political and social situation in Hungary does not seem supportive of large debates about climate policies and requisite political action.

DMEs as climate and innovation laggards: assessment and perspectives

In all three DMEs under consideration, GHG emissions have been drastically reduced since the beginning of the 1990s, which one can argue is mainly the outcome of an economic transformation crisis. We argue that even though this is correct, at the same time it is also true that the countries have continued on a decreasing emission path, albeit with less speed.

One concern that immediately emerged after 1990, was that the reduction in emissions could lead to the collapse of the economy. This collapse did happen and so did the reduction of emissions, but the latter was the result of former. Later on, all three ECE economies achieved strong economic growth rates and were still able to reduce emissions. Compared to the communist past, an environmental transformation has occurred, allowing these countries to achieve simultaneous GDP growth and emission reduction. There are still margins to reduce GHG emissions per unit of GDP, especially in Poland and the Czech Republic, and to bring them in line with the most developed European countries. It is difficult to forecast how the situation will evolve in the future.

First of all, we cannot attribute the reduction in GHG emissions in Poland, Hungary and the Czech Republic to an endogenous development of green innovations, to particular climate policies or to other environmental policies. The reduction occurred because of the structural change experienced in these countries, which has progressively led to a more efficient production system and more efficient use of resources. The influx of FDI and its implied technology transfer contributed to this success.

Second, there is no evidence that there was an active national innovation system working to generate, introduce or disseminate green innovations. The public component of the scientific and technological system has been at the margins of the environmental issue. The business component was active indirectly, and mostly because it had to satisfy standards and regulations coming from abroad. (Smarzynska Javorcik and Wei 2004). But the integration with the EU has allowed these countries to benefit from more efficient technology systems. The fleet of vehicles was almost totally replaced, household heating systems were changed, and industrial plants were restructured. Automobiles, turbines and appliances became more environmentally friendly, and incorporated green innovations, though most of these innovations were generated elsewhere (even when they were assembled in these ECE countries).

Third, we have noted that the speed of emission reductions has decreased, and that at the same time the share of renewable energy has continued to increase. This is an important result since it cannot be attributed merely to passive structural change, but it is the outcome of deliberate policies aimed at the introduction of new power generation plants. Still, in all three DMEs, electricity generation is provided mainly through 'old' technologies (coal and nuclear), and those sectors are heavily protected in economic, as well as in political, terms. Fourth, in none of the DMEs could we detect even nascent green political coalitions either driving policies, or even providing a political push.

In spite of the similarities, we have also identified some strong differences in national strategies. In Poland, the coal regime is rather persistent and is seen by political parties and trade unions as the most conducive to the national interest, because of its low cost. In Hungary, there is a strong propensity to believe that it is nuclear energy that will reduce the country's dependency on external sources. The Czech Republic is in-between these two strategies.

In a positive manner, we argue that 'outsiders' drive active climate policies in all three DMEs. Two drivers were identified:

1   *The predominant activities of TNCs.* Through acquisitions and greenfield investments, they have become a core part of the industrial complex. They have managed to transfer know-how and expertise to their newly acquired subsidiaries in Poland, Hungary and the Czech Republic, which has had an indirect environmental impact. TNCs are also using these countries both to serve the local market, and to organize their European and global production in intra-firm value-added chains. TNCs are therefore willing and prepared to apply the environmental standards and regulations of other European countries, and this has been a major force for the introduction and diffusion of their production techniques.
2   *European regulations and incentives.* The national authorities in Poland, Hungary and the Czech Republic did not have much room to maneuvre with regard to environmental rules and directives provided by the EU. This holds particularly true for programs that come with substantial financial funding that is tied to environmental and climate conditionality.

Even if emission decreases will probably be slower in the future, it is reasonable to assume that the combined effect of TNC activity, EU regulations and incentives, and regional trade will continue to instigate emission reductions. At the same time, it is obvious that the economies will have to deal with pertinent and potentially difficult unlocking processes, in order to simultaneously achieve their emission targets and modernize their production regimes.

Notes

1 The targets were set by the European Council in March 2007, and were enacted through a set of complementary legislation, the so-called climate and energy package. For details see Böhringer et al. 2009; Capros et al. 2011.

2 NIRs can be downloaded from the UNFCCC website: http://unfccc.int/ national_reports/annex_i_GHG_inventories/national_inventories_submissions/ items/6598.php.

3 The other flexible mechanisms are Joint Implementation and Clean Development. These are also known as project-based mechanisms, since they allow parties to acquire credits by financing reduction projects in Annex I countries in the former case and in non-Annex I parties in the latter.

4 The EU ETS is a milestone of EU climate policy and its main instrument for reducing industrial GHG emissions. It covers more than 11,000 power stations, industrial plants and airlines. It is based on the 'cap and trade' principle, that is a cap, or limit, is set on the total amount of GHG that can be emitted by the factories, power plants and other activities covered by the system. Within the cap, firms receive emission credits that they can exchange with one another. Each year, every company must buy enough credits to cover its emissions if it does not want to incur heavy fines. Launched in 2005, the EU ETS is now in its third phase, running from 2013 to 2020. The revision has harmonized the system, and has defined auctioning, not free allocation, as the default method for allocating allowances, and increased the sectors covered, which now represent 45 percent of total EU emissions.

5 See Carbon Finance and the World Bank, *Mapping Carbon Pricing Initiatives*, May 2013, World Bank report available from www-wds.worldbank.org; Carbon Finance and the World Bank, *State and Trends of the Carbon Market 2011*, *State and Trends of the Carbon Market 2012*, World Bank reports available from http://site resources.worldbank.org.

6 LULUCF, that is, land use, land use change, and forestry activities, are a GHG inventory sector that covers emissions and removals of GHG resulting from measures in such areas.

7 Information is based on interviews held from June–September 2013 with three top managers of TNCs. One of these managers was responsible for R&D, another for product development and one for quality control. All respondents were asked: "Will your company locate polluting production in countries, such as ECE, that have lower environmental rigorous standards?" Somewhat surprisingly, the answer was always "No."

8 See the PISA ranking at OECD, www.oecd.org/pisa/46643496.pdf.

9 The mismatch between the knowledge generated by scientists and the innovation needs of the production units has often been the argument of ironic films and novels. See Iskander 1975.

10 See OECD metadata for NABS 2007 http://stats.oecd.org/oecdstat_metadata/ showmetadata.ashx?dataset=gbaord_nabs2007.

11 Jan Cienski, "Poland Struggles to Break its Dependency on Coal Power," *Financial Times*, November 10, 2013.

12 Available at www.mg.gov.pl/files/upload/8134/Polityka%20energetyczna%20ost_ en.pdf.

13 See International Energy Agency report *Energy Policies of IEA Countries: Poland 2011 Review*, available on www.iea.org.

14 Coal accounts for 51% of Poland's primary energy supply and 90% of electricity generation.

15 See International Energy Agency report 2016b.

16 See: https://unfccc.int/process/transparency-and-reporting/reporting-and-review-under-the-kyoto-protocol/first-commitment-period/kyoto-protocol-base-year-data-for-the-first-commitment-period-of-the-kyoto-protocol.

17 Available: www.kormany.hu/en/ministry-of-national-development/news/national-energy-strategy-2030-published.

18 Available: www.mzp.cz/C125750E003B698B/en/sep_cz/$FILE/OPZP-SEP-2008 1229.pdf.

19 See the report commissioned by CEEP Available: www.ey.com/Publication/ vwLUAssets/Central_Europe_Energy_Partners_brochure/$FILE/CEEP%20 brochure.pdf.

20 See "Czech nuclear tender seen pivotal after Fukushima," *Reuters* 2012. Available: www.reuters.com/article/2012/06/29/czech-nuclear-idUSL6E8HP17N20120629.

Bibliography

Aardal, B. and Valen, H. (1995). *Konflikt og opinion*. Oslo: NKS-forlaget.

Abe, S. (2007). *Invitation to "Cool Earth 50" – 3 Proposals, 3 Principles*. Available: www.kantei.go.jp/foreign/abespeech/2007/05/24speech_e.html.

Abelshauser, W. (2004). *Deutsche Wirtschaftsgeschichte seit 1945*. München: Beck.

Ackerman, F. (2009). "Carbon Embedded in China's Trade." Working Paper WP-US-0906. Stockholm: Stockholm Environment Institute. Available: http://sei-us.org/Publications_PDF/SEI-WorkingProgressUS-0906.pdf.

Adressa (2013). "Mer penger til Enova." *Adressa*, October 14. Available: www.adressa.no/nyheter/politikk/article8440117.ece (accessed May 6, 2014).

Aftenbladet (2012). "CO₂-utslipp er blitt billigare." *Aftenbladet*, January 30. Available: www.aftenbladet.no/energi/klima/CO2-utslepp-er-blitt-billigare-2924197.html (accessed April 25, 2014).

Aftenposten (2014). "Hevder regnskogprosjektet har vært en 'kjempesuksess.'" *Aftenposten*, March 4. Available: www.aftenposten.no/nyheter/iriks/politikk/Hevder-regnskogprosjektet-har-vart-kjempesuksess-7489130.html#.U2EMUfl_uCk (accessed April 30, 2014).

Agency for Natural Resources and Energy, Ministry of Economy, Trade and Industry (2010). *Top Runner Program: Developing the World's Best Energy-Efficient Appliances*. March. Available: www.enecho.meti.go.jp/category/saving_and_new/saving/enterprise/overview/pdf/toprunner2011.03en-1103.pdf (accessed April 3, 2015).

Aghion, P., Veugelers, R. and Serre, C. (2009). *Cold Start for the Green Innovation Machine*. Bruegel Policy Contribution No. 2009/12. Brussels: Bruegel.

Aldrich, D. (2008). *Site Fights: Divisive Facilities and Civil Society in Japan and the West*. Ithaca, NY: Cornell University Press.

Aldrich, D. (2012). *Building Resilience: Social Capital in Post-Disaster Recovery*. Chicago IL: University of Chicago Press.

Altenburg, T. and Pegels, A. (2012). "Sustainability-Oriented Innovation Systems: Managing the Green Transformation." *Innovation and Development*, 2 (1): 5–22.

Amin, A., Cameron, A. and Hudson, R. (2002). *Placing the Social Economy*. London: Routledge.

Andonova, Liliana B. (2004). *Transnational Politics of the Environment. The European Union and Environmental Policy in Central and Eastern Europe*, MIT Press, Cambridge.

Andonova, L.B., Betsill, M.M. and Bulkeley, H. (2009). "Transnational Climate Governance." *Global Environmental Politics*, 9 (2): 52–73.

Andonova, L.B., Mansfield, E.D. and Milner, H.V. (2007). "International Trade and Environmental Policy in the Postcommunist World." *Comparative Political Studies*, 40 (7): 782–807.

Andor, M.A., Frondel, M. and Vance, C. (2017). "Germany's Energiewende: A Tale of Increasing Costs and Decreasing Willingness-To-Pay." *Energy Journal*, 38 (SII): 211–228.

Annesley, C. (2004). *Postindustrial Germany: Services, Technological Transformation and Knowledge in Unified Germany*. Manchester: Manchester University Press.

Antweiler, W. and Harrison, K. (2007). "Canada's Voluntary ARET Program: Limited Success Despite Industry Cosponsorship." *Journal of Policy Analysis and Management* 26 (4): 755–773.

Arbeitsgemeinschaft Energiebilanzen (2013). Bruttostromerzeugung in Deutschland von 1990 bis 2012 nach Energieträgern. Available: www.ag-energiebilanzen.de/index.brd_stromerzeugung1990_2012.pdf.

Arbeitsgemeinschaft Energiebilanzen (2017). Energieverbrauch in Deutschland im Jahr 2016. Available: www.ag-energiebilanezn.de/20-0-Berichte.html.

Arto, I., Rueda-Cantuche, J.M., Andreoni, V., Mongelli, I. and Genty, A. (2014). "The game of trading jobs for emissions." *Energy Policy*, 66: 517–525.

Asuka-Zhang, S. (2003). "Development Assistance and Japan's Climate Change Diplomacy: Priorities and Future Options." In P.G. Harris (ed.), *China's Responsibility for Climate Change: Ethics, Fairness, and Environmental Policy*. Bristol: Policy Press, 152–166.

Baek, S.W. (2005). "Does China Follow the East Asian Development Model?" *Journal of Contemporary Asia* 35 (4): 485–495.

Baeumler, A., Chen, M., Iuchi, K. and Suzuki, H. (2012). "Eco-Cities and Low-Carbon Cities: The China Context and Global Perspectives." In A. Baeumler, E. Ijjasz-Vasquez and S. Mehndiratta (eds), *Sustainable Low-Carbon City Development in China*. Washington, DC: World Bank, pp. 33–63. Available: http://siteresources.worldbank.org/EXTNEWSCHINESE/Resources/3196537-1202098669693/463 5541-1335945747603/low_carbon_city_full_en.pdf.

Bailey, I. (2007). "Market Environmentalism, New Environmental Policy Instruments, and Climate Policy in the United Kingdom and Germany." *Annals of the Association of American Geographers*, 97 (3): 530–550.

Baldwin, R. and Lopez-Gonzalez, J. (2014). "Supply-chain Trade: A Portrait of Global Patterns and Several Testable Hypotheses." *The World Economy*, doi: 10.1111/twec.12189.

Bank of England: Prudential Regulation Authority (2015). *The Impact of Climate Change on the UK Insurance Sector: A Climate Change Adaptation Report by the Prudential Regulation Authority*. London: Bank of England Prudential Regulation Authority.

Bárány, A. and Grigonytė, D. (2015). *ECFIN Economic Brief: Measuring Fossil Fuel Subsidies*. Brussels: European Commission DG Economic and Financial Affairs. Available: http://ec.europa.eu/economy_finance/publications/economic_briefs/2015/pdf/eb40_en.pdf.

Bassi, S., Dechezleprêtre, A. and Fankhauser, S. (2013). *Climate Change Policies and the UK Business Sector: Overview, Impacts and Suggestions for Reform, Policy Paper*. LSE Centre for Climate Change Economics and Policy, Grantham Research Institute on Climate Change and the Environment, London: LSE.

Bast, E., Makhijani, S., Pickard, S. and Whitley, S. (2014). The fossil fuel bailout: G20 subsidies for oil, gas and coal exploration. Report, Overseas Development Institute and Oil Change International. Available: http://priceofoil.org/content/uploads/2014/11/G20-Fossil-Fuel-Bailout-Full.pdf.

Bathelt, H. and Gertler, M.S. (2005). "The German Variety of Capitalism: Forces and Dynamics of Evolutionary Change." *Economic Geography*, 81 (1): 1–9.

Baumol, W. (2002). *The Free-Market Innovation Machine: Analyzing the Growth Miracle of Capitalism*. Princeton, NJ: Princeton University Press.

BBC (2012). "Norway Aims for Carbon Leadership." *BBC*, May 11. Available: www.bbc.co.uk/news/science-environment-18009623 (accessed August 15, 2013).

Begley, S., Conant, E. and Stein, S. (2007). "The Truth about Denial." *Newsweek*. Available: http://academic.evergreen.edu/curricular/energy/0708/articles/Truth DenialNewsweek07Aug.pdf (accessed January 12, 2014).

Beinhocker, E., Oppenheim, J., Irons, B., Lahti, M.a, Farrell, D., Nyquist, S., Remes, J., Nauclér, T. and Enkvist, P.-A. (2008). *The Carbon Productivity Challenge: Curbing Climate Change and Sustaining Economic Growth*. McKinsey Global Institute, McKinsey Climate Change Special Initiative. Available: www.mckinsey.com/insights/energy_resources_materials/the_carbon_productivity_challenge.

Beisea, M. and Rennings, K. (2005). "Lead Markets and Regulation: A Framework for Analyzing the International Diffusion of Environmental Innovations." *Ecological Economics*, 52 (1): 5–17.

Belitz, H. and Kirn, T. (2008). "Deutlicher Zusammenhang zwischen Innovationsfähigkeit und Einstellungen zu Wissenschaft und Technik im internationalen Vergleich." In *DIW Vierteljahreshefte zur Wirtschaftsforschung, Vol. 2: Nationale Innovationssysteme im Vergleich*. Berlin: Duncker und Humblot, pp. 49–64.

Bergek, A. and Jacobsson, S. (2011). "Fremmer grønne sertifikater ny teknologi?" In J. Hanson, S. Kasa and O. Wicken (eds), *Energirikdommens paradokser: Innovasjon som klimapolitikk og næringsutvikling*. Oslo: Universitetsforlaget.

Bergesen, H.O., Roland, K. and Sydnes, A.K. (1995). *Norge i det globale drivhuset*. Oslo: Universitetsforlaget.

Bijsterbosch, M. and Kolasa, M. (2010). "FDI and Productivity Convergence in Central and Eastern Europe: An Industry-Level Investigation." *Review of World Economics*, 145 (4): 689–712.

Bina, O. (2011). "Responsibilities for Emissions and Aspirations for Development." In P.G. Harris (ed.), *China's Responsibility for Climate Change: Ethics, Fairness, and Environmental Policy*. Bristol: Policy Press, pp. 47–70.

Blackwill, R. and O'Sullivan, M. (2014). "America's Energy Edge: The Geopolitical Consequences of the Shale Revolution." *Foreign Affairs*, 93 (2): 102–114.

Blanchard, B. and Stanway, D. (2014). "China to 'Declare War' on Pollution, Premier Says." Reuters. March 4. Available: www.reuters.com/article/2014/03/05/us-china-parliament-pollution-idUSBREA2405W20140305 (accessed April 3, 2015).

Bloomberg News (2014). "China Rushes to Harness Wind While Government Still Pays." Available: www.bloomberg.com/news/2014-10-29/china-rushes-to-harness-wind-while-government-still-pays.html (accessed April 3, 2015).

Boasson, E.L. (2011). *Norsk miljøpolitikk og EU: EØS-avtalen som inspirasjonskilde og maktmiddel*. Oslo: Europautredningen.

Boden, T., Marland, G. and Andres, B. (2010). *Global, Regional, and National Fossil-Fuel CO₂ Emissions*. Carbon Dioxide Information Analysis Center, Oak Ridge National Laboratory. doi 10.3334/CDIAC/00001.

Bogumil, P. (2014). *ECFIN Country Focus: Composition of Capital Inflows to Central and Eastern Europe (CEE) – is Poland Different?* Brussels: European Commission DG Economic and Financial Affairs. Available: http://ec.europa.eu/economy_finance/publications/country_focus/2014/pdf/cf_vol. 11_issue8_en.pdf.

Bohle, D. and Greskovits, B. (2007). "Neoliberalism, Embedded Neoliberalism and Neocorporatism: Towards Transnational Capitalism in Central-Eastern Europe." *West European Politics*, 30 (3): 443–466.

Böhringer, C. (2014). "Two Decades of European Climate Policy: A Critical Appraisal." *Review of Environmental Economics and Policy*, 8 (1): 1–17.

Böhringer, L. and Moslener, R. (2009). "EU Climate Policy up to 2020: An Economic Impact Assessment." *Energy Economics*, 31 (2): 295–305.

Bolesta, A. (2015). *China and Post-Socialist Development*. Bristol: Policy Press.

Booth, A. (2001). *The British Economy in the Twentieth Century*. London: Palgrave.

Borshchevska, Y. (2016). "Putting Competitive Advantage at Stake? Energiewende in the Discursive Practices of German Industrial Actors." *Journal of International Studies*, 9 (3): 99–113.

Bowen, A. and Rydge, J. (2011). *Climate Change Policy in the United Kingdom*. Policy Paper August 2011, Centre for Climate Change Economics and Policy and Grantham Research Institute on Climate Change and the Environment. London: LSE.

Boyd, B. (2017). "Working Together on Climate Change: Policy Transfer and Convergence in Four Canadian Provinces." *Publius: The Journal of Federalism* 47 (4): 546–571.

Boyer, R., Uemura, H. and Isogai, A. (eds) (2012). *Diversity and Transformations of Asian Capitalisms*. New York: Routledge.

Brachert, M. and Hornych, C. (2011). "Entrepreneurial Opportunity and the Formation of Photovoltaic Clusters in Eastern Germany." In R. Wüstenhagen and R. Wuebker (eds), *The Handbook of Research on Energy Entrepreneurship*. Cheltenham: Elgar, pp. 83–103.

Bradsher, K. (2010). "China Leading Global Race to Make Clean Energy." *New York Times*, 30 January.

Brady, D. and Eilperin, J. (2017). "EPA Chief Scott Pruitt Tells Coal Miners He Will Repeal Power Plant Rule Tuesday: 'The War against Coal is over'." *Washington Post*, October 9. Available: www.washingtonpost.com/news/energy-environment/wp/2017/10/09/pruitt-tells-coal-miners-he-will-repeal-power-plan-rule-tuesday-the-war-on-coal-is-over/?noredirect=on&utm_term=.e9e7f2929045.

Bramley, M. (2010). *Climate Leadership, Economic Prosperity: Final Report on an Economic Study of Greenhouse Gas Targets and Policies for Canada*. Available: http://dspace.cigilibrary.org/jspui/handle/123456789/27182 (accessed January 13, 2014).

Brand, U. and Wissen, M. (2013). "Crisis and Continuity of Capitalist Society–Nature Relationships: The Imperial Mode of Living and the Limits to Environmental Governance." *Review of International Political Economy*, 20 (4), 687–711.

Broadbent, G. (2002). "From Heat to Light? Japan's Changing Response to Global Warming." In J. Montgomery and N. Glazer (eds), *Sovereignty Under Challenge: How Governments Respond*. Piscataway, NJ: Transaction Publishers, pp. 109–142.

Broadbent, J. (1998). *Environmental Politics in Japan: Networks of Power and Protest*. Cambridge: Cambridge University Press.

Brulle, R.J. (2013). "Institutionalizing Delay: Foundation Funding and the Creation of US Climate Change Countermovement Organizations." *Climatic Change*, 124 (4): 681–694.

Bruvoll, A., Dalen, H.M. and Larsen, B.M. (2012). "Political Motives in Climate and Energy Policy." Discussion papers No. 721. Oslo: Statistics Norway.

Bundesministerium für Wirtschaft und Energie (2012). *First Monitoring Report "Energy of the Future" 2011 – Summary*. Berlin: BMWi.

Bundesministerium für Wirtschaft und Energie (2016). *Erneuerbare Energien in Zahlen: Nationale und internationale Entwicklungen im Jahr 2014.* Berlin: BMWi.

Bundesministerium für Wirtschaft und Energie und Arbeitsgruppe Erneuerbare Energien-Statistik (2017). *Aktuelle Informationen: Erneuerbare Energien im Jahre 2016.* Berlin: BMWi – AG EE-Stat. Available: www.bmwi.de/Redaktion/DE/Text sammlungen/Energie/arbeitsgruppe-erneuerbare-energien-statistik.html.

Bundesministerium für Umwelt, Naturschutz und Reaktorsicherheit (2012). *Green-Tech Made in Germany 3.0: Umwelttechnologie-Atlas für Deutschland.* Berlin: BMU.

Bundesnetzagentur (2010). *Monitoring Report 2010.* Bonn: Bundesnetzagentur.

Bundesverband der Energie- und Wasserwirtschaft (2016). *Erneuerbare Energien und das EEG: Zahlen, Fakten, Grafiken.* Berlin: BDEW.

Burck, J., Marten, F. and Bals, C. (2013). *The Climate Change Performance Index: Results 2014.* Berlin and Brussels: Climate Action Network Europe.

Burgess, Stephen (2011). "Measuring Financial Sector Output and its Contribution to UK GDP." *Bank of England Quarterly Bulletin.* Available: http://ssrn.com/abstract=1933710.

Busch, A. (2005). "Globalisation and National Varieties of Capitalism: The Contested Viability of the 'German Model'." *German Politics*, 14 (2): 125–139.

Butler, L. and Neuhoff, K. (2008). "Comparison of Feed-In Tariff, Quota and Auction Mechanisms to Support Wind Power Development." *Renewable Energy*, 33: 1854–1867.

Cabinet Office (2010). *The Coalition: Our Programme for Government.* London: Cabinet Office. Available: www.gov.uk/government/uploads/system/uploads/attachment_data/file/78977/coalition_programme_for_government.pdf.

Canadian Manufacturers and Exporters (2002). *Pain Without Gain: Canada and the Kyoto Protocol.* Ottawa: Canadian Manufacturers and Exporters.

Capros, P., Mantzos, L., Parousos, L., Tasios, N., Klaassen, G. and Van Ierland, T. (2011). "Analysis of the EU Policy Package on Climate Change and Renewables." *Energy Policy*, 39 (3): 1476–1485.

Carbon Trust and Shell (2013). *Low Carbon Entrepreneurs: The New Engines of Growth.* London: Carbon Trust. Available: www.carbontrust.com/resources/reports/technology/low-carbon-entrepreneurs.

Carlin, W. and Soskice, D. (2009). "German Economic Performance: Disentangling the Role of Supply-Side Reforms, Macroeconomic Policy and Coordinated Economy Institutions." *Socio-Economic Review*, 7 (1): 67–99.

Carter, N. (2008). "Combating Climate Change in the UK: Challenges and Obstacles." *The Political Quarterly*, 79: 194–205.

Carter, N. (2009). "Vote Blue, Go Green? Cameron's Conservatives and the Environment." *The Political Quarterly*, 80 (2): 233–242.

Carter, N. (2014). "The Politics of Climate Change in the UK." *WIREs Climate Change*, 5 (2): 423–433.

Casper, S. and Kettler, H. (2001). "National Institutional Frameworks and the Hybridization of Entrepreneurial Business Models: The German and UK Biotechnology Sectors." *Industry and Innovation*, 8 (1): 5–30.

Casper, S. and Murray F. (2004). *How Reflexive are Actors to Institutions: Policy Entrepreneurship and Marketplace Formation in German Biotechnology.* Cambridge, MA: MIT Press.

Casper, S., Lehrer, M. and Soskice, D. (1999). "Can High-Technology Industries Prosper in Germany? Institutional Frameworks and the Evolution of the German Software and Biotechnology Industries." *Industry and Innovation*, 6 (1): 5–24.

Cernat, L. (2006). *Europeanization, Varieties of Capitalism and Economic Performance in Central and Eastern Europe*. Basingstoke: Palgrave Macmillan.

Chen, G. (2009). *Politics of China's Environmental Protection: Problems and Prospects*. Singapore: World Scientific Publishing Co.

Chen, K. and Reklev, S. (2014). "China's National Carbon Market to START in 2016—Official." *Reuters*. August 31. Available: www.reuters.com/article/2014/08/31/china-carbontrading-idUSL3N0R107420140831 (accessed April 3, 2015).

Chenghui, Z., Zadek, S., Ning, C. and Halle, M. (2015). *Greening China's Financial System: Synthesis Report*. International Institute for Sustainable Development and Finance Research Institute, Development Research Center of the State Council of China. Available: www.iisd.org/sites/default/files/publications/greening-chinas-financial-system-synthesis-report_0.pdf.

China Council for International Cooperation on Environment and Development (2013). *CCICED Update*. Issue 6, May 31. Available: www.cciced.net/encciced/newscenter/update/2013/201307/P020130703540644566013.pdf (accessed April 3, 2015).

Chinese Civil Society Coalition on Climate Change (2009). *Chinese Civil Society on Climate Change: Consensus and Strategies*, 17 November. Available: www.eu-china.net/web/cms/upload/pdf/materialien/eu-china_2009_hintergrund_14.pdf (accessed April 3, 2015).

Christiansen, C.A. (2002). "New Renewable Energy Developments and the Climate Change Issue: A Case Study of Norwegian Politics." *Energy Policy*, 30: 235–243.

Christiansen, A.C. and Skjærseth, J.B. (2005). "Climate Change Policies in Norway and the Netherlands: Different Instruments, Similar Outcome." *Energy & Environment*, 16 (1): 1–25.

Christiansen, A.C. and Skjærseth, J.B. (2006). "Environmental Policy Instruments and Technological Change in the Energy Sector: Findings from Comparative Empirical Research." *Energy & Environment*, 17 (2): 223–241.

Císař, O. and Vráblíková, K. (2013). "Transnational Activism of Social Movement Organizations: The Effect of European Union Funding on Local Groups in the Czech Republic." *European Union Politics*, 14 (1): 140–160.

Citizens' Nuclear Information Center (2007). *Open Letter and Questions Concerning the Relevance of Nuclear Power in Addressing the Problem of Global Warming*. Available: www.cnic.jp/english/publications/pdffiles/lovelock.pdf (accessed April 3, 2015).

Citizens' Alliance for Saving the Atmosphere and the Earth (2010). *Japan's −25% GHG Emission Reduction Target can be Achieved Domestically. Results of CASA 2020 Model Simulation, Summary of Interim Report*. Available: www.bnet.jp/casa/teigen/paper/CASAModel2020Ver1%20clear%20version.pdf (accessed April 3, 2015).

Claes, D.H. and Vik, A. (2012). "Kraftsektoren: fra samfunnsgode til handelsvare." In D.H. Claes and P.K. Mydske (eds), *Forretning eller fordeling: Reform av offentlige nettverkstjenester*. Oslo: Universitetsforlaget.

Clark, P. (2015). "Carney on Climate: Stranded Fossil Fuel Theory Proves Potent." *Financial Times*. Available: www.ft.com/intl/cms/s/0/97ba13d4-6772-11e5-97d0-1456a776a4f5.html#axzz3n9FaYzSv.

Clark, P. (2015). "Mark Carney Warns Investors Face 'Huge' Climate Change Losses." *Financial Times*. Available: www.ft.com/intl/cms/s/0/622de3da-66e6-11e5-97d0-1456a776a4f5.html#axzz3qYaCzkdI.

Clean Coal Task Group (2011). *Roadmap for Coal*. London: TUC. Available: www.tuc.org.uk/industrial-issues/energy/regional-policy/clean-coal-task-group-cctg/roadmap-coal.

Clean Energy Canada (2014). *Tracking the Energy Revolution: Canada Edition 2014.* Available: http://cleanenergycanada.org/wp-content/uploads/2014/12/Tracking-the-Energy-Revolution-Canada-.pdf.

Clover, I. (2014). "Japan Installed 7 GW of solar capacity in last fiscal year." *PV Magazine,* June 19. Available: www.pv-magazine.com/news/details/beitrag/japan-installed-7-gw-of-solar-capacity-in-last-fiscal-year_100015475/ (accessed March 29, 2015).

Coates, D. (1999). "Models of Capitalism in the New World Order: The UK Case." *Political Studies,* 47 (4): 643–660.

Collier, P. and Venables, A. (2014). "Closing Coal Economic and Moral Incentives." *Oxford Review of Economic Policy,* 30 (3): 492–512.

Confederation of British Industries (2012). *The Colour of Growth: Maximising the Potential of Green Business.* London: CBI.

Conservative Party (2010). *The Conservative Manifesto 2010: Invitation to Join the Government of Britain.* London: Conservative Party. Available: http://conservativehome.blogs.com/files/conservative-manifesto-2010.pdf.

Copps, S. (2004). *Worth Fighting For.* Toronto: McClelland & Stewart.

Cornell University (2009). "Improved Air Quality during Beijing Olympics Could Inform Pollution-curbing Policies." *ScienceDaily,* August 5. Available: www.sciencedaily.com/releases/2009/07/090724113548.htm (accessed April 3, 2015).

Cox, E., Johnstone, P. and Stirling, A. (2016). "Understanding the Intensity of UK Policy Commitments to Nuclear Power." *Science Policy Research Unit Working Paper Series SWPS 2016–16.* Brighton: SPRU.

Crouch, C. (2005). *Capitalist Diversity and Change: Recombinant Governance and Institutional Entrepreneurs.* Oxford: Oxford University Press.

Crouch, C., Keune, M., Rafiqui, P.S., Sjöberg, Ö. and Tóth, A. (2009). "Three Cases of Changing Capitalism: Sweden, Hungary, and the United Kingdom." in C. Crouch and H. Voelzkow (eds), *Innovation in Local Economies: Germany in Comparative Context.* Oxford: Oxford University Press, pp. 43–69.

Cunningham, P. and Sweinsdottir, T. (2012). *Erawatch Analytical Country Report 2012: United Kingdom.* Brussels: European Commission. Available: http://erawatch.jrc.ec.europa.eu/erawatch/export/sites/default/galleries/generic_files/file_0387.pdf.

CzechInvest R&D Support Department (2016). *National R&D&I Policy.* Available: www.czech-research.com/rd-system/key-documents/national-research-development-and-innovation-policy-of-the-czech-republic-2016-2020/.

Dagger, S.B. (2009). *Energiepolitik und Lobbying.* Stuttgart : Die Novelle des ErneuerbareEnergien-Gesetzes (EEG).

Daly, H. (1975). "Developing Economies and the Steady State." *The Developing Economies* 13 (3): 231–242.

Dasgupta, S. and Wheeler, D. (1997). *Citizen Complaints as Environmental Indicators.* The World Bank, Policy Research Department, Environment, Infrastructure, and Agriculture Division, Policy Research Working Paper 1704. Washington, DC: The World Bank.

Dauvergne, P. (1997). *Shadows in the Forest: Japan and the Political Economy of Deforestation in Southeast Asia.* Cambridge, MA: MIT Press.

Davis, S.J., Peters, G.P. and Caldeira, K. (2011). "The Supply Chain of CO_2 Emissions." *Proceedings of the National Academy of Sciences,* 108 (45): 18554–18559.

De Carbonnel, A. (2017). "Exclusive: Polish 'Bluff' in EU Climate Talks Tests Bloc's Patience.". *Reuters,* February 3. Available: www.reuters.com/article/us-poland-eu-climatechange-exclusive/exclusive-polish-bluff-in-eu-climate-talks-tests-blocs-patience-idUSKBN15I2N7.

Dechezlepretre, A. and Sato, M. (2014). *The Impacts of Environmental Regulations on Competitiveness*. London: LSE. Available: www.lse.ac.uk/GranthamInstitute/wp-content/uploads/2014/11/Impacts_of_Environmental_Regulations.pdf.

den Elzen, M.G.J., Olivier, J.G.J., Höhne, N. and Janssens-Maenhout, G. (2013). "Countries' Contributions to Climate Change: Effect of Accounting for All Greenhouse Gases, Recent Trends, Basic Needs and Technological Progress." *Climate Change*, 121 (2): 297–412.

Department for Business, Energy and Industrial Strategy (2017). *Fuel Mix Disclosure Data Table*, August 2016. London: DBEIS. Available: www.gov.uk/government/uploads/system/uploads/attachment_data/file/542570/FuelmixdiFuelmixdisclosu 2016__3_.pdf.

Department for Business, Enterprise and Regulatory Reform (2009). *Impact of RDA Spending, National Report: Vol. 2, Regional Annexes*. London: DBERR. Available: www.berr.gov.uk/files/file50736.pdf.

Department of Business, Innovation and Skills (2009). "Government on Course to Create Europe's Largest Technology Venture Capital Fund." Press release, December 9. London: BIS. Available: www.capitalforenterprise.gov.uk/files/UKIIF.pdf.

Department of Business, Innovation and Skills (2010). *UK Low Carbon Industrial Strategy – Establishing an Industrial Policy for Greener Growth*. London: BIS. Available: www.oecd.org/sti/ind/45010315.pdf.

Department of Business, Innovation and Skills (2012). *Annual Innovation Report 2012*. London: BIS. Available: https://assets.publishing.service.gov.uk/government/uploads/system/uploads/attachment_data/file/34805/12-p188-annual-innovation-report-2012.pdf.

Department of Energy and Climate Change (2009). *The UK Low Carbon Transition Plan: National Strategy for Climate and Energy*. London: DECC.

Department of Energy and Climate Change (2011a). *The Carbon Plan: Delivering Our Low-Carbon Future*. London: DECC. Available: www.gov.uk/government/uploads/system/uploads/attachment_data/file/47613/3702-the-carbon-plan-delivering-our-low-carbon-future.pdf.

Department of Energy and Climate Change (2011b). *Planning Our Electric Future: A White Paper for Secure, Affordable and Low-Carbon Electricity*. London: DECC. Available: www.gov.uk/government/uploads/system/uploads/attachment_data/file/48129/2176-emr-white-paper.pdf.

Department of Energy and Climate Change (2012). *Electricity Market Reform: Policy Overview*. London: DECC. Available: www.gov.uk/government/uploads/system/uploads/attachment_data/file/65634/7090-electricity-market-reform-policy-overview-pdf.

Department of Energy and Climate Change (2013a). *Local Authority CO_2 Emissions Estimates 2011: Statistical Summary and UK Maps*. London: DECC. Available: www.gov.uk/government/uploads/system/uploads/attachment_data/file/211878/110713_Local_CO2_NS_Annex_B.pdf.

Department of Energy and Climate Change (2013b). *Fuel Mix Disclosure 2013*. London: DECC. Available: www.gov.uk/government/uploads/system/uploads/attachment_data/file/82783/Fuelmixdisclosure2013.pdf.

Department of Energy and Climate Change (2013c). *2012 UK Greenhouse Gas Emissions, Provisional Figures and 2011 UK Greenhouse Gas Emissions, Final Figures by Fuel Type and End-User*. London: DECC. Available: www.gov.uk/government/uploads/system/uploads/attachment_data/file/193414/280313_ghg_national_statistics_release_2012_provisional.pdf.

Department of the Environment, Transport and the Regions (2000). *Climate Change: The UK Programme*. London: DETR. Available: www.cne-siar.gov.uk/emergency planning/documents/ClimateChange-UKProgramme.pdf.

D'Este, P. and Patel, P. (2007). "University–Industry Linkages in the UK: What are the Factors Underlying the Variety of Interactions with Industry?" *Research Policy*, 36: 1295–1313.

Dietz, S. and Stern, N. (2014). *Endogenous Growth, Convexity of Damages and Climate Risk: How Nordhaus' Framework Supports Deep Cuts in Carbon Emissions*. Centre for Climate Change Economics and Policy Working Paper No. 180. Grantham Research Institute on Climate Change and the Environment Working Paper No. 159. London: LSE.

Directorate-General for Research and Innovation (2013). *Research and Innovation Performance in EU Member States and Associated Countries*. Brussels: European Commission.

Donat, L., Dreblow, E., Duwe, M., Wawer, T., Zelliadt, E. and Schachtschneider, R. (2013). *Assessment of Climate Change Policies in the Context of the European Semester, Country Report: Germany*. Berlin: eclareon.

Dore, R., Lazonick, W. and O'Sullivan, M. (1999). "Varieties of Capitalism in the Twentieth Century." *Oxford Review of Economic Policy*, 15 (4): 102–120.

Downs, A. (1972). "Up and Down with Ecology the 'Issue-Attention Cycle'." *The Public Interest*, 28: 38–50.

Dragsund, E., Aunan, K., Godal, O., Haugom, G.P. and Holtsmark, B. (1999). *Utslipp til luft fra oljeindustrien: Tiltak, kostnader og virkemidler*. CICERO Report 2. Oslo: University of Oslo.

Dreblow, E., Duwe, M., Wawer, T., Donat, L., Zelljadt, E., Ayres, A. and Tallat-Kelpsaite, J. (2013). *Assessment of Climate Change Policies in the Context of the European Semester, Country Report: United Kingdom*. Berlin: eclareon.

Dugan, J. (2014). "China Pledges to Cut Emissions at UN Climate Summit." *Guardian*. Available: www.theguardian.com/environment/chinas-choice/2014/sep/24/china-pledges-to-cut-emissions-at-un-climate-summit (accessed April 3, 2015).

Dunlap, R.E. and McCright, A.M. (2008). "A Widening Gap: Republican and Democratic Views on Climate Change." *Environment: Science and Policy for Sustainable Development*, 50 (5): 26-35.

DW (2013). "Norway's Electric Car Market Speeds Ahead." *DW Akademie*, November 18. Available: www.dw.de/norways-electric-car-market-speeds-ahead/a-17174540 (accessed May 5, 2014).

Earth Times (2008). *"Champion of Beijing's Olympic Air Cleanup Gets Award."* Earth *Times*, 12 November.

Ebner, A. (1999). "Understanding Varieties in the Structure and Performance of National Innovation Systems: The Concept of Economic Style." In J. Groenewegen and J. Vromen (eds), *Institutions and the Evolution of Capitalism: Implications of Evolutionary Economics*. Aldershot: Elgar, pp. 141–169.

Ebner, A. (2009). "Governance von Innovationssystemen und die politische Ökonomie der Wettbewerbsfähigkeit." In B. Blättel-Mink and A. Ebner (eds), *Innovationssysteme: Technologie, Institutionen und die Dynamik der Wettbewerbsfähigkeit*. Wiesbaden: VS, pp. 119–143.

Ebner, A. (2010). "Varieties of Capitalism and the Limits of Entrepreneurship Policy: Institutional Reform in Germany's Coordinated Market Economy." *Journal of Industry, Competition and Trade*, 10 (3–4): 319–341.

Ebner, A. (2014). *Shades of Green. Pathways to the Greening of Innovation Regimes in Germany and the United Kingdom.* Paper presented to the Seminar National Pathways to Low-Carbon Emission Economies, Berlin, 20 January.

Ebner, A. (2015). Editorial: Exploring Regional Varieties of Capitalism, *Regional Studies*, 50 (1): 3–6.

Ebner, A. and Täube, F. (2009). "Dynamics and Challenges of Innovation in Germany." In A. Fertel-Claros (ed.), *The Innovation for Development Report 2009–2010: Strengthening Innovation for the Prosperity of Nations.* London: Palgrave Macmillan, pp. 183–198.

Ecological Institute (2012a). *Assessment of Climate Change in the Context of the European Semester. Country Report: Poland.* Berlin: Ecological Institute.

Ecological Institute (2012b). *Assessment of Climate Change in the Context of the European Semester. Country Report: Hungary.* Berlin: Ecological Institute.

Ecological Institute (2012c). *Assessment of Climate Change in the Context of the European Semester. Country Report: Czech Republic.* Berlin: Ecological Institute.

Edahiro, J. (2008). "Vision for a Low Carbon Japan: Cutting Emissions by 60–80 Percent by 2050." *Journal for Sustainability Newsletter*, No. 71. Available: www.japanfs.org/en/news/archives/news_id027852.html (accessed March 29, 2015).

EEA (2012). EØS-komiteens beslutning nr. 152/2012 av 26. juli 2012 om endring av EØS-avtalens vedlegg XX (Miljø) (152/2012).

Égert, B. (2011). *France's Environmental Policies: Internalising Global and Local Externalities.* OECD Economics Department Working Papers No. 859. Paris: OECD.

Einsiedel, E., Boyd, A., Medlock, J. and Ashworth, P. (2013). "Assessing Sociotechnical Mindsets: Public Deliberations on Carbon Capture and Storage in the Context of Energy Sources and Climate Change." *Energy Policy*, 53: 149–158.

Electricity Info (2013). *Fuel Mix of UK Domestic Electricity Suppliers.* Available: www.electricityinfo.org/supplierdataall.php?year=latest.

Energy and Environment Council, Government of Japan (2012). *Innovative Strategy for Energy and the Environment in Session IL: Creating an Enabling Environment for a Job Centered Inclusive Growth and Economy.* UNDESA-ESCP-ILO-UNEP Expert Group Meeting on Green Growth and Green Jobs for Youth. Available: www.ilo.org/wcmsp5/groups/public/-asia/-ro-bangkok/documents/presentation/wcms_195560.pdf (accessed April 3, 2015).

Energy Information Administration (2015). *Frequently Asked Question: What is US Electricity Generation by Energy Source?* Available: www.eia.gov/tools/faqs/faq.cfm?id=427&t=3.

Engel, K. (2006). "State and Local Climate Change Initiatives: What Is Motivating State and Local Governments to Address a Global Problem and What Does This Say About Federalism and Environmental Law." *Urban Lawyer*, 38: 1015.

Engineering and Physical Sciences Research Council (2013). *Innovation and Knowledge Centres.* London: EPSRC. Available: www.epsrc.ac.uk/innovation/business/schemes/Pages/ikcs.aspx.

Environment and Climate Change Canada (2016). *National Inventory Report 1990–2014.* Ottawa: Environment Canada. Available: www.ec.gc.ca/ges-ghg/default.asp?lang=En&n=662F9C56-1-

Environment and Climate Change Canada (2017). *Canada's 2016 Greenhouse Gas Emissions Reference Case.* Ottawa: Environment Canada. Available: www.canada.ca/en/environment-climate-change/services/climate-change/publications/2016-greenhouse-gas-emissions-case.html

Environment Canada (2010). *Public Environment Analysis*. Ottawa: Environment Canada.

Environment Canada (2013). *Canada's Emissions Trends 2013*. Ottawa: Environment Canada. Available: www.ec.gc.ca/ges-ghg/985F05FB-4744-4269-8C1A-D443F8A 86814/1001-Canada's%20Emissions%20Trends%202013_e.pdf.

ESA (2013). "State Aid: Norwegian CO_2 Compensation Scheme Approved." Press release, September 25. Available: www.eftasurv.int/press-publications/press-releases/state-aid/nr/2082 (accessed May 6, 2014).

Eur-LEX (2009). Decision No. 406/2009/EC of the European Parliament and of the Council of 23 April 2009 on the effort of Member States to reduce their greenhouse gas emissions to meet the Community's greenhouse gas emission reduction commitments up to 2020. Available: http://eur-lex.europa.eu/legal-content/EN/TXT/?uri=uriserv:OJ.L_.2009.140.01.0136.01.ENG#page=12.

Europaportalen (2013). "Politisk enighet om Horisont 2020." *Regjeringen.no*, July 15. Available: www.regjeringen.no/en/sub/europaportalen/aktuelt/nyheter/2013/politisk-enighet-om-horisont-2020.html?id=732748 (accessed August 15, 2013).

European Commission (2009). *European Innovation Scoreboard 2009: Comparative Analysis of Innovation Performance*. Brussels: European Commission.

European Commission (2010). *Emissions Trading: Commission Accepts Polish National Allocation Plan for 2008–2012*, April 19. Brussels: European Commission. Available: https://ec.europa.eu/clima/news/articles/news_2010041901_en.

European Commission (2013). *Renewable Energy Progress Report*. COM(2013) 175 final. Brussels: European Commission. Available: https://eur-lex.europa.eu/legal-content/EN/TXT/?uri=celex:52014DC0015

European Commission (2014). *A Policy Framework for Climate and Energy in the Period from 2020 to 2030*. COM 2014/015 final. Brussels: Official Journal.

European Commission (2017). *Europe 2020 Targets: Statistics and Indicators for Hungary*. Available: https://ec.europa.eu/info/business-economy-euro/economic-and-fiscal-policy-coordination/eu-economic-governance-monitoring-prevention-correction/european-semester/european-semester-your-country/hungary/europe-2020-targets-statistics-and-indicators-hungary_en.

European Commission DG Climate (2013). *The EU Emissions Trading System (EU ETS)*. Brussels: European Commission. Available: http://ec.europa.eu/clima/publications/docs/factsheet_ets_en.pdf.

European Commission DG Climate Action (2017a). *Proposal for an Effort Sharing Regulation 2021–2030*. Available: https://ec.europa.eu/clima/policies/effort/proposal_en.

European Commission DG Climate Action (2017b). *Kyoto 2nd commitment period (2013–20)*. Available: https://ec.europa.eu/clima/policies/strategies/progress/kyoto_2_en.

European Commission DG Climate Action (2017c). *Kyoto 1st commitment period (2008–12)*. Available: https://ec.europa.eu/clima/policies/strategies/progress/kyoto_1_en.

European Commission DG Internal Market, Industry, Entrepreneurship and SMEs (2017). *Germany Innovation Scoreboard 2017*. Available: http://ec.europa.eu/growth/industry/innovation/facts-figures/scoreboards_en.

European Commission DG Regional and Urban Policy (2015). *Available Budget 2014–2020*. Available: http://ec.europa.eu/regional_policy/en/funding/available-budget/.

European Commission DG Regional and Urban Policy (2017a). *OP Infrastructure and Environment Poland*. Available: http://ec.europa.eu/regional_policy/en/atlas/programmes/2014-2020/poland/2014pl16m1op001.

European Commission DG Regional and Urban Policy (2017b). *Environment Czech Republic*. Available: http://ec.europa.eu/regional_policy/en/atlas/programmes/2014-2020/czech-republic/2014cz16m1op002.

European Commission DG Regional and Urban Policy (2017c). *Transport Czech Republic*. Available: http://ec.europa.eu/regional_policy/en/atlas/programmes/2014-2020/czech-republic/2014cz16m1op001.

European Commission DG Regional and Urban Policy (2017d). *Environmental and Energy Efficiency OP Hungary*. Available: http://ec.europa.eu/regional_policy/en/atlas/programmes/2014-2020/hungary/2014hu16m1op001.

European Council for an Energy Efficient Economy (2011). *National Energy Efficiency and Energy Saving Targets – Further Details on Member States*. Available: www.eceee.org.

European Environment Agency (2010). *Country Profile: Czech Republic*. Available: www.eea.europa.eu.

European Environment Agency (2010). *Country Profile: Hungary*. Available: www.eea.europa.eu.

European Environment Agency (2010). *Country Profile: Poland*. Available: www.eea.europa.eu.

European Environment Agency (2013). *Annual European Union Greenhouse Gas Inventory 1990–2011 and Inventory Report 2013*. Available: www.eea.europa.eu.

European Patent Office (2016). *Climate Change Mitigation Technologies in Europe – Evidence from Patent and Economic Data*. Munich: EPO.

Eurostat (2013). *Science, Technology and Innovation in Europe*. Brussels: European Commission.

Eurostat (2014). *Environment Data*. Available: http://epp.eurostat.ec.europa.eu/portal/page/portal/environment/data/main_tables.

Eurostat (2016a). *Electricity Generated From Renewable Sources*. Available: http://ec.europa.eu/eurostat/tgm/table.

Eurostat (2016b). *Primary Energy Consumption Environment Data*. Available: http://ec.europa.eu/eurostat/tgm/table.

Eurostat (2016c). *Resource Productivity*. Available: http://epp.eurostat.ec.europa.eu/portal/page/portal/environment/data/main_tables.

Expertenkommission Forschung und Innovation (EFI) (2009). *Gutachten zu Forschung, Innovation und technologischer Leistungsfähigkeit 2009*. Berlin: EFI.

Expertenkommission Forschung und Innovation (EFI) (2011). *Gutachten zu Forschung, Innovation und technologischer Leistungsfähigkeit 2011*. Berlin: EFI.

Fagerberg J.B., Mowery, D. and Verspagen B. (2009). "The Development of the Norwegian Petroleum Innovation System. A Historical Overview." In J.B. Fagerberg, B. Verspagen and D. Mowery (eds), *Innovation, Path Dependency and Policy: The Norwegian Case*. Oxford: Oxford University Press.

Fæhn, T., Hagem, C., Lindholt, L., Mæland, S. and Rosendahl, K.E. (2013). *Climate Policies in a Fossil Fuel Producing Country: Demand versus Supply Side Policies*. Discussion papers No. 747. Oslo: Statistics Norway.

Fankhauser, S., Bowen, A., Calel, R., Dechezleprêtre, A., Grover, D., Rydge, J. and Sato, M. (2012). *Who Will Win the Green Race? In Search of Environmental Competitiveness and Innovation*. Grantham Research Institute on Climate Change and the Environment, Working Paper 94. London: LSE. Available: www.lse.ac.uk/GranthamInstitute/publications/WorkingPapers/Papers/90-99/WP94-green-race-environmental-competitiveness-and-innovation.pdf.

Federation of Electric Power Companies Japan (2014). *Electricity Review Japan*. Available: www.fepc.or.jp/library/pamphlet/pdf/2014ERJ_full.pdf (accessed April 3, 2015).

Ferrouhki, R., Lucas, H., Renner, M., Lehr, U., Breitschopf, B., Lallement, D. and Petrick, K. (2013). *Renewable Energy and Jobs*. Abu Dhabi: International Renewable Energy Agency. Available: www.irena.org/rejobs.pdf.

Fertel, C., Bahn, O., Vaillancourt, K. and Waaub, J.-P. (2013). "Canadian Energy and Climate Policies: A SWOT Analysis in Search of Federal/Provincial Coherence." *Energy Policy*, 63: 1139–1150.

Finansdepartementet (2012). *Skatter, avgifter og toll 2013*. Prop. 1 LS (2012–2013).

Fioretos, O. (2011). "Historical Institutionalism in International Relations." *International Organization*, 65 (2): 367–399.

Fischer, D.R. (2003). "Beyond Kyoto: The Formation of a Japanese Climate Change Regime." In P.G. Harris (ed.), *China's Responsibility for Climate Change: Ethics, Fairness, and Environmental Policy*. Bristol: Policy Press, pp. 187–206.

Forsythe, M. (2017). "China Cancels 103 Coal Plants, Mindful of Smog and Wasted Capacity." *New York Times*, December 22. Available: www.nytimes.com/2017/01/18/world/asia/china-coal-power-plants-pollution.html.

Foxon, T.J. (2013). "Transition Pathways for a Low Carbon Electricity Future." *Energy Policy*, 52 (1): 10–24.

Foxon, T.J., Gross, R., Chase, A., Howes, J., Arnall, A. and Anderson, D. (2005). "UK Innovation Systems for New and Renewable Energy Technologies: Drivers, Barriers and Systems Failures." *Energy Policy*, 33 (16): 2123–2137.

Foy, H. (2014). "Poland on Course for Battle on New EU Climate Change Targets." *Financial Times*, October 1. Available: www.ft.com/content/4ec9373c-495e-11e4-8d68-00144feab7de.

Frankfurt School of Finance and Management – United Nations Environment Programme Collaborating Centre for Climate and Sustainable Energy Finance (2017). *Global Trends in Renewable Energy Investment 2017*. Frankfurt am Main: FS-UNEP Centre.

Frankhauser, S. and Jotzo, F. (2017). *Economic Growth and Development with Low-Carbon Energy*. Centre for Climate Change Economics and Policy, Working paper 301. London: LSE.

Fraunhofer Institut für Solare Energiesysteme ISE (2014). *Stromerzeugung aus Solar- und Windenergie im Jahr 2013*. Available: www.ise.fraunhofer.de/de/downloads/pdf-files/aktuelles/stromprodukton-aus-solar-und-windenergie-2013.pdf (accessed April 3, 2015).

Freeman, C. and Perez, C. (1988). "Structural Crisis of Adjustment, Business Cycles and Investment Behaviour." In G. Dosi (ed.), *Technical Change and Economic Theory*. London: Frances Pinter, pp. 38–66.

Friends of the Earth (2011). *The Dirty Half Dozen*. London: FoE. Available: www.foe.co.uk/resource/reports/dirty_half_dozen.pdf.

Fritsch, S. (2015). "Technological Innovation, Globalization, and Varieties of Capitalism: The Case of Siemens AG as Example for Contingent Institutional Adaptation." *Business and Politics*, 17 (1): 125–159.

Fuchs, G. and Wassermann, S. (2013). *Governance von Innovationen im Energiesektor, Zwischen Anpassung und Erneuerung, Helmholtz-Gesellschaft, Allianz ENERGY-TRANS Discussion Paper No. 01/2013*. Berlin: Helmholtz-Gesellschaft.

Fukuda, Y. (2008). Special Address – Annual meeting of the World Economic Forum, Congress Center, Davos, Switzerland. Available: www.mofa.go.jp/policy/economy/wef/2008/address-s.html (accessed March 29, 2015).

Galloway, G. (2015). "Harper Suggests Canada Likely Won't Match US Targets." *Globe and Mail*, 23 April.

Gamper-Rabindran, S. (2006). "Did the EPA's Voluntary Industrial Toxics Program Reduce Emissions? A GIS Analysis of Distributional Impacts and by-Media Analysis of Substitution." *Journal of Environmental Economics and Management*, 52 (1): 391–410.

Gang, H. (2008). "China's New Ministry of Environmental Protection Begins to Bark, but Still Lacks in Bite." *World Resources Institute*, 17 July.

Geels, W. (2014). "Regime Resistance against Low-Carbon Transitions: Introducing Politics and Power into the Multi-Level Perspective." *Theory, Culture and Society*, 31 (5): 21–40.

Geels, F.W., Kern, F., Fuchs, G., Hinderer, N., Kungl, G., Mylan, J., Neukirch, M. and Wassermann, S. (2016). "The Enactment of Socio-Technical Transition Pathways: A Reformulated Typology and a Comparative Multi-Level Analysis of the German and UK Low-Carbon Electricity Transitions (1990–2014)." *Research Policy*, 45 (4): 896–913.

Georgescu-Roegen, N. (1971). *The Entropy Law and the Economic Process*. Princeton, NJ: Harvard University Press.

German Federal Ministry of Education and Research (2014). *The New High-Tech Strategy Innovations for Germany*. August, 2014. Available: www.bmbf.de/pub/HTS_Broschuere_eng.pdf.

German Federal Ministry of Education and Research (2016). *Pact for Research and Innovation*. Available: www.research-in-germany.org/en/research-landscape/r-and-d-policy-framework/pact-for-research-and-innovation.html.

Glassmann, U. (2009). "Rule-Breaking and Freedom of Rules in National Production Models: How German Capitalism Departs from the 'Rhenish Equilibrium'." In C. Crouch and H. Voelzkow (eds), *Innovation in Local Economies: Germany in Comparative Context*. Oxford: Oxford University Press, pp. 22–42.

Global Commission on the Economy and Climate (2015). *Seizing the Global Opportunity: Partnerships for Better Growth and a Better Climate. The 2015 New Climate Economy Report*. Washington, DC: New Climate Economy, c/o World Resources Institute. Available: www.newclimateeconomy.report.

Global Wind Energy Council (2012). *Global Wind Report Annual Market Update 2012*. Available: www.gwec.net/wpcontent/uploads/2012/06/Annual_report_2012_LowRes.pdf.

Golden, J. and Wiseman, H. (2014). "The Fracking Revolution: Shale Gas as a Case Study in Innovation Policy." *Emory Law Journal*, 64 (4): 955–1040.

Goldenberg, S. (2009). "China and US Held Secret Talks on Climate Change Deal." *Guardian*, May 18. Available: www.theguardian.com/world/2009/may/18/secret-us-china-emissions-talks.

Goldenberg, S. (2014). "Secret Talks and a Private Letter: How the US–China Climate Deal was Done." *Guardian*. Available: www.theguardian.com/environment/2014/nov/12/how-us-china-climate-deal-was-done-secret-talks-personal-letter (accessed April 3, 2015).

Government of Canada (2013). *Highlights of Canada's Sixth National Communication and First Biennial Report on Climate Change*. Available: www.ec.gc.ca/cc/16153A64-BDA4-4DBB-A514-B159C5149B55/6458_EC_ID1180-MainBook_high_min%20FINAL-s.pdf

Government of Japan (1998a). Bill for the Promotion of Measures to Tackle Global Warming. Available: www.env.go.jp/en/earth/cc/jde.html (accessed April 3, 2015).

Government of Japan (1998b). Law Concerning the Promotion of the Measures to Cope with Global Warming, Law No. 117. (地球温暖化対策推進大綱、地球温暖化対策推進本部決定、平成１４年、３月１９日) Available (in Japanese): law.e-gov.go.jp. Available (in English): www.env.go.jp/en/laws/global/warming.html (accessed April 3, 2015).

Graham-Harrison, E. and Buckley, C. (2009). "China Unveils Carbon Target for Copenhagen Deal." *Reuters*, November 27.

Green Investment Bank (2012). *Our Investment Approach.* Available: www.green investmentbank.com/userfiles/files/Our-Investment-Approach.pdf.

Gresser, J., Fujikura, K. and Morishima, A. (1982). *Environmental Law in Japan.* Cambridge, MA: MIT Press.

Grosjean, G., Acworth, W., Flachsland, C. and Marschinski, R. (2014). "After Monetary Policy, Climate Policy: Is Delegation the Key to EU ETS Reform?" *Climate Policy*, 16 (1): 1–25.

Grupp, H., Schmoch, U. and Breitschopf, B. (2008). "Perspektiven des deutschen Innovationssystems: Technologische Wettbewerbsfähigkeit und wirtschaftlicher Wandel." In B. Blättel-Mink and A. Ebner (eds), *Innovationssysteme: Technologie, Institutionen und die Dynamik der Wettbewerbsfähigkeit.* Wiesbaden: Verlag für Sozialwissenschaften, pp. 249–266.

Gullberg, A.T. (2011). "Access to Climate Policy-Making in the European Union and in Norway." *Environmental Politics*, 20 (4): 464–484.

Haggard, S. (1990). *Pathways from the Periphery: The Politics of Growth in the Newly Industrializing Countries.* Ithaca, NY: Cornell University Press.

Hake, J.-F., Fischer, W., Venghaus, S. and Weckenbrock, C. (2015). "The German Energiewende – History and Status Quo." *Energy*, 92: 532–546. doi: 10.1016/j.energy.2015.04.027.

Hall, P. (2007). "The Evolution of Varieties of Capitalism in Europe." In B. Hancké, M. Rhodes and M. Thatcher (eds), *Beyond Varieties of Capitalism: Conflict, Contradictions, and Complementarities in the European Economy.* Oxford: Oxford University Press, pp. 39–85.

Hall, P. and Soskice, D. (2001). "An Introduction to Varieties of Capitalism." In P.A. Hall and D. Soskice (eds), *Varieties of Capitalism: The Institutional Foundations of Comparative Advantage.* Oxford: Oxford University Press, pp. 1–68.

Hall, P. and Soskice, D. (2003). "Varieties of Capitalism and Institutional Change: A Response to Three Critics." *Comparative European Politics* 1 (2): 241–250.

Hall, P. and Thelen, K. (2009). "Institutional Change in Varieties of Capitalism." *Socio-Economic Review*, 7 (1): 7–34.

Hancké, B., Rhodes, M. and Thatcher, M. (2007). "Introduction: Beyond Varieties of Capitalism" In B. Hancké, M. Rhodes and M. Thatcher (eds), *Beyond Varieties of Capitalism: Conflict, Contradictions, and Complementarities in the European Economy.* Oxford: Oxford University Press, pp. 3–38.

Hanson, P. and Pavitt, K. (1987). *The Comparative Economics of Research Development and Innovation in East and West: A Survey.* London: Routledge.

Hanson, J., Kasa, S. and Wicken, O. (2011). "Politikk for den store transformasjonen." In J. Hanson, S. Kasa and O. Wicken (eds), *Energirikdommens paradokser: Innovasjon som klimapolitikk og næringsutvikling.* Oslo: Universitetsforlaget.

Harding, R. and Soskice, D. (2000). "The End of the Innovation Economy?" In R. Harding and W.E. Paterson (eds), *The Future of the German Economy: An End to the Miracle?* Manchester: Manchester University Press, pp. 83–99.

Harris, P.G. (ed.) (2011). *China's Responsibility for Climate Change: Ethics, Fairness, and Environmental Policy.* Bristol: Policy Press.

Harrison, K. (2007). "The Road Not Taken: Climate Change Policy in Canada and the United States: Global Environmental Politics." *Global Environmental Politics*, 7 (4): 92–117.

Harrison, K. (2010a). "The Struggle of Ideas and Self-Interest in Canadian Climate Policy." In L. McIntosh Sundstrom and K. Harrison, (eds), *Global Commons, Domestic Decisions: The Comparative Politics of Climate Change.* Cambridge, MA: MIT Press, pp. 169–200.

Harrison, K. (2010b). "The United States as Outlier: Economic and Institutional Challenges to US Climate Policy." In L. McIntosh Sundstrom and K. Harrison, (eds), *Global Commons, Domestic Decisions: The Comparative Politics of Climate Change.* Cambridge, MA: MIT Press, pp. 67–104.

Harrison, K. (2011). *Passing the Buck: Federalism and Canadian Environmental Policy* (Google eBook). Vancouver: UBC Press.

Harrison, K. (2012). "A Tale of Two Taxes: The Fate of Environmental Tax Reform in Canada." *Review of Policy Research*, 29 (3): 383–407.

Harrison, K. (2013a). "Federalism and Climate Policy Innovation: A Critical Reassessment." *Canadian Public Policy*, 39 (Supplement 2): S95–S108.

Harrison, K. (2013b). *The Political Economy of British Columbia's Carbon Tax.* Paris: OECD Environment Working Papers.

Harrison, K. and McIntosh Sundstrom, L. (2010). "Conclusion: The Comparative Politics of Climate Change." In L. McIntosh Sundstrom and K. Harrison (eds), *Global Commons, Domestic Decisions: The Comparative Politics of Climate Change.* Cambridge, MA: MIT Press, pp. 261–290.

Harrison, N. and Mikler, J. (2014). *Climate Innovation: Liberal Capitalism and Climate Change.* Palgrave Macmillan.

Hasegawa, K. (2004). *Constructing Civil Society in Japan: Voices of Environmental Movements.* Melbourne: Trans Pacific Press.

Hashimoto, M. (1989) "History of Air Pollution Control in Japan." In H. Nishimura (ed.), *How to Conquer Air Pollution a Japanese Experience.* Amsterdam: Elsevier, pp. 1–93. doi: 10.1016/s0166-1116(08)70055-4.

Hatch, W. (2002). "Regionalizing the State: Japanese Administrative and Financial Guidance for Asia." *Social Science Japan Journal*, 5 (2): 179–197.

Hellevik, O. (2013). *Norsk monitor: Kulturelle hovedtrender i Norge.* Frokostmøte Ipsos MMI, April 4. Available: http://ipsos-mmi.no/files/Dokumentasjon/Frokost Seminar040413/IpsosMMI_Frokost_04042013_NorskMonitor_Ottar_Hellevik.pdf (accessed May 5, 2014).

Helm, D. (2014). "The European Framework for Energy and Climate Policies." *Energy Policy*, 64: 29–35.

Hempel, L.C. (2006). "Climate Policy on the Installment Plan." In N.J. Vig and M.E. Kraft (eds), *Environmental Policy: New Directions for the Twenty-First Century.* Washington: CQ Press, pp. 288–310.

Hepburn, C. and Teytelboym, A. (2017). "Climate Change Policy after Brexit." *Oxford Review of Economic Policy*, 33 (S1): S144–S154.

Hess, D. (2014). "Sustainability Transitions: A Political Coalition Perspective." *Research Policy*, 43: 278–283.

Heyman, E. and Khademi, P. (2015). "Talking Point, Carbon Bubble: Real Risk or Exaggerated Fears?" *Deutsche Bank Research*. Available: www.dbresearch.com/servlet/reweb2.ReWEB;RWSESSIONID=AC2E60C55C582C2907B0A8252282A97E. srv-tc2-dbr-com?rwsite=DBR_INTERNET_EN-PROD&rwobj=ReDisplay.Start.cl ass&document=PROD0000000000361779.

Hicks, B. (2004). "Setting Agendas and Shaping Activism: EU Influence on Central and Eastern European Environmental Movements." *Environmental Politics*, 13 (1): 216–233.

Higher Education Funding Council for England (2013). *UK Research Partnership Investment Fund*. London: HEFCE. Available: www.hefce.ac.uk/whatwedo/rsrch/howfundr/ukrpif.

Hirschhausen, C.V. (2014). "The German 'Energiewende' – An Introduction." *Economics of Energy and Environmental Policy*, 3 (2): 1–12.

Hoggan, J. (2009). *Climate Cover-up: The Crusade to Deny Global Warming*. Vancouver: Greystone Books.

Horbach, J., Chen, Q., Rennings, K. and Vögele, S. (2014). "Do Lead Markets for clean Coal Technology Follow Market Demand? A Case Study for China, Germany, Japan and the US." *Environmental Innovation and Societal Transitions*, 10: 42–58.

Hornby, L. (2015). "China Spells out Cost of Meeting Pollution Targets." *Financial Times*. Available: www.ft.com/intl/cms/s/0/f8f3337a-e8d7-11e4-b7e8-00144feab7 de.html#axzz3qYaCzkdI.

Houle, D. (2015). "Carbon Pricing in Canadian Provinces: From Early Experiments to Adoption (1995–2014)." PhD dissertation, University of Toronto.

Howell, C. (2007). "The British Variety of Capitalism: Institutional Change, Industrial Relations and British Politics." *British Politics*, 2 (2): 239–263.

Hubbard, C. (2014). *Fukushima and Beyond: Nuclear Power in a Low-Carbon World*. Farnham: Ashgate.

Huberty, M. and Zachmann, G. (2011). *Green Exports and their Global Product Space: Prospects for EU Industrial Policy*. Bruegel Working Paper 07. Brussels: Bruegel.

Huizi, L. (2009). "China Amends Law to Boost Renewable Energy." *Xinhua News*, December 26. Available: www.chinaview.cn. Available: www.news.xinhuanet. com/english/2009-12/26/content_12706612.htm.

Hübner, K. (2009). "Innovationssysteme und 'Varieties of Capitalism' unter Bedingungen ökonomischer Globalisierung." In B. Blättel-Mink and A. Ebner (eds), *Innovationssysteme: Technologie, Institutionen und die Dynamik der Wettbewerbsfähigkeit*. Wiesbaden: Verlag für Sozialwissenschaften, pp. 143–157.

Hübner, K. (2013). "'Grünes Wachstum' – Herausforderungen und Chancen." In B. Huber (ed.), *Kurswechsel für ein gutes Leben*. Frankfurt: Campus Verlag.

Hübner, K. (2015). "Die 'Wiederentdeckung' staatlicher Industriepolitik – eion globaler Politikwettbewerb." In W. Lermb (ed.), *Welche Industrie wollen wir? Nachhaltig produzieren – zukunftsorientiert wachen*. Frankfurt: Campus Verlag.

Imura, H. and Schreurs, M. (eds) (2005). *Environmental Policy in Japan*. Cheltenham: Edward Elgar Publishing.

Institute for Industrial Productivity (IPCC) (2015). *Industrial Efficiency Policy Database*. Available: iepd.iipnetwork.org (accessed August 1, 2015).

Intergovernmental Panel on Climate Change (2014). *Climate Change 2014 Synthesis Report, Fifth Assessment Report: Topic 1 Observed Changes and their Causes*. Available: http://ar5-syr.ipcc.ch/topic_observedchanges.php.

International Energy Agency (2010). *Energy Policies of IEA Countries: Czech Republic 2010 Review.* Paris: IEA. Available: www.iea.org.

International Energy Agency (2011). *Energy Policies of IEA Countries: Hungary – 2011 Review.* Paris: IEA Available: www.iea.org.

International Energy Agency (2012). *Energy Policies of IEA Countries: United Kingdom – 2012 Review.* Paris: IEA.

International Energy Agency (2013a). *World Energy Outlook.* Paris: IEA. Available: www.worldenergyoutlook.org/publications/weo-2013/.

International Energy Agency (2013b). *Energy Policies of IEA Countries: Germany – 2013 Review.* Paris: IEA.

International Energy Agency (2013c). *Redrawing the Climate-Energy Map: World Energy Outlook Special Report.* Paris: IEA.

International Energy Agency (2015). *Key Trends in IEA Public Energy Technology Research, Development and Demonstration (RD&D) Budgets 2015.* Paris: IEA.

International Energy Agency (2016a). *CO_2 Emission from Fuel Combustion.* Paris: OECD/IEA.

International Energy Agency (2016b). *Energy Policies of IEA Countries: Poland 2016 Review.* Available: www.iea.org/publications/freepublications/publication/Energy_Policies_of_IEA_Countries_Poland_2016_Review.pdf.

International Energy Agency (2017a). *Energy Policies of IEA Countries Poland 2016 Review.* Paris: IEA.

International Energy Agency (2017b). *Czech Republic – Energy System Overview.* Paris: IEA.

International Monetary Fund (IMF)) (2008). *World Economic Outlook, Chapter 4: Climate Change and the Global Economy,* Washington, DC: IMF

International Monetary Fund-Fiscal Affairs Department (2015). *How Large are Global Energy Subsidies? Country-Level Subsidy Estimates.* Available: www.imf.org/external/pubs/ft/survey/so/2015/new070215a.htm.

Iskander, F. (1975). *The Goatibex Constellation.* Ardis: New York.

Jackson, T. (2009). "Prosperity without Growth: The Transition to a Sustainable Economy." *Sustainable Development Commission.* Available: www.sd-commission.org.uk/publications.php?id=914.

Jackson, G. and Deeg, R. (2006). *How Many Varieties of Capitalism? Comparing the Comparative Institutional Analyses of Capitalist Diversity.* MPIfG Discussion Paper, No. 06/2.

Jackson, R.B., Canadell, J.G., Le Quéré, C., Andrew, R.M., Korsbakken, J.I., Peters, G.P. and Nakicenovic, N. (2016). "Reaching Peak Emission." *Nature Climate Change,* 6, pp. 7–10.

Jacobsson, S. and Lauber, V. (2006). "The Politics and Policy of Energy System Transformation – Explaining the German Diffusion of Renewable Energy Technology." *Energy Policy,* 34: 256–276.

Jakob, M. and Edenhofer, O. (2014). "Green Growth, Degrowth, and the Commons." *Oxford Review of Economic Policy,* 30 (3): 447–468.

Japan Center for Climate Change Actions (n.d.). Available: www.jccca.org/trend_japan/chronology/ (accessed April 3, 2015).

Japan Times (2014). "Japan's Fiscal '13 Greenhouse Gas Emissions, Worst on Record." *The Japan Times,* December 5. Available: www.japantimes.co.jp/news/2014/12/05/national/japans-fiscal-13-greenhouse-gas-emissions-worst-record/#.VRgAfSTlfFI (accessed April 3, 2015).

Jevnaker, T., Lunde, L. and Skjærseth, J.B. (2015). "EU–Norway Energy Relations towards 2050: From Fossil Fuels to Low Carbon Opportunities?" *Decarbonization in the European Union*. London: Palgrave Macmillan, pp. 222–243. doi: 10.1057/9781137406835_11.

Jiménez, V. (2004). *World Sales of Solar Cells Jump 32 Percent: Eco-Economy Indicators: Solar Power*. Washington, DC: Earth Policy Institute. Available: www.earth-policy.org/indicators/C47/solar_power_2004 (accessed April 3, 2015).

Jin, L. (2005). "Energy First: China and the Middle East." *Middle East Quarterly*, 12 (2): 3–10.

Johnson, C. (1982). *MITI and the Japanese Miracle: The Growth of Industrial Policy, 1925–1975*. Stanford, CA: Stanford University Press.

Johnson, C. (1987). "Political Institutions and Economic Performance: The Government–Business Relationship in Japan, South Korea, and Taiwan." In F. Deyo (ed.), *The Political Economy of the New Asian Industrialism*. Ithaca, NY: Cornell University Press, pp. 136–164.

Johnston, E. (2015). "Let's Discuss the Paris Climate Change Agreement." *The Japan Times*, June 12.

Johnstone, N., Haščič, I. and Popp, D. (2010). "Renewable Energy Policies and Technological Innovation: Evidence Based on Patent Counts in Environmental and Resource Economics." *Environmental and Resource Economics*, 45 (1): 133–155.

Jones, J.M. (2011). "In US, Concerns About Global Warming Stable at Lower Rates." *Gallup*, March 14.

Jordan, A. and Huitema, D. (2014). "Policy Innovation in a Changing Climate: Sources, Patterns and Effects." *Global Environmental Change*, 29: 387–394.

Jůn, D. (2017). "Czech Lower House Embarks on Fresh Attempt to Ratify Paris Climate Agreement." *Radio Prague*, July 10. Available: www.radio.cz/en/section/curraffrs/czech-lower-house-embarks-on-fresh-attempt-to-ratify-paris-climate-agreement.

Kahlenborn, W., Mewes, H., Knopf, J., Hauffe, P., Kampfmeyer, N., Fichter, K., Clausen, J., Weiß, R., Beucker, S. and Bergset, L. (2013). *Treiber und Hemmnisse für die Transformation der deutschen Wirtschaft zu einer "Green Economy": Endbericht an das Bundesministerium für Bildung und Forschung (BMBF)*. Berlin: adelphi/Borderstep Institut.

Kaiser, R. and Prange, H. (2004). "The Reconfiguration of National Innovation Systems – The Example of German Biotechnology." *Research Policy*, 33: 395–408.

Kameyama, Y. (2003). "Climate Change as Japanese Foreign Policy." In P.G. Harris (ed.), *Global Warming and East Asia: The Domestic and International Politics of Climate Change*. London and New York: Routledge, pp. 135–151.

Kasa, S. (1999). *Social and Political Barriers to Green Tax Reform: The Case of CO_2 Taxes in Norway*. CICERO Policy Note no. 5. Oslo: University of Oslo.

Kasa, S. (2000). "Policy Networks as Barriers to Green Tax Reform: The Case of CO_2 Taxes in Norway," *Environmental Politics*, 9 (4): 104–122.

Kasa, S. (2011). "Klimakamp blir innovasjonspolitikk." In J. Hanson, S. Kasa and O. Wicken (eds), *Energirikdommens paradokser: Innovasjon som klimapolitikk og næringsutvikling*. Oslo: Universitetsforlaget, pp. 153–171.

Katzenstein, P.J. (1985). *Small States in World Markets: Industrial Policy in Europe*. Ithaca, NY: Cornell University Press.

Keay, M. (2016). "UK Energy Policy – Stuck in Ideological Limbo?" *Energy Policy*, 94 (3): 247–252.

Kemfert, C., Opiz, P., Traber, T. and Handrich, L. (2015). *Research Report, Deep Decarbonisation in Germany: A Macro-analysis of Economic and Political Challenges of the "Energiewende" (Energy Transition)*. DIW Berlin: Politikberatung kompakt, No. 93. Available: www.diw.de/documents/publikationen/73/diw_01.c.497746.de/diwkompakt_2015-093.pdf.

Keohane, R. and Victor, D. (2011). "The Regime Complex for Climate Change." *Perspective on Politics*, 9 (1): 7–23.

Khatri, K. (2007). "Climate Change." In A. Seldon (ed.), *Blair's Britain 1997–2007*, Cambridge: Cambridge University Press, pp. 572–592.

Kiko Network (2008). *Greenhouse Gas Emissions in Japan: Analysis of First Data Reported (FY2006) from Emissions Accounting, Reporting and Disclosure System for Large Emitters and Japan's "The Law Concerning the Protection of the Measures to Cope with Global Warming."* Kiko Network, May. Available: www.kikonet.org/english/publication/archive/japansGHGemission_E.pdf (accessed April 3, 2015).

Kilisek, R. (2015). "Denmark Outstrips Germany as the 'Energiewende" Model Country." *Breaking Energy*. Available: http://breakingenergy.com/2015/01/06/denmark-outstrips-germany-as-the-energiewende-model-country/.

Kim, T. (2008). "Variants of Corporatist Governance: Differences in the Korean and Japanese Approaches in Dealing with Labor." *Yale Journal of International Affairs*, 3 (1): 78–94.

Kimura, O. (2010). *Japanese Top Runner Approach for Energy Efficiency Standards*. SERC Discussion Paper SERC09035, Socio-economic Research Center, Central Research Institute of Electric Power Industry. Available: www.denken.or.jp/en/serc/research_re/download/09035dp.pdf (accessed April 3, 2015).

King, D., Browne, J., Layard, R., O'Donnell, G., Rees, M., Stern, N. and Turner, A. (2015). *A Global Apollo Programme to Combat Climate Change*. London: LSE. Available: http://cep.lse.ac.uk/pubs/download/special/Global_Apollo_Programme_Report.pdf.

Kitschelt, H. and Streeck, W. (2004). "From Stability to Stagnation: Germany at the Beginning of the Twenty-First Century." In H. Kitschelt and W. Streeck (eds), *Germany: Beyond the Stable State*. London: Routledge, pp. 1–35.

Klein, C. (2012). *Climate Change Policies in Germany: Make Ambition Pay*. OECD Economics Department Working Papers No. 982. Paris: OECD.

Klif (2011). *Regler om tildeling av vederlagsfrie kvoter for perioden 2013 til 2020*. Oslo: Klif.

Klimaløftet (2011). Folks egne klimaløfter. January 20. Available: www.klimaloftet.no/Arkiv/2011/Folks-egne-klimalofter-/ (accessed May 6, 2014).

Knie, A. and Lengwiler, M. (2008). "Token Endeavors: The Significance of Academic Spin-Offs in Technology Transfer and Research Policy in Germany." *Science and Public Policy*, 35 (3): 171–182.

Knopf, B., Koch, N., Grosjean, G., Fuss, S., Flachsland, C., Pahle, M., Jakob, M. and Edenhofer, O. (2014). *The European Emissions Trading System (EU ETS): Ex-Post Analysis, the Market Stability Reserve and Options for a Comprehensive Reform*. Nota di Lavoro Working Paper Series Number 79.2014. Milan: Fondazione Eni Enrico Mattei.

Koch, N., Fuss, S., Grosjean, G. and Edenhofer, O. (2014). "Causes of the EU ETS Price Drop: Recession, CDM, Renewable Policies or a Bit of Everything? New Evidence." *Energy Policy*, 73: 676–685.

Kornai, J. (2006). "The Great Transformation of Central Eastern Europe." *Economics of Transition*, 14 (2): 207–244.

Kravtsova, V. and Radosevic, S. (2012). "Are Systems of Innovation in Eastern Europe Efficient?" *Economic Systems*, 36 (1): 109–126.

Kuramochi, T. (2014). *GHG Mitigation in Japan: An Overview of the Current Policy Landscape*. Working Paper. Washington, DC: World Resources Institute. Available: www.wri.org/publicationghg-mitigation-policy-japan (accessed March 29, 2015).

Kuramochi, T. (2015). "Review of Energy and Climate Policy Developments in Japan before and after Fukushima." *Renewable and Sustainable Energy Reviews*, 43: 1320–1332.

Labour Party (2010). *The Labour Party Manifesto 2010: A Future Fair for All*, London: Labour Party. Available: www.labour.org.uk/uploads/TheLabourPartyManifesto-2010.pdf.

Lachapelle, E., Borick, C.P. and Rabe, B. (2012). "Public Attitudes Toward Climate Science and Climate Policy in Federal Systems: Canada and the United States Compared." *Review of Policy Research*, 29 (3): 334–357.

Lamparter, D.H., Pinzler, P. and Tatje, C. (2013). *"Autoindustrie – Gift für das Klima." Die Zeit*, September 5. Available: www.zeit.de/2013/37/autoindustrie-bundesregierung-lobbyismus.

Länderarbeitskreis Energiebilanzen (2013) Available: www.lak-energiebilanzen.de.

Landis, F. and Heindl, P. (2016). *Renewable Energy Targets in the Context of the EU ETS: Whom Do They Benefit Exactly?* ZEW – Centre for European Economic Research Discussion Paper No. 16–026.

Lane, C. and Wood, G. (2009). "Capitalist Diversity and Diversity within Capitalism." *Economy and Society*, 38 (4): 531–551.

Lane, D. and Myant, M. (eds) (2007). *Varieties of Capitalism in Post-Communist Countries*. Basingstoke: Palgrave Macmillan.

Lardy, N. (2014). *Markets over Mao: The Rise of Private Business in China*. Washington, DC: Peterson Institute for International Economics.

Lazonick, W. (2008). *Entrepreneurial Ventures and the Developmental State: Lessons from the Advanced Economies*. Discussion Paper No. 2008/01. Helsinki: United Nations University: World Institute for Development and Economics Research. Available: www.wider.unu.edu/publications/working-papers/discussion-papers/2008/en_GB/dp2008-01/ (accessed March 29, 2015).

Lee, J.W. (2013). "The Contribution of Foreign Direct Investment to Clean Energy Use, Carbon Emissions and Economic Growth." *Energy Policy*, 55: 483–489.

Legler, H., Krawczyk, O. and Leidmann, M. (2009). *FuE-Aktivitäten von Wirtschaft und Staat im internationalen Vergleich*. Hannover: NIW.

Leijten, J., Butter, M., Kohl, J., Leis, M. and Gehrt, D. (2012). *Investing in Research and Innovation for Grand Challenges, Study to Assist the European Research Area Board*. Brussels: Joint Institute for Innovation Policy.

Lesbirel, H. (1998). *NIMBY Politics in Japan: Energy Siting and the Management of Environmental Conflict*. Ithaca, NY: Cornell University Press.

Lewis, J. (2010). "The State of US–China Relations on Climate Change: Examining the Bilateral and Multilateral Relationship." *China Environment Series (11)*. Washington, DC: Woodrow Wilson International Center for Scholars, pp. 7–39.

Li, L. (2008/2009). "China Youth Climate Action Network: Catalyzing Student Activism to Create a Low-Carbon Future." *China Environment Series (10)*. Washington, DC: Woodrow Wilson International Center for Scholars, pp. 114–116.

Liberal Democrats (2010). *Liberal Democrat Manifesto: Change that Works for You.* London: Liberal Democrats. Available: http://network.libdems.org.uk/manifesto2010/libdem_manifesto_2010.pdf.

Licht, G., Peters, B., Köhler, C. and Schwiebacher, F. (2014). *The Potential Contribution of Innovation Systems to Socio-Ecological Transition.* Work Package 303, Deliverable No. 4. Brussels: WWWforEurope.

Littlecott, C. (2016). *UK Coal Phase Out: The International Context.* E3G Briefing Paper, November 2016. Available: www.e3g.org/docs/UK_Coal_Phase_Out_-_ The_International_Context,_November_2016,_E3G.pdf.

Liu, X., Dong, Y., Wang, C. and Shishime, T. (2011). "Citizen Complaints about Environmental Pollution: A Survey Study in Suzhou." *China Journal of Current Chinese Affairs*, 40 (3): 193–219.

Lizza, R. (2010). "As the World Burns." *The New Yorker*, October 11.

Lopatka, J. (2012). "Czech Nuclear Tender Seen Pivotal after Fukushima." *Reuters*, June 29. Available: www.reuters.com/article/2012/06/29/czech-nuclear-idUSL6E 8HP17N20120629.

Lorenzoni, I., O'Riordan, T. and Pidgeon, N. (2008). "Hot Air and Cold Feet: The UK Response to Climate Change." In H. Compston and I. Bailey (eds), *Turning Down the Heat: The Politics of Climate Policy in Affluent Democracies.* London: Palgrave, pp. 104–124.

Lutzenhiser, L. (2001). "The Contours of US Climate Non-Policy." *Society & Natural Resources*, 14 (6): 511–523.

Macalister, T. and Harvey, F. (2013). "George Osborne Unveils 'Most Generous Tax Breaks in World' for Fracking." *Guardian*, July 19. Available: www.theguardian. com/politics/2013/jul/19/george-osborne-tax-break-fracking-shale-environment.

Macfarquhar, N. (2009). "Proposals Lag behind Promises on Climate." *New York Times*, September 22. Available: www.nytimes.com/2009/09/23/science/ earth/23climate.html.

Mander, S., Walsh, C., Gilbert, P., Traut, M. and Bows, A. (2012). "Decarbonizing the UK Energy System and the Implications for UK Shipping." *Carbon Management*, 3 (6): 601–614.

Mazzucato, M. (2013). *The Entrepreneurial State: Debunking Public vs. Private Sector Myths.* London: Anthem Press.

McCarthy, Shawn (2014). "Harper Calls Climate Regulations on Oil and Gas Sector 'Crazy Economic Policy.'" *The Globe and Mail*, December 9. Available: www. theglobeandmail.com/news/politics/harper-it-would-be-crazy-to-impose-climate-regulations-on-oil-industry/article22014508/.

McCracken, R. (2014). "Energy Economist: The Burden that Japan is Facing in its Higher Energy Costs." *The Barrel Blog.* Available: http://blogs.platts.com/2014/01/ 24/japan-energy/.

McCright, A.M. and Dunlap, R.E. (2003). "Defeating Kyoto: The Conservative Movement's Impact on US Climate Change Policy." *Social Problems*, 50 (3): 348–373.

McCrone, A., Usher, E., Sonntag-O'Brien, V., Moslener, U. and Grüning, C. (2013). *Global Trends in Renewable Energy Investment 2013.* Frankfurt School of Management and Finance UNEP Centre. Frankfurt am Main: FSMF-UNEP. Available: http://fs-unep-centre.org/publications/global-trends-renewable-energy-investment-2013.

McIntosh Sundstrom, L. and Harrison, K. (eds) (2010). *Global Commons, Domestic Decisions: The Comparative Politics of Climate Change.* Cambridge, MA: MIT Press.

McJeon, H., Edmonds, J., Bauer, N., Clarke, L., Fisher, B., Flannery, B.P., Hilaire, J., Krey, V., Marangoni, G., Mi, R., Riahi, K., Rogner, H. and Tavoni, M. (2014). "Limited IMPACT on Decadal-Scale Climate Change from Increased Use of Natural Gas." *Nature*, 415: 482–485.

McKibben, B. (2013). "Obama and Climate Change: The Real Story." *Rolling Stone*, December 17.

McKinsey (2013). *Disruptive Technologies: Advances That Will Transform Life, Business, and the Global Economy*. Boston, MA: McKinsey.

McMenamin, I. (2004). "Varieties of Capitalist Democracy: What Difference Does East-Central Europe Make?" *Journal of Public Policy*, 24 (3): 259–274.

McNamara, D. (1996). "Corporatism and Cooperation among Japanese Labor." *Comparative Politics*, 28 (4): 379–397.

Medve-Bálint, G. (2014). "The Role of the EU in Shaping FDI Flows to East Central Europe." *Journal of Common Market Studies*, 52 (1): 35–51.

Meeus, L., Azevedo, I., Marcantonini, C., Glachant, J.-M. and Hafner, M. (2012). "EU 2050 Low-Carbon Energy Future: Visions and Strategies." *The Electricity Journal*, 25 (5): 57–63. doi: 10.1016/j.tej.2012.05.014.

Meiritz, A. (2014). "Streit um Kohlekraft: Wirtschaftsflügel der CDU stützt Gabriels Kurs." *Spiegel-Online*, November 11. Available: www.spiegel.de/politik/deutschland/kohlekraftwerke-gabriel-und-hendricks-ringen-um-klimaschutzziele-a-1002336.html.

Michaelowa, A. and Betz, R. (2001). "Implications of EU Enlargement on the EU Greenhouse Gas 'Bubble' and Internal Burden Sharing." *International Environmental Agreements: Politics, Law and Economics*, 1 (2): 267–279.

Mikler, J. (2009). *Greening the Car Industry: Varieties of Capitalism and Climate Change*. Cheltenham: Edward Elgar.

Mikler, J. (2011). "Plus Ça Change? A Varieties of Capitalism Approach to Social Concern for the Environment." *Global Society*, 25 (3): 330–352.

Mikler, J. and Harrison, N.E. (2012). "Varieties of Capitalism and Technological Innovation for Climate Change." *New Political Economy*, 17 (2): 179–208.

Miljøverndepartementet (1995). *Om norsk politikk mot klimaendringer og utslipp av nitrogenoksyder (NOx)*. White Paper 41 (1994–95). Oslo: Miljøverndepartementet.

Miljøverndepartementet (1997). *Miljøvernpolitikk for en bærekraftig utvikling*. Dugnad for framtida, White Paper 58 (1996–97). Oslo: Miljøverndepartementet.

Miljøverndepartementet (2008). "Enighet om nasjonal klimadugnad." Press release, January 17. Available: www.regjeringen.no/nb/dokumentarkiv/stoltenberg-ii/md/Nyheter-og-pressemeldinger/pressemeldinger/2008/enighet-om-nasjonal-klimadugnad.html?id=496878 (accessed May 5, 2014).

Miljøverndepartementet (2009). "Norwegian Climate Policy: Carbon Capture and Storage (CCS)." Press release, December 2. Available: www.regjeringen.no/en/dep/md/Selected-topics/climate/internasjonale-klimaforhandlinger/norge-vil-spille-en-aktiv-rolle-i-klimaf/carbon-capture-and-storage-ccs.html?id=554250 (accessed August 15, 2013).

Miljøverndepartementet (2012). *Norsk Klimapolitikk [Norwegian Climate Change Policy]*. White Paper 21 (2011–2012). Oslo: Ministry of the Environment.

Ministry of Economy, Trade and Industry, Japan (2008). *Cool Earth Innovative Energy Technology Program*. Available: www.meti.go.jp/english/newtopics/data/pdf/031320CoolEarth.pdf.

Ministry of Environment of the People's Republic of China (2013). *The State Council Issues Action Plan on Prevention and Control of Air Pollution Introducing Ten Measures to*

Improve Air Quality. September 12. Available: http://english.mep.gov.cn/News_service/infocus/201309/t20130924_260707.htm (accessed April 3, 2015).

Ministry of Environment, Japan (1998). *Guidelines for Measures to Prevent Global Warming, Part II.* Available: www.env.go.jp/en/earth/cc/gw/part2.html (accessed April 3, 2015).

Ministry of Environment, Japan (2010). *Japan's National Greenhouse Gas Emissions in Fiscal Year 2010 (Final Figures).* Available: www.env.go.jp/en/headline/file_view.php?serial=451&hou_id=1763 (accessed April 3, 2015).

Ministry of Environment, Japan (2012). *Japan's National Greenhouse Gas Emissions in Fiscal Year 2012 (Preliminary Figures).* Available: www.env.go.jp/en/headline/file_view.php?serial=547&hou_id=2031 (accessed April 3, 2015).

Ministry of Environment, Japan (2013). *Japan's Climate Change Policies.* Available: www.env.go.jp/en/focus/docs/files/20130412-68.pdf (accessed April 3, 2015).

Ministry of Environment, Japan (n.d.*).* *Japan's Domestic and Global Initiatives toward Low Carbon Society.* Available: www.env.go.jp/earth/cop/cop19/event/file/131120/15301600/1120_1530_01_MOEJ.pdf (accessed April 3, 2015).

Ministry of Finance, Norway (2013). *National Budget 2013: A Summary.* Available: www.statsbudsjettet.no/Upload/Statsbudsjett_2013/dokumenter/pdf/NBudget_2013.pdf.

Mitchell, C., Bauknecht, D. and Connor, P.M. (2006). "Effectiveness through Risk Reduction: A Comparison of the Renewable Obligation in England and Wales and the Feed-In System in Germany." *Energy Policy,* 34: 297–305.

Molina, M., Zaelke, D., Sarma, K.M., Andersen, S.O., Ramanathan, V. and Kaniaru, D. (2009). "Reducing Abrupt Climate Change Risk Using the Montreal Protocol and Other Regulatory Actions to Complement Cuts in CO_2 Emissions." *Proceedings of the National Academy of Sciences of the United States of America,* 106 (49): 20616–20621.

Mooney, C. (2006). *The Republican War on Science.* New York: Basic Books.

Moore, M. (2009). "China's Middle-Class Rises up in Environmental Protest." *Telegraph,* November 23. Available: www.telegraph.co.uk/news/worldnews/asia/china/6636631/Chinas-middle-class-rise-up-in-environmental-protest.html (accessed April 3, 2015).

Moran, M. (2009). *Business, Politics, and Society: An Anglo-American Comparison.* Oxford: Oxford University Press.

Morgan, G. (2014). "Jim Prentice Says to Wind Down Carbon Capture Fund in Alberta, New Projects 'on Hold'." *National Post,* October 6. Available: http://business.financialpost.com/news/energy/jim-prentice-to-wind-down-carbon-capture-fund-in-alberta-new-projects-on-hold.

Morgan, K.J. (2007). "The Polycentric State: New Spaces of Empowerment and Engagement?" *Regional Studies,* 41 (9): 1237–1251.

Morgenstern, R.D. and Pizer, W.A. (eds) (2007). *Reality Check: The Nature and Performance of Voluntary Environmental Programs in the United States, Europe, and Japan.* Washington, DC: RFF Press. doi.org/10.1111/j.1477-8947.2007.00159_4.x.

Morris, C. (2014). "Renewable Energy Patents Boom in Germany." *Energy Transition Newsletter,* August 2014. Available: https://energytransitions.org/2014/08/renewable-energy-booms-in-germany.html.

Müller, J.-W. (2011). "The Hungarian Tragedy." *Dissent,* 58 (4): 5–10.

Munroe, K.B. (2012). "Risk and Advantage in a Changing Climate: Business Preferences for Climate Change Policy Instruments in Canada." Available: www.researchgate.net/publication/279421075_Risk_and_advantage_in_a_changing_climate_business_preferences_for_climate_change_policy_instruments_in_Canada.

Murray, B., Cropper, M., de la Chesnaye, F. and Reilly, J. (2014). "How Effective are US Renewable Energy Subsidies in Cutting Greenhouse Gases?" *The American Economic Review*, 104 (5): 569–574.

N8 Research Partnership (2013). *Industry Innovation Forum*. Available: www.n8 research.org.uk/industry-innovation-forum.

National Development and Reform Commission (NDRC) (2006). *The 11th Five-Year Plan: Targets, Paths, and Policy Orientation*. March 23. Available: http://en.ndrc.gov. cn/newsrelease/200603/t20060323_63813.html.

National Development and Reform Commission (NDRC) (2013). *China's Policies and Actions for Addressing Climate Change*. Available: http://en.ndrc.gov.cn/ newsrelease/201311/P020131108611533042884.pdf.

National Institute for Environmental Studies (2012). *Japan's National Greenhouse Gas Emissions in Fiscal Year 2012: Final Figures*. Available: www.nies.go.jp/whatsnew/ 2014/20140415/20140415-e.html (accessed April 3, 2015).

National Institute for Environmental Studies (2014). *Japan's National Greenhouse Gas Emissions in Fiscal Year 2013 (Preliminary Figures)*, December 4. Available: www.nies. go.jp/whatsnew/2014/20141204/20141204-e.html (accessed March 30, 2015).

Nationen (2012). "Regjeringen vil fjerne grønne sertifikater i 2020." *Nationen*, October 18. Available: www.nationen.no/2012/10/18/nyheter/gronne_sertifikater/ola_borten_ moe/senterpartiet/olje_og_energiminister/7736899/ (accessed August 16, 2013).

Natural Resources Defense Council (NRDC) (2007). *China's National Climate Change Programme*. Available: http://en.ndrc.gov.cn/newsrelease/200706/P020070604561191 006823.pdf.

Natural Resources Defense Council (NRDC) (2008). *Green Buildings and Sustainable Cities*. Available: www.nrdc.org/international/china/greenbuildings.pdf (accessed April 3, 2015).

National Roundtable on the Environment and the Economy (2012). *Reality Check: The State of Climate Progress in Canada*. Available: http://nrt-trn.ca/reality-check-the-state-of-climate-progress-in-canada.

Nee, V., Opper, S. and Wong, S. (2007). "Developmental State and Corporate Governance in China." *Management and Organization Review*, 3 (1): 19–53.

Neuman, K. (2008). "*Carbon Taxes: Panacea or Political Oblivion.*" *Environics Research*, September.

New Power Consulting (2011). *New Power Newsletter*, August 2011. Available: www. newpowerconsulting.com.

Nikkei (2014). "Japan Finally Talking Emission Reduction Target." *Nikkei Asian Review*, October 25. Available: http://asia.nikkei.com/Politics-Economy/Policy-Politics/Japan-finally-talking-emission-reduction-target (accessed April 3, 2015).

Nölke, A. and Vliegenthart, A. (2009). "Enlarging the Varieties of Capitalism: The Emergence of Dependent Market Economies in East Central Europe." *World Politics*, 6 (2): 670–702.

Nordhaus, W. (2007). "A Review of the Stern Review on the Economics of Climate Change." *Journal of Economic Literature*, 45 (3): 686–702.

Nordhaus, W. (2015). "Climate Clubs: Overcoming Free-riding in International Climate Policy." *American Economic Review*, 105 (4): 1339–1370.

NOU (2012). *Utenfor og innenfor: Norges avtaler med EU*. Available: https://www. regjeringen.no/contentassets/5d3982d042a2472eb1b20639cd8b2341/no/pdfs/ nou201220120002000dddpdfs.pdf.

NOU (2013). *Lønnsdannelsen og utfordringer for norsk økonomi.* Available: http://www. regjeringen.no/nb/dep/fin/dok/ nouer/2013/nou-2013-13.html?id=747181.

NVE and Energimyndigheten (2013). *Et norsk-svensk elsertifikatmarked: Årsrapport for 2012.* Available: http://publikasjoner.nve.no/rapport/2013/rapport2013_59.pdf.

O'Brien, T. (2011). "Sustaining Regional Environmental NGOs in Latin America and Eastern Europe: Considering the Experience of the FARN and the REC." *Space and Social Polity*, 15 (1): 49–63.

Obayashi, Y. and Miyakazi, A. "New Coal Power Plants May Block Japan's Carbon Emissions Goal." *Reuters*, June 29. Available: www.reuters.com/article/us-japan-environment-analysis/new-coal-power-plants-may-block-japans-carbon-emissions-goal-minister-idUSKBN19K15Z.

OECD (2007). *OECD Environmental Performance Reviews: China.* Paris: OECD.

OECD (2009). *Revealed Technology Advantage in Selected Fields.* Paris: OECD. Available: www.oecd-ilibrary.org/science-and-technology/data/oecd-science-technology-and-industry-outlook/revealed-technology-advantage-in-selected-fields_data-00673-en.

OECD (2010a). *Economic Surveys: Germany.* Paris: OECD.

OECD (2010b). *Measuring Innovation.* Paris: OECD.

OECD (2010c). *Main Science and Technology Indicators*, August 2010. Paris: OECD.

OECD (2011a). *Towards Green Growth.* Paris: OECD.

OECD (2011b). *Germany Environmental Performance Review.* Paris: OECD.

OECD (2012a). *OECD Science, Technology and Innovation Outlook 2012.* Paris: OECD.

OECD (2012b). *Main Science and Technology Indicators*, August 2012. Paris: OECD.

OECD (2014). *The Cost of Air Pollution: Health Impacts of Road Transport.* Paris: OECD.

OECD (2016). *Triadic Patent Families.* Paris: OECD. Available: https://data.oecd.org/rd/triadic-patent-families.htm.

OECD (2017). *Gross Domestic Expenditure on R&D by Sector of Performance and Source of Funds.* Paris: OECD. Available: http://stats.oecd.org/Index.aspx?DataSetCode=GERD_FUNDS.

OED (2011). *Fornybardirektivet en del av EØS-avtalen* (110/11). Oslo. Available: www.regjeringen.no/nb/dep/oed/pressesenter/pressemeldinger/2011/fornybardirektivet-en-del-av-eos-avtalen.html?id=667482 (accessed May 5, 2014).

OED (2013). "Ønsker ny vurdering av CO_2-håndtering." Press release, November 1. Available: www.regjeringen.no/nb/dep/oed/pressesenter/pressemeldinger/2013/onsker-ny-vurdering-av-co2-handtering.html?id=744870 (accessed November 2, 2013).

Oei, P.-Y., Reitz, F. and von Hirschhausen, C. (2014). *Risks of Vattenfall's German Lignite Mining and Power Operations: Technical, Economic, and Legal Considerations.* Policy report on behalf of Greenpeace Germany. DIW Berlin: Politikberatung kompakt, No. 87.

Office of Gas and Electricity Markets (2013). *The Final Report of the Carbon Emissions Reduction Target (CERT) 2008–2012.* London: OFGEM. Available: www.ofgem.gov.uk/ofgem-publications/58425/certfinalreport2013300413.pdf.

Oliver, J.G.J., Janssens-Maenhout, G., Muntean, M. and Peters, J.A.H.W. (2013). *Trends in Global CO_2 Emissions, 2013 Report.* The Hague, PBL Netherlands Environmental Assessment Agency; Ispra: Joint Research Centre, 8–14. Available: http://edgar.jrc.ec.europa.eu/news_docs/pbl-2013-trends-in-global-co2-emissions-2013-report-1148.pdf (accessed March 29, 2015).

Oljedirektoratet (2014). Petroleumsressursene på norsk kontinentalsokkel: Felt og funn. Available: www.npd.no/Global/Norsk/3-Publikasjoner/Ressursrapporter/Ressursrapport2014/RessRapp. 2014nett.pdf (accessed May 6, 2014).

Oreskes, N. and Conway, E.M. (2010). *Merchants of Doubt: How a Handful of Scientists Obscured the Truth on Issues from Tobacco Smoke to Global Warming.* London: Bloomsbury Press.

Ostrom, E. (2012). "Nested Externalities and Polycentric Institutions: Must We Wait for Global Solutions to Climate Change before Taking Actions at Other Scales?" *Economic Theory*, 49 (2): 353–369.

Pahle, M. (2010). "Germany's Dash for Coal: Exploring Drivers and Factors, Energy Policy." *Energy Policy*, 38: 3431–3442.

Pan, L. (2005). *The New 11th Five-Year Guidelines*, November 9. Available: www.gov. cn/english/2005-11/09/content_247198.htm (accessed August 2, 2015).

PBL Netherlands Environmental Assessment Agency and European Commission Joint Research Centre (2013). *Trends in Global CO$_2$ Emissions: 2013 Report*. Available: http://edgar.jrc.ec.europa.eu/news_docs/pbl-2013-trends-in-global-co2-emissions-2013-report-1148.pdf (accessed April 3, 2015).

Pekkanen, R. (2006). *Japan's Dual Civil Society: Members without Advocates*. Stanford, CA: Stanford University Press.

Pemberton, B. (2017). "Control, Historic Pitfalls, and the UK Nuclear Renaissance." *International Journal of Public Administration*, 40 (6): 481–489.

Pempel, T.J. (1998). *Regime Shift: Comparative Dynamics of the Japanese Political Economy*. Ithaca, NY: Cornell University Press.

Pempel, T.J. and Tsunekawa, K. (1979). "Corporatism without Labor? The Japanese Anomaly." In G. Lehmbruch and P.C. Schmitter (eds), *Trends Toward Corporatist Intermediation*. Beverly Hills, CA: Sage, pp. 231–270.

Peters, G.P. and Hertwich, E.G. (2008). "CO$_2$ Embodied in International Trade with Implications for Global Climate Policy." *Environmental Science & Technology*, 42 (5): 1401–1407.

Pielke, A.R. (2009). "The British Climate Change Act: A Critical Evaluation and Proposed Alternative Approach." *Environmental Research Letters*, 4 (2): 024010. doi: 10.1088/1748-9326/4/2/024010.

Pigou, A.C. (1920). *The Economics of Welfare*, 1st edn. London: Macmillan.

Pindyck, R. (2013). *Climate Change Policy: What do the Models Tell Us?* Working Paper 19244. Cambridge, MA: National Bureau of Economic Research. Available: http://web.mit.edu/rpindyck/www/Papers/Climate-Change-Policy-What-Do-the-Models-Tell-Us.pdf.

Pitt-Watson, D. (2015). "'Fossilist' Finance Blocks 'Clean Trillion'." *Financial Times*, October 7. Available: www.ft.com/cms/s/0/dc5d09d2-6b65-11e5-8171-ba1968cf791a.html.

Plumer, B. (2015). "How Obama's Clean Power Plan Actually Works – A Step-by-Step Guide." *Vox*, August 5. Available: www.vox.com/2015/8/4/9096903/clean-power-plan-explained.

Pollitt, H., Summerton, P. and Billington, S. (2013). *The Economics of Climate Change Policy in the UK: An Analysis of the Impact of Low-Carbon Policies on Households, Businesses and the Macro-Economy*. Cambridge: Cambridge Econometrics.

Prange, H. (2005). *Wege zum Innovationsstaat: Globalisierung und der Wandel nationaler Forschungs- und Technologiepolitiken*. Baden-Baden: Nomos.

Price, L., Xuejun, W. and Yun, J. (2008). *China's Top-1000 Energy-Consuming Enterprises Program: Reducing Energy Consumption of the 1000 Largest Enterprises in China*. Ernest Orlando Berkeley National Laboratory, Environmental Energy Technologies Division.

Pritchett, L. and Summers, L. (2014). *Asiaphoria Meets Regression to the Mean*. NBER Working Paper 20573. Cambridge: National Bureau of Economic Research.

Qi, Y. (ed.) (2013). "Chinese Research Perspectives on the Environment." *Annual Review of Low Carbon Development in China* (2011–12), Special Volume. Leiden: Brill.

Qi, Y., Li, M., Huanbo, Z. and Huimin, L. (2008). "Translating a Global Issue into Local Priority: China's Local Government Response to Climate Change." *The Journal of Environment and Development*, 17 (4): 379–400.

Rabe, B.G. (2004). *Statehouse and Greenhouse: The Emerging Politics of American Climate Change Policy*. Washington, DC: Brookings Institute Press.

Rabe, B.G. (2007). "Beyond Kyoto: Climate Change Policy in Multilevel Governance Systems." *Governance*, 20 (3): 423–444.

Rabe, B.G. (2008). "States on Steroids: The Intergovernmental Odyssey of American Climate Policy." *Review of Policy Research*, 25 (2): 105–128.

Radosevic, S. (2011). "Science-Industry Links in Central and Eastern Europe and the Commonwealth of Independent States: Conventional Policy Wisdom Facing Reality." *Science and Public Policy*, 38 (5): 365–378.

Radosevic, S. and Lepori, B. (2009). "Public Research Funding Systems in Central and Eastern Europe: Between Excellence and Relevance." *Science and Public Policy*, 36 (9): 667–681.

Rammer, C., Polt, W., Egeln, J., Licht, G. and Schibany, A. (2004). *Internationale Trends der Forschungs- und Innovationspolitik: Fällt Deutschland zurück?* Baden-Baden: Nomos.

Rankin, J. (2015). "Mark Carney Defends Bank of England over Climate Change Study." *Guardian*, March 10. Available: https://www.theguardian.com/environment/2015/mar/10/mark-carney-defends-bank-of-england-climate-change-study.

Rapp, T., Schwägerl, C. and Traufetter, G. (2010). "The Copenhagen Protocol: How China and India Sabotaged the UN Climate Summit." *Spiegel Online International*, May 5. Available: www.spiegel.de/international/world/the-copenhagen-protocol-how-china-and-india-sabotaged-the-un-climate-summit-a-692861.html (accessed April 3, 2015).

Regjeringen (2012). "CO_2-kompensasjonsordning for industrien." Press release, September 11. Available: www.regjeringen.no/nb/dep/smk/pressesenter/presse meldinger/2012/co2.html?id=698862 (accessed May 5, 2014).

Reiche, D. (2004). *Rahmenbedingungen für erneuerbare Energien in Deutschland*. Frankfurt am Main : Möglichkeiten und Grenzen einer Vorreiterpolitik.

Reiche, D. (2006). "Renewable Energies in the EU-Accession States" *Energy Policy*, 34 (3): 365–375.

Reitan, M. (1998). "Interesser og institusjoner i miljøpolitikken." PhD dissertation 5/98, Oslo: Akademika/University of Oslo.

REN21 (2013). *Renewables 2013: Global Status Report*. Paris: REN21 Secretariat. Available: www.ren21.net/Portals/0/documents/Resources/GSR/2013/GSR2013_lowres.pdf (accessed June 8, 2018).

REN21 (2017). *Renewables 2017: Global Status Report*. Paris: REN21 Secretariat. Available: www.ren21.net/wp-content/uploads/2017/06/17-8399_GSR_2017_Full_Report_0621_Opt.pdf

RenewableUK (2014). *About RenewableUK*. London: RenewableUK. Available: www.renewableuk.com/en/about-renewableuk/index.cfm.

Research Councils UK (2013). *RCUK Energy Programme*. London: RCUK. Available: www.rcukenergy.org.uk/home/research-councils-energy-program.html.

Reuters (2014). "Complaints about Air Pollution in China's Capital Double in Five Months." *Reuters*, June 14. Available: www.reuters.com/article/2014/06/14/us-china-pollution-beijing-idUSKBN0EP0A320140614 (accessed April 3, 2015).

Reuters (2016). "Germany Risks Missing 2020 Climate Targets, Ministry Report Shows." *Reuters*, December 14. Available: www.reuters.com/article/us-germany-environment-carbon/germany-risks-missing-2020-climate-targets-ministry-report-shows-idUSKBN1431EN.

Rhys, J. (2013). "Current German Energy Policy – The 'Energiewende': A UK and Climate Change Perspective." *Oxford Energy Comment* April 2013. Oxford: The Oxford Institute for Energy Studies.

Riksrevisjonen (2013). "Cost Management of CCS Must be Improved." Press release, September 17. Available: www.riksrevisjonen.no/en/Formedia/PressReleases/Pages/CCS.aspx (accessed May 5, 2014).

Rodrik, D. (2014). "Green Industrial Policy." *Oxford Review of Environmental Policy*, 30 (3): 469–491.

Rodrik, D. (2015). "From Welfare State to Innovation State." *Project-Syndicate*, January 14. Available: www.project-syndicate.org/commentary/labor-saving-technology-by-dani-rodrik-2015-01.

Rootes, C. and Carter, N. (2010). "Take Blue, Add Yellow, Get Green? The Environment in the UK General Election of 6 May 2010." *Environmental Politics*, 19 (6): 992–999.

Ruhkamp, C. and Rossbach, H. (2013). "Erfolgreiche Lobbyarbeit – Wie die Autoindustrie sich in Berlin und Brüssel durchsetzt." *Frankfurter Allgemeine Zeitung*, June 29. Available: www.faz.net/aktuell/wirtschaft/wirtschaftspolitik/erfolgreiche-lobbyarbeit-wie-die-autoindustrie-sich-in-berlin-und-bruessel-durchsetzt-12264332.html.

Sanna-Randaccio, F. and Sestini, R. (2011). "Foreign Direct Investment and Environmental Policy: Have Location Factors Been Neglected?" *Journal Asia-Pacific Journal of Accounting & Economics*, 18 (1): 45–60.

Sapir, A., Aghion, P., Bertola, G., Hellwig, M., Pisani-Ferry, J., Rosati, D., Viñals, J. and Wallace, H. (2003). *An Agenda for a Growing Europe: Making the EU Economic System Deliver. Report of an Independent High-Level Study Group Established on the Initiative of the President of the European Commission.* Brussels: European Commission.

Sato, A. (2003). "Knowledge in the Global Atmospheric Policy Process: The Case of Japan." In P.G. Harris (ed.), *China's Responsibility for Climate Change: Ethics, Fairness, and Environmental Policy*. Bristol: Policy Press, pp. 167–186.

Saunders, C. (2012). "Reformism and Radicalism in the Climate Camp in Britain: Benign Coexistence, Tensions and Prospects for Bridging." *Environmental Politics*, 21 (5): 829–846.

Schienke, E.W. (2011). "Evaluating Ethical Obligations across Scales of Governance." In P.G. Harris (ed.), *China's Responsibility for Climate Change: Ethics, Fairness, and Environmental Policy*. Bristol: Policy Press, pp. 123–146.

Schneider, L. and Kollmuss, A. (2015). "Perverse Effects of Carbon Markets on HFC-23 and SF6 Abatement Projects in Russia." *Nature Climate Change*, 5 (12): 1061–1063.

Schneider, M.R. and Paunescu, M. (2012). "Changing Varieties of Capitalism and Revealed Comparative Advantages from 1990 to 2005: A Test of the Hall and Soskice Claims." *Socio-Economic Review*, 10 (1): 1–23.

Schreurs, M.A. (2002). *Environmental Politics in Japan, Germany, and the United States.* Cambridge: Cambridge University Press.

Schreurs, M.A. (2008). "From the Bottom Up: Local and Subnational Climate Change Politics." *The Journal of Environment and Development*, 17: 343–355.

Schreurs, M.A. (2012). "Breaking the Impasse in the International Climate Negotiations: The Potential of Green Technologies." *Energy Policy*, 48: 5–12.

Schreurs, M.A. (2014). "The Fukushima Nuclear Accident: Trigger of an *Energiewende* in Japan?" In A. Brünnengräber, A. and M.R. Di Nucci (eds), *Im Hürdenlauf zur Energiewende: Von Transformationen, Reformen, und Innovationen.* Wiesbaden: Springer VS, pp. 429–437.

Schreurs, M.A. and Yoshida, F. (2013). *Fukushima: A Political Economic Analysis.* Sapporo: Hokkaido University Press.

Schultz, S. (2012). "Twilight of an Industry: Bankruptcies have German Solar on the Ropes." *Spiegel-Online*, April 3. Available: www.spiegel.de/international/business/q-cells-bankruptcy-heralds-end-of-german-solar-cell-industry-a-825490.html.

Schumacher, K. and Sands, R. (2006). "Innovative Energy Technologies and Climate Policy in Germany." *Energy Policy*, 34: 3929–3941.

Schwartz, F.J. and Pharr, S. (2003). *The State of Civil Society in Japan.* Cambridge: Cambridge University Press.

Section for Science, Research and Innovation of the Government of the Czech Republic (2016). *National Research, Development and Innovation Policy of the Czech Republic 2016–2020.* Available: www.vyzkum.cz/FrontClanek.aspx?idsekce=782691.

Sieminski, A. (2014). *Outlook for US Shale Oil and Gas.* Washington, DC: US Energy Information Administration. Available: www.ncac-usaee.org/pdfs/2014_01Sieminski.pdf.

Simmie, J., Sternberg, R. and Carpenter, J. (2014). "New Technological Path Creation: Evidence from the British and German Wind Energy Industries." *Journal of Evolutionary Economics*, 24 (4): 875–904.

Skjærseth, J.B. (2014). *Implementing EU Climate and Energy Policies in Poland: From Europeanization to Polonization?* FNI Report 8/2014. Lysaker: Fridtjof Nansen Institute. Available: www.fni.no/pdf/FNI-R0814.pdf.

Skjærseth, J.B. (2013). "Governance by EU Emissions Trading: Resistance or Innovation in the Oil Industry?" *International Environmental Agreements: Politics, Law and Economics*, 13 (1): 31–48.

Skjærseth, J.B. and Skodvin, T. (2003). *Climate Change and the Oil Industry: Common Problem, Varying Strategies.* Manchester: Manchester University Press.

Small Business Research Initiative (2013). *About SBRI.* London: TSB. Available: https://sbri.innovateuk.org/about-sbri.

Smarzynska Javorcik, B. and Wei, S.-J. (2004). "Pollution Havens and Foreign Direct Investment: Dirty Secret or Popular Myth?" *Contributions to Economic Analysis & Policy*, 3 (2): 1–32.

Smith, K. (2011). "Den vanskelige transformasjonen." In J. Hanson, S. Kasa and O. Wicken (eds), *Energirikdommens paradokser: Innovasjon som klimapolitikk og næringsutvikling.* Oslo: Universitetsforlaget.

Soskice, D. (1994). "Innovation Strategies of Companies: A Comparative Institutional Approach of Some Cross-Country Differences." In W. Zapf and M. Dierkes (eds), *Institutionenvergleich und Institutionendynamik.* Berlin: edition sigma, pp. 271–289.

Spiegel Online (2015). "Klimaabgabe: IWF-Chefin plädiert für CO_2-Steuer." *Spiegel Online*, Wirtschaft Forum. Available: www.spiegel.de/wirtschaft/soziales/co2-iwf-chefin-lagarde-fordert-kohlesteuer-a-1056776.html.

SSB (2012). *Kildefordelte utslipp til luft: 2010.* Available: www.ssb.no/klimagassn/tab-2012-05-08-02.html (accessed September 4, 2012).

SSB (2013). 283 *Bruttonasjonalprodukt. Bruttoprodukt, etter hovednæring. I basisverdi. Mill. kr.* Available:www.ssb.no/a/aarbok/tab/tab-283.html (accessed December 2, 2013).

Staffell, I. (2017). "Measuring the Progress and Impacts of Decarbonising British Electricity." *Energy Policy,* 102 (4): 463–476.

Statistics Norway (2016). *Oslo.* Available: www.ssb.no/en/forskning/discussion-papers/_attachment/254379.

Steinmo, S. (1993). *Taxation and Democracy: Swedish, British, and American Approaches to Financing the Modern State.* New Haven, CT: Yale University Press.

Steltzner, H. (2013). "Energiewende. Zu viel ist zu viel." *Frankfurter Allgemeine Zeitung,* September 14. Available: www.faz.net/aktuell/politik/bundestagswahl/energiewende-zu-viel-ist-zu-viel.

Stern, N. (2006). *Stern Review Report on the Economics of Climate Change.* London: HM Treasury. Available: http://web.archive.org/web/20081211182219/www.hm-treasury.gov.uk/stern_review_final_report.htm.

Storesletten, K. and Zilibotti, F. (2014). "China's Great Convergence and Beyond." *Annual Review of Economics,* 6: 333–362.

Stortinget (2012). *Møte i Europautvalget torsdag den 18. oktober 2012 kl. 08.30.* Available: www.stortinget.no/no/Saker-og-publikasjoner/Publikasjoner/Referater/Europautvalget/2012-2013/121018/ (accessed May 5, 2014).

Storz, C., Amable, B., Casper, S. and Lechevalier, S. (2013). "Bringing Asia into the Comparative Capitalism Perspective." *Socio-Economic Review,* 11 (2): 217–232.

Streeck, W. (1997). "German Capitalism: Does it Exist? Can it Survive?" *New Political Economy,* 2 (2): 237–256.

Streeck, W. (2009). *Re-Forming Capitalism: Institutional Change in the German Political Economy.* Oxford: Oxford University Press.

Streeck, W. and Thelen, K. (2005). Institutional Change in Advanced Political Economies. In W. Streeck and K. Thelen (eds), *Beyond Continuity: Institutional Change in Advanced Political Economies,* Oxford: Oxford University Press, pp. 1–39.

Streimikiene, D., Klevas, V. and Bubeliene, J. (2007). "Use of EU Structural Funds for Sustainable Energy Development." *New EU Member States, Renewable and Sustainable Energy Reviews,* 11 (6): 1167–1187.

Strong, L. (2010). "Understanding the Role of the Business Community in the Making of UK Climate Policy between 1997 and 2009." PhD thesis, University of Sheffield.

Strunz, S., Gawel, E. and Lehmann, P. (2015). *The Political Economy of Renewable Energy Policies in Germany and the EU.* UFZ Discussion Paper No. 12/2015. Available: www.ufz.de/export/data/global/69411_DP_12_2015_Strunzetal.pdf.

Sugiyama, N. and Takeuchi, T. (2008). "Local Policies for Climate Change in Japan." *Journal of Environment and Development,* 17: 424–441.

Sun, Y. and Zhao, D. (2008). "State-Society Relations and Environmental Campaigns." In J. O'Brien (ed.), *Popular Protest in China.* Cambridge, MA: Harvard University Press, pp. 144–162.

Sussman, G. 2004. "The USA and Global Environmental Policy: Domestic Constraints on Effective Leadership." *International Political Science Review,* 24 (4): 349–369.

Szent-Iványi, B. (ed.) (2017). *Foreign Direct Investment in Central and Eastern Europe Post-crisis Perspectives.* Berlin: Springer.

Takahashi, T. and Nakamura, M. (2001). "Rising to the Kyoto Challenge: Is the Response of Canadian Industry Adequate?" *Journal of Environmental Management,* 63: 149–161.

Tallberg, J. (2012). "Europeiseringen av Norge i et jämförande perspektiv." *Internasjonal politikk*, 70 (3), 287–303.

Taylor, M.Z. (2004). "Empirical Evidence against Varieties of Capitalism's Theory of Technological Innovation." *International Organization*, 58 (3): 601–631.

Technology Strategy Board (2013). *Priority Areas: Transport*. London: TSB. Available: www.innovateuk.org/transport.

Tenfjord, A.P. (1995). *CO_2-saka: Økonomisk interessepolitikk og miljøpolitiske målsetjingar*. Report 9507. Bergen: LOS-senteret.

The Economist (2014). "Sunny, Windy, Costly and Dirty: Germany's New 'Super Minister' for Energy and the Economy has His Work Cut Out." *The Economist*, January 18. Available: www.economist.com/node/21594336/print.

The Institute of Energy Economics, Japan (2015). "Toward Choosing Energy Mix." *The 419th Forum on Research Work*, Institute of Energy Economics, Japan. Available: http://eneken.ieej.or.jp/data/5886.pdf.

Theurer, M. (2013). "Britische Energiewende." *Frankfurter Allgemeine Zeitung*, October 22. Available: www.faz.net/aktuell/wirtschaft/wirtschaftspolitik/neue-atomkraftwerke-britische-energiewende-12627208.html.

Thomson, V.E. and Arroyo, V. (2011). "Upside-down Cooperative Federalism: Climate Change Policymaking and the States." *Virginia Environmental Law Journal* 29: 1.

Tjernshaugen, A. and Langhelle, O. (2011). "CCS som politisk lim." In J. Hanson, S. Kasa and O. Wicken (eds), *Energirikdommens paradokser: Innovasjon som klimapolitikk og næringsutvikling*. Oslo: Universitetsforlaget.

Tianje, M. (2009). "Environmental Mass Incidents in Rural China: Examining Large-Scale Unrest in Donyang, Zhejiang." *China Environment Series* (10). Washington, DC: Woodrow Wilson International Center for Scholars, pp. 33–49.

Tiberghien, Y. and Schreurs, M.A. (2007). "High Noon in Japan: Embedded Symbolism and Post-2001 Kyoto Protocol Politics." *Global Environmental Politics*, 7 (4): 70–91.

Tiberghien, Y. and Schreurs, M.A. (2010). "Climate Leadership, Japanese Style: Embedded Symbolism and Post-2001 Kyoto Protocol Politics." In L. McIntosh Sundstrom and K. Harrison (eds), *Global Commons, Domestic Decisions: The Comparative Politics of Climate Change*. Cambridge, MA: MIT Press.

Tienhaara, K. (2014). "Varieties of Green Capitalism: Economy and Environment in the Wake of the Global Financial Crisis." *Environmental Politics*, 23 (2): 187–204.

Tiezzi, S. (2014). "China Revises Environmental Law for the First Time since 1989." *The Diplomat*, April 25. Available: http://thediplomat.com/2014/04/china-revises-environmental-law-for-the-first-time-since-1989/ (accessed April 3, 2015).

Toke, D. (2011). "UK Electricity Market Reform: Revolution or Much Ado about Nothing?" *Energy Policy*, 39: 7609–7611.

Tokyo Electric Power Company (2014). *Nuclear: TEPCO Power Plants*. Available: www.tepco.co.jp/en/challenge/energy/nuclear/plants-e.html (accessed March 29, 2015).

Tollefson, J. (2015). "China's Emissions Overestimated." *Nature*, 524 (7565): 276.

Toyhama, H. and Harada, Y. (2013). "Effect of Institutional Configuration on Innovation Activities in East Asian Firms: A Study of the Institutional Diversity of Asian Economies" *International Journal of Asian Business Management and Information Management*, 44 (2): 16–34.

Trade Union Congress (2013). *Industrial Issues: Energy*. London: TUC. Available: www.tuc.org.uk/industrial-issues/energy.

Trading Economics. *China GDP Annual Growth Rate, 1989–2015*. Available: www. tradingeconomics.com/china/gdp-growth-annual (accessed April 3, 2015).

TU (2012a). "Grønn bløff eller klimatiltak?" *TU*, August 31. Available: www.tu.no/ meninger/tumener/2012/08/31/gronn-bloff-eller-klimatiltak (accessed August 16, 2013).

TU (2012b). "NVE forsvarer elsertifikatene." *TU*, August 31. Available: www.tu.no/ energi/2012/08/31/nve-forsvarer-elsertifikatene (accessed August 16, 2013).

TU (2012c). "Vi må ha full fart på utbygging av kablene." *TU*, September 19. Available: www.tu.no/energi/2012/09/19/-vi-ma-ha-full-fart-pa-utbygging-av-kablene (accessed August 16, 2013).

TU (2012d). "Krever større klimafond." *TU*, August 16. Available: www.tu.no/ industri/2012/08/16/krever-storre-klimafond (accessed May 6, 2014).

TU (2014a). "Norwea advarer Finansdepartementet mot å ignorere Stortingets ønske om fornybarutbygging." *TU*, 11 February. Available: www.tu.no/kraft/2014/02/11/ norwea-advarer-siv-jensen-mot-a-ikke-hore-pa-stortinget (accessed May 6, 2014).

TU (2014b). "Bakgrunn: Dragkampen om kraft fra land." *TU*, 4 February. Available: www.tu.no/petroleum/2014/02/04/bakgrunn-dragkampen-om-kraft-fra-land (accessed May 5, 2014).

Tylecote, A. and Visintin, F. (2008). *Corporate Governance, Finance and the Technological Advantage of Nations*. London: Routledge.

UD (2012a). *EØS-avtalen og Norges øvrige avtaler med EU: Sentrale prioriteringer og virkemidler i norsk europapolitikk*. Meld. St. 5 (2012–2013). Oslo.

UD (2012b). *Samtykke til deltakelse i en beslutning i EØS-komiteen om innlemmelse i EØS-avtalen av direktiv 2009/29/EF for å forbedre og utvide ordningen for handel med utslipp-skvoter for klimagasser i Fellesskapet (revidert kvotedirektiv)*. Prop. 77 S (2011–2012).

Ui, J. (1998). "Minamata Disease." In S. Large (ed.), *Shōwa Japan: Political, Economic, and Social History, 1926–1989*, Vol. III, 1952–1989. New York: Routledge, pp. 206–235.

Ui, J. (1992). *Industrial Pollution in Japan*. Tokyo: United Nations University Press.

Umweltbundesamt (2010). *Umweltbewusstsein in Deutschland 2010: Ergebnisse einer repräsentativen Bevölkerungsumfrage*. Berlin: Umweltbundesamt.

Umweltbundesamt (2012). "Emissions Trading: CO_2 Emissions Fall in 2011 Despite Strong Economy." Press release 16/2012. Berlin: Umweltbundesamt.

Umweltbundesamt (2013a). "Treibhausgasausstoß im Jahr 2012 um 1,6 Prozent gestiegen." Press release Nr. 9/2013. Berlin: Umweltbundesamt.

Umweltbundesamt (2013b). "Emissionshandel: CO_2-Emissionen 2012 knapp über dem Niveau von 2011." Press release Nr. 15/2013. Berlin: Umweltbundesamt.

Umweltbundesamt and Deutsche Emissionshandelsstelle (2012). *Pressehintergrundpapier VET 2011*. Berlin: Umweltbundesamt. Available: www.dehst.de/SharedDocs/ Downloads/DE/Publikationen/Pressehintergrund_VET-2011.pdf.

Union of Concerned Scientists (2012). *Ripe for Retirement: The Case for Closing America's Costliest Coal Plants*. Cambridge, MA: Union of Concerned Scientists Available: www.ucsusa.org/clean_energy/smart-energy-solutions/decrease-coal/ripe-for-retirement-closing-americas-costliest-coal-plants.html#.WxsnCyAnaUk.

United Nations Framework Convention on Climate Change (n.d.). *CDM Statistics*. Available: http://unfccc.int/kyoto_protocol/mechanisms/clean_development_mech anism/items/2718.php (accessed April 3, 2015).

United Nations Framework Convention on Climate Change (n.d.). *Distribution of CERs by host country*. Available: https://cdm.unfccc.int/Statistics/Public/CD Minsights/index.html (accessed April 3, 2015).

United Nations Framework Convention on Climate Change (2008). *Kyoto Protocol Reference Manual on Accounting of Emissions and Assigned Amounts.* Available: www.unfccc.org.

United Nations Framework Convention on Climate Change (2011a). *National Inventory Report to UNFCCC 2011 – Czech Republic.* Available: www.unfccc.org.

United Nations Framework Convention on Climate Change (2011b). *National Inventory Report to UNFCCC 2011 – Hungary.* Available: www.unfccc.org.

United Nations Framework Convention on Climate Change (2011c). *National Inventory Report to UNFCCC 2011 – Poland.* Available: www.unfccc.org.

United Nations Framework Convention on Climate Change (2014a). *Frequently asked questions relating to the Doha Amendment to the Kyoto Protocol,* November 21. 2014. Available: http://unfccc.int/files/kyoto_protocol/doha_amendment/application/pdf/frequently_asked_questions_doha_amendment_to_the_kp.pdf.

United Nations Framework Convention on Climate Change (2014b). *Kyoto Protocol Targets for the First Commitment Period.* Available: https://unfccc.int/process/transparency-and-reporting/reporting-and-review-under-the-kyoto-protocol/first-commitment-period/kyoto-protocol-base-year-data-for-the-first-commitment-period-of-the-kyoto-protocol.

United Nations Framework Convention on Climate Change (2014c). *Time Series – Annex I.* Available: http://unfccc.int/ghg_data/ghg_data_unfccc/time_series_annex_i/items/3814.php.

United Nations Framework Convention on Climate Change (2017a). Interim NDC Registry. Available: www4.unfccc.int/ndcregistry/Pages/All.aspx.

United Nations Framework Convention on Climate Change (2017b). *Time Series – Annex I.* Available: http://di.unfccc.int/time_series.

United Nations Treaty Collection (2017). *Doha Amendment to the Kyoto Protocol.* Available: https://treaties.un.org/pages/ViewDetails.aspx?src=TREATY&mtdsg_no=XXVII-7-c&chapter=27&lang=en.

US Department of Energy (2014). *Life Cycle Greenhouse Gas Perspective on Exporting Natural Gas from the United States.* DOE/NETL-2014/1649.

US Department of State (2009). *US-China Memorandum of Understanding to Enhance Cooperation on Climate Change, Energy and the Environment,* July 28. Available: www.state.gov/r/pa/prs/ps/2009/july/126592.htm (accessed April 3, 2015).

US Energy Information Administration (2013). *Annual Energy Outlook 2014.* Wshington, DC: US EIA.

US Energy Information Administration (2014). *China.* Available: www.eia.gov/countries/analysisbriefs/China/china.pdf (accessed April 3, 2015).

US Energy Information Administration (2015). *Japan.* Available: www.eia.gov/countries/cab.cfm?fips=ja (accessed April 3, 2015).

US Energy Information Administration (2017). *Annual Energy Outlook 2017 with Projections to 2050.* Washington, DC: US EIA.

US Environmental Protection Agency (2015). *Fact Sheet: The Clean Power Plan.* Available: www3.epa.gov/airquality/cpp/fs-cpp-overview.pdf.

Van Vuuren, D.P., Cofala J., Eerens, H.E., Oostenrijk, R., Heyes, C., Klimont, Z., den Elzen, M.G.J. and Amann, M. (2006). "Exploring the Ancillary Benefits of the Kyoto Protocol for Air Pollution in Europe." *Energy Policy,* 34 (4): 444–460.

Vasagar, J. (2015). "Renewables Take Top Spot in Germany Power Supply Stakes." *Financial Times,* January 7. Available: www.ft.com/cms/s/0/cc90455a-9654-11e4-a40b-00144feabdc0.html#axzz3qYaCzkdI.

Veugelers, R. (2011). *Europe's Clean Technology Investment Challenge*. Bruegel Policy Contribution No. 2011/06. Brussels: Bruegel.

Vitols, S. (2001). "Varieties of Corporate Governance: Comparing Germany and the UK." In P. Hall and D. Soskice (eds), *Varieties of Capitalism: The Institutional Foundations of Comparative Advantage*. Oxford: Oxford University Press, pp. 337–360.

Vitols, S. (2006). "Das 'deutsche Modell' in der politischen Ökonomie." In V. Berghahn and S. Vitols (eds), *Gibt es einen deutschen Kapitalismus? Tradition und globale Perspektiven der sozialen Marktwirtschaft*. Frankfurt am Main: Campus, pp. 44–61.

Vitols, S. and Engelhardt, L. (2005). *National Institutions and High Tech Industries: A Varieties of Capitalism Perspective on the Failure of Germany's Neuer Markt*. WZB Discussion Paper SP II 2005–03. Berlin: Wissenschaftszentrum Berlin.

Vivodo, V. (2011). "Japan's Energy Security Predicament in the Aftermath of the Fukushima Disaster." *Journal of Energy Security*, December 14.

Vogel, E. (1979). *Japan as Number One: Lessons for America*. Cambridge, MA: Harvard University Press.

Wade, R. (1990). *Governing the Market: Economic Theory and the Role of Government in East Asian Industrialization*. Princeton, NJ: Princeton University Press.

Wallach, P. (2015). *Which States Lose from the Changes to the EPA's Clean Power Plan?* Washington, DC: Brookings Institute. Available: www.brookings.edu/blogs/fixgov/posts/2015/08/05-state-losers-clean-power-plan-wallach.

Weale, A. (1992). *The New Politics of Pollution*. Manchester: Manchester University Press.

Weidner, H. and Mez, L. (2008). "German Climate Change Policy: A Success Story with Some Flaws." *The Journal of Environment Development*, 17 (4): 356–378.

Weitzman, M. (2014). "Fat Tails and the Social Cost of Carbon." *The American Economic Review*, 104 (5): 544–546.

Welch, E.W. (2000). "Voluntary Behavior by Electric Utilities: Levels of Adoption and Contribution of the Climate Challenge Program to the Reduction of Carbon Dioxide." *Journal of Policy Analysis*, 19 (30): 407–425.

Wen, J. (2006). "Address to the 6th National Conference on Environmental Protection." *News Xinhua Net*, April 23. Available: http://news.xinhuanet.com/english/2006-04/24/content_4465638.htm (accessed April 3, 2015).

White House, Office of the Press Secretary (2014). *Fact Sheet: US–China Joint Announcement on Climate Change and Clean Energy Cooperation*. Available: www.whitehouse.gov/the-press-office/2014/11/11/fact-sheet-us-china-joint-announcement-climate-change-and-clean-energy-c (accessed April 3, 2015).

Wicken, O. (2011). "Kraft fra infrastruktur til marked." In J. Hanson, S. Kasa and O. Wicken (eds), *Energirikdommens paradokser: Innovasjon som klimapolitikk og næringsutvikling*. Oslo: Universitetsforlaget, pp. 126–144.

Wilson, G. and Staffell, I. (2017). "The Year Coal Collapsed: 2016 was a Turning Point for Britain's Electricity." *The Conversation*, January 6. Available: http://theconversation.com/the-year-coal-collapsed/.

Witt, M. (2010). *China: What Variety of Capitalism?* INSEAD Working Paper No. 2010/88/EPS. Available: http://papers.ssrn.com/sol3/Papers.cfm?abstract_id=1695940.

Witt, M. and Redding, G. (2013). "Asian Business Systems: Institutional Comparison, Clusters and Implications for Varieties of Capitalism and Business Systems Theory." *Socio-Economic Review*, 11 (2): 265–300.

Wong, S.F. (2005). "Obliging Institutions and Industry Evolution: A Comparative Study of the German and UK Wind Energy Industries." *Industry and Innovation*, 12: 117–145.

Woo-Cummings, M. (ed.) (1990). *The Developmental State*. Ithaca, NY: Cornell University Press.

Wood, T. (2010). "Good Riddance to New Labour." *New Left Review*, 62 (March–April): 256–261.

World Bank (2012). *State and Trends of the Carbon Market*. Washington, DC: World Bank. Available: http://siteresources.worldbank.org.

World Bank (2013). "Japan Announces Development of the New Joint Crediting Mechanism." *Climate Finance Options*. Available: www.climatefinanceoptions.org/cfo/news/japan-announces-development-new-joint-crediting-mechanism-3490 (accessed April 3, 2015).

World Bank (2013). *Mapping Carbon Pricing Initiatives*, May 2013. Washington, DC: World Bank Available: www-wds.worldbank.org.

World Bank (2014). *Bringing China's Energy Efficiency Experience to the World: Knowledge Exchange with Asian Countries*. Washington, DC: World Bank. Available: www.worldbank.org/en/news/feature/2014/06/27/bringing-chinas-energy-efficiency-experience-to-the-world-knowledge-exchange-with-asian-countries (accessed April 3, 2015).

World Bank (2017a). *CO_2 Emissions (kt): World Development Indicators*. Washington, DC: World Bank. Available: http://databank.worldbank.org/data/reports.aspx?source=2&series=EN.ATM.CO2E.KT&country=.

World Bank (2017b). *Energy Use (kg of Oil Equivalent per Capita): World Development Indicators*. Washington, DC: World Bank. Available: https://data.worldbank.org/indicator/EG.USE.PCAP.KG.OE.

World Bank and Development Research Center of the State Council (2014). *The People's Republic of China. Urban China: Toward Efficient, Inclusive, and Sustainable Urbanization*. Washington, DC: World Bank.

World Bank and State Environmental Protection Administration, P.R. China (2007). *Cost of Pollution in China: Economic Estimates of Physical Damages*. Washington, DC: World Bank. Available: https://siteresources.worldbank.org/INTEAPREGTO PENVIRONMENT/Resources/China_Cost_of_Pollution.pdf.

World Energy Council (2013). *World Energy Perspective: Energy Efficiency Policies – What Works and What Does Not*. London: World Energy Council.

Wörlen, C. and Gebauer, K. (2017). *Kurzanalyse der nationalen Treibhausgasemissionen für das Jahr 2016*. Berlin: arepo.

Wu, R., Geng, Y., Dong, H., Fujita, T. and Tian, X. (2015). "Changes of CO_2 Emissions Embedded in China–Japan Trade: Drivers and Implications." *Journal of Cleaner Production*, 112: 4151–4158.

WWF Japan. "WWF ジャパン について." Available: www.wwf.or.jp/aboutwwf/japan/ (accessed April 3, 2015).

Xinhua News Agency (2009). "Copenhagen Accord Marks New Starting Point for Global Fight against Climate Change." *Xinhua*, December 26. Available: http://news.xinhuanet.com/english/2009-12/26/content_12706317.htm (accessed April 3, 2015).

Xue, L., Simonis, U.E. and Dudnek, D.J. (2007). "Environmental Governance for China: Major Recommendations of a Task Force." *Environmental Politics*, 16 (4): 669–676.

Yamamura, K. and Hatch, W. (1997). "A Looming Entry Barrier: Japan's Production Networks in Asia." *NBR Analysis* 8(1). Seattle, WA: National Bureau of Asian Research.

Yamamura, K. (2003). "Germany and Japan in a New Phase of Capitalism: Confronting the Past and the Future." In K. Yamamura and S. Wolfgang (eds), *The End of Diversity? Prospects for German and Japanese Capitalism.* Ithaca, NY: Cornell University Press, pp. 115–146.

Yi, H. and Yuan, L. (2015). "Green Economy in China: Regional Variations and Policy Drivers." *Global Environmental Change*, 31: 11–19.

Yoon, E., Seunghwan, L. and Fengshi, W. (2007). "The States and Nongovernmental Organizations in Northeast Asia's Environmental Security." In In-taek Hyun and Schreurs M.A. (eds), *The Environmental Dimension of Asian Security: Conflict and Cooperation over Energy, Resources, and Pollution.* Washington, DC: United States Institute of Peace Press, pp. 207–232.

Zhang, H. (2015). "CO_2 Emission Embodied in International Trade: Evidence for China." *International Journal of Economics and Finance*, 7 (2): 138–143.

Zhang, J. and Peck, J. (2014). "Variegated Capitalism, Chinese Style: Regional Models, Multi-scalar Constructions." *Regional Studies*, 50 (1): 52–78. doi: 10.1080/00343404.2013.856514.

Index

Page numbers in **bold** denote tables, those in *italics* denote figures.

For Product Safety Concerns and Information please contact our EU
representative GPSR@taylorandfrancis.com Taylor & Francis Verlag GmbH,
Kaufingerstraße 24, 80331 München, Germany

Printed and bound by CPI Group (UK) Ltd, Croydon, CR0 4YY

01/05/2025

01858438-0005